INDIA

INDIA
AT THE DEATH OF AKBAR

(An Econmic Study)

by

W. H. MORELAND
C.S.I., C.I.E.

GYAN

Published by

Gyan Publishing House
5, Ansari Road
Daryaganj, New Delhi-110002
Phone: 011-47034999, 9811692060
E-mail: books@gyanbooks.com

Distribution Network
gyanbooks.com
India, USA, Canada, UK, Australia, France

ISBN : 978-81-212-2637-0 (PB)
First Published, 1920

2nd Impression 2021

Printed at: Gyan Press, Delhi.

India
Author: W. H. Moreland

INDIA

AT THE DEATH OF AKBAR

AN ECONOMIC STUDY

BY

W. H. MORELAND

C.S.I., C.I.E.

LATE OF THE INDIAN CIVIL SERVICE

AUTHOR OF

"THE AGRICULTURE OF THE UNITED PROVINCES,"

"THE REVENUE ADMINISTRATION OF THE UNITED PROVINCES,"

AND "AN INTRODUCTION TO ECONOMICS FOR INDIAN STUDENTS"

MACMILLAN AND CO., LIMITED

ST. MARTIN'S STREET, LONDON

1920

PREFACE

THE aim of this book is to present a sketch of the economic life of India at the opening of the seventeenth century, that is to say, at the period immediately antecedent to the first appearance of those new forces which were destined to exercise an increasing and eventually predominant influence on the development of the country. If it be permissible to assign a precise date to what is essentially a gradual transition, we may say that the medieval history of India ended, and the modern history began, in the year 1608, when the English ship *Hector* reached Surat. Starting from this date, it is possible to trace the economic story of the next three centuries, first in the narratives of travellers and the early Letter-Books of the East India Company, and then in the more copious official records and publications of later times, so that a well-defined period for study is within the reach of our schools and universities, provided that a suitable beginning can be made. This book attempts to supply such a beginning, by furnishing an account of the economic position at the close of Akbar's reign; there is, I fear, little prospect that adequate materials for a similar study of earlier periods will ever become available, but our knowledge of the closing years of the sixteenth century appears to be sufficient to justify the attempt which I have made.

Whether the attempt is successful is a question for the reader. The materials which I have used seem to me to provide the basis for a coherent and consistent account of the main currents of the economic life of India, but I cannot claim that the account now offered is definitive. It is a sketch rather than a finished picture; there is room for more intensive study of some of the authorities, and there is a reasonable prospect of the discovery of additional facts among sources to which I have not at present access, such as the records of the Portuguese administration and of the Jesuit missionaries, or the vernacular literature of the East and South and West. The period thus offers opportunities for further research, much of it of a kind well suited to the schools of economics now growing up in the Indian Universities, and while there are obvious arguments for deferring publication until the sources have been more fully explored, it seems to me that the balance of advantage lies in offering the sketch for use until the schools have got to work; it will serve at the least as a frame-work on which additional results can be arranged, and as an index to the topics on which further information is required.

A few words are necessary regarding the point of view. I have tried to write from the standpoint of readers who have a general knowledge of recent conditions in India, and to state the past in terms of the more familiar present, or, to speak more precisely, in terms of the years between 1910 and 1914, before the occurrence of the sudden economic disturbances resulting from the war. Comparisons are, however, difficult to draw when the earlier period is described in superlatives; the wonderful capacities of India could not fail to stir the imagination of visitors from the West, and the exuberant language of the sixteenth century may give a very misleading impression if the adjectives are taken at their modern value. The only possible corrective is to fix the attention on quantities, and I have attempted throughout to arrive at numerical estimates, actual or relative as the available data permit, of the various factors which composed the stream of economic life. The dangers attendant on this form of political arithmetic can best be realised by those who have practised it, and I am not so sanguine as to hope that I have escaped them all; the justification for offering such estimates is that they may assist the reader to see the past more nearly in its true perspective, and while they may be at variance with the facts, they will usually indicate the order of magnitude of the quantities under consideration, and will at any rate direct attention to an aspect of the subject which is almost wholly neglected by popular writers on the period. I ask only that these estimates should be regarded as first approximations, and that readers to whom they may appear to be improbable should test them in the light of the original authorities.

It would be unfair, however, not to add a word of warning for the benefit of any one who may accept this invitation. One of the difficulties surrounding this period is the diversity of language employed by the authorities. I have worked on them in English, French, Latin, Persian and Portuguese, and I have found that translations (where they exist) must be used with caution; they may be sufficiently accurate for all ordinary purposes, and yet miss the technical sense of words in which economists are specially concerned, while even standard dictionaries may fail to indicate the precise shade of meaning intended by a writer of the sixteenth century. It is advisable, therefore, to go to the original text wherever possible, and if I have myself failed to do this in the case of the Italian, Spanish and Russian travellers, I can offer only the plea that I am ignorant of those languages. What I have said regarding translations applies particularly to the English versions of the *Ain-i Akbari*, in which the technical force of many expressions is lost, and I fear that some knowledge of Persian must be regarded, for the present at least, as indispensable for the detailed study of this particular period.

The subject which I have treated is extensive, and has involved a certain amount of exploration in unfamiliar byepaths of literature and science. I have received cordial assistance from almost every one to whom I have applied, and I take this opportunity of expressing my gratitude to the friends and the strangers on whose resources I have drawn, —to Mrs. C. M. Knowles of the London School of Economics, Sir David Prain and Dr. Stapf of Kew, Dr. Barnett of the British Museum, Mr. P. S. Allen of Merton College, Oxford, Mr. R. W. Dana, the Secretary of the Institution of Naval

Architects, Mr. J. H. Dickenson of Manchester, and Mr. F. Lauder, the Honorary Secretary of the India Section of the Manchester Chamber of Commerce; also to the following past and present members of my old Service (which, by the way, is sometimes said to have lost its interest in study and research),—Sir George Grierson, Sir Edward Maclagan, Mr. Vincent Smith, Mr. R. Sewell, Mr. M. Longworth Dames, Mr. R. Burn, Mr. A. C. Chatterjee, and Mr. A. Yusuf Ali. I have also to thank Mr. D. T. Chadwick, the Indian Trade Commissioner, for his readiness to place his knowledge at my disposal; and finally I have to acknowledge the unvarying kindness of Mr. W. Foster of the India Office.

CONTENTS

CHAPTER I

PAGE

THE COUNTRY AND PEOPLE 1

1. The Country 1
2. The Numbers of the People 9
3. The Classes of the Population 23

CHAPTER II

THE ADMINISTRATION 31

1. The Form of Administration . . 31
2. The Course of Justice 35
3. Security in the Cities 37
4. Security in the Country 41
5. Customs and Transit-Dues . . . 46
6. Effect on Trade and Industry . . . 50
7. Weights, Measures, and Currency . . 52

CHAPTER III

THE CONSUMING CLASSES 63

1. The Court and the Imperial Service . . . 63
2. Other Forms of State Employment . . . 73
3. The Professional and Religious Classes . 83
4. Servants and Slaves 87

CHAPTER IV

AGRICULTURAL PRODUCTION 96

1. Land Tenures 96
2. The System of Agriculture 100
3. Peasants and Labourers . . . 109
4. Agriculture in its Local Aspects 118
5. The Environment as affecting Agriculture . . . 124
6. The Conditions of Life in the Villages . . 136

CHAPTER V

PAGE

Non-agricultural Production 141

1. The General Position 141
2. Forests and Fisheries 143
3. Mines and Minerals 146
4. Agricultural Manufactures . . . 155
5. Handicrafts in General . . . 160
6. Production of Means of Transport . 166
7. Textile Manufactures—Silk, Wool, and Hair . 171
8. Textile Manufactures—Hemp, Jute, and Cotton . 178
9. Industrial Organisation . . 184
10. Urban Wages . . . 189

CHAPTER VI

Commerce 196

1. General Features . 196
2. The Principal Indian Seaports . 203
3. The Principal Foreign Ports in the Indian Seas 212
4. Trade Routes on the Land Frontier 218
5. The Direct Trade with Europe 221
6. The Volume of Foreign Commerce 227
7. Coasting and Internal Trade . 240
8. The Organisation of Indian Commerce 245

CHAPTER VII

The Standard of Life 253

1. Introductory . . 253
2. The Upper Classes 256
3. The Middle Classes . . 263
4. The Economic Position of the Lower Classes . 265
5. Food, Clothing, and other Details . . . 270

CHAPTER VIII

The Wealth of India 282

1. Contemporary Ideas . . . 282
2. Modern Ideas . . 286
3. Distribution 294
4. Conclusion . . 299

APPENDICES

PAGE

A. The Crops grown in India in the Sixteenth Century 303

B. "Indian Corn" in Vijayanagar 305

C. The Seaports of Bengal . . . 307

D. The Shipping Ton 310

E. List of Authorities 313

INDEX 319

MAPS

TO FACE PAGE

Map of India 1

Sketch Map showing Foreign Seaports . 203

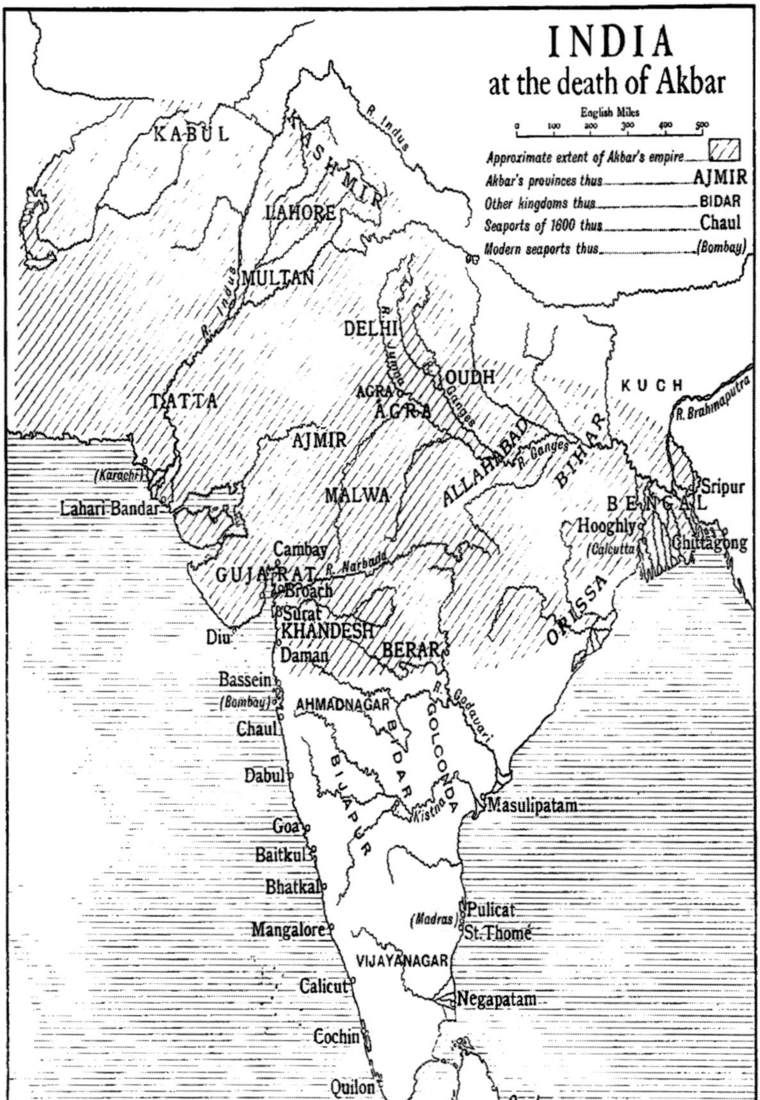

Emery Walker Ltd. sc.

CHAPTER I

THE COUNTRY AND PEOPLE

I. The Country

I attempt in this book to present a sketch of the economic life of India at the close of Akbar's reign, that is to say, to show how the people spent their incomes, and the sources from which those incomes were derived. In order to do this, it is necessary first of all to define the meaning of "India," for the word has not always conveyed the precise signification which it bears to-day. In the Middle Ages the ordinary European, if he thought of India, or the Indies, at all, probably thought merely of some vague region lying somewhere to the east of Syria, which supplied various costly commodities, and in particular the spices used in preparing his food. With the progress of geographical discovery the Indies were in time subdivided into East and West, and the word India was gradually restricted (at least in English use) to the former area, which comprised in a general way all the country lying between the Persian Gulf and the Malay Peninsula. This extensive area was further subdivided by geographers into various regions, the mouths of the Indus and the Ganges being commonly taken as dividing points, so that the "second" or "middle" India of some writers of the sixteenth century corresponds roughly to the modern meaning of the word. The Portuguese, however, and also some travellers of other nations who visited the country under Portuguese auspices, gave the word a much narrower signification: to them India meant primarily the west coast and the land lying immediately behind it, so that we may read of journeys from Sind to "India," or from "India" to Bengal, and we have to be on our guard in order to grasp the precise meaning of writers of this class. In the present book I use India in the modern and familiar sense as denoting the country lying between the sea and the Himalayas, and not extending farther into the mainland of Asia than Baluchistan on the west and the vicinity of Chittagong on the east. The modern Indian Empire includes, also, Burma, but in the sixteenth century the country which now bears that name was composed of kingdoms entirely independent of India, and for my present purpose it is most conveniently treated as a foreign land. The subject of this book is, then, the economic life of the country whose limits I have indicated, or, speaking generally, of the modern Indian Empire including the States, but excluding the province of Burma.[1]

At the time of which I write the bulk of this area was divided between the Mogul Empire in the north, the Hindu territories of the south, and the Moslem kingdoms of the Deccan. The Hindu territories might at this period still be justly described as the Empire of Vijayanagar. It is true that the military power of this Empire had been finally broken in the Battle of Talikot (A.D. 1565), but the dynasty continued to claim supremacy over what was left of its dominions, and we read of the Empire, under the current name of "Narsinga," for some time after Akbar's death. This supremacy was, however, little more than nominal, and the Imperial officers or local chieftains enjoyed a large measure of independence, and were concerned chiefly in strengthening themselves and enlarging the areas subject to their jurisdiction. The Moslem kingdoms of the Deccan had not as yet definitely submitted to the Moguls: one of them, Ahmadnagar, was claimed as a province in the latter part of Akbar's reign, but its independence was reasserted a few years later: another, Khandesh, was more definitely, but still incom-

[1] References to the authorities on which the statements in the text are based will be found in the list of Authorities printed at the end of each chapter.

pletely, incorporated in the Mogul Empire: the remainder, Golconda, Bijapur, and Bidar, were separate and independent States.

The Mogul Empire, which covered nearly all the rest of India, was at this time still a novelty. When Akbar came to the throne in 1556, he had at most a precarious footing in parts of the country between Agra and Peshawar, as well as in what is now Afghanistan, and the territories conquered during his long reign were by no means completely assimilated at its close. The position which then existed in regard to administration has sometimes been compared to the intermingling of British provinces and Indian States familiar at the present day, but the analogy is by no means exact. Under the Moguls administration meant primarily the collection of the land revenue, and the administrative ideal of the period was that the Emperor, or his nominees, should collect the revenue from the actual cultivators of the soil, but this ideal was not always realisable in practice, and in various parts of the Empire we find that the local administration was in the hands of men who are spoken of consistently as "zamindars." As used by the writers of Akbar's reign, this word ordinarily denotes something different from the land-holder of the present day, but it would be a mistake to regard these zamindars as necessarily equivalent to Princes or Chiefs; the word covers everybody, other than a grantee or an official, who stood between the peasants and the Emperor, and it may mean a land-holder in the modern sense, a chief, or a rebel, while it is occasionally used to signify an independent king. Akbar's administration was severely practical: a Chief or a Raja who submitted and agreed to pay a reasonable revenue was commonly allowed to retain his position of authority: one who was recalcitrant or rebellious was killed, imprisoned, or driven away, and his lands taken under direct control. The existence of zamindars is not therefore by itself significant of any precise constitutional arrangements: we hear of them in the Gangetic plain, where Akbar's supremacy was definitely established; we hear of them in the borderlands where his rule was little more than nominal;

and we find them in Rajputana, and in the mountainous country south of Allahabad and Benares, where his administration was compelled by circumstances to be content with a somewhat dubious position. They serve to remind us that the Empire was very far from being a homogeneous entity, and if we possessed detailed knowledge of the position of individuals, we should probably find a wide variety of superior tenures, ranging from what would now be termed landholders to rulers in subordinate alliance with the Emperor, and linked together only by the universal obligation to pay revenue or tribute.

In addition to these main divisions, there were various smaller States scattered through the country, some of them important from the economic standpoint. The strength of Vijayanagar had lain mostly in the interior, and along the west coast the political situation at this time was intricate. The Portuguese were established as a sovereign power in Goa and other settlements: the "pirate" chiefs, whose position will be described in a later chapter, owed allegiance to no superior authority; while the Zamorin of Calicut also maintained a position of independence, sometimes allied with the Portuguese, sometimes in open hostility, but always giving secret support to the piratical communities. On the east coast the position was more regular, though the Portuguese had informally assumed jurisdiction over portions of the territory of Vijayanagar, but farther north we find a few petty Hindu States situated between Golconda and the Mogul province of Orissa.

In Northern India the existence of separate States at this period is usually little more than a question of words. A zamindar who paid revenue to the Mogul was clearly in a position of dependence, and if he wished to establish a claim to sovereignty, the first step was to refuse, or omit, to pay revenue. Such an omission might, however, arise from various other causes, and it is probable that in Rajputana, Central India, and Chota Nagpur there were numerous chiefs and tribes occupying what constitutional lawyers would regard as an anomalous position, sometimes paying the stipulated revenue, sometimes in open rebellion, and sometimes enjoying practical independence because the Mogul authorities found it inconvenient to undertake active measures of coercion. An exception to these general remarks is, however, presented by the State of Kūch, lying in the valley of the Brahmaputra, over which the Moguls did not claim to exercise jurisdiction.

I have not attempted to indicate more than a few of these minor States on the map prefixed to this chapter, nor have I tried to lay down the boundaries of even the larger territorial areas with any approach to precision. Boundaries are, in fact, frequently obscure, and in many cases all that can be said is that a frontier was indeterminate, jurisdiction being commonly claimed by two parties and exercised sometimes by one and sometimes by the other. A cursory survey of the boundaries of the Mogul Empire will illustrate this statement, and will assist the reader to understand the political conditions of the period. On the west, Akbar's dominions included a portion of what is now Baluchistan, but the westward limit of the actual jurisdiction is not precisely indicated in any authority within my reach. Farther north, the Empire included what is now Afghanistan, from Kabul southwards, but the narratives of travellers make it clear that the hill-country west of the Indus was then, as now, more or less independent, the Moguls endeavouring at most to keep open the caravan routes through the passes. The southern portion of Kashmir was effectively administered, and this is also perhaps true of parts of Southern Kumaun, but much of this mountainous tract was subject to no real control. From Kumaun eastward, the northern limit of the Empire was, in practice at least, set by the Himalayan forests as far as the valley of the Brahmaputra, where the boundary turned southward, skirting the State of Kūch and the territory occupied by the tribesmen of Hill Tippera. From this point the authorities are conflicting, but there seems to be little doubt that Chittagong was outside the Empire, and probably Akbar's jurisdiction was limited in practice by the estuary of the Meghna. From the Meghna, the boundary followed the coast to a little south of Puri, whence it struck westwards across the Peninsula to Bombay. The position between the Mahanadi and Godavari rivers is uncertain: some chiefs in this area were certainly independent, while others paid revenue, and only an approximate line can be drawn. The boundary then followed roughly the line of the Godavari to Ahmadnagar, and reached the west coast between Surat and Bombay, but in this part of India the extension of the Empire was in progress, and as has been said above the latest conquests had not been fully assimilated.

The uncertainties regarding frontiers, of which some illustration has just been given, are of interest mainly to the political historian, and in the present state of our knowledge it cannot be said that these boundaries were of any particular importance from the economic point of view. We have fairly full descriptions of the life of Vijayanagar in the first half of the sixteenth century: we know something of life in the Deccan kingdoms of Golconda and Bijapur; and I cannot see that either of them differed in essentials from life in Akbar's Empire. The quality of the administration varied from place to place and from time to time, but its framework was substantially identical, and the people lived under it as best they could. I shall not, therefore, attempt to describe the life of each region separately: the period is marked by uniformity rather than diversity, and the available materials can best be employed to present a sketch of the position in India as a whole.

Leaving, then, political boundaries out of account, what was the surface of India like at the time of Akbar's death? I should answer that on the whole it was very like the India which we know to-day. There are, of course, important differences to be borne in mind. There were no railways: the great canal systems of the Punjab and the United Provinces did not exist; and there were no metalled roads, though the main routes of land travel were clearly defined, in some cases by avenues of trees, and more generally by walled enclosures, known as *sarais*, in which travellers and merchants could pass the night in comparative security. In Northern India these routes were, in some cases at least, suitable for wheeled traffic, and long lines of carts might occasionally be seen, but from Golconda southwards to Cape Comorin carts were practically unknown, and pack-animals or porters were the only means of transport by land. Navigable rivers such as the Indus, the Ganges, and the Jumna were at this time important highways, and carried a large volume of heavy traffic throughout the north of India, while the waterways of Bengal were perhaps even more frequented than now. There was certainly more forest or jungle than exists at the present day, but this statement is not equally true of all portions of the country. In some parts forest predominated, and the groups of settled villages might be described with accuracy as clearings in the jungle, but it appears probable that in others, such as Bengal, Gujarat, and the upper Gangetic plain, the bulk of the country was under regular cultivation, and the jungles, though more extensive than now, were not the principal feature of the landscape. One point in the topography of Northern India is worthy of notice: the submontane forests extended much farther into the United Provinces and Bihar than is now the case, and the frontier of settled cultivation might be defined roughly by a line drawn very little to the north of Bareilly, Gorakhpur, and Muzaffarpur. The prevalence of forest land meant necessarily the presence of large numbers of destructive animals: herds of elephants were not uncommon in the hilly country south of the Ganges and the Jumna, lions could be shot in the province of Malwa, rhinoceros were found on the Gogra, and tigers were killed, though not I think very frequently, in portions of the Gangetic plain. Extensive hunting-grounds were maintained near the Imperial capital of Agra, and probably near other administrative centres, and Jahangir tells in his *Memoirs* how antelope overflowed from one of his preserves into the cultivated tracts, "and were not subject to any kind of molestation."

The general aspect of the settled country must have been very similar to that of the present day. The fields were as a rule unenclosed, or "champion country" in the phrase of contemporary English travellers. The crops grown and the trees planted at the present time were to be seen with a few exceptions of minor importance; and apart from trees and crops there is little in the landscape to attract the eye. The villages too have probably changed but little. There were of course no roofs of corrugated iron such as now strike the observer in Bengal and some other parts of the country: walls of mud or wicker-work, with tiled or thatched roofs, were universal, and the inferiority of the accommodation, together with the lack of furniture, is commented on by Europeans of the period who had occasion to seek temporary hospitality. In regard to the towns and cities there are perhaps greater changes to be noticed. Calcutta and Bombay, Cawnpore and Karachi have all come into existence since Akbar's death, and the modern Madras was represented in his time only by Mylapore and S. Thomé. Some ancient capital cities, like Kanauj and Vijayanagar, were already in a state of decay, others like Jaunpur still retained some portion of their earlier importance, while Fatehpur Sikri, the most recent capital of all, had been deserted within a few years of its establishment. The Imperial capital of Agra, the Deccan capitals of Golconda and Bijapur, and such provincial centres as Multan, Lahore, Delhi, Allahabad, Patna, Ujjain, Ahmadabad, and Ajmer, were large and populous cities, and European observers did not hesitate to compare the largest of them with London or Paris or Constantinople, the greatest cities with which they were familiar. These Indian cities did not as a rule include anything corresponding to a modern "civil station" or residential suburbs: extensive gardens commonly lay outside their walls, but families and places of business were safer within, and though the city houses were in some cases large and luxurious, their importance was not usually visible from the outside. Father Monserrate, who had travelled from Surat to Agra and had accompanied Akbar on his march through Lahore to Kabul, sums up the results of his observations somewhat as follows: "The cities look attractive from a distance, but inside them all the splendour is lost in the narrowness of the streets and the hustling of the crowds. The houses have no windows. Rich men have gardens, ponds, and fountains within their walls, but externally there is nothing to delight the eye. The common people live in huts and hovels, and to have seen one city is to have seen all." That description is substantially applicable at the present day to those cities which have not as yet passed under the hands of the town-planning expert, or developed residential areas on the familiar Anglo-Indian lines.

A few words may be added regarding India's neighbours. On the west, Persia was at this time a powerful State, in friendly relations with the Mogul, but at war with the Turks, who were endeavouring to extend their borders to the south and east, and already dominated the Arabian coast. On the north-west lay Bokhara, which like Persia maintained intercourse with India. Of Tibet we hear little beyond vague tales; a caravan route between Bengal and China was theoretically in existence, but I have found no record of its actual use at this period, and travellers from Agra for China were advised to journey by way of Kabul and the main east-and-west road through Central Asia.[1] To the east of Bengal lay the kingdom of Arakan, and south-east of it was Pegu, the two States covering much of the country now known as Burma. Pegu was at this period desolate as the result of a series of disastrous wars: Arakan appears to have been prosperous, and its king was described (perhaps with some exaggeration) as the most powerful prince in India next to the Great Mogul, but its traffic by land was unimportant. Apart then from the intercourse with Persia and Bokhara, the relations of India with other nations were then as now maintained by sea rather than by land, and since they were based principally on commerce their description may appropriately be postponed to the chapter dealing with that subject.

II. The Numbers of the People

It is scarcely necessary to say that no records exist showing the numbers of the population of India in the sixteenth or

[1] Intercourse with China was, however, conducted principally by the sea route, which will be described in a later chapter.

seventeenth century. I have not read of anything approaching to a census of any part of the country, and our information consists mainly of comparative estimates made by individuals, which are subject to large errors, even larger perhaps in India than in the Europe of the same period. Indian chroniclers throw little light on the question because they had no standard of comparison, and the most they can tell us is something about the relative density in different parts of the country: such facts as I have gathered from them in this respect are adequately represented in a saying recorded by the historian M. de Faria y Sousa, who wrote in the latter part of the seventeenth century. "The heathens," he tells us, "say that God granted these particular prerogatives or blessings to five kingdoms—to that of Bengala, infinite numbers of foot: to Orixa, elephants: to Bisnagar, people skilled in sword and buckler: to Delhi, abundance of towns, and to Cou, innumerable horses."[1] Some further information can be obtained from the observations of European travellers, provided we can ascertain the standard of comparison which was in their minds, a matter of some uncertainty, since the census was not yet an established institution in Europe, and the estimates of population framed by later students are by no means always in agreement. It is perhaps fair to say that at the period of which I am writing the population of France was somewhere about half its present size, while that of England may have been as much as one-eighth, and if it be assumed that Western Europe as a whole lay between these somewhat wide limits, we obtain a rough measure of what was in the minds of travellers when they spoke of Eastern countries as densely or sparsely populated: their observations do not mean that the population of India was large or small judged by Europe at the present day, but that it was large or small when compared with a Europe which had at any rate much less than half its present population.

Judged by this standard, there can be no doubt that the

[1] The quotation is from Stevens's translation of *The Portuguese Asia*, i. 415. Orixa is of course Orissa; Bisnagar is Vijayanagar; Delhi is the Mogul Empire; while Cou is most probably Kūch, the State mentioned in the preceding section.

territory of Vijayanagar had been very densely populated for at least two centuries. Conti, writing soon after the year 1400, said that "the numbers of the people exceed belief"; the Persian Envoy, Abdur Razak, who was in Vijayanagar about the same period, wrote that the Empire contained so great a population that it would be impossible to give an idea of it, and, a century later, Paes observed that the whole country was thickly populated with cities and towns and villages. A temporary reduction in numbers must have followed on the famine of 1540, which was very severe on the Coromandel coast, but I have found no record of a similar calamity in the next sixty years, and the observations of the Jesuit missionaries about the year 1597 show that the description given by Paes was still in the main applicable: the pearl fishery at Manar attracted a crowd estimated at 60,000, and the impression left by the narratives of Pimenta and Simon Sa is one of numerous towns and fully occupied country. As regards the narrow strip of land below the Western Ghats, the presence of a dense population must be assumed in order to explain the facts recorded in the *Decadas*, and is expressly affirmed by Barbosa among European writers.

For the Deccan kingdoms, there is very little evidence relating directly to our period. In the fifteenth century the Russian monk Nikitin commented on the number of small towns, and said (if the translation is to be trusted) that "the land is overstocked with people." Throughout the greater part of the sixteenth century these kingdoms maintained a bitter, and eventually successful, struggle with Vijayanagar, and must have been able to draw upon a large population to swell their armies to the necessary size; while half a century after Akbar's death the French traveller Thévenot found the population dense from Aurangabad to Golconda, but sparse from Golconda eastward to Masulipatam. The narrative of Tavernier's travels in the Deccan gives a general impression of density, and his account of the crowds at the diamond fields suggests that there was no scarcity of labourers in this part of the country.

As regards the Mogul Empire we have a considerable number

of incidental observations made by travellers along certain routes. Taking first the journey from Surat to Agra, it is clear that Gujarat was thickly peopled. Della Valle, writing of Surat, says it "is very populous as all other cities and places are in India, which everywhere abounds with people." This writer uses the word India in the restricted sense favoured by the Portuguese, and his travels did not extend northwards, but his evidence is relevant to the condition of Gujarat and the west coast. Finch counted a city, seven "great towns," and three other "towns" on his march from Surat to Burhanpur, and his narrative leaves the impression of a closely settled country. From Burhanpur northwards to Gwalior the population was less dense; parts of Malwa were indeed fully occupied, but much of the broken country on both the north and the south of the plateau was very nearly desolate. The alternative route through Rajputana was in general sparsely inhabited, at least as far north as Ajmer, and travellers found little to notice in this part of the country. The route from Agra to Lahore, on the other hand, lay through a dense population, and the same statement holds good from Lahore as far as Multan, and down the Indus to Bhakkar, but from Bhakkar onwards most of Sind was desert. In this case also there was an alternative route across the desert from Ajmer to Tatta, but the country traversed was, as might be expected, uninhabited or occupied only by nomads.

Of the routes eastwards from Agra we have much scantier knowledge. Finch gives an itinerary through Kanauj and Lucknow to Jaunpur, but it is hearsay and throws little light on the state of the country: he mentions, however, that the road from Jaunpur to Allahabad lay through a continuous forest, a fact of which the significance will appear later. Fitch some years earlier travelled by river from Agra to Bengal, and he notes that the country from Allahabad to Patna was populous, but this remark applies only to the river-banks, and I have found no other description of Bihar and the east of what is now the United Provinces.

So far then we have reached a rough general idea of the relative density of the population in different parts of the country, and we may say that Bengal, the north-western plains, Gujarat, and Southern India were thickly, or very thickly, populated when judged by contemporary European standards. As regards the size of the great cities, it is possible to make a further approximation: travellers compared Indian cities with others which they knew, and though such comparisons are liable to large errors, they are not therefore entirely to be neglected. To take a modern parallel, we should not expect a traveller unprovided with statistical information to discriminate between the great cities of Northern India: to him, Lahore and Delhi, Agra and Lucknow would all appear to be of about the same size. On the other hand, a man of ordinary intelligence could hardly fail to observe that all of them are much inferior in population to Calcutta or Bombay, and larger than places like Jullundur or Saharanpur, and we may fairly allow to earlier travellers a corresponding exactitude of discrimination. Speaking generally, they class the largest cities of India with the largest cities of the West. Jourdain says Agra was one of the biggest cities of the world: Coryat says that Lahore was larger than Constantinople, and that Agra was not so large as Lahore: Paes says that Vijayanagar was as large as Rome: Bernier (rather later than our period) says that Delhi was not much less than Paris, and that Agra was larger than Delhi: Ralph Fitch says that Agra and Fatehpur Sikri were each much greater than London: Monserrate says that Lahore was second to no city in Europe or in Asia; and other travellers offer similar comparisons. Now the population of European cities about this period is by no means accurately known, but it appears reasonable to say that Paris contained not more than 400,000 inhabitants at the outside, and that no other city in Europe had more than 200,000; we may therefore conclude that the greatest Indian cities were most probably of the quarter-million to half-million standard, and that in any case their inhabitants were not to be counted by the million.[1]

[1] The population of European cities about this period is discussed in the *Handwörterbuch der Staatswissenschaften*, ii. 882-898. *Levasseur* gives a

This conclusion, vague as it is, will serve at least to correct the exaggerated ideas which grew up in Europe during the period when intercourse with India was rapidly increasing, and which are not even now entirely discarded. Thévenot, writing in the middle of the seventeenth century, took pains to test the accuracy of some of these stories by inquiries among people likely to know the facts, and his results are in general agreement with the view which has just been expressed. Of Agra, probably the largest city in India, he writes that it was populated as befits a great town, but the current story that it could furnish 200,000 armed men was an exaggeration: the gardens within the city gave a false impression of size, while the streets were so narrow that they were necessarily crowded when the Imperial Court was present, though at other times they were empty. Similarly, in considering Delhi he lays stress on the number of people who accompanied the Court, and concludes that without the Court the city was of small importance; if the population amounted to 400,000 when the Emperor was present, it might be less than one-sixth of that number when the Emperor was elsewhere. An example of the exaggerations current during the seventeenth century is the statement made by various writers that the city of Gaur in Bengal contained 1,200,000 houses, a figure which would indicate a population approximating to that of modern London. In the previous century, however, Barros, the Portuguese annalist, gave its population at 200,000, and since the city was of no particular importance at this epoch, it is safe to conclude that the number of houses indicated in the later story was either a wild exaggeration or took into account the ruins of the various capitals which had existed in the neighbourhood. At any rate I have been unable to find any reasonable grounds for inferring that any city in

variety of estimates of the population of Paris, which taken together suggest a maximum figure of 400,000 in the year 1600. In his *History of the City of Rome in the Middle Ages* (translation, Hamilton, viii. 407) Gregorovius quotes with apparent approval an estimate putting the population of Rome in 1520 at about 85,000: Paes's account of Vijayanagar is of about the same date. Paes also states (*Sewell*, p. 290) that there were more than 100,000 houses in Vijayanagar; this would mean a population of half a million or somewhat more, and probably the truth lay between the two numbers.

India had a resident population of as many as half a million. It is probable, indeed, that an influx of troops or pilgrims might result, as happens to-day, in temporary aggregations of people in excess of this number, but for comparative purposes such incidents must be disregarded: the population of modern Allahabad is correctly taken as less than 200,000, though over a million persons may gather there for a religious festival, and the same basis must be adopted in estimating the population of Indian cities at the earlier period.

A general idea of the magnitude of the city population can thus be drawn from the particulars within our reach. From the nature of the case, the question of rural density cannot be determined on similar considerations, and we must look elsewhere for information which may enable us to give somewhat greater precision to the vague conclusions at which we have already arrived. Such information may be drawn from two sources, the strength of armies and the extent of cultivation, and it so happens that from the first source we can learn something about the south of India, while the second throws some light on the position in the north. I shall examine these sources in order, but at the outset it is necessary to utter a word of warning as to the degree of exactitude which may be expected in these calculations, and in others of a similar nature which will be found in subsequent chapters. A certain amount of statistical information was indeed recorded in India at this period, but we have not access to the original records, and we do not always know the basis on which they were compiled. We have to be content, as a rule, with secondary and partial evidence in the shape of facts stated by contemporary writers, who may have made mistakes in the figures, or may have been misled as to their precise significance; and we can interpret their statements only by the aid of assumptions, the validity of which may be open to question. We can scarcely ever say that a conclusion is certain or that a particular number is unquestionably correct; we have to estimate probabilities and seek for limits within which the truth may lie. Data, assumptions, and conclusions are alike open to criticism, and if I sometimes appear to speak too confidently in matters of number or of quantity, the reader must bear in mind that this preliminary caution applies throughout, and that we are not travelling on the broad road of modern statistical information, but are trying to find a path through a hitherto untrodden jungle.

The information at our disposal regarding the strength of the armies of Southern India has been set out by Mr. Sewell, who, without committing himself to a numerical estimate, concludes that "all the chroniclers believed that the King of Vijayanagar could, if he so desired, put into the field immense masses of armed men. They were probably not all well armed or well trained or well disciplined, but as to large numbers there can be little reasonable doubt." The statements on which this conclusion is based fall into two groups: some authorities tell us the nominal strength of the army of Vijayanagar, while others give the numbers actually put into the field on particular occasions, and the evidence under these two heads is on the whole reasonably consistent. Five writers, of whom four at least may be regarded as independent, put the nominal strength of the army at about one million, while two of them add that it could be increased to two millions if necessary. Now it is possible that these round numbers may be mere vague guesses having no relation to the truth, but to my mind it is more probable that they represent a notorious fact. The great bulk of the army was organised on the quota system, which will be described in a subsequent chapter; each Imperial officer was bound, as a condition of his tenure, to produce on demand a fixed number of troops, and the most reasonable interpretation of the statements we are considering appears to me to be that the total of these contingents amounted on paper to about a million, that this fact was common knowledge in the city, so that all strangers received approximately the same answer to their questions, and that the possibility of doubling the numbers was added by men who were jealous for the reputation of the Empire. This interpretation does not, of course, imply that an army of a million ever took the field. Nuniz tells us, what we might in any case have guessed, that some of the officers kept smaller forces than their obligations required, and we should regard the number of a million as a theoretical limit, not perhaps in excess of the capacity of the country, but not likely to be reached in any particular campaign. This view is borne out by such details as we possess of the actual strength mobilised. The array of the army in the year 1522 is described by Nuniz with a fulness which shows that he must have had access to detailed sources of information; he mentions eleven separate bodies of the main army, which aggregate just over 600,000 men, and in addition there were other contingents of 10,000 or 12,000 men, as well as a strong advance-guard, so that on this showing about 650,000 men, or say two-thirds of the nominal strength of the Empire, were put into line in a very serious emergency. At Talikot forty years later, when the danger to the Empire was known to be even greater, we are told on Portuguese authority that the army was 700,000 strong, a number which accords generally with the description quoted by Mr. Sewell of the final campaign, when the force marched in three bodies, an advance guard of 120,000, then another "large army," and then "the whole power" of the Empire. These independent statements appear to me to justify a view of the military organisation which is in harmony with all that we know as to the activities of the great Empire of the south, and also with the relation of performance to promise prevalent at this period—a huge army provided for, and in the utmost emergency an array of perhaps two men out of three, presumably because some contingents failed to appear, and the others were substantially below the obligatory strength.[1]

[1] We may presume that the Emperor's personal troops were present at Talikot in approximately full strength, but they formed only a small proportion of the whole army. The strength of the personal troops employed forty years earlier in the attack on Raichur was 46,000, but this was a picked force (*Sewell*, 327), and the total number was probably about 100,000, as stated by *Barbosa* (p. 300). Mr. Longworth Dames, in his translation of this passage (i. 211 *note*), takes this number as indicating the total strength of the trained army, but I read it as referring to the personal troops, those paid directly by the Emperor, and not those paid by his nobles: Barbosa (p. 300) says the Emperor had this number "continually in his pay," and further on (p. 306) he says that the same number accompanied the Emperor when travelling. In his account of Vijayanagar he does not refer to the contingents provided by the nobles.

Similar data are not available for the opposing armies of the Deccan. They must obviously have been numerous, since they maintained the struggle for so many years and at last gained a decisive victory, but I am disposed to infer from the imperfect accounts of particular battles that the northern forces were usually in a minority, and that they owed their success in part to their strength in cavalry, and in part to greater skill; the Portuguese account of the battle of Talikot says that the Deccan had half the numbers of Vijayanagar, and this proportion is not in itself improbable, but allowance must be made for the wastage of the invading armies, which had marched some distance from their bases to the scene of the battle. Taking then the Deccan and Vijayanagar together, it is not unreasonable to infer that this part of India could actually put something like a million men in the field, though it could not have maintained this number throughout a long campaign; and armies of this strength would not represent what it has become the fashion to call the "man-power" of the country, for the figures which have been given for Vijayanagar exclude numerous camp-followers, while the brahmans, merchants, and artisans, constituting in the aggregate a substantial proportion of the population, were exempted from service. These forces were drawn from an area consisting of the greater part of the Presidencies of Madras and Bombay (excluding Sind) together with the States of Mysore and Hyderabad, and containing according to the last census a population of between sixty and seventy millions;[1] the question is what numbers were contained in this area at the period under consideration. So far as I know, there are no data to show directly what forces could be raised from a given population in the conditions which prevailed in India at this period, and European analogies must be used with a certain amount of caution. We may, however, be sure that the latest European experience must be set aside; the world has now learned that a proportion as

[1] It is not easy to define the area exactly in terms of the modern administrative units for which the population is recorded, but the numbers almost certainly lie between these limits.

great as one-sixth of the total population can be armed, but that this requires progressive organisation extending over a series of years, and it is practically impossible that any similar proportion could have been attained in the short and sudden campaigns characteristic of Indian warfare. A closer analogy is the number of men which European States were prepared to mobilise on the outbreak of war: according to the published figures, France had arranged before the year 1914 to mobilise one out of 31, and Germany one out of 32, so that, if the recruiting organisation of the Deccan and Vijayanagar was as efficient as that of modern France and Germany, their united strength of a million would imply a population of about thirty millions, while the population would be greater if the efficiency was less. The degree of efficiency attained in India at this period is entirely a matter of conjecture: on the one hand the quota system was calculated to distribute the demand for men over all portions of the country, and it is improbable that a high standard of physique was required, but on the other hand the exempted classes were, as we have seen, considerable in point of numbers, and speaking for myself, I find it difficult to believe that the Indian system can have been the more efficient of the two. At any rate, if we accept the inference that the Deccan and Vijayanagar could together put somewhere about a million men into the field, we must agree that they could draw on a population of over thirty millions (or about half the present numbers), unless we are prepared to maintain that their military system was more efficient than those of modern Europe so far as the enrolment of recruits is concerned. This inference is of course based on data drawn from the period ending with the battle of Talikot in 1565, but, as has been said already, there is no record of any serious calamity between that date and the end of the century, and since the country cannot be described as overcrowded with about half its present population, we should not be justified in concluding that the numbers had decreased largely in the interval; a moderate increase is in fact the more reasonable inference.

To my mind then the available information suggests that the population of the southern territories was at least thirty millions, and probably substantially more. No similar inference can be drawn regarding Northern India, for the sufficient reason that the strength of the Mogul forces is unknown. Akbar, at least in his later years, never had occasion to put his whole power into the field; he was indeed frequently at war, but the operations were of a secondary nature, and it is no more possible to deduce from them the potential strength of his army than it is possible to calculate the forces of modern India from the details of successive expeditions on the frontiers. It is true that the *Ain-i Akbari* contains much information in regard to Akbar's military organisation, but unfortunately the account is not complete, and after working up all the figures furnished by Abul Fazl, I have found myself compelled to assent to the conclusion reached by Mr. Irvine that the numbers of the army cannot be estimated with any approach to precision. For the north, however, we have access to the alternative source of information to which I have already alluded, for the statistics preserved in the *Ain-i Akbari* suffice, if we can interpret them correctly, to give a general idea of the extent of cultivation in those provinces of the Mogul Empire in which the regulation system of revenue assessments had been effectively introduced. Unfortunately, these statistics have not yet been thoroughly studied, and I can offer only my individual interpretation of the figures which relate to a portion of Northern India. My conclusions may be stated as follows:

(1) A detailed study of the statistics for the western portion of the United Provinces, that is to say, the area lying between the Jumna and a line joining Bareilly and Agra, indicates that the cultivated area in settled country was about three-fourths of the present standard, the proportion being more than eight-tenths in the tract between the Ganges and the Jumna known as the *duāb*, and almost seven-tenths in Rohilkhand, the country lying east of the Ganges. The area of settled cultivation was less, because as has been said in the preceding section the line of the Himalayan forests lay nearer the Ganges than

is now the case, but the *duāb*, and also a strip of country on the left bank of the Ganges, may almost be described as fully occupied.

(2) A general survey of the statistics for the Punjab suggests that the density of cultivation found in the *duāb* extended westwards across the Jumna, at any rate as far as Lahore, but that on the other hand the South and West Punjab was very sparsely occupied.

(3) The statistics for the centre of the United Provinces present difficulties which I have not yet been able to surmount, but they suggest a rapid decline in cultivation in the *duāb* from Agra eastwards.

(4) In the east of the Provinces, the amount of cultivation north of the Gogra was very small, while between the Gogra and the Ganges, eastwards of a line joining Allahabad and Fyzabad, the proportion was less than one-fifth.

(5) The figures for Bihar suggest on a general examination that this proportion of one-fifth extended as far as Monghyr, at which point the statistics come to an end.

In order to translate density of cultivation into density of population, it is necessary to anticipate the conclusion reached in Chapter IV., that, while there have been many changes in detail, the main lines of the Indian system of agriculture have persisted during the last three centuries, and consequently the area placed under crops is a rough index to the numbers of the rural population. If this conclusion is provisionally accepted, it follows that the western Gangetic plain was almost as full of people in Akbar's time as it is to-day, and consequently was very densely populated when judged by the European standard of the sixteenth century, while on the other hand the eastern Gangetic plain as far as the confines of Bengal was not, as it now is, a congested area, but supported a population of about one-fifth the present density. We have already seen that European travellers found a dense population in that portion of the former area which was visited by them, and on the other hand we have here an explanation of the statement made to Finch that the road from Jaunpur to Allahabad lay through a continuous forest, as well as of the fact recorded in the *Akbarnama* that forests were traversed and various strange beasts seen during a march along the southern bank of the Gogra in what is now the congested district of Azamgarh. The conclusions drawn from contemporary statistics are thus not entirely uncorroborated, and it is possible that further study of the literature of the period will furnish other statements of a similar nature.

If now we apply these conclusions to the figures of the last census, we shall find that the population of the northern plains from Multan to Monghyr must have been well over 30 millions and probably little less than 40 millions at the period to which the statistics relate.[1] We have thus a total of, at any rate, more than 60 millions in sight for the northern and southern areas taken together, but without allowing anything for two populous regions, Bengal and Gujarat, or for any part of the more sparsely peopled but extensive intervening area; and when we bring these excluded tracts into account, we are justified in concluding that there must have been at the least somewhere about 100 millions of people in India in order to carry on the activities disclosed by contemporary authorities. The number is absolutely very great, and would have appeared almost incredible to European observers of the period, but it is only one-third of what the same area contained in the year 1911; various arguments could be adduced in favour of a higher figure, but the nature of the data compel us to be content with indefinite estimates, and it appears to me that we shall run no risk of serious error if we take 100 millions as indicating a total, not indeed attained by careful enumeration, but rendered probable by a consideration of all the relevant facts which are available.

[1] The date of the statistics is not absolutely certain, but they are earlier than the famine of 1596, which caused heavy mortality in the north-west, and consequently the population at the end of the century must have been less than the figures disclose. The extent of country affected by this famine is not known, but I think I have discounted it adequately by taking little over 30 millions where the figures would justify nearly 40 millions; I can find nothing to suggest that this famine extended to Bengal or to Gujarat.

III. The Classes of the Population

The population of whose numbers we have been trying to form some idea was by no means homogeneous. Among the Hindus, who formed the great majority, the caste system existed substantially as it exists to-day, and the differences among castes and races were such that we find travellers speaking of baniyas or of Gujaratis as "nations" distinct from brahmans or rajputs. The Sikhs were at this time regarded merely as a sect of Hindus, and from the economic point of view the Christians of the South may apparently be classed as resembling in essentials the people among whom they lived. Jews and Armenians were few in numbers, but important in commercial life. The position of the Parsis is not altogether clear. Terry, writing of his experiences about 1616, says that "their profession is, for the generality, all kinds of husbandry"; Mundy, a little later, speaks of them as cultivating palm-trees, and Monserrate was unable to distinguish them from the rest of the crowd of what he calls heathens, meaning, I take it, the ordinary Hindu population of the country round Navsari, in which they were at that time settled. On the other hand, in Thévenot's time they were conspicuous figures in Surat, essentially a commercial city, while in the middle of the sixteenth century Garcia da Orta knew some of them as traders in Cambay and Bassein, and notes that they were regarded as Jews by the Portuguese. Apparently, therefore, they were at this period passing from the pursuit of agriculture to the commercial career in which they have since achieved such remarkable success.

Two other elements of the population, the Moslems and the Portuguese, require to be noticed in greater detail. Among the Moslems we must distinguish between the Arabs and Persians of the coast and the men of Northern India, and the latter again must be divided into old-established inhabitants and recent immigrants. In the centuries preceding the year 1500 Arabs and Persians had acquired a position of predominance in the sea-borne trade of the whole Indian Ocean from Mozambique to the Straits of Malacca. They had settlements at the seaports on both sides of India, wherever they could come to arrangements with the local authorities, and the value of their trade to those authorities was so great that they were commonly welcomed and in some places at least enjoyed special favours. The Moslem population of these settlements did not however consist wholly, or even mainly, of foreigners. The merchants came primarily for trade, but they did not neglect the interests of their faith, and at the seaports which they frequented larger or smaller groups of converts were to be found, increased as the result of intermarriages or less formal unions with the people of the country. Early in the sixteenth century the Portuguese had ousted these Moslems from their predominant position in the Indian Ocean, but had not succeeded in driving them out of trade, and we meet with Moslems at practically every seaport in India, even in some of those where the Portuguese had acquired territorial jurisdiction. From the seaports Moslems made their way into the interior, chiefly as distributors of the commodities their ships brought to India, and Vijayanagar in the days of its prosperity included a considerable Moslem quarter.

Altogether apart from these sea-borne influences, a large number of Moslems had entered India from the north-west in the five or six centuries preceding the establishment of Akbar's Empire, and had effected conversions on a very large scale. The descendants of the early arrivals were already well assimilated when the Moguls first appeared on the scene, and as a rule took the Indian side in the struggles against Babur and Humayun: in the time of Akbar, they may be described with substantial truth as Indian Moslems, in contradistinction to the men who had come with him to India or who followed him there on the establishment of his authority. Akbar's Court was essentially foreign, and even in his later years the Indian element, whether Hindu or Moslem, constituted only a small proportion of the whole.[1] Such influence as was exerted by the Court in the economic sphere came from the predominant party, whose tastes and

[1] Details on this point are given below in Chapter III.

habits led to the patronage of foreign merchants and the use of foreign commodities, as will be explained in the following chapters.[1]

The coming of the Portuguese at the opening of the sixteenth century was the result of a variety of motives. At that time eastern commodities for Europe were carried up the Red Sea or the Persian Gulf, and, after paying heavy duties to the Moslems in authority in Turkey and Egypt, were distributed by the Italian merchants who dominated the trade of the Eastern Mediterranean. The Portuguese desired to carry these commodities in their own ships round the Cape of Good Hope: by doing this, they would at once enrich themselves and strike a heavy blow at the prosperity of the Moslem States, which were still regarded as the enemies of Christendom, but at the same time they hoped to secure a position whence the Christian religion could be propagated, and thus their enterprise was at once commercial and missionary in its nature. They did not attempt to found an empire on land: the root-idea of their policy was such supremacy in the Indian seas that they could control and direct the course of trade, and with this object they established maritime settlements, protected by forts sufficiently strong to resist attack, and large enough to provide the supply of soldiers and sailors which their policy required. These settlements existed on the east coast of Africa, at the mouth of the Persian Gulf, on the western coast of India, in the Straits of Malacca, and even farther east. Their capital city was Goa; they occupied several other ports on the west coast, and while they were not established in the Gulf of Cambay, they controlled its traffic from their posts at Daman and Diu. On the east coast they were established less formally but effectively at S. Thomé and elsewhere; they had trading establishments at the mouths of the

[1] In contemporary European records the distinction between the various strains of Moslem influence is obscured by the use of the term Moor. The Portuguese learned to know Islam, and to hate it, from the Moors who penetrated into their country from Northern Africa, and to them every Moslem was a Moor, and consequently an enemy. This use of the word was adopted by Dutch and English visitors to the East, and throughout our period a Moor is merely a Moslem, without any reference to race or nationality. See *Hobson-Jobson* under the word.

Indus and the Ganges, while Portuguese subjects occupied an anomalous position at Chittagong and elsewhere in the Bay of Bengal, depending for their livelihood largely upon piracy. In the interior of the country they were rarely met with. They had representatives engaged in trade at a few places like Lahore, and missionaries from Goa were at Court for long periods towards the end of Akbar's reign, but apart from such cases the only mention I have found of their presence up the country is Terry's remark that he occasionally met Portuguese "who would beg relief"; they were usually men who had deserted from one of the settlements or had absconded to avoid punishment for some crime.

To complete the enumeration of the races found in India, mention should be made of the imported slaves. Abyssinians were in much demand, and we read of them frequently—sometimes in very responsible positions—in the chronicles of the time; a regular traffic existed in the inhabitants of Mozambique, and there was also an import trade from Persia and the countries lying beyond. Finally it may be noted that the number of temporary residents must have been considerable. Merchants from Arabia, Armenia, Persia and other countries to the north-west, and Europeans travelling for pleasure, profit, or adventure appear in various places, and in numbers greater than might be expected, while there are a few references to the presence of Chinese and Japanese on the west coast. India was very far from being a closed country, and access to it could be obtained by men of any nation who cared to face the dangers and discomforts of the journey.

When we turn from the racial to the economic classification of the people, the first point to arrest our attention is the comparative insignificance of the middle classes. Bernier, writing half a century later, remarked that "in Delhi there is no middle state. A man must be either of the highest rank or live miserably"; and this is the impression left by a perusal of the narratives and chronicles relating more particularly to our period.[1] There were at this time no lawyers, very

[1] This statement is possibly less applicable to Bengal than to other parts of India. I have been told that contemporary Bengalee literature

few if any professional teachers, no journalists or politicians, no engineers, no forms of employment corresponding to the modern railway, postal or irrigation services, or to factories and large workshops, few landholders in the modern sense, and, unless I am mistaken, scarcely any families living upon accumulated property; and if we remove these elements from the middle classes as they exist to-day, we shall find that there is very little left, beyond the families dependent on the various public offices. Materials do not exist for a precise or scientific classification of the remaining elements of the population, but for our present purposes they can be studied most conveniently in two groups, the first of which is of interest mainly from the point of view of consumption, while the second comprises the classes whose principal importance is found in production. The former group includes (1) the Court and the Imperial Service, (2) the professional and religious classes, including mendicants and ascetics, and (3) domestic servants and slaves. In the second group we have to consider the classes engaged in (1) agriculture, (2) industry, and (3) commerce. The precise economic position of the men known in Akbar's days as zamindars may fairly be regarded as arguable; there are very few definite data as to their activities, and what little there is to say can be said appropriately in connection with the agricultural interest. Another class which is not provided for in this scheme consists of the tribes inhabiting the mountains and the forests, but they are scarcely mentioned in the authorities and can be left out of account in an economic study.[1]

---

suggests the presence of something like a middle class, but my ignorance of the language has prevented me from following up the subject in detail. There is no trace of such a distinctive feature in the authorities within my reach, but they are not conclusive on this particular point.

[1] Some idea of the importance attached to these classes may be gathered from the story current in the early years of Jahangir's reign that in hunting the men of the jungle were on the same footing as the beasts. A favourite form of sport was the *Kamargha*, which consisted in enclosing a tract of country by a line of guards, and then gradually contracting the enclosure until a large quantity of game was encircled in a space of convenient size. Finch, writing at Agra about 1610, says (*Purchas*, I. iv. 430): "Whatever is taken in this enclosure is called the King's *shikar* or game, whether men

The classification which I have indicated will furnish the framework of the remainder of this book, but before we take up the study of the first group it is necessary to say a little about the nature of the administration, so far as it influenced the conditions under which the processes of production and consumption were carried on, and this subject is dealt with in the following chapter.

AUTHORITIES FOR CHAPTER I

NOTE.—*In these Notes on Authorities, reference is made by means of abbreviations or key-words, which are printed in italics, and are explained in alphabetical order in Appendix E.*

SECTION 1.—For an account of the various meanings of the word India, the article with that heading in *Hobson-Jobson* may be consulted. For Vijayanagar at this period, see *Sewell*, 199 ff. Father N. Pimenta, in reporting on his missionary journey of 1598, noted that Vijayanagar was regarded as King of Kings (*Hay*, 741), and Father Simon Sa, writing in the same year, described his visit to the Imperial Court (*Hay*, 762 ff.).

The constitutional organisation of Akbar's Empire has to be inferred from a detailed study of the *Ain* and the *Akbarnama.* Some of the passages bearing on it were discussed by Mr. Yusuf Ali and the present writer in the *Journal of the R.A.S.* (January, 1918, "Akbar's Land-Revenue System," etc.). As regards the smaller Indian States, the position on the west coast can best be studied in the later *Decadas* (x.-xii.), while Portuguese activities on the east coast are referred to frequently in the same work, and also in *Hay*, 737. The existence of Hindu States to the south of Orissa is mentioned by Jahangir (*Tuzuk*, i. 433); for Kūch, see the "Account" of Bengal in the *Ain* (translation, ii. 117), Fitch's journey (*Purchas*, II. x. 1736), and *Hobson-Jobson* (*s.v.* Cooch Bahar).

For the boundaries of the Mogul Empire, I have made use of the map facing p. 322 of Mr. Vincent Smith's *Akbar, the Great Mogul*, but the details have been drawn mainly from the *Ain*, especially the "Account of the XII. Subas." The conditions in the hills beyond the Indus are clearly indicated in the narratives of travellers such as Steel and Crowther (*Purchas*, I. iv. 521). As regards the portion of Bengal lying east of the Meghna estuary, the *Ain* includes the country as far as Chittagong in the revenue roll of Bengal (translation, ii. 139), and twice mentions Chittagong itself

---

or beasts. . . . The beasts taken, if man's meat, are sold, and their money given to the poor; if men, they remain the King's slaves, which he sends yearly to Kabul to barter for horses and dogs: these being poor, miserable, thievish people, that live in woods and deserts, little differing from beasts." I do not know if this story be true: other writers tell it besides Finch, but the fact that it was told may be safely accepted as evidence of the estimation in which these unfortunate people were held by their more highly civilised brothers.

specifically as part of the Empire (ii. 116, 125), but it also states (ii. 119) that the port was held by Arakan. *Pyrard* (translation, i. 326) visited the port in 1607 and found that it was held subject to Arakan by a petty king; while the Jesuit missionaries whose narratives are quoted by Father N. Pimenta in 1597–98 (*Hay*, pp. 730-33, 840-47) seem to have known nothing of Mogul jurisdiction after leaving Hooghly, but dealt with various "Kinglets" (*reguli*) in the country they traversed, and obtained concessions from "the Most High and Mighty King of Arakan, Tippera, Cucoma and Bengal," a title which indicates the claim of Arakan to, at any rate, a portion of the Delta.

As to the country between the Mahanadi and the Godavari, Mr. Vincent Smith shows on the map mentioned above the territory of Gondwana (which was a Mogul province in later times), as held by "Chiefs mostly independent, some tributary," and carries it nearly as far north as Allahabad. This description is borne out in a general way by the portions of the "Account" in the *Ain* referring to the frontiers of the adjoining provinces: it is fairly certain that many of the Chiefs in this area had not submitted to Akbar, but I am inclined to include the area as a whole in his "sphere of influence," though not in his actual dominions.

The general description given of the surface of India is really the impression left on my mind by the accounts of all the contemporary writers named in the list of authorities, and it is not worth while quoting the references in detail. The absence of wheeled traffic in Southern India is vouched for in particular by *Tavernier*, 121. The extension of forest land is referred to in *Elliot, Races*, ii. 149, also in a paper by the present writer on "The Agricultural Statistics of Akbar's Empire," which is being published in the *Journal* of the United Provinces Historical Society.

Jahangir has much to say of sport in Northern India: the passage quoted in the text is from the *Tuzuk*, i. 190. *Monserrate's* summary of the aspect of Indian cities is on p. 651; unfortunately this careful observer seems to have been more interested in the towns than in the country.

As regards neighbouring countries, a few references may be given to supplement the ordinary authorities. Steel and Crowther (*Purchas*, I. iv. 522 ff.), among other writers, tell something of Persia at this period. For the country north of India, *Yule's Cathay* is of course indispensable. The land routes from India to China are discussed in letters printed by *Hay*, 798 ff. The ruin of Pegu is mentioned by various writers: details are given by Father A. Boves (*Hay*, 850), and a portion of his letter is translated in *Purchas* (II. x. 1748) along with other information on the subject. Various details as to Pegu are scattered through the Xth and XIIth *Decadas*. The description of the King of Arakan as second only to the Mogul is given by *Pyrard* (translation, i. 326), but this accurate writer makes it plain that during his short stay in Chittagong he could learn only what was said in the port, and he does not vouch for the details which he records.

SECTION 2.—For the population of France I follow *Levasseur*; for that of England I have been guided mainly by the figures in *Cunningham*, i. 331 (note), and by the suggestions of Mrs. C. M. Knowles, the Reader in Economic History in the University of London. The observations regarding the general population quoted in the text will be found in *Major* (Conti, 26, Abdur Razak, 32, Nikitin, 14); *Sewell*, 237; *Hay*, 735-738; *Barbosa*, 294; *Thévenot*, 104, 129, 231, 312; *Tavernier*, 336 ff.; *della Valle*, 30; *Manrique*, lxi, lxix; *Purchas* (Finch, I. iv. 423 ff.; Steel and Crowther, I. iv. 520 ff.; Fitch, II. x. 1734 ff.); *Mundy*, ii. 55, 245. It is advisable, however, to read the entire narratives of these and other travellers in order to obtain a just idea of the state of the country through which they passed.

For references to Indian cities, see *Jourdain*, 162; *Sewell*, 256; *Bernier*, 282, 284; *Monserrate*, 622; *Purchas* (Coryat, I. iv. 493 ff.; Fitch, II. x. 1733). The exaggerated statement as to the size of Gaur will be found in *Faria y Sousa*, i. 415; Barros' estimate is in *Decadas*, IV. ix. c. 1, and is quoted in *Hobson-Jobson* under *Gour*.

For the strength of the army of Vijayanagar, see *Sewell*, 147-150, and the authorities there enumerated; for maintenance of inadequate forces, *idem*, 384; and for exemptions from service, *idem*, 279. The strength of Akbar's army is discussed in *Irvine*, 87 ff., the data being scattered through many sections of the *Ain*. The present writer's study of the agricultural statistics in the *Ain* is referred to above under Section 1.

SECTION 3.—The institution of caste is referred to by practically all the European writers who made any attempt to describe India. For the Parsis, see *Terry*, 377; *Mundy*, ii. 306; *Monserrate*, 550; *Thévenot*, 46; *Garcia da Orta*, 445; *Jourdain*, 128.

Moslems at the Indian seaports are referred to in all descriptions from *Barbosa* (*passim*) downwards. For their settlements in Africa, see *Decada*, X. i. 42, and *passim*. Accounts of the spread of Islam in Malaysia will be found in Clifford's *Further India*, 16 ff., and (by R. O. Windstedt) in the *Journal of the R.A.S.* (Straits Branch) for December 1917. The position of Moslems on the west coast is stated by *Whiteway* (3 ff. and *passim*): for Moslems in Goa, see *Purchas*, II. x. 1758; and in Vijayanagar, see *Sewell*, 256. The position of Moslems in Northern India must be gathered from the chronicles of the period, as represented in *Elliot*, *History*, iv.-vi., the *Akbarnama*, and the *Ain*.

General accounts of the Portuguese in India are given by *Whiteway* and *Danvers*, while for more detailed information it is necessary to refer to the *Decadas* and other contemporary authorities. For their possessions at this period, see *Decada*, X. i. 42 ff., where the position on the east coast is clearly distinguished from that on the west. For the Indus, see *Purchas*, I. iv. 496; for the Ganges and Chittagong, see in particular *Hay*, 727-733, 840-847, also *Pyrard*, translation, i. 334. For the missionaries at Akbar's Court, see the full account in *V. Smith*, *Akbar*, and the references there given, especially *Monserrate*. *Terry's* reference to Portuguese being met up the country is on p. 154.

The presence of foreigners in India is noted incidentally in most of the authorities; for examples, see *Garcia da Orta*, 442, and Finch, in *Purchas*, I. iv. 427. *Pyrard* (translation, ii. 38) mentions "a goodly number" of Chinese and Japanese at Goa, and Father Pimenta records (*Hay*, 832) that a famous Malabar pirate employed a Chinese secretary.

CHAPTER II

THE ADMINISTRATION

I. The Form of Administration

The word administration denotes the organisation and methods by which a State endeavours to attain its objects, and consequently the nature of the administration at any given time depends in great measure on the objects in view. In the India of Akbar's time, two objects were of paramount importance: one was the assessment and collection of sufficient revenue, the other was the supply of adequate contingents for the army, and these two primary functions were largely in the hands of a single set of officers, who also discharged most of the remaining duties, and in particular were responsible for the preservation of internal peace. The administration was thus of the centralised or unified type which is still familiar in India, though its nature is now to some extent obscured by the multiplication of departments, the partial separation which has been effected between judicial and executive functions, and the introduction of the rudiments of local self-government. The foundation of the Indian administrative system lay in the division of the State territory into provinces, or districts, of varying size, and the appointment in each area of officers to carry out the orders of the central authority. The conditions of appointment differed, but throughout the whole country they may be classified as belonging to one of two types, the distinction between which is marked by the Indian words *kachcha* and *pakka* or their Persian equivalents *khām* and *pukhta*. An officer who held his post *kachcha* was remunerated by a salary which, in theory at least, was a fixed sum, while he had to account to his superior for all the revenue he collected; on the other hand an officer who held *pakka* had to pay a fixed sum to his superior, and was entitled to retain all that he could collect in excess of that amount. In Akbar's time, both systems of appointment were followed, but the information which is available suggests that the former prevailed in Northern India and the latter in the south.

The description left by Nuniz indicates that the territory of Vijayanagar was parcelled out among the nobles of the Empire. The nobles, he says, "are like renters, who hold all the land from the King: they also pay to him every year 60 lakhs of rents as royal dues. The lands, they say, yield 120 lakhs, of which they must pay 60 to the King, and the rest they retain for the pay of soldiers and the expenses of the elephants which they are obliged to maintain. For this reason the common people suffer much hardship, those who hold the lands being so tyrannical." In other words, a noble to whom a district was entrusted was bound to pay a fixed sum and provide a certain force: so long as he fulfilled these obligations, he could do very much what he liked. This account refers to the early part of the century, but it is probable that the system survived,[1] and that the final collapse of the Empire meant merely that the nobles at last ceased to pay the fixed revenue, and by that act became independent sovereigns of the territories already in their possession.

In the case of the Deccan kingdoms, accounts of the administrative system prevailing at the end of the sixteenth century are not available. Barbosa wrote that the whole kingdom of the Deccan was divided among Moorish (Moslem) lords, and that the King took no part in the Government, but this description refers to the last days of the Bahmani kingdom which was then rapidly disintegrating, and it is uncertain

[1] Father N. Pimenta (*Hay*, 740) noted in 1598 that S. Thomé or Mylapore belonged to the King of Vijayanagar, who had made it over to the Naik of Tanjore to govern on fixed terms, and various incidents of the missionary journeys made about this time fit in well with the theory that the country was still held *pakka* under the nominal authority of the Emperor.

whether a similar system of devolution was practised in the new States which emerged. There is, however, no doubt that by the middle of the seventeenth century the nobles in Golconda at least enjoyed a large measure of independence. On passing from Mogul territory into the Deccan, Thévenot was at once struck by the insolence of the tax-collectors acting in the name of the lords to whom the villages had been granted, and later on he noted that the King granted the land to the highest bidder, or to his favourites, and that the nobles made "extraordinary exactions" on their grants, while the weakness of the central government allowed them to commit occasional outrages even in the capital city. It is of course possible that the nobles attained this position only a short time before Thévenot wrote, but I think it is more probable that the system was of old standing, and that we are justified in regarding the greater part of India south of the latitude of Bombay as governed by nobles, who so long as they paid the revenue and maintained the requisite forces could do very much as they chose. The King or Emperor had doubtless unlimited power to reverse their acts and to remove them from their positions: the extent to which these powers were exercised must have depended on the personality of the ruler, but they should be regarded as ordinarily held in reserve, and counting for comparatively little in the every-day business of the country.

The position in the Mogul Empire was so far different that office was ordinarily held on the terms described as *kachcha*, and that under Akbar the rudiments of departmental organisation had come into existence. Akbar divided his Empire into Sūbas, or provinces, and the Governor of the Sūba was responsible for every part of its administration, but the actual administrative unit was the Sarkār or district, each of which had a military commander (Faujdār) distinct from the revenue officer (Amalguzār). Further, the principal cities and seaports were in charge of separate officers, but taking the Empire as a whole, the separation of functions was rudimentary compared with the present state of things in India. As has been said in the previous chapter, the administrative ideal favoured direct relations between the State and the individual peasant, the assessment and collection of revenue being controlled from the centre, and officers having to account in detail for all receipts. There are, however, numerous indications that this ideal was not fully realised in practice, and it is probable that in many areas where the zamindars were left in charge of the administration they were responsible only for the payment of a fixed revenue.

In the Mogul Empire the relation between collection of revenue and provision of troops was so far maintained that the administration of each sarkār or district was held responsible for the supply of the local force known as Būmi, which consisted mainly of infantry, but included also cavalry and elephants, and in some localities guns and boats. The bulk of the fighting army was, however, provided on a slightly different system: the officers of the State were required to maintain contingents in proportion to their cash salaries, and this liability was personal and independent of the particular locality in which an officer might be employed. This organisation is explained in a subsequent chapter, and for the moment it is sufficient to point out that while Akbar's system resembled that of the south in requiring the local authorities to provide certain forces, it relied mainly on contingents more directly amenable to the Emperor's disciplinary authority.

Judicial organisation had at this period made little progress, and the redress of individual grievances was the duty of the King or Emperor, that is to say in practice of the Executive. Akbar maintained judicial officers known as the Kāzi and the Mir Adl, but the extent of their jurisdiction is not clearly described,[1] and I suspect that they dealt mainly with questions arising out of Moslem law; at any rate the litigation, both civil and criminal, described by visitors was usually conducted before executive officers, and very commonly before the Kotwal, or City Governor, who is found in Vijayanagar and in the Deccan as well as in the north, and whose functions will be discussed in the next section but one.

[1] The fact that these officers had not exclusive jurisdiction is indicated by Akbar's instructions for the procedure of his Governors in judicial investigations (*Ain*, translation, ii. 37, 38).

II. The Course of Justice

From the economic point of view the details of the framework of the administration are comparatively unimportant; the merchant or the producer is concerned mainly with the questions: Can justice be obtained, and how? Are the cities safe for residence and business? What are the conditions affecting the transit of men and goods? Answers to these questions must be sought chiefly in the records left by foreign visitors, for the chroniclers of the country were apt to take such things for granted, and where they allude to them they have no standard of comparison even when their statements are not coloured by obvious flattery. Foreign visitors compared conditions in India with those they knew at home, and it is important to bear in mind that, about the year 1600, Western Europe was very different from what it is to-day; in England, for instance, judicial integrity and impartiality cannot be said to have been finally established at that period, while the modern security of travel is little older than the railway system. Allowing, however, for the influence of the point of view, we are told enough to enable us to form a general impression of the conditions in which business was carried on.

As regards the measure of justice obtainable, a merchant who wished to enforce a contract or recover a debt could not put his case into the hands of a professional lawyer, for the simple reason that the profession did not exist; he would have to appear and plead his cause in person. The idea is at first sight attractive, but the experience of the world has shown that it does not work well in practice, and in India suitors knew that even a good case must be supported by bribery or by influence of some description: they might pay something to the authority who would dispose of the case, or they might induce some influential person to speak to that authority on their behalf. Bribery was almost universal in India at this time. Regarding Vijayanagar Nuniz tells us this in plain words, Sir Thomas Roe found practically the same conditions at Jahangir's court, and between these two authorities I have found no assertion to the contrary. Roe indeed mentions an exception, speaking of one man as "no briber, reported honest," but it is the only exception that I can recall. The same writer gives a good illustration of the power of influence. There was no court in the Mogul Empire in which the English merchants could recover their debts, and for a long time the executive officers took very little trouble in the matter. When, however, Roe had secured the friendship of the Vazir, matters moved more rapidly: an order to the Kotwal secured the prompt imprisonment of the defaulters, and their objections were disposed of summarily by the Vazir himself. Assuming that a suitor was able to out-bribe or out-influence his opponent, it seems probable that a decision could be obtained more speedily than at the present day, but it must have been difficult to judge beforehand whether it would be worth while to set the authorities in motion.[1]

Foreign observers comment on the absence of any body of written law, but we may doubt whether this was a serious evil to residents of the country. The Emperor's will was supreme, but the official record of Akbar's institutions contains very little that can be described as civil law, and we must assume that courts and officers were guided by Hindu or Moslem law, by custom, and by their personal views, but in all cases subject to the condition that they should not risk incurring the displeasure of the Emperor. The ruler of the time was accessible to private appeals, and we read of cases where such appeals were successfully made, but distances were great, travel was in some instances dangerous, and the dissatisfied suitor must have had to consider in each case whether an appeal was worth the cost and risk. An unsuccessful appellant might get into serious trouble: Finch, after describing the well-known bells provided for the use of appellants in the palace at Agra, adds: "But let them be sure their cause be good, lest he be punished for presumption that trouble the King." The threat of appeal to the ultimate

[1] See *Hakluyt*, v. 52, for a somewhat later instance of the employment of influence. The captain of an Indian boat, having a complaint against the English ships visiting Cuttack, paid a fee to one of the nobles to represent his case before the Governor.

authority seems to have been most important when it was made by a community rather than an individual. We find occasional suggestions of communal pressure on the officers concerned in the revenue administration, a practice which still survives in the tradition of the country, and a vivid illustration of its working is on record in the year 1616. An officer employed in the custom-house at Surat in that year did "some violence" to a leading Hindu merchant, whereupon "the whole multitude assembled shut up their shops and (as their custom) after a general complaint to the Governor left the city, pretending to go to the Court for justice, but with much fair usage and fairer promises were fetched back." In this way, if in no other, public opinion might be brought to bear on the side of justice: officials were above all things anxious to avoid a scandal at the Emperor's Court.

Practical men are more interested in the execution of a decree than in the law on which it rests, or even the means by which it has been obtained. In the Mogul Empire execution processes were drastic: we read not merely of the sale of a debtor's goods and house-property, but of his imprisonment, along with his family and servants, while he might be sold into slavery or handed over to the creditor in satisfaction of the decree. These processes, however, did not run as a matter of course: bribes and influence were necessary to set them to work, and to keep them working when they had started, and the general conclusion must be that while individuals could look to the State to redress their private wrongs, proceedings required careful judgment throughout or they might prove unfruitful, or cost more than they brought in.

III. Security in the Cities

When we ask what was the position of men of business in the cities, the answer must be that almost everything depended on the personality of the Kotwal, or, where there was no Kotwal, of the officers in charge of the local administration. The description of the Kotwal's duties contained in the *Ain-i Akbari* shows that he was intended to be very much more than the head of the city police, to which office the term is now usually restricted: it was his duty to prevent and detect crime, but he had also power to punish offenders, to perform many of the functions now assigned to municipal boards, to regulate prices, to set the idle to work, and speaking generally to interfere in almost every detail of the daily life of the city. The regulations are somewhat rhetorical, and must be read as setting out Akbar's ideal of city government: we may fairly question whether the ideal was often realised in practice, but there can be no doubt that, with these regulations in his hands, and so long as he possessed the confidence of his superiors, the Kotwal was a very powerful autocrat, and could make life either pleasant or intolerable for the individual citizen. The scope for bribery and influence must have been enormous, but provided that an individual took care to maintain friendly relations with the authorities, the cities appear to have been reasonably comfortable places for residence and business, and foreign merchants were on the whole favourably impressed with the extent to which order was maintained.

The title of Kotwal was in use in the Deccan as well as in the north, and Thévenot describes the Kotwal of Golconda as the chief officer of the city, and also the chief judge. I do not know what designation was used in Vijayanagar, but that city was administered by a single officer substantially on the lines subsequently laid down by Akbar, and visitors to it recorded that thieves were few, and that the property of foreign merchants was well protected. This latter statement appears to be of general application: visitors would have been careful to record any losses or oppression suffered by them, and their silence may reasonably be taken as showing that they had no serious grounds for complaint. It is not possible to speak with equal certainty of the experience of Indian merchants: there is no doubt that the Kotwal had extensive powers, but the degree of integrity with which they were exercised must remain a matter of conjecture.

One incident of the Kotwal's position deserves mention, because it seems to have given rise to rather exaggerated ideas regarding the security of property in Indian cities. Various travellers state that the Kotwal was personally liable to make good the value of any stolen property which he was unable to recover, and that this is something more than a traveller's tale is shown by Akbar's regulation that the Kotwal should discover stolen goods or be responsible for the loss. The practical value of this system of State insurance against theft was, however, very slight. Thévenot, who examined its working at Surat, came to the conclusion that any one who took the post would understand how to avoid the necessity of payment, and he tells a story which puts the matter in what I take to be the true light. While Thévenot was at Surat, an Armenian merchant was robbed, and the Kotwal failed to detect the offenders. The Armenian was disposed to press the case: the Governor in effect told the Kotwal that there must be no scandal: the latter thereupon proposed to torture the complainant so as to clear up some uncertainty as to the precise value of the stolen property: the Governor approved of this course, and the case came to an abrupt conclusion because under the threat of torture the Armenian withdrew his complaint. "That," says Thévenot, "is a fair sample of the Kotwal's conduct."

Torture of witnesses and suspected persons was in fact one of the two methods on which the police administration principally relied, as indeed was the case in parts of Europe at the same period. Thévenot, pursuing his account of the practical working of the administration, gives a precise description of the way in which suspects were whipped, the torture continuing for several days until either a confession had been secured, the stolen property recovered, or suspicion diverted in some other direction. Apart from torture, the police depended upon espionage, a subject on which Akbar's regulations are clear and detailed. An "obscure resident" was to be appointed as a spy in each quarter of the city; detectives were to watch all arrivals at the inns or *sarais*; the lives of individuals were to be carefully scrutinised; and speaking generally, it was the Kotwal's business to know everything that happened and to act on his knowledge.

Punishments were as drastic as in Europe at the same period, and were perhaps even more cruel. Their nature can best be indicated by the following quotation from the *Memoirs* of the Emperor Jahangir regarding the arrest of an habitual offender by the Kotwal of Ahmadabad. "He had committed several thefts before, and each time they had cut off one of his members: once his right hand, the second time the thumb of his left hand, the third time his left ear, the fourth time they hamstringed him, and the last time his nose; he with all this did not give up his business, and yesterday entered the house of a grass-seller in order to steal. By chance the owner of the house was on the look-out and seized him. The thief wounded the grass-seller several times with a knife and killed him. In the uproar and confusion his relatives attacked the thief and caught him. I ordered them to hand over the thief to the relatives of the deceased that they might retaliate on him."

It will be seen that the Kotwal occupied a strong position in regard to the repression of crime, since his powers for detection were reinforced by the threat of such punishments as these; and we need not be surprised that foreign merchants, whose presence was usually welcomed by the administration, should have had little cause for complaint in regard to the security of life and property. While, however, order was fairly well maintained in normal times, there was always a feeling of uncertainty as to the future. Governments were less stable than they are to-day, and the administration of a town or province might collapse with very little warning. Akbar's Empire had been in serious danger as late as 1581 from rebellions in Bengal and Kabul, while Gujarat was in revolt in 1584, and, after a short period of comparative tranquillity, the early years of Jahangir were marked by internal disorders in various localities from Delhi to Bengal. Sir Thomas Roe when ambassador to this Emperor laid down a policy for the English merchants in view of the civil disturbances which he apprehended, advising them to make few debts and to hold together instead of scattering themselves over the country, and similar considerations must have had weight with Indian men of business throughout the Empire. The results of a collapse of the administration may perhaps be inferred from the account given by an English merchant named Salbank of the condition of Agra during a great epidemic in 1616; he tells how his life was daily in danger "by reason of the licentiousness of certain impious villains, that after people were gone [from] their houses . . . did not stick to break up the same and carry all such movable goods as they found. This they did, not only in houses where all the people had fled, but also in other houses where few were left to defend their goods." That is to say, the forces of disorder were present, even in the capital of the Empire, just as they are present to-day, but the chances of their activity were very much greater, and required to be taken into account by any prudent man of affairs: so long as the administration stood firm, he had merely to keep on friendly terms with the Kotwal and his numerous subordinates, but he must be prepared to shift for himself in the not improbable event of a collapse.

IV. Security in the Country

Outside the large cities, there was no officer corresponding to the Kotwal, and the maintenance of law and order was, in the Mogul Empire at least, included in the functions of the revenue administration. The degree of security attained in the country generally can be inferred only from the observations of travellers: the information they give us is far from being complete, but it is sufficient to justify the statement that conditions varied very greatly from place to place and also from time to time, so that the personality of the local officers was probably the most important single factor to be taken into account. In studying the evidence on this subject allowance must be made for the fact that the standard of the seventeenth-century traveller was not that of the present day: highway robberies were to be expected in Europe as well as in India, and conditions which would now be regarded as almost intolerable might be described as satisfactory by a traveller of the time of Jahangir. Allowance must also be made for the estimation in which Europeans were at this time held in India. As yet they enjoyed no such prestige as was gradually built up by the experience of the next two centuries: the official world regarded them with somewhat disdainful interest as merchants who might have goods worth buying and who probably had some money to spend: by the populace the foreigners were, I take it, regarded chiefly as rather dangerous curiosities. On the other hand, Europeans in general did not regard Indians with disdain: the impression left by the available narratives is one of open-mindedness, and where an unfavourable verdict is expressed, as in the later portions of Sir Thomas Roe's journal, it is based on experience and not on prejudice.[1] European merchants then started on a journey on practically the same footing as Persians, Arabs, or travellers from other parts of India, and it is permissible to accept their experience as typical of the time and place where it was obtained.

As an example of these experiences, we may follow the travels of a merchant named William Finch as recorded in his journal, which is printed in *Purchas His Pilgrimes*. Finch was careful to note details which interested him, and I can trace no sign of prejudice in his journal. He sailed from England on the third voyage of the East India Company, and reached India in August 1608. Sixteen months later he travelled to Agra, and after staying in that neighbourhood for nine months, buying indigo and performing other duties for the Company, he marched to Lahore, where his personal record ends, though he describes various other routes from hearsay.[2]

[1] It must be admitted that the Portuguese regarded Indians with disdain, but this is true of their attitude to the world at large and not merely to a particular race: they despised Indians, not because they were Indians, but because they were not Portuguese. Pyrard states this definitely from personal experience, affirming that the Portuguese in India "hold themselves in the greatest respect and honour, despising not merely the Indians, but all other European nations" (*Pyrard*, translation, ii. 128), and the fact is established by the accounts of their bearing towards Englishmen (see, for an instance, Hawkins' narrative in *Purchas*, I. iii. 207).

[2] In the extracts which follow, I have retained Finch's terse and picturesque language, but I have modernised his spelling and punctuation.

From Surat to Agra there were two well-known routes, the western through Ahmadabad and Ajmer, and the eastern by way of Burhanpur and Gwalior. Finch chose the latter, and following the line of the Tapti, reached Burhanpur in sixteen marches. For the first four stages he tells us nothing of interest: in the fifth he came to broken country, where, he says, "Ba[ha]dur keepeth, holding divers strong forts thereon that the king with all his force cannot hurt him."[1] In the sixth stage he passed "a troublesome stony river," and at the seventh he halted in Badur [Bhadwar] "a filthy town and full of thieves." He mentions that this point was the limit of the jurisdiction of a petty Raja; Akbar had "besieged" him for seven years, but "in the end was forced to compound with him," and left him in possession of certain villages "for the safe conducting of his merchants along this plain." The next stage was Nandurbar, an important town, of which he tells us nothing; the next "a beastly town with thievish inhabitants, and a dirty castle"; while the following march led to "a great, dirty town," where he contracted dysentery by drinking bad water. In this march he had an adventure: "In the way the Governor of Lingull [Nimgul] (with others as honest as himself) would have borrowed some money of me, but, seeing it prove powder and shot, gave over, and we drew on our carts without trouble." The next march was "a thievish way," and then he joined the party of the Governor of Nandurbar: the roads were dangerous just then, for Jahangir's General, the Khān Khānān, had been defeated in the Deccan and had retired on Burhanpur, "whereupon the Deccanis grew so insolent that they made roads [inroads] into this way and spoiled many passengers." Four more marches followed, during which Finch nearly died of dysentery, and then he reached Burhanpur, the base of Jahangir's army of the Deccan, and at this time thought to be in danger of an attack. "The city is very great but beastly, situated in a low unwholesome air, a very sickly place." Two days after his arrival came news that some of the towns where he had halted

[1] Bahadur's rebellion is mentioned by Jahangir in *Tuzuk*, i. 49. Finch uses "keep" in the old sense of living or residing.

had been sacked by the enemy, so that he was fortunate in getting over this part of the journey when he did.

At Burhanpur the road left the Tapti and struck north-west for Mandu and Malwa, crossing the Satpura range and the Narbada river, and then ascending the steep scarp of the Vindhyas. The track was very bad, successive marches being described as "stony and steep way," "stony troublesome way," "bad way," and "steep way"; while the ascent to Mandu was "up a steep stony mountain, having way but for a coach at most." After Mandu there was one more bad stage, and then a good road to Ujjain. Finch had joined the camp of the Governor of Burhanpur, and up to this point says nothing of thieves, but on the second march northwards to Gwalior he found the "way much stony and thievish" and a group of travellers was saved from the hill-robbers only by the approach of his party. Two marches followed without incident, then we read "the way for the last five koses thievish, hilly, stony, the other pleasant plains," and then three more marches brought him to Sironj. From Sironj to Sipri travel was easy and pleasant until the last day, when the way was "thievish, stony, full of trees, a desert passage": here "two nights before some 60 or 70 thieves, mistaking for a late-passed caravan, assailed in a dark night 150 Patan soldiers, and fell into the pit they digged for others." The next stage, to Narwar, was worse, "a desert rascally way, full of thieves"; there were guard-houses in the jungle, but the watchmen were not to be trusted, for "the fox is often made the goose-herd." From Narwar to Gwalior there were no incidents, and from Gwalior to Agra the only danger was among the ravines at the passage of the Chambal. The whole journey from Surat to Agra occupied about ten weeks.

A little later we find Finch buying indigo near Biana, a town lying south-west of Agra, and in those days a well-known market for the commodity. His notes on this journey are chiefly of agricultural interest, but he mentions that Fatehpur Sikri "still standeth fair, but all ruinate," and that Biana too was decayed, "save two sarais and a long bazar, with a few straggling houses, many fair ones being quite fallen and many others not inhabited except by rogues or thieves." Returning to Agra, he started for Lahore to collect debts due to the Company. The march to Delhi up the right bank of the Jumna was without incident, but just north of the city the country was disturbed: "some report being given out of the King's death, many rogues with false alarms were abroad; we met the Faujdar [military governor] of Delhi, with some 2000 horse and foot in their pursuit . . . and the next day at breakfast we were like to be surprised by thieves." At the entrance to Panipat he saw "the heads of some hundred thieves newly taken; their bodies set on stakes, a mile in length." The way to Karnal was "thievish, where but for our peece-language[1] we had been assaulted"; but from Karnal to Lahore there was no trouble, though at the latter place he heard news of a rebellion in Kabul.

Finch's experience then was that you might travel long distances in India without serious danger, but that caution was always necessary. Robbers were to be expected in hilly and wooded country, but they might be met with at any time in the open plains; a false rumour might set the countryside ablaze; and the road watchmen were by no means to be trusted without reserve. Other travellers tell substantially the same story: some were more fortunate than others, and their impressions vary accordingly, but the general result of their experiences is summed up accurately in the preceding sentence. A few of these experiences may be quoted. Varthema and Nuniz assure us that Vijayanagar was safe in the prosperous period of the Empire, but it is possible that the weakening of the central authority may have resulted in some deterioration in this respect. Fitch (1583–91) mentions the abundance of thieves near Patna, while in Bengal he travelled to Hooghly through the jungle because the ordinary road was infested by thieves. Withington (1613) attempted to march from Ahmadabad to Lahari Bandar on the Indus, but found the population utterly lawless, and was at last taken prisoner

[1] This expression does not mean conciliatory language. "Peece" signifies a gun or musket, and I take it that Finch's party made their weapons speak.

by the guard he had hired for his protection. About the year 1615 the English merchants found the roads from Surat to Ahmadabad and Broach exceedingly dangerous owing to large gangs of robbers: about the same time, Steel and Crowther reported that the road from Agra to Lahore was "dangerous in the night for thieves, but in the day secure"; and in 1617 the Golconda country was entirely shut off from the north by wars and disturbances. As regards the general impressions of travellers, we may compare the favourable view taken by Terry (about 1616), whose camp was only attacked on one occasion, with the report of Hawkins a few years earlier that "the country is so full of thieves and outlaws that almost a man cannot stir out of doors throughout all his [Jahangir's] dominions without great forces."[1] Hawkins admits that conditions had deteriorated since the death of Akbar, but they had not been perfect in Akbar's time, for one of Jahangir's first orders on his accession was intended to improve the control of roads where thefts and robberies took place: we may doubt whether his orders were effective, but their issue is reasonably good evidence that matters were not entirely satisfactory.

V. Customs and Transit Dues

A few words must now be said regarding the charges borne by merchants in return for the degree of security which they enjoyed. The attitude of the central administrations towards foreign commerce was at this period usually favourable, and the prescribed scales of customs duties were distinctly moderate. Abul Fazl states that under Akbar the duties did not exceed 2½ per cent, and the charges of which we read as actually paid

[1] Salbank gives a still more unfavourable picture, asserting it to be "well known that no country in the whole world is more dangerous to travel in than this, by reason of many thousand blood-sucking villains, that for so much as one of their brass pieces of money as countervaileth the third part of a penny sterling will cut a man's throat" (*Letters Received*, vi. 196). Salbank, however, was labouring under a sense of grievance when he wrote this, and probably exaggerated the dangers he had faced in the service of the Company.

do not appear to have been materially higher.[1] At the sea-ports, however, as throughout the country, the personality of the local officers counted for very much, the more so that the customs seem to have been commonly let on contract, or in Indian phrase were held *pukhta*. An individual officer might welcome merchants and give them all facilities for trade: he might also refuse to admit their goods at all; and he might claim, apart from customs, a large share of the profits for himself. A good example of the position occupied by the customs officers is furnished by the story of the attempt made by English merchants to open trade at the Indus port of Lahari Bandar, in the year 1613. The Portuguese were already established in trade at this port, and they objected very strongly to competition by merchants of any other nation; they threatened the Governor that they would abandon his port if he allowed the English to trade, and this put him in a difficulty, because they paid large sums as duty, and "he having farmed the customs of that port from the King, unto whom he stood bound for the payment of certain sums of money yearly for the same, whether it came in or not, it behoved him carefully to be circumspect in ordering these businesses." He offered therefore to admit the English trade if it could be guaranteed to be more remunerative than that conducted by the Portuguese, but the merchants were not in a position to promise this, and so they sailed southward without transacting any business. In the same year one of the Company's merchants named Flores, writing from the Coromandel coast, insisted on the risks resulting from the personality of the officers in authority. A Governor might allow open trade, or he might claim it for himself, taking over the goods to be sold for his own profit; and if he chose the latter course there was a risk of default, "these Governors' debts being good while they continue their place: otherwise doubt-

[1] Finch says the charges at Surat were 2½ per cent on goods, 3 per cent on provisions, and 2 per cent on money (*Purchas*, I. iv. 423). The rates were increased during the seventeenth century, but not to an excessively high level: in Thévenot's time they ranged from 4 to 5 per cent (*Thévenot*, p. 7). At Masulipatam in 1616 the rates ranged from 3½ to 5 per cent (*Letters Received*, iv. 28).

ful." Again, in a protest drawn up in 1615 by the merchants at Surat against the conduct of the local authorities, it was alleged that "the Governor and Customer do lay aside the choicest and principal wares so brought [that is, to the custom-house], and send them to their houses without making price unto the merchant, and after long (if ever payment be made) it shall be very under rates, and less than they cost." Sir Thomas Roe too complained that the Governor of Surat required better presents than were at first offered before he would permit trade to be opened; and the conclusion may fairly be drawn that the authorised scale of customs duties counted for little in the calculations of ordinary merchants, compared with the payments which would have to be made in one form or another in order to secure the favour of the officers on the spot.

This conclusion applies to the principal ports under Indian rule. Where the Portuguese were in authority, the cost to merchants was probably, if anything, rather higher, because the administration was exceedingly corrupt, and the control of important ports furnished some of the greatest prizes of the service. On the other hand, abuses were rare at some of the Malabar seaports, and particularly at Calicut, which had reached prosperity by the development of the transhipment trade between the Red Sea and the Straits of Malacca, and where the organisation of the custom-house received high praise from European visitors such as Pyrard.

In regard to inland transit dues the position of merchants, whether Indian or foreign, was much less favourable. The tradition of the country was in favour of this method of raising revenue, and though transit dues were from time to time remitted, the fact that identical dues were remitted by successive rulers makes it difficult to attach much importance to such concessions. Akbar remitted transit dues on at least two occasions during his reign, and the evidence seems to justify Mr. Vincent Smith's inference [1] that "the benevolent intentions of the autocrat were commonly defeated by distant governors enjoying practical independence during their term

[1] *Akbar, the Great Mogul*, p. 377.

of office;" but it is also possible that such concessions were not intended to have more than temporary effect, and certainly no merchant would have been justified in relying on their permanence. At any rate it is clear that transit dues were charged towards the end of Akbar's reign, though they may not have reached the Imperial Treasury; for one of Jahangir's first orders after his accession was to forbid the levy of road and river tolls, as well as "other burdens which the *jagirdars* [grantees] of every province and district had imposed for their own profit." River tolls, indeed, are expressly stated in the *Ain* to have been retained by Akbar, as well as fees for the use of ferries.

When we turn from official records to the evidence of travellers, we are met by the fact that transit dues were such an ordinary feature of the period as to be scarcely worth mentioning in narratives designed to show the peculiarities of Indian life. We can, however, infer their existence from incidental allusions, such as the complaint of a Portuguese priest that the Mogul's practice of collecting taxes on inland vessels was accompanied by peculation and extortion, or Monserrate's remark that the low prices prevailing in Akbar's camp were due in part to the exemption from taxes of goods brought in for sale. At a later period travellers like Mundy, Thévenot, and Tavernier, who took an interest in such topics, show us a regular system of transit dues in force throughout large portions of the country, and Father Sebastian Manrique tells how the passport granted to him as an ecclesiastic to travel from Lahore to the mouth of the Indus was used by a merchant of his party to evade many demands during the journey.

Transit and city dues were certainly heavy in Vijayanagar during the sixteenth century. When a new city was founded, we are told that "nothing comes through the gate that does not pay duty, even men and women as well as head-loads and merchandise"; while no one could enter the capital without paying whatever the tax-contractors chose to ask. At the end of the century, too, the missionaries insist on the need for passports in this part of India in order to avoid infinite trouble regarding dues and taxes. As regards the Deccan, I have found no information about the sixteenth century, but in Thévenot's time the system was exceedingly vexatious, and on the road from Aurangabad to Golconda he counted sixteen taxing posts in twenty-three leagues. Taking then India as a whole, a merchant of the period would naturally calculate on having to pay fairly often in the course of a journey of any length, though he might hope to escape occasionally, if the local administration happened at the moment to be in favour of free passage. Apart, too, from official charges, there were other burdens to be taken into account. We have seen already that the road watchmen were regarded as untrustworthy, and in places it seems to have been the practice to compel merchants to pay heavily for escorts over roads reputed to be dangerous. In the wilder parts of the country, blackmail was paid to the local chieftains, and we may perhaps infer its more general existence from Jahangir's order directing that the bales of merchants should not be opened on the roads without informing them and obtaining their leave. In one way then or in another, the burdens on inland trade were substantial, quite apart from the actual cost of carriage, but the data which are available do not enable us to form even a vague idea of their amount.

VI. Effect on Trade and Industry

The conditions which have been described in the preceding sections, and which sound so nearly intolerable at the present day, did not in all probability suffice to interfere very seriously with internal or foreign commerce as conducted at the end of the sixteenth century. Bribes, presents, taxes, and even thefts in transit can all be brought into account, and in the long run these charges had to be borne by the consumer. The English factors at Surat reported to the Company that Indian merchants "in regard of danger *etcetera* by travel deal not in any commodity without apparency of great profit," and that remark really sums up the position: goods would not be carried unless the transaction would leave a profit after meeting all expenses, and if the expenses were high the selling price must be high enough to cover them. Then as now, the success of a merchant depended on his ability to forecast costs and prices, and these items of cost could be forecasted with some approach to accuracy. There was, however, another risk which wealthy merchants had to take into account. Sir Thomas Roe remarks that the Mogul was the heir of all his subjects, and though this statement is too wide, the Emperor certainly claimed the goods left by the wealthier merchants as well as by his nobles and officers. The successful man was therefore under the necessity of concealing his wealth if he wished to transmit it to his family, and in some parts of India at least the risk was not limited to the case of death: one observer remarks that merchants known to be wealthy were liable to be used as "fill'd sponges," or in modern slang, to be "squeezed," and I know of nothing to make this suggestion appear improbable. It was good to be rich, but it might be bad to let your wealth be known: "let the profit be ever so great, the man by whom it has been made must still wear the garb of indigence."

It is obvious that these conditions would have been very unfavourable to the establishment of industry on a capitalist basis: a wealthy man would have been exceedingly unwise to invest largely in fixed capital when the administration might at any time collapse, or when a change of local officers might expose him to a campaign of ruinous extortion. This question, however, has no practical interest, for the day of capitalist enterprise had not dawned. The industrial production of India at this period was large and valuable, but so far as I can gather it was entirely in the hands of the artisans, presumably financed by merchants and middlemen, but individually of too little importance to attract the hostility or cupidity of the higher officials. The city artisan had doubtless to secure the favour of the subordinates and spies detailed by the Kotwal for the supervision of the locality in which he lived, and outside the cities there were other minor officials to be propitiated; but it is reasonable to assume that these matters were adjusted on a customary basis, and that the position was not felt to be particularly irksome. The peasant cultivators, then as now by far the most important section of the population, were much more directly concerned with the quality of the administration, but it is more convenient to postpone the discussion of their position until we come to examine the agricultural and land-revenue system in detail.

VII. Weights, Measures, and Currency

Before leaving the subject of administrative conditions it will be well to say something of the systems of weights, measures, and currency, which were already, in part at least, regulated by the various Indian governments, and some knowledge of which is essential to a proper understanding of the contemporary authorities. The matter is, however, one of detail, and this section can be passed over lightly by readers who do not intend to study those authorities for themselves. In the sixteenth century, as in the twentieth, the leading characteristic of the Indian systems of weights and measures is diversity: then as now we find old local standards existing side by side with those which had been officially prescribed, and we find further that as a rule scales are more uniform than units, the maund, for instance, usually containing forty sers, but the weight of the maund, and consequently of the ser, varying from place to place. The diversity is more noticeable at the seaports, where units introduced by foreign merchants had become established side by side with the local systems; but in all the contemporary authorities where quantities are stated it is necessary to ascertain the unit to which reference is made. Apparently most Indian administrations were content with this position, and I have not found any record of attempts to secure uniformity of weights and measures either in Vijayanagar or in the kingdoms of the Deccan. Akbar, however, took a more modern view, and prescribed the principal units of weight, length, and surface measure: there is no doubt that his units were employed in the neighbourhood of his capital, but, as we shall see, they had not become established in the seaports up to the time of his death, and it appears to be probable that, as has happened occasionally in later times, the final result of his action was to increase the previous complexity by the introduction of yet another series of competing units.

Before the change introduced by Akbar the commonest maund of Northern India appears to have weighed about 28 or 29 lb. avoirdupois. Akbar fixed the weight of the ser at 30 dams, the dam being the principal copper coin: the maund of 40 sers thus weighed 388,275 grains, or practically 55½ lb. avoirdupois, and for ordinary rough comparisons it may be thought of as 56 lb., or just half a hundredweight, so that 40 of Akbar's maunds would make a ton as against 27 of the maunds now in ordinary use. It is safe to assume that this maund is used in the *Ain-i Akbari*, which is an official record, and there is evidence to show that it was employed in mercantile transactions in the neighbourhood of the Imperial capital, but it does not appear to have spread to distant parts of the Empire. At Surat and the other Cambay ports there were two maunds in ordinary use, the smaller being 27 lb. and the larger about 33 lb.: the latter is based on a ser weighing 18 dams, and this relation was known to some of the earliest English merchants. In reading of the west coast, therefore, the smaller local maund should be thought of as a quarter of a hundredweight, and the larger as two-sevenths of that unit.

The maund appears to have been known at least as far south as Goa, where it varied between 20 and 30 lb., but the unit of weight most commonly mentioned in Southern India is the candy, which also varied greatly, but may be taken as somewhere about 500 lb. The bahar, which is also frequently referred to, was a foreign unit, introduced by the Arab merchants throughout the Indian seas: its weight varied with the mercantile customs governing the sale of different commodities, but it usually indicates something less than a candy. Contemporary European writers refer also to the quintal (or kintal), which represented about 130 lb., and may be thought of as somewhat larger than a hundredweight. Lastly, it must be remembered that in the authorities the pound itself does not always mean exactly the same thing. English writers of the period mean the pound avoirdupois which is still in use, but in translations from the French the word denotes the *livre*, a unit which varied from time to time, but at this period was nearly equivalent to half a modern kilogram, or say 1·1 lb. Differences such as this may be important in the interpretation of particular statements, but for a general study of the economic circumstances of the time it is probably sufficient to bear in mind that the pound means what it means now, that the maund means 56 lb. at or near the Mogul capital, and about 30 lb. elsewhere, while candy and bahar mean much larger quantities, approximating to one-fifth or one-quarter of a ton.

The unit of length in Northern India was the gaz: the word is frequently translated "yard," and the unit may be thought of in this sense, but there is a substantial difference. The history of the gaz is given in the *Ain-i Akbari*, but here it is sufficient to say that Akbar eventually introduced a compromise unit which he named the *Ilahi gaz*, and which measured 30¾ inches. That this unit was in fact used in Northern India may be inferred from Prinsep's statement made in 1834 that "in a great degree it still maintains its position as the standard of the Upper Provinces"; it was not, however, used in the commercial centres of the west coast where transactions were effected in terms of the covad. The covad varied in length with the class of merchandise: for cotton cloth it was about 26 inches, while for woollens it was larger, about 35 inches, or "a yard within an inch"; uniformity was, however, not to be expected, and the merchant who gives this description of the covad at Surat expresses a doubt whether the covad at Broach has the same value. In regard then to measures, as to weights, it was a merchant's business to find out the value of the unit in each market where he proposed to deal. The unit of surface measure is important only for the interpretation of contemporary statistics of area, and its consideration need not detain us.

Akbar's administration led the way in currency as in weights and measures, and the detailed description of the Imperial mints which is given in the *Ain-i Akbari* makes it possible to form an accurate idea of the system established in the Mogul Empire. The coins in regular use were silver and copper. Gold coins were also struck, but most of the twenty-six denominations may be described as "fancy," and the three which were struck regularly were rarely found in circulation, being too large for retail transactions, and being sought mainly in order to be hoarded. The chief silver coin was the rupee of 172½ grains, which in weight (but not in purchasing power) was practically identical with the coin now known by that name: the chief copper coin was the dam, and in each case there were subsidiary coins, the smallest silver piece being $\frac{1}{20}$ rupee, and the smallest copper ⅛ dam. The copper coins were not as now tokens, but, like the silver, circulated at the value of the metal they contained, and consequently there were two independent standards (or three if we include gold), the rates of exchange between which might vary from time to time or from place to place. In the official accounts forty copper dams were taken as equivalent to one rupee, and the fluctuations in the rate were not at this time serious, at least in Upper India, but there was apparently something in the nature of a constant difference between the rate at the headquarters of the Empire and that ruling on the west coast. This difference arose from the position in regard to the supply of the two metals: the silver used for coinage was imported by sea, and had to bear the cost of carriage up-country, while the copper was obtained from the mines of Rajputana, and increased in value as it was carried southwards; consequently at any given time a rupee would exchange for more dams at Delhi or Agra than at Surat or Cambay. The difference was not, however, very great, and the general reader can safely take forty dams as the equivalent of a rupee, especially as Gujarat, then the chief centre of oversea trade, had not at this period adopted the rupee, but transacted business in the mahmudi, a silver coin of rather less than half its value. Stated in terms of contemporary English currency, the rupee was worth about 2s. 3d., and the mahmudi about 11d., subject in each case to fairly large fluctuations.

Even the smallest copper coin (the *damri* or $\frac{1}{8}$ dam, or $\frac{1}{320}$ rupee) did not suffice either for the detailed items of the Imperial accounts or for the small transactions of everyday life. For the former purpose, the dam was subdivided on paper into twenty-five jitals, so that the accounts could be kept to the one-thousandth part of a rupee: for the latter, cowries were used, as is still the case, their value in terms of silver or copper depending on the distance from the coast. On the other hand, there is no trace of larger aggregates of money corresponding to the modern currency notes: merchants who had to remit large sums could usually do so by bills of exchange, while as an alternative they could carry pearls or precious stones for sale at their destination. The need for large aggregates was also reduced by the high purchasing power of the rupee. It is not possible to speak with absolute precision on this point, but an examination of the statistics of prices given in the *Ain-i Akbari* indicates that towards the end of the sixteenth century a rupee would purchase in the vicinity of the capital at least seven times as much grain as could be bought in Upper India in the years 1910–12, at least eleven times as much oilseeds, and probably five times as much cloth, while on the other hand metals were little cheaper than now and imported goods were actually dearer. On this basis it may be said that to the very poorest classes a rupee of the year 1600 was worth as much as seven rupees of 1912: to the classes just above the line of extreme poverty it was worth about six rupees, and to the middle classes about five rupees or possibly more. For general purposes therefore it is reasonable (at least, until these conclusions shall be upset by the discovery of new data) to think of one of Akbar's rupees as equivalent in purchasing power to six rupees in the period before the war, or in other words, to recognise that a monthly income of five rupees would provide the same quantity of necessaries as could be purchased from an income of thirty rupees in 1912.

The currency of Southern India at this period, unlike that of the Mogul Empire, was based essentially upon gold, which was also the chief circulating medium. The standard coin was known variously as varāhu or as hūn, but in European writings it is usually spoken of as pagoda, and its average value may be taken as about equal to 3½ of Akbar's rupees. There was also a smaller gold coin known as fanām, and subsidiary coins of silver and copper were in circulation, but their names and values are unimportant for our present purpose. In addition to this indigenous coinage, the commerce of the coast was concerned largely with coins of foreign origin. In the sixteenth century, as throughout history, India may be said to have traded largely for cash, that is to say, the precious metals, coined or uncoined, were among the principal imports, and any one who wished to take part in external commerce required to know something of the currencies of various countries, and to be familiar with at least the larin, the sequin, the ducat, and the Spanish real-of-eight, as well as with the somewhat complicated system maintained by the Portuguese at Goa.

The larin was Persian money, and reached India in large quantities through the trade with that country. It was not a coin in the ordinary sense of the word, but a bent rod or bar of silver stamped at the end, and was worth rather less than half of one of Akbar's rupees. The sequin (or chickeen) was a Venetian gold coin, worth about four of Akbar's rupees, and travelled to India by way of the Red Sea or the Persian Gulf, in connection with the overland trade to Europe. Italian ducats came by the same route; the gold ducat was worth nearly as much as the sequin, while the silver ducat was of about half that value, or say two of Akbar's rupees. Spanish reals-of-eight,[1] on the other hand, reached India chiefly by sea: their value was about the same as that of the silver ducat.

The Goanese currency is a very intricate subject, mainly because successive Governors manipulated the coinage to meet financial exigencies, but while fluctuations in value were

[1] The name real (or rial) of eight, which is used by contemporary writers, is apt to mislead. The coins would be more properly described as pieces of eight reals; the Spanish real was worth slightly more than sixpence in English money, so that a piece of eight reals was equivalent to about four shillings and sixpence, or practically two rupees.

frequent, the general trend was steadily towards depreciation. The system was based on a unit known as the real, which was much smaller than the Spanish unit bearing the same name, being, in fact, only a small fraction of a penny, but the standard coin was the pardao, which was at first identical with the pagoda. By about the year 1600, however, the real, and with it the gold pardao, had depreciated, so that the pagoda was then worth 570 instead af 360 reis,[1] and thus the gold pardao was at this time equivalent to about 2¼ of Akbar's rupees, while another pardao, not made of gold, and having a slightly lower value, had also come into existence. In practice a pardao of this period may be thought of as two rupees, but when a *gold* pardao is specified, it may be taken as 2¼ rupees.

I have not found sufficient data to furnish even a rough measure of the purchasing power of these coins in Southern India. Various travellers note that prices were low in Surat and the neighbourhood, but it must be remembered that Europe was at this time experiencing the effects of the continued influx of silver from America; prices, that is to say, were rising in Europe, and it is exceedingly difficult to make out the particular standards in the minds of individual travellers. Some figures given by the first English merchants suggest that prices were much higher at Surat than in Northern India, but it would be unsafe to base conclusions on these isolated transactions, especially as the merchants were strangers, and it is not improbable that they were cheated. Further, as will appear in a subsequent chapter, trade at the seaports was marked by very sudden fluctuations, so that it would be dangerous to use figures which may represent purchases made in exceptional circumstances; it is probable that prices were higher on the coast than up the country, but until further materials become available, the difference cannot be stated quantitatively.

It will be noticed that I have not attempted to give precise equivalents for the various coins circulating in India. The

[1] *Reis* is the plural form of the Portuguese word *real*. At the beginning of the sixteenth century the Portuguese real was worth about 0·27 or 0·28 of a penny, but by the year 1600 its value had fallen to 0·16d.

omission is deliberate, for under the methods of transacting business which prevailed coins did not pass current as a matter of course; weighing and assaying were necessary elements of ordinary transactions, and the value of a particular coin or parcel of coins must often have been a matter of negotiation. Foreign coins were received at the value of the metal they contained, and consequently new coins were worth more than those which had suffered by wear. Indian coins of former rulers were received on the same terms, and even current issues were liable to discount if for any reason the amount of metal fell below the accepted standard. Some idea of the position can be formed from the long account of Akbar's efforts to improve it contained in the *Ain-i Akbari.* The rules for valuing current coins were modified on several occasions, and as is so frequently the case, it is not possible to accept Abul Fazl's courtly assurance that the latest regulations were universally approved; we can take them as proof of the existence of malpractices, but we cannot be certain that they operated to ensure honesty throughout the Empire. They indicate that officers of the mint were suspected of issuing light coins, that the official treasurers reduced the weight of coins received by them, and that dealers followed the same practice, and also used false weights; they show further that treasurers occasionally insisted on the State dues being paid in coins of particular denominations, presumably those of which they and their friends possessed a temporary local monopoly, and that the rules regulating the permissible deficiency in weight were occasionally ignored. It is not surprising therefore to find that the business of dealing in money was highly developed throughout India, and that travellers notice the presence of expert dealers in all centres of trade.

In order then to realise the conditions in which business was carried on, it is well to bear in mind that coins were not at this period regarded as fixed standards of value, but rather as a form of merchandise, of which the equivalent in other commodities depended upon the weight and the quantity of the coins tendered. A merchant who offered payment in money was in fact entering on a particular kind of barter;

he knew that the other party to the bargain would usually accept the money, but he knew also that it would be accepted as so much metal, and that the amount of metal would have to be determined before the transaction was completed. To readers familiar with modern conditions this method of doing business appears to be exceedingly cumbrous and inconvenient, but it would probably be a mistake to suppose that the merchants of the sixteenth century looked at it in the same light: I cannot recall any complaints regarding it in the narratives of Europeans, while to Indians the arrangement would be familiar, and must, I think, have been regarded as a natural incident of their business. The various coins which they handled had in their eyes approximate relations, based on the quantity of gold, or of silver, which they might be expected to contain, but the precise value of the coins passing in a particular transaction would have to be ascertained.

It is these approximate relations which I have endeavoured to indicate. The student who wishes to obtain a general view of the economic condition of India at this period will probably find it simplest to think in terms of Akbar's rupee. So far as Upper India is concerned, he need then remember merely that the rupee was worth about forty copper dams, and that the ordinary gold mohur was worth about ten rupees, but that the purchasing power of these coins was about six times as great as in the present century. Travelling southwards, he will meet the silver mahmudi (about 2½ to the rupee), and the gold varāhu or pagoda worth about 3½ rupees. Of foreign silver coins, it is sufficient to remember that a larin was about the same as a mahmudi, while Italian ducats and Spanish reals-of-eight were worth about two rupees in each case. Among gold coins the sequin and the ducat were each equivalent to about four rupees; and lastly the Goanese pardao was worth about 2¼ rupees if of gold, but otherwise about two rupees. Of the purchasing power of these coins in the South of India all that can at present be said is that the nominal value should not be increased to the same extent as that of the northern rupee; the proportion by which it should be raised must remain doubtful until further data come to light.

AUTHORITIES FOR CHAPTER II

SECTION 1.—For the Vijayanagar administration, see *Sewell*, 373 and *passim*. For the Deccan, see *Barbosa*, 289, and *Thévenot*, 279, 301-307. Akbar's system must be studied in the *Ain*: some of the difficulties in that work are discussed in a paper by Mr. Yusuf Ali and myself in *Journal R.A.S.*, January 1918, and I follow the conclusions there given. References on the organisation of the Mogul Army will be given in the next chapter.

SECTION 2.—For bribery, see in particular *Sewell*, 380; *Letters Received*, iv. 9; *Roe*, 263. *Manrique* (lxxi.) tells how when he had been arrested by the Kotwal of Multan, a way of release was found "through some mollifying gratifications." For the value of influence, see *Roe*, 416, 436, and *Letters Received*, vi. 117. For the risk of appealing to the Emperor, see Finch in *Purchas*, I. iv. 439. The account of an instance of communal pressure is from *Letters Received*, iv. 320, while details as to execution are mentioned in *Letters Received*, i. 25; vi. 117, and in *De Laet*, 124.

SECTION 3.—Akbar's regulations for the Kotwal are in Book III. of the *Ain* (translation, ii. 41). The reference to the Kotwal of Golconda is in *Thévenot*, 290: police administration in Vijayanagar is referred to in *Major*, 30, and *Sewell*, 381. The account of the actual working of the system is in *Thévenot*, 59, 60: the quotation regarding punishments will be found in *Tuzuk* (translation, i. 432). Regarding the danger of lawlessness, see in particular *Roe*, 295. Salbank's account of Agra is in *Letters Received*, vi. 198.

SECTION 4.—The only direct mention I have found of police administration in the country is the statement in the *Ain* (translation, ii. 47), that should there be no Kotwal, the Revenue Officer (Amalguzar) should perform his duties.

The inland portion of Finch's travels begins on I. iv. 424 of *Purchas*. The other authorities quoted are *Varthema*, 130; *Sewell*, 381 (for Nuniz); *Purchas*, II. x. 1735, 1736 (for Fitch); I. iv. 484 (for Withington); I. iv. 520 (for Steel and Crowther); *Letters Received*, ii. 254, and *passim* (for the roads from Surat); v. 323 (for Golconda); *Terry*, 160, 171; *Hawkins*, 434; and *Tuzuk*, i. 7.

SECTION 5.—Akbar's orders regarding customs and river dues are in the *Ain* (translation, i. 281). The experience of the English merchants on the Indus is told at length in *Purchas*, I. iv. 497; Flores' advice is in *Letters Received*, iv. 78, while *Roe's* complaint is on p. 68 of his Journal. I have not found a clear statement of the official charges levied by the Portuguese, but in practice they were matters of negotiation: as *Pyrard* says (translation, ii. 240), the Governors let everything pass for money. Pyrard's account of the Calicut custom-house is i. 238.

Jahangir's orders as to transit dues are in *Tuzuk* (translation, i. 7). For dues and extortion on inland vessels, see *Hay*, 730; for exemptions, see *Monserrate*, 581; for transit dues at a later period, see Mundy, ii. 39, and *passim*; *Thévenot*, 15; *Tavernier*, 81, 305, and *Manrique*, lxxi. For duties in Vijayanagar, see *Sewell*, 364, 366, and *Hay*, 738; for the Deccan, see *Thévenot*, 279. Charges for escorts are mentioned in various places, *e.g.* *Letters Received*, iv. 78.

Section 6.—The quotation regarding the need for large profits is from *Letters Received,* v. 116. The Mogul rule of inheritance is discussed at some length by *Bernier* (p. 116). *Tavernier* (ii. 15 and *passim*) insists on the incentive to hoarding furnished by the rule, and *Manrique* (lxxi) gives a vivid picture of its actual working. The expressions quoted in the text regarding it are from *Terry,* 391, and *Bernier,* 229.

Section 7.—For Akbar's maund, see *Thomas, Chronicles,* 430; *Purchas,* I. iii. 218; *Letters Received,* iii. 1, 84; *De Laet,* 137. The Surat maunds are mentioned frequently in *Letters Received, e.g.* i. 30; those of Goa are shown in the table prefixed to *Garcia da Orta.* For the candy and the bahar, see *Hobson-Jobson* under those words; for the quintal, see (*e.g.*) *Letters Received,* i. 30. For references to the *livre,* see *Tavernier,* 290 and *passim*; I take its value from the *Grande Encyclopédie* (Art. *Livre*).

For the gaz, see *Ain,* translation, ii. 58 ff., and *Useful Tables,* 87 ff. For the covad, see *Letters Received,* i. 34, ii. 230.

Akbar's coinage is dealt with at length in the first Book of the *Ain* (translation, i. 16 ff.). The rarity of gold coins is referred to by various writers, *e.g. Terry,* 112, 113, and *Tavernier,* ii. 14 ff.; Tavernier illustrates the difference in ratio of silver to copper. For the mahmudi, see *Letters Received,* i. 34, and *passim.* The system of bills of exchange is dealt with fully in *Tavernier,* ii. 24, and referred to incidentally in most of the English accounts, *e.g. Letters Received,* ii. 228, 266; iii. 281. The purchasing power of the rupee is discussed in a paper by the present writer in the *Journal of the R.A.S.,* for October 1918, pp. 375 ff.

For the money current in Southern India, see *Hobson-Jobson,* under Pagoda, Fanam, Pardao, Chick, Larin, and other notices referred to therein. For the Goanese currency, see also *Whiteway,* ch. iv., and Mr. Longworth Dames' notes to *Barbosa* (translation, i. 191). References to low prices on and near the coast will be found in *Terry,* 175, and *Della Valle,* 42. For prices paid by the English at Surat in 1611, see *Letters Received,* i. 141. For malpractices in connection with the coinage, see in particular *Ain,* translation, i. 32 ff.

CHAPTER III

THE CONSUMING CLASSES

I. The Court and the Imperial Service

From the working of the administration we pass to consider the economic position of the men by whom it was conducted, the first class of those into which the population of India has been divided for the purpose of this study. The inclusion in a single class of courtiers and officials may excite surprise, but in India at this period no valid distinction can be drawn. Men came to Court in search of a career, or at the least a livelihood; if the search was unsuccessful, they withdrew, while success meant the attainment of military rank, administrative functions, and remuneration, sometimes in the form of a cash salary, and sometimes by the grant of the whole or a portion of the revenue yielded by a particular area. There was no independent aristocracy, for independence was synonymous with rebellion, and a noble was either a servant or an enemy of the ruling power. The present section will deal with the position of those high officials who had a recognised standing at Court, leaving for subsequent consideration the minor functionaries, both civil and military, who may be regarded as officials pure and simple.

In regard to these high officials, something very like uniformity appears to have prevailed throughout India. Descriptions of Vijayanagar in the first half of the sixteenth century show us the Emperor surrounded by a body of nobles, who occupied the principal posts in the administration, governed portions of the Empire, retained a large part of the revenue of their charges, and were liable to maintain a military force of a prescribed size and composition; accounts of the Deccan kingdoms in the sixteenth and seventeenth centuries give glimpses of practically the same arrangements, while we have full details of the corresponding organisation maintained by Akbar. We are justified therefore in regarding this as the typical Indian system of the period, and it will be sufficient for the present purpose if we study it in detail for the Mogul Empire, regarding which our information is almost complete. A few illustrations may, however, be given of the positions held by the nobles in Vijayanagar, as described by Nuniz about the year 1535. The Emperor's Chief Minister then governed the Coromandel coast, Negapatam, Tanjore, and other districts, from which, after paying the share claimed by the treasury, he was supposed to draw annually 733,000 gold pardaos, or say 20 lakhs of rupees;[1] out of this sum he had to maintain a force of 30,000 infantry and 3000 cavalry, but the chronicler mentions that he economised in this direction. Similarly the Keeper of the Jewels, who had charge of an extensive area in the Deccan, retained nominally 200,000 gold pardaos, and was responsible for 12,600 men, while a former Minister, who held the country about Udaigiri, had 500,000 gold pardaos and a force of 26,500. The significance of these figures depends on the cost of maintaining the troops; precise data on this point are not available, but a rough estimate suggests that on paper the surplus left to the nobles was not very great, perhaps two or three lakhs of rupees annually for the Minister, and lesser sums for the other nobles. In all probability, however, their real income depended largely on two sources, what they could save on their troops, and what they could collect in addition to the nominal revenue of their districts: there is good evidence that both these sources were important, and it is reasonable to conclude that able and unscrupulous men were about as well off in Southern India as Akbar's nobles were in

[1] At this time the pardao had not depreciated to the level reached at the end of the century. In 1510 it had been worth about 3½ rupees: I do not know the precise equivalent in 1535, but it cannot have been much less than three rupees.

the North. It is true that these accounts relate to the period before the battle of Talikot, but the permanent effect of that disaster on the income of the nobles was probably not great,[1] and the incidental pictures furnished by the Jesuit missionaries of the life at the end of the century leave an impression of wealth and profusion similar to what we shall find in those parts of India where the evidence is more detailed.

When we turn to Northern India, we are struck by the minuteness of the organisation maintained by Akbar. All the great men of the Empire were graded in what may fairly be regarded as an Imperial Service, the conditions of which were laid down by the Emperor in great detail, but the Service differed in essentials from the types familiar in India at the present day, and for that reason its structure is at first sight a little difficult to understand. A person admitted to this Service was appointed to a rank (*mansab*) as commander of a certain number of cavalry: he had thereupon to enrol and produce the men and horses corresponding to his command, and on producing them he became entitled to draw the salary of his rank. The force for which he was thus made responsible was usually less in number than his title indicated; a commander of 1000 for instance was not required to maintain a body of 1000 cavalry out of his official salary, but some lesser number, which seems to have been gradually reduced as time went on. In the middle of Akbar's reign the highest ordinary rank was commander of 5000, but the Imperial princes might hold higher positions, and when the *Ain-i Akbari* was compiled Prince Salim, afterwards Jahangir, stood at the head of the list as commander of 10,000; the limit of 5000 was relaxed towards the close of Akbar's reign, and under his successors subjects could rise to considerably higher positions. From the lowest rank, that of commander of 10, up to the rank of 400, a commander was known as *mansabdār*, from 500 to 2500 as *Amīr*,[2] and from

[1] It is quite possible that some of the nobles were benefited financially by the defeat of the Emperor; their gross income was not affected, and they may have been able to withhold part of the revenue which they formerly paid.

[2] Foreign visitors speak of the high officers collectively as Omrah, or some other variant of *Umara*, the Arabic plural of Amīr.

3000 upwards as *Amīr-i-Azam* or *Umda.* Apart from the force appropriate to his personal rank, an officer might be permitted to maintain an additional force known as *suwār.* This was a privilege: the pay of the additional force was drawn from the treasury, the commander was allowed to retain 5 per cent of the pay-bill, and probably had various other perquisites, while his own salary varied to some extent with the strength of his additional force.

I have spoken of the salaries of the various ranks as if they were fixed sums, and in fact they are so stated by Abul Fazl, but it is difficult to ascertain even approximately the amount which can be regarded as the net income of officers holding any particular rank. The following table shows the sanctioned monthly salaries of a few grades; the figures are in the rupees of Akbar's time, and as explained in the last chapter must be multiplied by five or six in order to obtain the equivalent purchasing power in Northern India at the standard of the present day.

Rank.	Monthly Salary.[1]			Cost of Appropriate Force.
	First Class.	Second Class.	Third Class.	
5000	30,000	29,000	28,000	10,600
3000	17,000	16,800	16,700	6,700
1000	8,200	8,100	8,000	3,000
500	2,500	2,300	2,100	1,170
50	250	240	230	185
10	100	82½	75	44

In order to get an idea of the income represented by these salaries, we have firstly to deduct the cost of maintaining the force appropriate to an officer's personal rank. I have shown this cost in the last column of the table, calculated on the

[1] The "class" depended on the *suwār* rank: a commander of 5000, for instance, was entitled to draw Rs. 30,000, only if his *suwār* rank also was 5000; if his *suwār* rank was 2500 or over, he drew Rs. 29,000, and if it were less than 2500, he drew Rs. 28,000. These differences in salary are comparatively insignificant, and for our present purposes they may be ignored.

monthly expenditure allowed for similar forces on the Imperial establishment, but we may be confident that these figures are maxima, and that a competent officer could maintain, or appear to maintain, his force for a substantially smaller sum. Early in Akbar's reign there were very great irregularities in this matter: Badaoni gives a pungent account of the malpractices in vogue, and his statements are in substance confirmed by the more discreet phrases used by Abul Fazl. Akbar introduced various regulations to secure that the prescribed forces should be in fact maintained, but it would probably be a mistake to assume that his success was complete, and we may take it that the actual cost was less than that shown in the table. Secondly, we have to consider the manner in which these salaries were paid. The traditional practice of the country was to pay by way of *jāgīr*, that is to say, an officer was granted the revenue of a village or group of villages, or of a pargana, or some larger area, calculated to yield him the sanctioned salary. Like other financial reformers, Akbar disliked this system, and endeavoured to introduce cash payments in its place; I doubt whether he was ever entirely successful, and in any case the *jāgīr* system quickly regained its lost ground under Jahangir. Cash payments were unpopular with the Service largely because of the delays of the treasury; an officer felt greater certainty when in possession of a *jāgīr*, and he could often hope to obtain one which was really worth, or which could be made to yield, more than the official records showed. There was in fact no small amount of fraud in connection with these allotments, and from a financial point of view, Akbar was undoubtedly right in objecting to the whole system.[1] So far, however, as the officers of his period were concerned, we may fairly say that they could expect to receive at least the

[1] Hawkins, who represented the East India Company at Court about 1611, and who was made a commander of 400 by Jahangir, writes very bitterly on this subject. The Vazir, he says, continually put him off with grants in "places where outlaws reigned," and when, at the Emperor's express order, he was given a *jāgīr* at Lahore, he was soon deprived of it on some pretext. An Indian commander would probably have managed the business more successfully. (*The Hawkins' Voyages*, p. 411; see also his account of the system in *Purchas*, I. iii. 221.)

salaries recorded by Abul Fazl,[1] while those of them who had secured profitable *jāgīrs* might hope for something more; on the other hand, their troops probably cost less than the estimates I have given, and consequently their net incomes were greater than the figures suggest.

Bearing these uncertainties in mind, we can attempt to form a rough idea of the incomes enjoyed by officers of various classes. A commander of 5000 could count on at least Rs. 18,000 a month, and he might be able to increase this sum by judicious economies in his military expenditure, or as the result of good fortune in securing a profitable *jāgīr*; this income would enable him to purchase about as much as a monthly income of a lakh would have bought in the years before 1914, and he was thus very much more highly paid than any officer now employed in India. A commander of 1000 could similarly count on receiving Rs. 5000 a month, equal to from Rs. 25,000 to Rs. 30,000 in 1914, or say three times the pay of a modern Lieutenant-Governor, while a commander of 500 would have received the equivalent of Rs. 5000 to Rs. 6000 at the present day. While therefore the precise figures are uncertain, it appears to be reasonable to conclude that the higher ranks of the Imperial Service were remunerated on a scale far more liberal than that which now prevails in India, or for that matter in any portion of the world: certainly there was at the time no other career in

[1] Some recent writers hold that a substantial deduction must be made from the sanctioned figures on the ground that many officers received salary for less than twelve months in the year; Mr. Vincent Smith, for instance, writes that the pay " was seldom, if ever, drawn for the whole year, and in some cases only four months' pay was allowed," and Mr. Irvine makes a similar statement, but without specific reference to the reign of a particular Emperor. The authority relied on by these writers dates from the reign of Shahjahan, and I have been unable to trace any contemporary authority showing that the statement in question is true of Akbar's officers; the fact that Abul Fazl says nothing about it in his minute account of the system appears to me to be practically conclusive, and until contemporary evidence is adduced I think it is safe to regard such deductions as a subsequent development, possibly introduced in order to neutralise the unauthorised gains from assignments of revenue. Even, however, if such deductions were made under Akbar, the scale would remain extraordinarily liberal when judged by modern standards. See on this point, V. Smith's *Akbar, the Great Mogul,* p. 363; Irvine's *The Army of the Indian Moghuls,* pp. 7, 11; Blochmann's Note on the Mansabs in *Ain,* translation, i. 238 ff.

India which could offer the prospect of such prizes, and we need not wonder that the Service should have attracted to the Court the ablest and most enterprising men from a large portion of Western Asia.

Appointments to the Service were made by the Emperor personally, the rank being fixed in accordance with the circumstances of each case; Raja Behari Mal, for instance, was appointed direct to the rank of 5000, the highest position open to any one outside the Imperial family. In ordinary cases, however, a candidate had to find a patron who would introduce him to the Emperor, and if he won favour, his appointment followed after a somewhat lengthy series of formalities. There appears to have been no recognised test of fitness, certainly nothing in any way corresponding to the modern usage of requiring some evidence of educational or other qualifications; Akbar had great faith in his own powers of discerning character, and he appears to have acted uniformly on his own judgment. In the same way there were no rules regarding promotion; an officer might be advanced, or degraded, or dismissed at the Emperor's pleasure.

The Service was not by any means confined to men of Indian nationality, and in Akbar's time it was predominantly foreign. Akbar himself was a foreigner in India; his father entered the country as a conqueror, and his adherents came from beyond the frontiers. Writing in the middle of the seventeenth century, Bernier insisted that the Mogul was even then a foreigner in Hindustan, and he states that "the Omrahs consist mostly of adventurers from different nations who entice one another to Court." The approximate composition of the Service under Akbar can be ascertained from Blochmann's laborious notes to the lists of amirs and mansabdars given by Abul Fazl; these lists include all appointments made during the reign to ranks above 500, and also those holders of inferior rank who were alive when the *Ain* was compiled about 1595. Omitting a small number of officers whose origin is not on record, I find that just under 70 per cent of the remainder belonged to families which had either come to India with Humayun, or had arrived at Court after the accession of Akbar; the remaining 30 per cent of the appointments were held by Indians, rather more than half by Moslems and rather less than half by Hindus. Akbar has often been praised for the enlightened policy which offered such scope for advancement to his Hindu subjects, and the praise is deserved, provided that proper stress is laid on the element of policy. In the course of about forty years he appointed in all twenty-one Hindus to ranks above 500, but of these, seventeen were Rajputs, that is to say, the great majority of the appointments were made in order to consolidate his hold over the chiefs who submitted to his rule. Of the remaining four appointments, one was held by Raja Birbal, the Court wit, the second by Raja Todar Mal, the great revenue administrator, the third by his son, and the fourth by another khattri, whose origin is not recorded, but who may be assumed to have been brought in by Todar Mal. In the lower ranks there were thirty-seven Hindus, of whom thirty were Rajputs. While, therefore, it is true that the Service offered a career to Hindus, it is also true that in practice the career was limited to Rajputs, apart from a few very exceptional cases drawn from other castes. The entire list contains only two brahmans for the whole Empire; one was Birbal, the other was Birbal's spendthrift son. The Imperial Service in fact consisted in the higher ranks of foreigners, Moslems, Rajputs, Birbal, and Todar Mal.

The primary duty assigned to the Service was simply to obey the Emperor's orders, though officers in the junior ranks were commonly placed under the orders of a senior. Two lists of officers were kept, one of those in attendance, the other of those holding appointments. Officers on the first list had nothing to do beyond appearing regularly at Court, maintaining their military force, and being ready to carry out any order which the Emperor might give. The appointments held by those on the second list were of very various kinds; they might be employed on strictly military duties, they might hold governorships or other posts in the provinces, or they might be attached to one of the departments of the Imperial Household, in the band, or the stables, or the fruitery as the case might be. There was very little specialisation of appointments, and an officer might be transferred at a moment's notice to an entirely novel form of employment: Birbal, after many years at Court, met his death in command of troops on the Frontier, while Abul Fazl, the most eminent literary man of the time, did excellent service when sent to conduct military operations in the Deccan. The whole Service was directly under Akbar's orders, and he chose from it the officers whom he considered best suited for the work of the moment; the success of his administration on these lines is the best evidence of his power of judging men.

A general view of the prospects of Akbar's Imperial Service suggests a comparison with the Bar rather than State employment at the present day. There was nothing approaching to the orderly promotion which is now so familiar; there were huge prizes to be won, but there were also many blanks in the lottery. It must have been very difficult to make a start, and from a subordinate position attract the favourable notice of the Emperor, but the start once made promotion might be rapid, and success could be commanded by the exercise of the indispensable qualities. The biographical notices collected by Blochmann, to which reference has already been made, afford instances of the possibilities which Akbar's Service offered. Hakim Ali, for instance, came from Persia to India poor and destitute, but won Akbar's favour, and from being his personal servant rose to the rank of 2000. Peshrau Khan again was a slave who was given to Humayun as a present; he rendered service in many different capacities and died a commander of 2000, leaving a fortune of 15 lakhs (equivalent to nearly a crore of rupees at modern values). The Service was undoubtedly by far the most attractive career in India, but at the same time it had its drawbacks. The Emperor was heir to his officers, and neither rank nor fortune could be passed on; the most that could be hoped for was that enough would be left for the maintenance of the family, and that the sons would be given a start in consideration of the father's services. Some officers may have accumulated secret hoards to meet this and other emergencies, but at any rate it was impossible to establish a family in a position of open independence, and each generation had practically to start afresh. The expenses of keeping up appearances and living in accordance with the fashionable standard were very great, as we shall see later on; payments were irregular, *jāgīrs* might almost be termed a gamble, and there was every possible inducement to take advantage of any momentary prosperity, and get together a sum of money which would tide over evil days or perhaps purchase the favour of men of influence and authority. Money spent on bribes and presents might prove a most profitable investment; money saved was money wasted, unless it could be concealed from the knowledge of the world.

I have tried to indicate the position of Akbar's high officers in some detail. My reason for dwelling on it is that these officers administered the Empire, and that the fortunes of the masses of the people were in their hands. The questions of real economic importance regarding the great men of the Empire, and indeed of India taken as a whole, concern the many rather than the few. What qualities were brought out among the successful officers by the system which has been described? Could it be counted on to produce administrators who would have the good of the people at heart, or did it tend to equip the country with exploiters rather than cherishers of the poor? On these questions the verdict must I think be unfavourable. The student of the chronicles of the time, while he recognises that some rulers watched for and rewarded honest work, must also recognise that honest work was not the only, or the easiest, road to preferment. In order to rise, an officer needed readiness of speech, plausibility, and the capacity for carrying on, or at least withstanding intrigue, and Akbar, like other rulers, was surrounded by men of this type. They preferred to remain at Court, and a province or a *jāgīr* served mainly to replenish their resources; they were less concerned to promote the prosperity of their charges than to keep things quiet, to see that complaints did not reach the Emperor's ears, and meanwhile to amass, or to spend, as much wealth as could be collected under these conditions. Making every allowance for Akbar's gift of discernment, it cannot have operated for long enough to work any permanent alteration, and there is abundant evidence that under his successor things got rapidly worse; Jahangir believed in frequent transfers, and the certainty of a speedy change meant increased activity in exploitation. But even in Akbar's time I find it impossible to believe that officers of the type best adapted to the environment were likely to carry out any steady policy of development such as the condition of the people rendered desirable. Akbar recognised the need for such a policy, mainly I take it on financial grounds, but his regulations to secure its realisation are remarkable for their vagueness, and the single instance of definite action furnished by the appointment of the Karoris [1] is also the most conspicuous of his administrative failures. Probably the most that the peasants could hope was that their Governor would leave them to themselves, and not exploit them more than his predecessor had done, but it is impossible to gather from the records whether this hope was often realised.

II. Other Forms of State Employment

The remaining forms of State employment require perhaps less detailed notice, for while in the aggregate they furnished the livelihood of a large section of the people, they were of comparatively slight importance for the economic welfare of the country as a whole. It now becomes possible to draw a distinction, though not an absolutely clear distinction, between military and civilian employment, and under the former head the class which calls for the earliest mention is the body of gentlemen-at-arms known as the Ahadis, which was a distinctive feature of Akbar's organisation. In the Mogul Empire a young man of position, who for any reason was unable to secure a *mansab*, might still hope to be appointed Ahadi, becoming one of "the immediate servants" of the Emperor, and from this position he might hope

[1] The Karoris are noticed in the next section.

to be promoted to a *mansab* later on. Ahadis were employed on a great variety of work; some of them performed duties analogous to those of a modern aide-de-camp or King's Messenger, while others were appointed to positions of trust in the Household departments, as guards over the harem, or with the camp, in the fruitery, or the library, and so on. Their pay was substantially higher than that of ordinary troopers, and Abul Fazl says that many of them received more than Rs. 500 a month; their salaries were paid for nine and a half months in the year, the remainder being set off against the cost of horses and equipment, and they received special consideration in various ways. Their importance from the economic point of view is not great; the position offered the beginning of a career to men who could not make a better start, but patronage was necessary to secure appointment, and it may fairly be assumed that Ahadis were chosen mainly from the same classes as the *mansabdārs*.

In considering the economic importance of the bulk of the Mogul army, I think it is safe to leave out of account the four millions of infantry included in the *būmī* or local forces. Abul Fazl says only that these forces were furnished by the zamindars of the country, and I can find no suggestion in the authorities that the men received pay, or that they were withdrawn from production by being called up for any regular training. In the literature of the time the word foot-soldier has a very wide meaning, and covers both fighting men and the camp-followers who were employed in enormous numbers: the enumeration of these "foot-soldiers" in the *Ain* means, I take it, that the local authorities might be required in case of need to produce the prescribed number of men, in other words, that the peasantry of a particular area might be impressed temporarily when military operations were in progress in that part of the Empire. The position of the local cavalry was probably more regular; their distribution over the provinces corresponds roughly with the importance of zamindars, and it may be inferred that the forces enumerated under this head were of substantial military value, consisting of troops maintained by zamindars at their own cost, but liable to be called on by the Emperor in case of need.[1] Possibly the whole number was not permanently maintained, but the force represents a withdrawal from production of a substantial number of men.

Apart from these local forces, we have to take into account the comparatively small number of troops maintained by the Emperor himself, and the much larger number maintained by his officers, partly at their own cost and partly paid for by the Imperial treasury. We know the sanctioned pay of the troops paid by the State, and we may assume that the officers got their men at rather cheaper rates. The pay of mounted men included the cost of maintaining their equipment and horses; deducting this item, the monthly pay of a trooper owning a single horse was on paper about 7 or 8 rupees, though it might be as much as 13 rupees if he owned an imported animal, but various deductions and frequent fines would operate to reduce these figures considerably. In the artillery, which was entirely Imperial, and was administered as a department of the Household, and not of the Army, the pay ranged from about 7 to 3 rupees. The infantry may fairly be described as a miscellaneous force; the ranks included matchlock-men (from 3 to 6 rupees monthly), porters (2½ to 3 rupees), gladiators and wrestlers (from 2 to 15 rupees), and slaves (from a dam to a rupee daily). The significance of these rates will be considered when we come to examine the standard of remuneration in other careers, and for the present it is sufficient to note that the higher pay sanctioned for the cavalry is in part at least an index to a difference in social position; service in the cavalry was respectable, and a gentleman could enter it, but the other branches of the army may almost be classed as menial, though a partial exception may be made of the artillery, in which foreign experts were employed in increasing numbers as time went on.

As has been said in the last chapter, the strength of the Mogul army cannot be calculated with any approach to

[1] Out of 343,000 local cavalry enumerated in the *Ain*, 86,500 belong to the single province of Ajmer, where the position of the zamindars was particularly strong: Oudh, on the other hand, was expected to produce only 7600 horsemen.

precision; the effective cavalry forces may have numbered somewhere about a quarter of a million, while the numbers of the infantry can only be conjectured. The amount of employment provided was, however, substantial. The dismounted ranks were probably recruited from the ordinary classes of peasants and townsmen, but in the cavalry Pathans and Rajputs predominated, apart from the numerous adventurers of foreign origin, and it may be noted that Akbar's regulations gave a substantial preference to foreigners in certain departments.

The armies of Southern India differed from those of the north mainly in the small proportion of cavalry which they contained. The chief reason for this difference was the scarcity of horses; they were not to any appreciable extent bred in the southern kingdoms, and importation from Arabia and Persia was a costly and risky business, while throughout the sixteenth century the trade was controlled entirely by the Portuguese, who in this way used their predominance at sea to secure a footing in the politics of their neighbours, obtaining various important concessions in return for promises of supply. Horses were in fact a luxury in the south; in Goa they cost about 500 pardaos (or say 1000 of Akbar's rupees), and it is significant that Pyrard, who gives this figure, puts the price of a slave-girl at from 20 to 30 pardaos in the same market. Apart from the predominance of infantry, the status of the soldiers appears to have been similar to that of the Mogul army; I have not found a record of the scale of pay about the year 1600, but half-a-century later Thévenot wrote that the soldiers in Golconda received 2 or 3 rupees monthly, which would leave them rather worse off than the corresponding ranks of Akbar's troops. It is not to be supposed that the numbers permanently employed in military duties were equal to the war strength of the southern country, which I have calculated at about a million men, but the forces maintained at the end of the sixteenth century must still have been considerable; the Deccan kingdoms had then to face the increasing menace of the southward expansion of the Mogul power, while the nobles of Vijayanagar were engaged in strengthening their position, and were occasionally at war among themselves. If then we reckon together the regular forces of the Moguls, the cavalry (but not the infantry) of their local forces, the permanent troops of the Deccan kingdoms, and those of the nobles of Vijayanagar, it seems reasonable to conclude that the total for the whole of India would at any rate greatly exceed a million of men, or more than double the strength of the various armies maintained about the year 1914. Allowing for the probable increase of population in the interval, the permanent draft on the productive power of the country was thus proportionately very much greater at the earlier period than at the later; fewer workers had to supply the needs of more fighters, and the difference appears to be sufficiently great to affect materially the distribution of India's annual income regarded as a whole.

When we turn from military to civil administration, the first difference to be observed from the conditions of the present day is the absence of specialised departments. We hear of nothing corresponding to the modern educational [1] or medical services, to the excise department, or (outside the large cities) to the police, nor, it need scarcely be added, was there any organisation for the management of the forests, or the provision of technical assistance for peasants or artisans. Notwithstanding the absence of such careers as these, the amount of employment provided by the civil administration must have been large. In Northern India the various departments of the Household were indeed staffed mainly from the Army, the superior posts being usually held by amirs, mansabdars, or ahadis, and the rank and file being drawn from the infantry, but there were large clerical establishments at the

[1] Some writers have inferred a large educational development from a regulation (*Ain*, translation, i. 278), in which Akbar sketched out an exceedingly ambitious curriculum for schools. Serious students of the period will scarcely be disposed to accept this view: had such a development taken place, the details would certainly have been recorded in the *Ain*, and in their absence the natural interpretation of this chapter is that, in the evolution of his theological views, Akbar formed the opinion that the schools (then religious institutions) were wasting time, and dictated his ideas as to their better organisation; it is fairly safe to conclude that the matter went no further.

various administrative headquarters, while the assessment and collection of the revenue required a numerous outdoor staff. Of the offices at headquarters Abul Fazl tells us practically nothing, and since the *Ain* purports to be a complete compilation of Akbar's administrative orders, we may conclude that he did not alter the organisation of these offices, but maintained the system which he found at work. The employment of a large staff of clerks can, however, be inferred with confidence from Abul Fazl's description of the course of official procedure, which was exceedingly complex and involved much copying and the use of many registers, features which still distinguish the practice of Indian public offices. As an example of the way in which things were done, we may follow the steps required before a newly appointed mansabdar could draw his allowances. The appointment, having been made by the Emperor personally, would first be recorded in the diary, in which all his orders were entered. The diary having been checked and passed, an extract (*yāddāsht*) of the order was then made, signed by three officials, and handed over to the copying office, where an abridgement (*tālīqa*) was prepared, signed by four officials, and then sealed by the Ministers of State. The *tālīqa* then passed to the military office, which called for estimates and descriptive rolls of the troops to be furnished; when these were ready, a statement of salary (*sarkhat*) was made out, and after being entered in the records of all sections of the office was sent on to the financial department. There an account was drawn up, and a report submitted to the Emperor, and on an allowance being formally sanctioned, a pay-certificate (*tālīqa-i tan*) was drafted, and passed through the hands of the Finance Minister, the Commander-in-Chief, and the Military Accountant. This last officer prepared the final document, the *farmān*, which required six signatures from three separate departments, and would at last be accepted by the Treasury as authority for payment of the salary.

This elaborate procedure will remind the reader of the methods of modern Indian public offices at their worst. That it was not confined to the disbursing departments may be gathered from the account of the revenue administration furnished by Abul Fazl, who mentions among other details that the assessment statements, which were prepared twice yearly for every village, were to be sent to Imperial headquarters as soon as they were ready; the examination and registration of such a mass of records implies by itself a small army of clerks, apart from those who were required to deal with other branches of the revenue business of the Empire.[1] Nor were these large offices peculiar to the north of India. Pyrard writes enthusiastically of the secretariat maintained by the Zamorin at Calicut. "I often wondered," he says, "to see the great number of men who have no other business and do nothing else all day long but write and register. Their position is very honourable. . . . Some write down the goods which come for the King, others the taxes and tributes paid day by day, others the money for the expenses of the King's household, others the most noteworthy events from day to day at Court or in the rest of the kingdom, and in short all the news; for everything is registered, and each has its own place. They register also all strangers who arrive, taking their names, and their country, the time of their arrival, and the object which brings them, as they did in our case; and it is a surprising thing to see their number, the good order kept among them, and how quickly they write. . . . The King has similar clerks in all the towns, seaports, harbours, and routes of the kingdom; they correspond with the clerks in the palace, and everything is organised, the former obeying the latter, and also having superiors among themselves. They have the same method of writing and the same organisation all along the Malabar Coast." In another passage describing the

[1] Mr. Vincent Smith conjectures (*Akbar, the Great Mogul*, p. 376) that these statements were sent to provincial headquarters only, but the language of the *Ain* appears to be quite definite, and it is not likely that the authorities who drafted these sections of the work would make a mistake on a point of current practice. If, however, we assume that the clerks who handled the statements were distributed in the provinces and not concentrated at the Capital, the volume of work would not be materially affected; and Mr. Smith recognises (p. 375) that there must have been "a gigantic statistical office" at Imperial headquarters, a statement which is amply borne out by the contents of the *Ain*.

custom-house at Calicut, Pyrard noted that fraud or mistake was rendered difficult by the number of clerks and officials, and that clerks were posted at the very smallest seaports, who spent their whole time making inventories of the goods which were brought. Other travellers, too, give us glimpses of elaborate formalities implying a fully organised administration, and we may conclude that in Akbar's time, as at the present day, clerical service afforded employment to a substantial proportion of the population of the country, although as it happens we have no information as to the prevailing rates of remuneration or other terms of their engagements.

Apart from the clerical service, a large amount of employment was provided by the methods of assessing and collecting the revenue, and we obtain occasional glimpses of the subordinate executive staff of the Mogul Empire; I know of no similar information regarding the south, but there also the business of the revenue must have required numerous officials, though in view of the system of administration they were probably servants of the nobles rather than of the central authority.[1] One item of information which has been preserved relates to the kanungos, who constituted as I understand the permanent localised element in the revenue administration. They were at one time paid from a cess, but Akbar gave them assignments (*jāgīr*) calculated to yield monthly salaries of from Rs. 20 to Rs. 50, so that allowing for changes in purchasing power they were very much better off than their successors of the present day. Apart from the kanungos, Akbar does not appear to have altered the subordinate organisation brought into existence by Sher Shah, and we meet with the designations of large numbers of officials—*shikkdār*, *amīn*, *karkūn*, *munsiff*,[2] etc.—without any details

[1] Reference has been made in a previous chapter to *Thévenot's* observations (p. 279) on the great number of tax-collectors met with in the kingdom of Golconda.

[2] The *munsiff* was an executive officer, not as now a judge. It is not clear to me whether the posts established by Sher Shah (Elliot, *History*, iv. 413) were in all cases continued by Akbar; this course would have involved a duplication of offices, and it is possible that a single officer appears under different names, being spoken of sometimes under the old title, and at other times under the designation introduced by the new régime.

regarding their position. We have more information regarding the staff employed in preparing the seasonal crop-statistics, which were an essential feature of the regulation-system of assessment. These statistics were not compiled by the village accountants, who were at this period servants of the village, and not of the State; season by season the measurers and writers appeared on the scene, and if, as I conjecture, their emoluments were in part at least a charge on the peasants, the burden must have been heavy. Akbar laid down a scale of diet to be provided for the measuring parties, and also fees to be paid in cash, but as the amount of the season's revenue depended on the records so prepared, it is reasonable to suppose that in practice payments were limited less by any orders than by the appetite of the subordinate officials, and thus the persistent tradition of the country that land-measurement means loot may well have its roots in the system of assessment introduced by Sher Shah and elaborated under Akbar by Raja Todar Mal.

No account of our knowledge of the local administrative staff would be complete without a reference to Akbar's disastrous experiment of appointing Karoris, of which incidental mention has already been made. The idea underlying this experiment was undoubtedly sound; large portions of the Empire were inadequately cultivated, and since every field brought under the plough meant an almost immediate increase in revenue, it was a reasonable financial measure to appoint what would now be termed Colonisation Officers with the primary duty of fostering the extension of cultivation, although the time-limit of three years assigned for the undertaking indicates a failure to appreciate the difficulty and complexity of the task. The annalists record these appointments under the year 1574, but say nothing as to the result, but the Karoris are nowhere alluded to in the revenue sections of the *Ain*, and must therefore have disappeared before its compilation. What actually happened is told by Badaoni; the officers appointed to the post used the opportunity to further their own interests rather than those of the Empire, and the experiment ended in disaster. "A great portion of the country was laid waste through the rapacity of the Karoris, the wives and children of the *raiyats* were sold and scattered abroad, and everything was thrown into confusion. But the Karoris were brought to account by Raja Todar Mal, and many good men died from the severe beatings which were administered and from the tortures of the rack and pincers. So many died from protracted confinement in the prisons of the revenue authorities that there was no need of the executioner or swordsman, and no one cared to find them graves or grave-clothes." This account is doubtless highly coloured, as is so much of Badaoni's work, but the main facts alleged are in themselves probable, and the fact of failure is to my mind established by the entire omission of any reference to the appointments in the historical account of the revenue system given by Abul Fazl; had the measure succeeded, he would certainly have seized the opportunity of attributing its success to the insight of his Imperial Master, but as things turned out the topic was one to be altogether avoided.

At this point we may leave the consideration of the classes who depended on State employment for their livelihood: our knowledge of them is in many respects incomplete, but we know enough to recognise their importance from the economic point of view. The higher ranks, while comparatively few in numbers, controlled the expenditure of a large proportion of the income of the country, and on their attitude depended the welfare of the classes by whom that income was produced. The lower ranks were at least sufficiently numerous to make up in the aggregate a substantial portion of the population; from the economic standpoint they must be regarded as parasites, feeding upon the fruits of the workers' toil, and, beyond an imperfect and precarious measure of security, contributing nothing to the common stock. In the remaining sections of this chapter we have to consider the other classes to whom the same description may in general be applied.

III. The Professional and Religious Classes

Mention has already been made of the fact that some of the most important modern professions, notably law, education, and journalism, were non-existent in Akbar's time. There were doubtless learned students of both Moslem and Hindu texts, but there were no advocates or pleaders practising in the courts; there were teachers, but the profession had not yet been separated off from more definitely religious pursuits; while ignorance of the art of printing would suffice to account for the absence of journalists even if other conditions had been favourable to their appearance.[1] Following the *Ain-i Akbari*, we may describe the established professions as medicine, learning, literature, art (including caligraphy), and music, but it must be understood that the lines of separation were not very clearly drawn, and a versatile man might be equally famous as a poet and a physician. When these professions are regarded from the point of view of the economist, the most striking fact is the narrowness of the market for their products or services. The educated middle class was very small, and the physician or artist or literary man could hope to obtain an adequate income only by attaching himself to the Imperial Court or to one of the provincial Governors who organised their surroundings on its model. Patronage was the one road to worldly success,[2] and patronage had usually to be paid for in the form of flattery or otherwise.

Akbar's reign was a favourable period for these professions. The Emperor was interested in everything, and he was a generous patron, while the Court inevitably followed his example and was guided by his taste. At the same time it must be remembered that the atmosphere was predominantly foreign, and while Indian talent was not neglected, a large share of patronage was secured by visitors from Persia and

[1] The Jesuits had recently introduced the art of printing in the south of India, but the press was used solely for religious purposes, and it had not yet been carried to the north.

[2] The *Ramayana* is sufficient evidence that pure literature of the highest class might be produced at this epoch, but Tulsi Das was not "discovered" by the Court during Akbar's lifetime, though he was received by Jahangir.

other parts of Asia.[1] This patronage took three practical forms, the conferment of rank (*mansab*), the grant of stipends in land or cash, and the gift of rewards for particular performances. The lists of eminent men in the *Ain-i Akbari* show that official rank might be conferred on physicians, artists, poets, and scholars, as well as on soldiers and administrators, while we read from time to time of rewards conferred in the traditional style on the production of a poem or other work of art. The remaining form of patronage, the grant of stipends, requires a rather longer notice. Stipends were sometimes given in the form of cash allowances, but the ordinary course was to grant an assignment of the revenue of a particular area of land. These assignments were known by the Turki name of *swyūrghāl*, by the Persianised expression *madad-i-ma'āsh*, and by various other names; they differed from the assignments to officers (*jāgīr*) in being granted for an indefinite period, and were in theory hereditary, but it would be a great mistake to regard them as permanent in the sense which that word bears in modern administration. Almost throughout the whole period of Moslem rule the policy in regard to these assignments seems to have followed a more or less definite cycle; there would be a long period of lavishness in granting, coupled with every conceivable variety of fraud in the details of the allotments, and then there would be a shorter interval of vigorous financial reform, in the course of which many of the existing grants would be either cancelled or greatly reduced in value. The allocation of the assignments was vested in one of the chief officers of the Empire, designated the Sadr, and the history of this post furnished by Abul Fazl is a consistent record of corruption.

In Akbar's Empire, then, the chief characteristic of a professional career was insecurity. Success depended on favour,

[1] Abul Fazl gives lists of the artists and professional men who had been received at Akbar's Court. Three-fourths of the poets were foreigners, more than one-third of the doctors, and about the same proportion of the musicians; see Blochmann's notes in *Ain*, translation, i. 537 ff. At the same time it must be allowed that Akbar had an eye for local talent, and Abul Fazl tells how he noticed a youth, the son of a menial servant, drawing pictures on walls, and handed him over to be trained as an artist; the youth was Daswanth, who "became the first master of the age."

which might be withdrawn as quickly as it was granted, and even the most stable forms of income were in practice held only during pleasure, and were liable to be cut off summarily on a change in the personnel of the administration. The economist is not directly concerned with the bearing of this system on the quality of the work produced, and for my present purpose it is sufficient to lay stress on the insecurity of the career. I think it is probable that conditions in the south of India were essentially similar, but I have found little direct evidence bearing on the subject.[1] We may, however, note Tavernier's observation, half a century later, that in all the countries traversed in the course of his journey through the Carnatic, Golconda, and Bijapur there were scarcely any doctors except for kings and princes; the common people doctored themselves with herbs which they gathered, while a large town might contain one man—or possibly two—with some practice in medicine. The opinion may be hazarded that in Akbar's time the prospects of artists and professional men were more favourable in the north than in the south; the Deccan kings of the period do not stand out as patrons, while the decay of the central authority in Vijayanagar must have diverted the thoughts of the nobles from literature and art.

The influence of the Court, which so largely dominated the professions, becomes comparatively unimportant when we turn to examine the position of the religious classes. The main subdivisions of these—the ascetics and mendicants—appear from contemporary accounts to have been proportionately as numerous as at the present day, and travellers comment on their abundance in various parts of the country; they concern the economist only as representing a withdrawal from the productive forces of the country. Of priests as distinct from ascetics the authorities tell us little. Mr. Sewell records that in the first half of the sixteenth century

[1] The position of the medical profession in the Deccan may be illustrated by the story that Sultan Ibrahim at Bijapur during his illness put to death several physicians who had failed to cure, beheading some and causing others to be trodden to death by elephants, so that all the surviving medical practitioners fled from his dominions (*Sewell*, p. 192).

a large number of grants were made by the nobles of Vijayanagar to temples throughout Southern India, and we may fairly assume that in the north and centre the religious foundations continued to enjoy the ancient grants and assignments, at least wherever the local administration was in the hands of zamindars. Akbar also appears to have continued the practice of making grants of this kind. The *Ain-i Akbari* speaks of his liberality in general terms, but does not say definitely that he gave religious grants to Hindus. Badaoni, however, in describing the revision of grants made by Shaikh Abd-un Nabi on his appointment as Sadr states that while learned Moslems had to be content with small portions of their former allotments, "the ordinary run of ignorant and worthless fellows, even down to Hindus, would get as much land as they asked for without question"; and the same writer indicates that the articles used in the ceremonial weighments of the Emperor were distributed to brahmans among other persons. We may conclude, therefore, that some share of the Emperor's liberality reached Hindu religious endowments.

Moslem institutions had benefited very largely by grants and assignments made by Akbar's predecessors, and in the early part of his reign they must have consumed a substantial portion of the revenues of the State. Akbar's later attitude was, however, hostile, and, if we may believe Badaoni, the revisional operations to which reference has just been made were very unfavourable to the Moslems, and must have resulted in a serious diminution of the income enjoyed by their institutions. The *Ain-i Akbari* gives statistics of the assignments of revenue in force towards the end of the reign. It is not possible to draw quantitative conclusions from these figures, partly because the text is still uncertain, and partly because they do not distinguish between the objects of the various assignments, but give only the totals assigned for objects of very different classes; all that can be said is that, in spite of the energy of financial reformers, a considerable portion of the State revenue remained alienated for the support of religious institutions, professional and learned men, and others whose claim to charity rested solely on their poverty. Of the economic position of the beneficiaries we have no contemporary information. Certainly many temples in India had accumulated large resources, for their plunder was a recognised means of securing wealth, but to my mind it is equally certain that there were many good men of all ways of thinking, doing their best according to their light, and living in a state of poverty which might be either compulsory or voluntary; in this respect, at least, there is no reason for supposing that India has changed materially in the course of the last three centuries.

IV. Servants and Slaves

The amount of labour expended in the performance of personal services is, if I am not mistaken, one of the outstanding economic facts of the age of Akbar. Some of the men thus employed were free, while others were slaves, but the functions assigned to the two classes were to a great extent interchangeable, and for the present purpose it is sufficient to treat them as a single group. In order to realise fully the extent to which productive forces were diverted to serve the purposes of luxury and display it is necessary to acquire a thorough familiarity with the conditions of life in India at this period, and the subject might be illustrated by quotations from practically every writer who has said anything at all about the country or the people. To collect all the contemporary statements would, however, involve much and tedious repetition, and I shall attempt to give only such a selection as will enable the reader to appreciate the nature of the evidence which is available. So far as Northern India is concerned, it will suffice to refer to some of the details of Akbar's Court recorded by Abul Fazl, bearing in mind that, as is shown abundantly in the chronicles of the time, the Emperor set the standard in such matters, and that every one who occupied or aspired to a position at Court followed that example so far as his means allowed. The first section of the Imperial Household described in the *Ain-i Akbari* is the *zanana*, which contained more than 5000 ladies, each of whom had separate apartments; they were attended by an adequate staff of servants, and watched in successive circles by female guards, eunuchs, Rajputs, and the porters at the gates, apart from the troops stationed on all four sides of the buildings. Next we come to the Imperial camp, which employed between 2000 and 3000 servants in addition to a guard of cavalry; there was one tent in particular which required 1000 men for a week for its erection. Supplies for the Household were obtained from distant sources, apparently regardless of the amount of labour expended. Wherever the Emperor might be, water for his use was brought from the Ganges, while ice came daily by post carriages and by runners from the snowy mountains to Lahore, and fruit was supplied regularly from Kashmir and Kabul, and even from more distant sources, such as Badakhshan and Samarqand. The stables swarmed with men as well as animals; each ordinary elephant, for instance, had four servants, but this number was increased to seven in the case of animals chosen for the Emperor's use.[1] The number of men employed in connection with sport and amusement cannot be calculated accurately, but was in the aggregate very large; a thousand swordsmen and many wrestlers were constantly in attendance at Court, a numerous staff was employed specially for hunting and shooting, another for hawking, another for pigeon-flying, and provision was made for training the fighting instincts of a variety of animals down to frogs and spiders. These instances are drawn from departments where the organisation had received the Emperor's personal attention, and it is easy to understand that his principal officers modelled their establishments on similar lines, one employing 500 torch-bearers, another having a daily service of a thousand rich dishes, and so on. A Mogul army in the field had on the average two or three servants for each fighting man; and that the fashion was not confined to the entourage of the Emperor is shown by della Valle's statement that at Surat servants and slaves were so numerous and so cheap that "everybody, even

[1] *Terry* (p. 141) tells how Jahangir assigned four attendants to each of the dogs brought to him as presents from England.

of mean fortune, keeps a great family, and is splendidly attended."

Such glimpses as we have of life in the Deccan at this period disclose an essentially similar picture. Pyrard, for instance, tells of the state maintained at Goa by the Bijapur envoy, who was accompanied about the town by a crowd of servants, pages, bearers, grooms, and musicians, and he adds that all the great men of the Deccan indulged in similar display. Thévenot, writing of a later period, gives a corresponding description of life in Golconda; the nobles had large followings, and every one, whether Hindu or Moslem, who had any sort of position imitated the nobles, having at the very least an umbrella-bearer, a cup-bearer, and two attendants to drive away flies. Life in Vijayanagar was organised on the same lines as may be seen from the accounts of visitors to that city before its destruction, and the narratives of missionaries show similar profusion at the courts of the Southern nobles towards the end of the sixteenth century. On the Malabar coast again we find that to European observers the number of attendants was the most striking feature; Pyrard, for instance, says that the Zamorin of Calicut travelled with about 3000 men in his train, and that on the coast generally the prominent men had always a large following. Similar fashions prevailed at Goa, where the Portuguese imitated the social life of their neighbours, and we are shown the men of quality attended through the streets by pages, lacqueys, and slaves in great number, with a led-horse and a palanquin behind even when the master preferred to go on foot. It will thus be understood that the profusion of servants, which attracts attention in India at the present day, is no modern phenomenon, but is in fact an attenuated survival of the fashions prevailing in the time of Akbar and doubtless dating from a much earlier period.

As has already been said, these servants were in some cases free, and in other cases slaves. Free men were hired at rates which sufficed for a little more than a bare existence, and consequently look absurdly low when stated in terms of modern currency; a servant with no special qualifications cost about 1½ rupees monthly at Akbar's Court, and perhaps 2 rupees on the west coast. The data on record regarding the price of slaves are too scanty to furnish a similar generalisation; Pyrard, as we have seen, puts the price of a slave-girl at the equivalent of about 50 rupees in Goa, which was a very busy market for such commodities, but the rate must have varied between very wide limits, depending as it did partly on the qualities of the individual and partly on fluctuations in the supply. To speak, however, of human beings as commodities is likely to produce an instinctive feeling of revolt in the minds of modern readers, and in truth the idea of slavery has become so unfamiliar in modern British India that it may be well to say a few words regarding the position formerly occupied by the institution. Its disappearance may fairly be described as recent; until the passing of Act V. of 1843 the British Courts in India were occupied in deciding questions arising out of the servile status of individuals, and the leading text-books on Hindu and Moslem law discussed these questions on precisely the same footing as those arising out of adoption, or partition, or inheritance. Nor was the institution a rare survival at that period: the Report on which Act V. was based affirms that slavery prevailed more or less throughout the territories forming the Presidency of Bengal as well as in Madras and Bombay, and gives instances of bodies of 2000 slaves being owned by individual proprietors; yet its disappearance is so complete that the subject is scarcely mentioned in the current text-books of Indian history.

In discussing the institution as it existed in Akbar's time it is convenient to distinguish clearly between urban and rural servitude. So far as I can see, two distinct systems had grown up in India side by side. In the villages the labourer was, at least in practice, in the position of a serf, and I do not think that Akbar's officers can have been troubled with questions affecting his legal status; in the towns and cities slaves were employed for many domestic purposes, and the incidents of their position were governed, at least to some extent, by the principles of law. The interest of rural serfdom arises from its importance in primary production, and it can be discussed most conveniently in connection with the organisation of agriculture: for the present I shall deal only with what may be called urban or domestic servitude, which was concerned almost exclusively with luxury and display.

Slavery must be accepted as a Hindu institution, though in Akbar's time at least it did not secure the approval of all Hindus, and the text-writers refine and distinguish according to their practice regarding its origin and incidents. The institution is also sanctioned, though on a more restricted basis, by Moslem law, and in either case Akbar and his contemporaries had legal justification for its recognition; in the Mogul Empire, however, its basis was wider than strict Moslem lawyers would have been disposed to authorise, and we may take it that, the institution itself being accepted as natural and reasonable, the local customs regarding it were adopted without much scrutiny of their legality. The existence of slavery in Vijayanagar is testified to by the travellers Abdur Razak, Conti, and Barbosa. It would be safe to assume that it prevailed in the Deccan, because it prevailed farther north in the country whence the Deccan dynasties sprung, and we may believe Nikitin's statement that in his time there was a trade in "black people" in Bidar. The Portuguese in this matter as in others followed the custom of the country: Linschoten recorded that they never worked, but employed slaves, who were sold daily in the market like beasts, and della Valle notes that the "greatest part" of the people in Goa were slaves. Various accounts could be quoted to prove the prevalence of slavery in the Mogul Empire, but its formal recognition in the *Ain-i Akbari* is sufficient evidence of the fact. We may infer from della Valle's statements that the principal Hindus at Surat—perhaps the most humane people that ever lived—disapproved entirely of slavery, but I do not think this remark can be extended to Hindus generally; many of them are known to have held slaves up to the time when legal recognition of the institution was withdrawn.

Slaves were obtained from various sources. The import

trade from Africa and Western Asia was of substantial importance, as has been noticed in a previous chapter, while there was also an export trade westwards; foreign slaves were costly, and were essentially articles of luxury. As regards Indian slaves, the status was hereditary under both systems of law, while the number could be increased in various ways, such as capture and voluntary or involuntary surrender. Capture was recognised by both Hindu and Moslem law, and in India this recognition led to serious abuses, for it became the fashion to raid a village or group of villages without any obvious justification, and carry off the inhabitants as slaves: early in his reign Akbar found it necessary to issue orders prohibiting the soldiery from taking part in such forays.[1] Under involuntary surrender may be classed condemnation for criminal offences, and sale of insolvent debtors (with their families), as well as the persons and families of revenue-defaulters, instances of such procedure being occasionally met with in contemporary narratives. Voluntary surrender has a more painful interest; its commonest occurrence was in the sale of children by their famine-stricken parents, a course which may fairly be described as normal in Akbar's time and for two centuries after.[2] We read of a Persian envoy taking home a large number of Indian children, because famine had made them cheap during his visit; and Barbosa tells us that when the people on the Coromandel coast were starving, the ships of Malabar used to carry food there and return laden with slaves, the people selling their own children for provisions. In ordinary times, however, children were stolen or kidnapped as well as purchased, and Bengal in particular was notorious for this

[1] *Akbarnama*, translation, ii. 246. Abul Fazl describes these orders as "the abolition of enslavement," but the expression is not, I think, meant to be taken literally; the limited scope of the orders is sufficiently plain from their wording.

[2] In 1785 Sir William Jones in a charge to a jury spoke of "large boats filled with children, mostly stolen from their parents or bought perhaps for a measure of rice in a time of scarcity, coming down the river for open sale in Calcutta"; and the Report on Slavery from which I take this quotation mentions (p. 17) that in the same city during the inundations of 1834 children were commonly hawked about the streets for sale.

practice in its most repulsive form.[1] There were still other sources from which slaves might be obtained, but enough has perhaps been said to show that the market must have been adequately supplied, and that a member of the upper classes who desired to make a display would have little difficulty in obtaining as many as he was prepared to buy. With the details of the slave's position the economist is not directly concerned, but I know of no evidence suggesting that the class was badly treated as a whole. Slaves were largely interchangeable with free men, and it is reasonable to conclude that the two classes of servants were treated on the whole alike, as was the case at the time when the existence of the institution was at last brought to a close.[2]

We have now passed in review the classes composing the first of the two main groups into which the population of India has been divided, that which is of interest chiefly from the standpoint of consumption, and we have seen that the effect of the existing social and political system was to withdraw from useful employment a large share of the energy and resources of the people, and to direct them towards unprofitable expenditure. In regard to labour, we have to take into account the man-power employed in official and domestic service, or engaged in religious pursuits; these avocations may indeed be classed as "necessary," but all essential needs could have been met with very much smaller forces. The armies were in the aggregate certainly much more numerous than those now maintained, but the men were wasted for lack of proper organisation and training; much of the domestic service rendered was sheer waste; and from the economist's point of view the throngs of religious mendicants can be

[1] Bengal is mentioned as a source of eunuchs by such different writers as *Marco Polo* (*Yule*, ii. 115), *Barbosa* (p. 363), and *Pyrard* (translation, i. 332); the facts are set out in the Account of Bengal included in the *Ain-i Akbari* (translation, ii. 122).

[2] This seems to me the general result of the statements in the *Slavery Report*. Masters differed, and choleric men, as the Rohillas are aptly described, might break bones in beating their menials, but I do not suppose that the status of the individual delinquent had any influence on the severity of his punishment.

placed on no higher plane. Turning to the upper ranks, we have seen that the only career open to men of ability and enterprise was the service or the bounty of the State, and that the dominant note of this career was consumption rather than production of wealth. A wealthy upper class may render substantial economic services if they use their wealth wisely, and direct a steady flow of savings into productive channels, but there are no signs that such services were rendered in the India of Akbar's time, and where savings were accumulated they took the useless form of stores of gold and silver and gems. In the aggregate, a very substantial proportion of the income of the country was spent on waste and superfluities, the cost of which fell in the long-run on the producing classes, the peasants, artisans, and merchants; the next stage in this study is to examine the conditions under which these classes fed and clothed the population and provided the surplus to pay for this extravagance and waste.

AUTHORITIES FOR CHAPTER III

SECTION 1.—The position of the nobles in Vijayanagar is indicated in *Barbosa*, 296-97, and in more detail in *Sewell*, especially 280, 373, 384. The position at the end of the sixteenth century can be gathered from incidental references in *Hay*, 733-780. For the Deccan, see *Thévenot*, 290 ff.

The *Ain* (translation, i. 233-265) gives full details as to Akbar's organisation; Blochmann's notes on this subject are most valuable, but by themselves are inadequate, and should be supplemented by *Irvine*. Badaoni's account of the irregularities is reproduced in Blochmann's translation of the *Ain* (i. 242). As regards *jagirs*, a perusal of the chapters in the *Ain* quoted above leaves the impression that assignments were commonly given, but the word *jagir* may in this case be used to signify a post traditionally remunerated by assignment, but actually carrying a salary. More important perhaps is the account given by Jahangir (*Tuzuk*, translation, i. 7) of the orders issued on his accession, confirming the *jagirs* held by his father's servants.

For the composition of the Imperial Service, see *Bernier*, 212, and *Ain*, translation, i. 309-528. References to the Emperor's claim to inherit have been given above under Chapter II. 6; the rule appears to have been of Mogul and not of Indian origin, for Sikandar Lodi is represented as having ruled that the property (though not the offices or *jagirs*) of a deceased noble should pass to his heirs (Elliot, *History*, iv. 327). Jahangir's practice in regard to *jagirs* may be gathered from his own account which is scattered through the *Tuzuk*: Hawkins (in *Purchas*, I. iii. 221) gives a graphic but perhaps prejudiced account of the frequency of transfers, and other European authorities write in the same sense. For the Karoris, see *Badaoni* (Lowe's translation, ii. 192). Badaoni's account is translated also in Elliot, *History*, v. 513, and the same volume contains (p. 383) the reference in the *Tabakat-i-Akbari.* The subject is noticed in the *Journal, R.A.S.*, for January 1918, p. 27.

SECTION 2.—The position of the Ahadis is stated clearly in the *Ain* (translation, i. 249); we meet them occasionally in the narratives of European travellers, the name taking various forms, *e.g.* "haddies" (*Purchas*, I. iii. 216). The local forces (*būmi*) are referred to in the opening chapter of Book II. of the *Ain* (translation, i. 232), and their numbers are specified in the "Account of the XII. Subas" (*idem*, ii. 115 ff.). Information regarding the rest of the troops is scattered through Books I. and II. of the *Ain*; the best summary will be found in *Irvine*. For the preference to foreigners, see the *Ain*, *passim*, *e.g.*, translation, i. 321; "Turanis and Persians get 25 rupees, and Hindustanis 20 rupees."

The horse-supply of Southern India is a common topic in the *Decadas*, and is discussed in *Whiteway*, ch. vii. viii.; the trade is referred to in the treaties made by the Portuguese, see for an instance *Sewell*, 186. The prices given by *Pyrard* will be found in translation, ii. 66, 67; a few years earlier *Linschoten* put the price of horses in Goa at 400 to 500 pardaos. For the pay of soldiers in Golconda, see *Thévenot*, 301. For instances of fighting among the nobles of Vijayanagar, see *Hay*, 759, 781.

The procedure at Akbar's headquarters is detailed in the *Ain* (translation, i. 258 ff.): that of the revenue administration is given in ii. 43-49. The passages quoted from *Pyrard* are translated from i. 258, 297. References to the subordinate executive service are scattered through the *Ain*; see especially translation, ii. 45, 66. The passages regarding the Karoris have been given under the preceding section.

SECTION 3.—The position of artists and professional men at Akbar's Court is dealt with in the *Ain* (translation, i. 96 ff. 537 ff.), and much light is thrown on it by Blochmann's notes to these sections as well as to the list of *mansabdars* (*idem*, i. 308 ff.). For *sayurghals*, see i. 268 ff., and the references given in Blochmann's notes.

Tavernier's observations on doctors in the south will be found in ii. 213. For grants to religious institutions, see *Sewell*, 178; *Ain*, translation, i. 266 ff.; Elliot, *History*, v. 522.

SECTION 4.—The first two books of the *Ain* (beginning at i. 44 of the translation) contain the details of Akbar's establishment. The other illustrations given of the fashion of keeping many servants are drawn from *Purchas*, I. iv. 432: *della Valle*, 42, 82; *Pyrard* (translation, i. 376, ii. 75, 80, 135); *Thévenot*, 307; but, as indicated in the text, practically every contemporary writer has something to say on the topic.

For the legal aspect of slavery in British India, readers may consult *Macnaghten*, while the *Slavery Report* contains a large though incomplete collection of facts. For slavery in the south, see *Major*, 29, 30, 31; *Barbosa*, 309, 358; *Linschoten*, c. 29; *della Valle*, 157; *Pyrard*, translation, ii. 39. For slaves under Akbar, see *Ain*, translation, i. 253-254. The sale of children is a commonplace; the instances given in the text are from *Bernier*, 151, and *Barbosa*, 358.

CHAPTER IV

AGRICULTURAL PRODUCTION

I. Land Tenures

Before we enter on an examination of the system of agriculture prevailing in India during the reign of Akbar, a few words must be said regarding the subject of land tenures. The terms on which land is held have everywhere an important bearing on the degree of success attained in its utilisation, and there is a special reason for noticing the subject in the case of India, because much of our knowledge of agriculture is derived from records relating to the assessment and collection of the land revenue, and the information which they supply cannot be fully appreciated unless we possess some idea of the conditions in which it was obtained. At the close of Akbar's reign, Indian tenures showed some development from the traditional system of the country, but no revolutionary changes had occurred, and the influence of the old ideas was still predominant. Traditionally there were two parties, and only two, to be taken into account; these parties were the ruler and the subject, and if a subject occupied land, he was required to pay a share of its gross produce to the ruler in return for the protection he was entitled to receive. It will be observed that under this system the question of ownership of land does not arise; the system is in fact antecedent to that process of disentangling the conception of private right from political allegiance which has made so much progress during the last century, but is not even now fully accomplished.[1] Nor was the occupation of land necessarily a right in the juridical sense of the word: the king required revenue, and the cultivation of sufficient land to supply his needs might be regarded rather as a duty, and might in some cases be enforced by appropriate penalties. In most parts of India the demand for land has become so great that the mention of duty in this connection may strike the reader as grotesque, but even in the present century there have been occasions in some of the more thinly populated States when this aspect of the relation was of practical importance, and when peasants were liable to get into trouble if they failed to cultivate a sufficient area: that the duty of cultivation might be rigorously enforced at an earlier period may be inferred from the incidental report made by an English merchant on the east coast in the year 1632, that the local Governor had with his own hands cut a village headman in two pieces for not sowing his ground; it may be presumed that such a measure of severity was exceptional, but the story illustrates a side of Indian land-tenure which has now passed into almost complete oblivion.

The development of this original and simple form of tenure may be associated with the aggregation of small States into great Empires, which recurred periodically in India during the historical period. A conqueror might either step into the place of a vanquished king, or he might leave the king in possession but require him to pay tribute. In neither case would the change necessarily affect the position of the peasant, but the result of such political adjustments was not uncommonly an alteration either in the share of the produce claimed, or in the method of its assessment and collection, and these were matters in which the peasant was deeply interested. No argument is required to show that his economic position was affected by the share which had to be

[1] This process may be followed in Northern India by observing the change in the significance of the word *raiyat*. In the literature of Akbar's time the word means primarily a subject: nowadays it usually means a tenant, but modern landholders are still occasionally influenced by the older implication, and tend to regard, and to treat, their tenants as their subjects.

set apart, which might be one-tenth as under Firoz Shah or one-half as under Alauddin Khalji, but it is desirable to realise that changes in methods of assessment might be almost equally important, and as a matter of fact it is to such changes that the appearance of the modern Indian landholder must be in great measure attributed. The revenue system prevailing in Vijayanagar may be taken as a type of one of the alternative methods of Imperial organisation. The revenue was collected by the nobles, who may be regarded as representing the successors of the kings formerly absorbed in the Empire; they paid a certain amount to the Imperial treasury and retained the rest, so that we may regard the Empire as having been super-imposed on the system previously existing; and when, a few years after Akbar's death, the Southern Empire finally ceased to exist, the nobles remained in possession and resumed the position of kings. Whether the super-position of the Empire involved any change in the tenure of the peasants is a question which I am unable to answer: we do not know what share of the produce they had to pay before the Empire came into existence, and we can be sure of only one fact, that under the Empire the share was exceedingly high. Nuniz states definitely that the peasants paid nine-tenths to the nobles, who paid one-half of what they received to the Emperor: there is no doubt that this writer had access to good sources of information, but I can conceive of no form of agriculture in which producers could live on so small a proportion as one-tenth of the gross produce of their holdings, and I am inclined to think that the expression should not be taken in its strict numerical sense, but rather as signifying a demand which seemed extraordinarily heavy. I feel a similar difficulty in accepting in its literal sense the statement made by de Laet that the Mogul authorities took nearly three-fourths of the gross produce, "leaving only one-fourth for the wretched peasants, so that they sometimes receive nothing in return for their labour and expenditure." Most of de Laet's information on such matters seems to have come from the maritime districts, and I think that his statement, like that of Nuniz, is best read as indicating a very severe revenue demand rather than a demand of the precise proportion stated, though it is possible that (including extra payments) three-fourths were actually demanded in some parts of the country.

In the north of India Akbar's administrative ideals favoured, as has been said in an earlier chapter, substitution rather than superposition; he aimed, that is to say, at entering into direct relations with the peasants who came under his rule, but his policy was guided largely by practical considerations, and his revenue system was therefore by no means uniform. In Sind he maintained the original Indian practice, and took a share of produce from the peasants: in Bengal, Berar, and Khandesh he continued the revenue systems which he found in force—systems the exact nature of which is doubtful; while in the heart of the Empire he introduced his own methods, based on those of his predecessor, Sher Shah, pushing them as far as could safely be done, but coming to terms with the zamindars when local conditions rendered this course desirable. It is not always possible to ascertain what system was in force in a particular area, but it is probably correct to say that in the most productive portion of Northern India, from Bihar to Lahore and Multan, the standard of revenue payments was set by the *zabt*, as the regulation system of assessment was termed. In this system Akbar fixed his claim at one-third of the gross produce, and in order to realise the revenue on this basis his officials determined the average yield of every crop grown in the country, and fixed cash rates representing one-third of this average yield valued on the results of ten years' experience. The area sown with each crop was recorded season by season, and the demand on each peasant was calculated by applying the sanctioned rates to the area which he had cultivated; thus a peasant cultivating land in the neighbourhood of Agra knew that he would be charged at the rate of 67 dams[1] on each bigha

[1] The figures given in the text are rounded: the actual schedules give the rates in dams and jitals, that is to the nearest thousandth of a rupee. There is some uncertainty whether these rates were meant to be collected in all individual cases, or were intended to set a standard for the guidance

sown with wheat, 49 dams on barley, 156½ dams on indigo, 239 dams on sugar-cane, and so for each separate kind of produce, and similar schedules of rates were fixed for each agricultural tract to which the system was applied. Under the original Indian system, in which the produce was divided at harvest, the peasant and the State shared the risk of the enterprise; under the system introduced by Akbar, the peasant took most of the risk, and (in theory) all the extra profit, since his payments were determined by the crops sown and not by the harvests gathered, subject only to the possibility of a remission being granted in the event of a failure of the crop. The change thus operated, on the one hand, to increase the peasant's interest in the success of his undertaking, and, on the other, to minimise seasonal fluctuations in the Imperial revenue, and while it did not amount to the establishment of a regular system of rents, it marks a definite step towards the transformation of the peasant into what is known as a cash-paying tenant; he did not know his liabilities definitely in advance, but he could calculate them for the season as soon as he had made his plans for sowing. Of the practical working of this system we shall speak later on; for the moment we may leave it with the remark that its introduction involved the collection of a large mass of data regarding the land, and that through the preservation of much of this information in the *Ain-i Akbari* we are able to arrive at a better understanding of the condition of the industry than if we were dependent solely on the casual observations of individuals.

II. The System of Agriculture

The literature of the period does not, so far as I am aware, include anything which can be described as a complete account

---

of collectors, but the question is not of much practical importance, since it is reasonably certain that the sums actually demanded were nearly if not quite as large as the standard rates. The bigha was the unit of land-measurement, and was intended to be a little more than half an acre.

of the system of Indian agriculture.[1] It would indeed be matter for surprise if such an account existed: the subject was not one to attract Indian writers of the time, while foreign visitors, whose interests centred for the most part in commerce, were content to enumerate and describe the products of the country without entering into details regarding the conditions under which they were produced. Writers of both classes, however, give us many partial glimpses of the subject, sufficient in the aggregate to furnish some approach to a general account provided that we have an outline or framework on which they can be arranged. This outline can, if I am not mistaken, be found in the theory of continuity. India did not experience between 1600 and 1900 an agricultural revolution such as in some other countries coincided with the adoption of a policy of enclosure, or followed on the development of the modern ocean-borne commerce: enclosure is only now becoming a question of practical interest, while the main results of modern conditions of transport are accurately known, dating as they do, for the most part, from the years following on the opening of the Suez Canal. The changes since Akbar's time have indeed been numerous, and some of them have been important, but they have not sufficed to transform the system as a whole; the plough and the ox, the millets and rice, the pulses and oilseeds, and the whole tradition of the countryside link us with the sixteenth century and with far earlier times in the history of the people, and almost every detail mentioned by the authorities for our period can be realised instantly by any one who is moderately familiar with the life of the peasants at the present day. Take as an example the Emperor Babur's description of the method of irrigation practised in the country round Agra: "At the well-edge they set up a fork of wood, having a roller adjusted between the forks, tie a rope to a large bucket, put

[1] Terry set out to give such an account, but the result is rather disappointing. He had seen very little of the country—only that part of it which lies between Surat and Mandu; much that he says is interesting, but its application is limited, and he either failed to observe or omitted to record many things which are indispensable to a proper appreciation of the conditions prevailing even in the small area he had seen.

the rope over the roller, and tie its other end to the bullock. One person must drive the bullock, another empty the bucket": that is as true of the twentieth century as of the time to which it relates. Or take Garcia da Orta's note on tillage in the Deccan uplands behind Goa: "They do not till the land with manure and labour as we do. They sow on the face of the earth with very little tillage." Turning to the *Imperial Gazetteer*, we may read of this country that "a field of black soil requires only one ploughing in the year, and is seldom manured." In the same way the reader will find that each detached observation falls into place on the assumption that the general system has been maintained, and it follows that, if we can arrive at a knowledge of the changes which have occurred, we shall be able to reconstruct the main outlines of the industry as it was practised three centuries ago.

Turning first to the crops grown, Abul Fazl has preserved for us lists giving the name of every crop which was assessed to revenue in Northern India, and we may be confident that no crop which was widely grown escaped assessment. These lists are very nearly identical with those contained in the agricultural statistics of the present day.[1] We find the cereals, rice, wheat, and barley; the two tall, and several small millets; the familiar pulses, and the usual kinds of vegetables. We find also sugar-cane (both thick and thin), the fibres cotton and hemp, the usual oilseeds, and such miscellaneous crops as indigo, poppy, *pān*, and *singhāra*. For the south we have no contemporary official records, but a compilation from the narratives of various travellers gives a similar list, nearly, but again not quite, identical with that of modern times. Taking the two lists together, it will be found that the only crop which can be said to have disappeared since Akbar's time is *āl* (*Morinda tinctoria*), the dye-yielding shrub which was formerly of importance in parts of Central India, but which was driven out of cultivation in the last

[1] I have given in Appendix A a single list based on those which occur in the *Ain*, and also a list of the crops of Southern India compiled from contemporary accounts.

century by the competition of manufactured dyes. To set against this loss there are substantial gains, the "planters' crops," tea and coffee, such widely-grown staples as potatoes, tobacco, groundnuts, and sweet potatoes, and the food-grains, oats and maize. Indian agriculture has thus been enriched since the sixteenth century, but not to such an extent as to transform its permanent characteristics.

The statistics preserved by Abul Fazl render it possible to obtain a rough idea of the relative value of the crops grown in those parts of Northern India where the revenue was assessed on Akbar's regulation system. That system aimed, as we have seen, at taking for the State the average money value of one-third of the gross produce, so that the sums demanded on equal areas of the different crops indicate the prevalent official view as to the proportionate value of each: the assessment of a bigha of wheat, for instance, at 60 dams meant that the assessors regarded the average value of a bigha of wheat as 180 dams; and if we put the assessment on wheat as equal to 100, we can show the assessments on other crops in a convenient form so as to bring out the relation in question. The figures for some of the principal crops stand as follows: they are based on the average of the various assessment rates in force under Akbar in the Mogul provinces of Allahabad, Agra, and Delhi.

Crop.	Comparative Value.	Crop.	Comparative Value.
Wheat	100	Linseed	51
Barley	67	Rape	53
Gram (common)	60	Poppy	210
Jowār	59	Sugar-cane (ordinary)	213
Bājra	42	Cotton	150
Mandua	44	Indigo	254
Sāwan	22		

So far as the food-grains are concerned, comparative values have changed very little; an acre of barley, or jowār, or gram is now worth, roughly speaking, 60 to 70 per cent of an acre of wheat, as was the case in Akbar's time, and the small millets, acre for acre, are worth substantially less.[1] Oil-

[1] Bājra was placed by Akbar's assessors on a lower level than we should have expected, presumably because of some difference in price.

seeds were proportionately less valuable than they are now, when a great and profitable export trade has grown up: sugar-cane, on the other hand, shows little change in the relative position, being still worth rather more than double the value of wheat. It is noteworthy that in Akbar's time poppy was as valuable as sugar-cane: its present value in a free market is unknown because the price paid to the grower has long been fixed by the State on considerations of a different order, but if we take into account the revenue realised until recently from the sale of the drug, the position occupied by the crop will occasion no surprise. The high level of the comparative value of cotton is a point to be considered in connection with the industrial development of the country; it is clear that the raw material of ordinary clothing was expensive when judged by the prices obtainable for food-grains. Indigo also was highly valued, but in this case the cause is to be sought in commerce rather than in industry, for even in the sixteenth century this crop was grown mainly for the export market. It is tempting to pass from relative to actual values, and deduce from these data figures for the average yield of crops in Akbar's time. Such a calculation is indeed possible on paper, but the uncertain factors are relatively large, and the result depends mainly on the values assigned to them by the individual calculator: in the present state of our knowledge, therefore, it is better to resist the temptation offered by the figures, and to be content with the conclusion that on the whole the relative values of the various crops show little alteration, and that in cases where the change is marked an explanation can usually be found in the known history of the intervening period.

We know then that, apart from the exceptions already indicated, India taken as a whole yielded the same agricultural produce as she yields now. We know also that the distribution of the various crops followed the main lines determined by the conditions of soil and climate: Bengal depended mainly on rice, Northern India on cereals, millets, and pulses, the Deccan on jowār and cotton, the south on rice and millets; and indications drawn from various sources justify the inference that there was less specialisation of cropping than is found at the present time. Specialisation was not indeed entirely unknown, for Bengal supplied sugar to many parts of India, while the production of indigo was to a large extent concentrated in two localities, Biāna near Agra, and Sarkhej in Gujarat, and both these instances throw light on the conditions affecting the process. Sugar was carried mainly by water, whether it went westwards to Agra or southwards to the ports of Malabar, that is to say, the trade was to a great extent independent of the high cost of land transit; indigo, on the other hand, was carried by land from Agra to the Cambay ports or across the frontier to Persia, the export value of the commodity being exceptionally high in proportion to its bulk; and thus we have in these instances early manifestations of the process of specialisation which has made such progress since the development of means of communication in the course of the past century. On the other hand, we look in vain for anything corresponding to the modern wheat tracts or cotton tracts, which are essentially the results of railway enterprise: cotton, at least, was more widely grown than is now the case, though the aggregate of production was probably less, and it is reasonable to infer that most parts of the country were nearly self-sufficing in the matter of clothes as well as of food and other requisites. We can therefore arrive at a general idea of the system of cropping practised in a particular part of India if we eliminate those staples which are known to have been subsequently introduced, and make due allowance for the progress of specialisation, and for the changes in regard to irrigation which we are about to discuss.

When we pass to a consideration of the implements used by the peasants of Akbar's time, we can see at once that few changes can have taken place, for even at the present day the peasant's equipment is so nearly the bare minimum required for his work that it is impossible to believe he was ever much worse off, while there are no grounds whatever for thinking that any useful implements have disappeared in the interval. Ploughs and hoes, water-lifts and minor implements generally, all bear their age upon their face: their minute adaptation to the circumstances of each locality must be the result of slow growth, and their most striking characteristic, the economy of iron, finds its explanation in the high cost of that metal during the period when India depended for it on her own resources. As it happens, we have a striking confirmation of this inference in regard to water-lifts. Babur's description of the ordinary plane-and-bucket lift has already been quoted, and his account of the Persian wheel used in the Punjab is equally convincing, so that there is no doubt that the existing implements were in use at any rate before Akbar was born; and though similar direct evidence in regard to ploughs has not come to my notice,[1] their antiquity is not likely to be seriously disputed. Whether implements in general cost the peasant more or less is a question which cannot be answered in terms of figures, but the difference either way was probably small: on the one hand, wood was easier to get than now, but iron was certainly much more expensive in terms of grain, while the cost of manufacture measured in the same currency has probably changed very little, and, on the whole, the quantity of produce required to maintain the supply of the necessary implements cannot have altered materially during the last three centuries.

As regards the supply of power, the peasant is probably somewhat worse off now than under Akbar. In most parts of the country, though not everywhere, there was more waste land available for grazing, and it is reasonable to infer that cattle could be obtained more cheaply and easily than is now possible. As to the quality of the stock, no precise information has come to my notice. Various travellers describe one or other of the famous breeds of what may be termed carriage oxen, but these were luxuries for the rich, and, so far as I know, there is no description of the animals which drew the ploughs.

[1] Terry says (*Purchas*, II. ix. 1469), "They till their ground with oxen and foot-ploughs." The English foot-plough of the period must have been very like the Indian plough as we know it, being made chiefly of wood and having neither wheel nor mould-board, but I have not found a sufficiently clear description of it to show whether there was any important difference.

Quality apart, it may be recognised as probable that plough cattle were easier to get, and also to feed, than is the case at present. I do not think that we should be justified in inferring that the supply of manure was larger. Assuming that there were more cattle for an equal area of cultivation, it does not follow that their manure was available, for in that case there must have been more grazing and less stall-feeding, and the manure would have been left where it was dropped. I have found nothing to show that less dung was burnt in the sixteenth century: it was certainly used as fuel, as indeed was the case in parts of Europe about the same period, but the comparative extent of the practice remains a matter of conjecture.

When we turn to the supply of water for irrigation, we must draw a sharp distinction between what is now the main canal tract and the rest of the country. In reading the narratives of writers who travelled north and west of Allahabad, we are at once struck by the scantiness of the allusions to this subject. The practice of irrigation was probably unfamiliar to most of the visitors, and we should naturally expect that they would record it as a novelty, but, as a matter of fact, they say very little about it. In some cases their silence may be explained by the season: Steel and Crowther, for instance, who travelled from Agra to Persia in 1615, and write enthusiastically about the system of irrigation in the latter country, performed the journey as far as Lahore in April and May, when little irrigation would have been seen. This explanation cannot, however, apply to a case like that of Finch, who marched from Agra to Lahore in January, and noticed only that a small water-channel had been cut to irrigate one of the royal gardens; and taking all the accounts together, it is difficult to resist the inference that in this part of the country irrigation was a much less conspicuous feature of the winter landscape than it is to-day. The meagre descriptions of agriculture contained in the *Ain-i Akbari* give a similar impression: in these the general emphasis is on the rains crops, and almost the only definite statement regarding irrigation in the *Account of the XII. Provinces* is that in Lahore irrigation was chiefly from wells. Babur, writing early in the sixteenth century, comments on the absence of artificial canals in India, and hazards the explanation that water is not absolutely requisite, the autumn crops being nourished by the rains, while "spring crops grow even when no rain falls." This observation, which could be made by no modern visitor to the Punjab, is in accordance with what is known about the sources from which water could be obtained. Practically the whole canal system is of later date: in Akbar's time there were some inundation channels on the Indus, and there were the remnants of the aqueducts constructed by Firoz Shah to supply the gardens and cities established by him, but the value of these works was essentially local, and the country as a whole depended either on wells or on the minor streams which were utilised by means of temporary dams. We must therefore picture conditions in the north as approximating to those which now prevail in the centre of the country, large expanses of dry cropping with patches of more productive land in places where a stream could be utilised or where efficient wells had been made.

The change in the rest of India has been much less striking. The face of the country supplies sufficient proof that the construction of wells and reservoirs is no novelty, and it is probable that in proportion to population the area irrigated in the time of Akbar was of about the same order of magnitude as at the beginning of the present century: it may have been substantially less, it may possibly have been somewhat greater, but I do not think that the difference can have been very marked. In peninsular India embankments have been built and have burst, wells have been sunk and have collapsed, for an indefinite number of centuries. So far, then, as regards the material conditions, the information which is available points to a system of agriculture generally similar to that which prevails to-day. In the next section we will consider the personal element in the industry.

III. Peasants and Labourers

A knowledge of the system of agriculture prevailing in the sixteenth century enables us to arrive at certain conclusions regarding the numbers of the population by whom it was carried on, but before we take the facts of our period into consideration, we must glance at the general relation subsisting between the numbers of a community and the area cultivated by its members. Putting aside instances of the commercial use of land, and confining our attention to agriculture pursued as a means of direct subsistence, we find that the particular system followed in any region depends partly on the soil, climate, and other durable elements of the environment, and partly on the capacities of the people by whom it is carried on. We find also that the area cultivated under such a system is limited by the quantity of labour available, and that this limitation operates at the seasons of maximum pressure. Unlike most industries, agriculture of the type we are considering does not offer an unvarying amount of employment throughout the year, but is marked by an alternation of slack and busy times; in some cases the pressure is greatest at seed-time, in others at harvest, and in others at some intervening period, but the result in each case is the same. The area cultivated will never be much greater than can be dealt with: it may fall far below this standard in unfavourable years, but so long as the motive to cultivate exists at all, the tendency will be to sow as large an area as can be matured, but no more. If, while other conditions remain substantially unchanged, the numbers of the rural population decline, then the area cultivated will fall off; if the population rises, the area will also rise, until no more land remains within reach, and the resulting congestion will tend to restore the balance, whether it leads to migration or to an increase in mortality, but, short of congestion, the relation between numbers and cultivation will remain approximately constant.

Even at the present day Indian agriculture is still very

largely in the "subsistence stage," that is to say, the production of food for the family is still the first care of the individual peasant, and we shall be justified in concluding that the relation between numbers and cultivation has not varied greatly during the last three centuries, provided that we find reason for thinking that the conditions have remained substantially unchanged. There are no grounds for supposing that the permanent conditions of soil and climate have altered in any way, and we have seen in the last section that the changes in crops and methods have not been marked; it remains to inquire whether the men themselves have changed. There is no evidence to show that Indian peasants and labourers were either more or less efficient in Akbar's times than at the present day. As we shall see in a later chapter they ate the same food then as now, and it is probable that they got a little less to eat rather than a little more; there were fewer influences in operation to stimulate the growth of intelligence; as we shall find later on, there was much less hope of keeping the fruits of additional effort; and in the absence of direct evidence it is reasonable to infer that the quantity and quality of the work done by ordinary men were at any rate not greater than they are. To take concrete illustrations, I do not think that it would be possible to show grounds for holding that there has been a material change in the time spent in ploughing an acre of land, in transplanting an acre of rice, in weeding an acre of cotton, in hoeing an acre of sugar-cane, or in harvesting an acre of wheat; and if so much be granted it follows that, in those parts of India where agriculture has not greatly changed, a given cultivated area implies somewhere about the same rural population at any period in the last three centuries. This conclusion does not involve uniformity in extent, but only in point of time; at the present day we find considerable variations in the numbers of people required in different localities, and the implication is that these variations have persisted without substantial change. At the beginning of the present century there were from 100 to 120 persons to each 100 acres of "normal cultivation" in some of the western districts of the United Provinces,[1] while there were from 60 to 70 persons to 100 acres in other districts lying farther south; the difference between these figures is adequately explained by permanent features of the environment, and the conclusion is that it has probably persisted with relatively little change, and that the western districts required somewhere about 100 to 120 persons, and the southern somewhere about 60 to 70 persons, to cultivate 100 acres in the time of Akbar and throughout the intervening period.

The position we have now reached is that, taking a wide view of India as a whole, the system of agriculture has not changed materially, and that in any particular region the numbers of the rural population have varied approximately with the area under cultivation. In theory this result is compatible with a very wide range of variation in the average size of holdings; it could be reached if the entire rural population held land, and also if the land were occupied by a small number of substantial farmers employing numerous landless labourers, but I do not think either of these extremes is in accordance with the facts of Akbar's age, and there are indications that, while landless labourers existed in numbers, the bulk of the cultivators were, as they are now, small men with limited resources. To take the latter point first, the recurring references to the village headmen in Akbar's administrative instructions appear to me to indicate the presence of numerous cultivators in each village, and I draw the same inference from the fragmentary accounts of life in Southern India, while a further reason for regarding the holdings as small is that in the literature of the time we do not meet with substantial capitalist farmers, who would almost certainly have made their appearance if they had been the predominant class. Where we meet the cultivator he is an inconspicuous unit very much as he is to-day, and he is also commonly short of ready money. Akbar directed his revenue officers to advance money to needy cultivators, and we may take his instructions as evidence of a deficiency of capital, though we

[1] "Normal cultivation" here means the area which has in fact been cultivated on the average of a series of favourable years.

cannot infer from them that the need was adequately met by State loans. Again, there is the story told by Jauhar how peasants living near Lahore were accustomed to give their wives and children in pledge to the bankers for money advanced on account of the revenue collections; that story indicates a financial position familiar at the present time, though the particular form of security offered has now become obsolete. Again, when an English merchant went into the villages near Agra to buy indigo in the year 1614, we are told that he followed the custom of the country and distributed advances, to be adjusted when the indigo should be ready for delivery; and about the same time another merchant, writing from Ahmadabad, advised that capital must be provided for daily purchases of indigo from the country people, "who are constrained to sell to engrossers at very low prices for want of money to supply the needful." Similarly we read that the Portuguese missionaries at Thana found it necessary to provide for their converts clothes and food, seed, cattle, and ploughs, in fact to find all the capital required to enable them to pursue their occupation. These instances are few, but they cover a fairly wide area, and I cannot recall any passage which suggests a contrary inference. The evidence is undoubtedly scanty, but what evidence exists is consistent with the predominance of small holdings and needy peasants rather than with large farmers in command of the capital required by the size of their undertakings.

On the other hand, it appears to me to be certain that in the sixteenth century, as at the present day, the rural population included a large number of landless labourers. It is true that I have failed to find any mention of such a class in contemporary literature, but in this case silence does not justify the inference that the agricultural labourer did not exist; it indicates merely that the topic had no interest for the writers whose works we possess. The argument in support of the existence of landless labourers may be summarised as follows. We know that early in the nineteenth century India was full of such labourers, occupying or emerging from the position of serfs. This servile class must either have existed in Akbar's days, or have come into existence in the intervening years. The latter hypothesis is very highly improbable, since such a social revolution must have left its mark on the history of the time, and until any evidence of its truth is produced, we must believe that village serfdom is an institution of old standing, dating from a period far earlier than that of Akbar. This belief is in accordance with what we know of the social history of the world at large, and of India in particular; it is in itself probable, and there is no reasonable alternative.

The evidence of fact on which this argument is based will be found mainly in the *Report on Slavery*, to which reference has been made in a previous chapter. That Report does not indeed give a complete view of the position: the Commissioners relied mainly on information obtained from judicial officers, and it is only in a few localities that they recorded the observations of men who had studied the question at first hand; their inquiries did not extend to the whole of what is now British India, and there are obvious gaps within the area which they cover. The Commissioners distinguished between regular slavery and the institution which they described sometimes as predial slavery, sometimes as agricultural bondage, and sometimes by the use of the law-Latin phrase, *adscripti glebae*, and the result of their investigations was that rural serfdom, or its trace, was found practically wherever it was looked for. Thus in some districts of Bengal it was reported that the agricultural slaves were generally sold with the land, and it may be remarked that Sir William Macnaghten lays it down as settled law that hereditary serfs are subject to the laws of ancestral real property. Sir Edward Colebrooke spoke of the claims of landholders in Bihar over their hereditary serfs as at that time nearly obsolete. The Commissioners obtained "no evidence of the present existence of the institution in the Western Provinces" (that is in parts of the United Provinces), but they thought it probable that "something of the kind prevailed up to the period at which they were brought under British rule." "During the government of the Nawab the people on each property were held in a great measure to be *adscripti glebae*." In Azamgarh the low-caste villagers were still required to render the landholder "many personal services. . . . Under former governments . . . they were predial slaves. . . . A *chamar* can now sue his zamindar in the criminal court. Nothing vexes or annoys the zamindars in our whole system as much as this." In Kumaun no free labour was procurable, but the "slaves of the plough" were distinguished from domestic slavery. In Assam there was much slave labour, but no free labour was employed in agriculture. So much may be said regarding Northern India. In Madras the Board of Revenue reported that "throughout the Tamil country as well as in Malabar [1] and Canara, far the greater part of the labouring classes of the people have from time immemorial been in a state of acknowledged bondage, in which they continue to the present time." The Board did not know of serfdom in the north of the Presidency, but the Commissioners had reason to believe in its existence. In Coorg also predial slavery had existed from time immemorial. In Bombay the evidence recorded was scanty and unsatisfactory, but it disclosed the existence of serfdom in Surat and the southern Maratha country.

These facts appear to me to prove that a servile labouring class was a normal element in the rural population up to the introduction of British rule, and consequently in the time of Akbar. Further confirmation of this view can be drawn from the systems of paying wages in kind, which prevailed so widely in the last century and which are still far from being extinct. Those systems can be explained convincingly as a natural development from the time when cultivators had merely to feed and clothe their serfs: they can scarcely be explained at all on any other hypothesis. Existing social relations point in the same direction, and in my opinion we are justified in regarding the rural population of Akbar's time as constituted of peasant cultivators, artisans, labourers, and menial servants, very much as it is constituted now, the main difference being that labourers and servants were not then free to choose their

[1] *Barbosa* (p. 335) and other writers of the sixteenth and seventeenth centuries describe the cultivators as well as the labourers of Malabar as slaves or serfs.

masters, but were bound to work for the cultivator or cultivators to whom they were assigned by the custom or tradition of the village. We cannot be certain of the precise proportion borne by each of these classes to the total population: it is possible that there were fewer cultivators and more labourers, but it is equally possible that cultivators were relatively more numerous than now, and in any case we are justified in concluding that, taking cultivators and labourers together, the proportion of workers to work has not undergone any material alteration.

We must now attempt to form some idea of the income of commodities obtained by the rural population, a matter which is largely independent of the precise distribution of the produce between cultivators and labourers. We have found reason to conclude that the part played by man has undergone little change; he has on the whole grown the same crops by the same methods, and has probably expended about the same amount of energy in the process, so that if there has been any material change in the average income[1] per head of the rural population, the cause must be sought in the response of the land. The question whether the return yielded by the land has altered materially in the course of the last three centuries is one to which popular opinion is prepared to give an immediate answer, but in this case, as in some others, popular opinion is not based on exact thinking, and it is necessary to draw some distinctions before we accept the current view that fertility has decreased. The average yield of land estimated over a long period may be affected by (*a*) change in fertility of the land under cultivation throughout the period, (*b*) change in the quality of the land under cultivation at different times, or (*c*) changes in crops and methods. Popular opinion has fastened on the first of these factors, and asserts that acre for acre the land yields less than it did, but this assertion rests on no objective evidence, and it is rendered improbable by what is known regarding the course of "fertility." Peasants in India, as elsewhere, will

[1] It is perhaps desirable to point out that in this and similar passages the word "income" refers to commodities and not to cash.

indeed always tell a sympathetic audience that the yield of their land has fallen off; such statements are not evidence of fact, but only of the psychological attitude of the people who make them, and they will continue to be made so long as the golden age is sought for in the past. They find, however, a certain excuse in what is known about the course of agricultural production. When new land is brought under cultivation the yield is in the early years [1] abnormally high, and then falls to a lower level at which it remains approximately constant, so long as the methods of treatment are not altered: a cultivator whose ideals are founded on the distant epoch when his land was virgin soil can thus say with truth that the yield is less than it was, since it is certain that at some period or other all the land in India was in this condition, and we may agree that whatever land was newly brought under cultivation in the latter years of Akbar's reign yielded more largely then than it yields now, provided that cultivation has been continuous throughout the intervening period. On the other hand, it is highly probable that the land which was already under regular cultivation at that period has, under similar conditions, given an approximately constant return, and clear, positive evidence would be needed to establish the fact that a decline has occurred over the bulk of the old-established cultivation. No such evidence being in existence, we are justified in concluding that there has been no marked general change in fertility other than the reduction which resulted when the land ceased to be "virgin soil." [2]

[1] By "early years" is meant not the first or second year, when initial difficulties of tillage commonly result in a low yield, but the few years which follow after these difficulties have been overcome. Akbar's assessments provided for these initial difficulties: a merely nominal sum was claimed as revenue in the year when new land was broken up, and the full revenue was taken only in the fifth year (*Ain*, translation, ii. 68).

[2] This statement requires formal qualification in regard to land where the slope is sufficient to permit of gradual denudation, because in such cases the decline in fertility may be progressive. The qualification will not, however, affect materially the general argument in the text, because denudation in one place is largely compensated by enrichment elsewhere, and while masses of good soil are annually being carried out to sea, other masses are being brought down from the higher levels and deposited in accessible positions. When land is eroded so much that it becomes unculturable, the effect is, of course, to increase *pro tanto* the average yield of the rest of the country, although the total income is reduced.

The position is essentially different in regard to the second factor: cultivation has certainly extended since Akbar's time in large parts of India, and extension of cultivation ordinarily implies a decrease in the average yield when the whole area, old and new, is taken together, for the obvious reason that the best land is usually the first to come under the plough, and that people cultivate inferior soils only when the best land no longer suffices. We may agree then that this cause has operated to reduce the average yield, and attempt to form a rough idea of its importance by calculating the effect on the lines adopted in Akbar's assessment of the land revenue, which assumed approximately equal areas under the three classes of land recognised as "good," "middling," and "bad." If we take the yield of some particular crop to be 12 maunds per bigha on good, 9 on middling, and 6 on bad land, and assume the areas in each class to be equal, then the average yield is 9 maunds; if cultivation extends by 20 per cent, all "bad" land, the average falls to 8·5 maunds; if the extension is 33 per cent, the average is 8·25 maunds; if 50 per cent, it is 8 maunds. Thus with moderate extensions of cultivation, such as we have seen in Chapter I. are probable in the country between Agra and Lahore, the average yield might have been reduced by an amount of the order of 10 per cent on the rather violent assumption that all the new land is of the worst class. In cases where the extension has been very great, as in Bihar and the east of the United Provinces, this assumption becomes inadmissible, because, in clearing large areas of waste, land of all classes will be reached, and the proportionate reduction in the average will be considerably less. The figures given are of course an illustration only, but if the reader will take the trouble to vary them in accordance with agricultural probabilities, and to generalise the results so obtained, he will find that the reduction in average yield is a small figure compared with the percentage of increase in cultivation. In other words, the effect of extension of area to poorer soils is very apt to be exaggerated; it does in fact reduce the average yield, but not as a rule to the extent that a casual observer would suppose.

On the other hand, the effect of the third factor—changes in crops or methods—may be very great. To take a single illustration: Let us suppose that while cultivation extends by 50 per cent, a canal system is introduced irrigating one-third of the total area, which we assume to have been originally dry. The increase of cultivation would, as we have seen, by itself reduce the yield from 9 maunds to 8, but the additional water-supply would more than counterbalance this, and the new average would on these figures be about $9\frac{1}{3}$ maunds, while if, as is probable, the canal led to improved cropping, the increase in average yield might be very substantial notwithstanding the extension of cultivation to poorer soils. My object in giving these illustrations is to bring out the fact that in the period under consideration two opposing tendencies have been at work to affect the average yield of the land: on the one side, extension of cultivation has tended to reduce the average by a relatively small amount over large areas; on the other side, improvements in cropping and in water-supply have tended to raise it very substantially in the tracts where they have come into operation. It would be absurd to strike a balance offhand for the whole of India and assert that the average yield has either risen or fallen, but it is safe to say that these opposing tendencies have had very different results in different parts of the country, and in the next section I shall attempt to carry the matter a little further, so as to obtain a more definite idea of the condition of the agricultural industry in those parts of the country for which the requisite data are available.

IV. Agriculture in its Local Aspects

In this attempt to indicate the condition of agriculture in certain parts of India, it is convenient to follow, so far as it goes, the arrangement of the "Account of the XII. Subas," included in the *Ain-i Akbari*, an account which, with all its omissions and imperfections, is still the nearest approach we possess to a systematic survey. The first province dealt with is Bengal and Orissa, and here Abul Fazl records merely that rice predominated, and that the harvests were always abundant, information which, so far as it goes, agrees essentially with the conditions prevailing at the present day. From other sources we learn that sugar-cane was a common, and valuable, crop, as is still the case, but beyond these facts there is no precise information, while, in the absence of any statistics of the area under cultivation, our knowledge of the numbers of the population is too vague to furnish any assistance. We can, however, be sure that maize and tobacco have both assumed their present position since the time of Akbar, while the extension in area and the rise in value of the jute crop are so recent that the facts can readily be ascertained. So far as I know, this fibre is not named by any contemporary writer, but it was probably grown in Akbar's time, since Abul Fazl tells us that "a kind of sackcloth" was produced in what is now the district of Rangpur, and we may infer that it was used to make clothes from the fact that jute-clothing was the ordinary wear of the poorer classes as lately as the beginning of the nineteenth century. Its transformation from a low-grade fibre grown for local consumption to one of the great staples of the commerce of the world is the outstanding fact in the agricultural history of the province, and there can be no reasonable doubt that the change has resulted in a substantial increase in the average of production per head of the rural population.

Conditions in Bihar show a more radical alteration. According to the statistics in the *Ain-i Akbari*, the area under cultivation was very much less than now, probably not more than one-fifth for the province as a whole, and there are good reasons for thinking that the class of crops was comparatively high: there was indeed little indigo,[1] and no potatoes, tobacco, or maize can have been produced, but poppy was widely grown, and (apart from rice), wheat, sugar-cane, and cotton seem to have been among the principal staples. Fitch tells us that Patna exported cotton, much sugar, and very much opium; the *Ain* mentions the abundance and

[1] The development of indigo cultivation in Bihar is quite recent, *vide Imperial Gazetteer*, iii. 70.

high quality of the sugar-cane, and though it says nothing about wheat, I believe that the Mogul capital was supplied largely from this part of the country. This last point needs a little explanation. So far as I know, none of the travellers who visited Bengal noticed a large surplus of wheat, but observers in other parts of India write of wheat coming from Bengal. Sir Thomas Roe, speaking of the Mogul Court, says that Bengal "feeds this country with wheat and rice," and the factors at Surat wrote about the same time, "we deny not but that Bengalla brings wheat, rice and sugar to India," India being in this passage used in the restricted sense to denote the west coast. Now, it is possible that at this time [1] Bengal may have produced wheat for export in some quantity, but it appears to me to be more probable that the wheat really came from Bihar, and was carried both up the river to Agra and down the river to the Bengal ports. The Surat factors would naturally hear of the point where the sea-voyage began, not of the locality of production, and we need assume only that Roe was told in general terms that provisions came from the direction of Bengal.[2] However this may be, I think there can be little doubt that the average value of the crops grown was at least as high as now, if not higher, and that the average yield per acre was substantially greater, because with a very small area under cultivation the quality of the land must have been on the average superior. The probabilities are therefore that in Bihar the average of production per head was distinctly higher than now, though the total production must have been very much smaller.

The Mogul province of Allahabad corresponds roughly to the eastern districts of the United Provinces, now a typically congested area. The land was certainly not crowded in Akbar's time, when cultivation reached only about one-fifth of the present standard, and in this respect the conditions

[1] Writing about half a century later, *Bernier* stated (p. 437) that Bengal had enough wheat for consumption and for provisioning ships, but he does not say anything to support the view that it had a large surplus for export.

[2] An example of this vague use of the word Bengal may be found in Hawkins's description of Patna as a city "upon the borders of Bengala" (*Purchas*, I. iii. 221). A few years later the same city is spoken of as "the chiefest mart town of all Bengala" (*English Factories*, 1618–21, p. 212).

approximated to those which prevailed in Bihar, though judging from the revenue statistics the cropping was of a less remunerative type. The *Ain* tells us that agriculture was in a flourishing state, but does not indicate any particular feature except the absence of jowār and bājra, crops which are still very rare in this part of the country; such general assertions of prosperity count for very little, and I do not know of any references to the subject in other contemporary authorities. It is, however, certain that the large stretches of inferior clay which characterise this part of the country were for the most part untilled in Akbar's time; the yield given by these soils is very small, and their exclusion would raise the average of production by an appreciable amount, so that here, as in Bihar, the average was probably greater than now.

Of the province of Oudh we are told very little. Abul Fazl remarks again that agriculture was flourishing, but he mentions only the superior varieties of rice obtainable in the northern districts. There is no hint of the remarkable system of well irrigation which now characterises the south of the province, and of course there was no maize, while the revenue statistics suggest that rice and millets were much more important than the winter crops, such as wheat. No definite inference can be drawn from these scanty data, but I am inclined to think that the average of production may have been even less than now in those parts of the province where cultivation had long been established.

The Mogul province of Agra was not homogeneous, including as it did part of the Gangetic plain and also a portion of what is now Rajputana, and for our present purpose it is convenient to neglect the latter area, and consider the northern portion along with the adjoining province of Delhi. In this tract the changes which have occurred amount very nearly to an agricultural revolution. The area cultivated in Akbar's time was, as we have seen, about three-fourths of the present standard, but the cropping appears to have been of an inferior grade. Neither Abul Fazl nor any other authority tells us of any production of special note, and the fact that wheat and sugar were imported from the eastern provinces shows that the country was not even self-sufficing in what are now two of its staple exports. The change must be attributed mainly to the construction of canals, which has rendered possible the developments on which the tract now depends, great expanses of wheat and sugar-cane, and of irrigated cotton and maize, forming a marked contrast to the millets, pulses, and oilseeds which must have been the staples at the earlier period. Some idea of the productivity of this tract, taken as a whole, can be formed from the fact that the revenue claimed from it by Akbar ranged from 20 to 30 dams a bigha,[1] while the average rate was over 50 dams in Allahabad, and probably well over 60 dams in Bihar; these rates are, it will be remembered, proportionate to the produce as valued by the assessors, who thus considered that a bigha near Jaunpur or Benares yielded as much as 2 bighas between Agra and Saharanpur. In this case there can be no doubt whatever that the average of production has greatly increased since the time of Akbar, and the same conclusion holds, though perhaps not to the same extent, of the adjoining province of Lahore.[2]

Up to this point it is possible to form a general idea of the position of agriculture in the time of Akbar, but when we turn to the country lying south of the great plains, we find that our sources of information begin to fail us. Of Ajmer we can say only that agriculture was very backward, and that winter crops were scarcely grown; in this case, it is probable that the average of production has not changed to a material extent. Malwa, too, probably shows little change, for the antiquity of its present system of agriculture is apparent

[1] These rates are adjusted to remove certain apparent errors in the manner explained in the present writer's paper on "The Agricultural Statistics of Akbar's Empire," referred to in the List of Authorities for Chapter I. The rates calculated directly from the statistics give an even greater difference in favour of the eastern provinces.

[2] It is at first sight difficult to believe that so great a change has occurred in this area, but the position is explained by the history of the intervening period. The old agricultural system of the country round Delhi was practically wiped out during the political disturbances of the eighteenth century, and the country made a fresh start after the establishment of British rule. A vivid picture of the conditions prevailing about the year 1794 is given in Twining's *Travels in India.*

to any observer, and the few statements made by Abul Fazl concerning it are still substantially true. The Mogul province of Berar has developed into an extensive cotton tract within the last two centuries, but I have found no data on which to base even a guess at its average production in Akbar's time: Gujarat, on the other hand, was certainly highly cultivated, but here, too, data for a comparison are wanting. The difficulty becomes greater in the case of the Deccan and of Vijayanagar, where there is nothing to take the place of the *Ain-i Akbari*, and we can say in a general way only that the country produced the same staples as it yields to-day. Thévenot, for instance, noted rice and cotton everywhere, and sugar-cane in some places, in the Deccan, while Portuguese narratives [1] tell us that the upland of Vijayanagar yielded rice, cotton, jowār, and other grains and pulses of whose names the writers were ignorant, and on the coast we hear frequently of coco palms, and, in Malabar, pepper. Of all this vast tract of country we know only that (apart from a few later introductions such as groundnuts) methods and products alike show little change; we cannot say whether the average of production has risen or fallen, but the variations which we have found farther north should serve as a warning against the assumption that there has been a uniform movement in either direction. In the north we have seen that the resultant of the opposed forces at work has been different in different parts of the country: Bengal probably yields more, and Upper India certainly does so, but much if not all of the intervening country has a lower average to-day than in the time of Akbar, and within these limits individual villages or parganas have probably been affected in different ways; it is reasonable to conclude that something of the same sort has happened in the south, and that while some portions of it are on the average richer, others are poorer than they were.

The final result of this analysis cannot be stated in precise or arithmetical form. We do not know the income of com-

[1] The translation of these narratives (*Sewell*, 237, 333) speaks of "Indian Corn," but the Portuguese expression so rendered undoubtedly signified jowār, as I have explained in Appendix B.

modities which India yielded at the close of the sixteenth century, and any dogmatism as to its amount would be unjustifiable, but the data appear to me to be sufficient to indicate that, taking the country as a whole, the average per head cannot have been greatly different from what it is to-day. The main lines of agriculture have not changed, and the tendencies affecting the amount of production have operated in opposing directions. On the one hand there is the undoubted fact of a great increase in population, which has necessitated the cultivation of inferior soils, and thereby reduced the average of production per head; on the other hand there have been the introduction of new and more remunerative crops, the provision of increased facilities for irrigation, and other changes in detail, which have increased the average income of large portions of the country to an extent more than sufficient to mask the operation of the former tendency. We cannot state the results in quantitative terms, but it is obvious that the change on balance is not very great. Individual students may fairly form different opinions on the question whether the average income of commodities produced by the rural population of India is on the whole a little greater, or a little less, than it was, but the available data indicate that the order of magnitude has not altered materially; a given number of people, peasants and labourers together, raise somewhere about the same amount of produce as the same number raised in Akbar's time, and if producers were in a position to consume all the produce they raised, we should reach the conclusion that their economic condition has not greatly changed. At this point, however, we must take the environment into account, and ascertain the proportion of the gross income which was left to the rural population after the claims of other parties had been met.

V. The Environment as affecting Agriculture

Hitherto we have looked at the agriculture of the period as an entity complete in itself, and we have now to enlarge our view by taking account of the relations between the peasants and other portions of the community, and to inquire to what extent the townsmen and the administrations of the sixteenth century promoted or retarded the success of the industry. We must not of course look for a policy of direct and conscious improvement such as has recently been initiated; that is essentially a modern development, and in Akbar's days there were no men of science investigating the peasant's problems, no skilled engineers designing implements to meet their needs, and no financial talent devoted to organising their markets or facilitating the supply of capital. Probably the only scope for action of the kind lay in the construction of irrigation works, and in this matter I am inclined to think that while the advantages of action were recognised in theory, very little was accomplished in practice. Akbar directed his provincial governors to be energetic in "the making of reservoirs, wells, watercourses, gardens, *sarais*, and other pious foundations," and no doubt this direction expresses his administrative ideal, while Abul Fazl states in general terms that "many wells and tanks are being dug," but his silence may be taken as proving that there was no special organisation for the purpose and that no detailed regulations had been issued. We have seen that the administrative arrangements of the Empire were not of a kind to produce officers who would display a vigorous initiative in such directions as these, and it appears to be probable that such action as was taken was spasmodic, and that where wells and reservoirs were made at the public cost, they were usually, and in accordance with precedent, designed for the comfort and convenience of townsmen and travellers rather than for the needs of the ordinary peasant. I have found nothing to suggest that conditions in the Deccan kingdoms were in this respect different from those prevailing in Northern India. In the south, Mr. Sewell tells us that in the first half of the sixteenth century the Emperor Krishna Raya had busied himself in improving irrigation in the neighbourhood of his capital, and it is possible that after the collapse of the central authority some of the lords of Vijayanagar may have pursued a similar policy in the interests of their own estates. In his picturesque account of a visit to Olala near Mangalore, della Valle mentions that the Queen was engaged in superintending the construction of a reservoir, and similar examples of individual effort were doubtless to be found in other parts of India, but there is no trace of anything like a consistent policy directed to meeting the needs of the country systematically, nor, it may be added, do we find any suggestion of arrangements for keeping existing works in proper repair.

We may consider next the influence exerted by the system of commerce: it makes a very great difference to agriculture whether the peasant has access to a free market and can count on getting price for quality, or is in the hands of a practical monopoly interested chiefly in buying at the cheapest possible rate. It is not altogether clear how far the peasant was dependent on the market in Akbar's time: in some places he paid his revenue in kind, and then the market meant comparatively little, since, as we shall find, he had not much to spend, but in the Mogul Empire at least payment in cash was common,[1] though its precise extent is doubtful, and cash payment involved finding a market for at least one-third of the gross produce of the season. The internal commercial system of the country appears to have been organised much as at present, but with two main differences: transport was more costly and dangerous, and consequently the merchants required a much wider margin between the prices at which they bought and sold, while the buyers for export houses, who have made things distinctly better for the peasant, had not come into existence at this time.[2] So far then as the

[1] The "Account of the XII. Subas," included in the *Ain*, tells us that in Bengal the revenue was paid in coin (ii. 122), and that in Bihar the peasant paid *zar* (ii. 151), which must I think bear the same meaning; in Ajmer cash payments were rare (ii. 267), while the subject is not mentioned in connection with other provinces. We must, however, remember that the local officials had to account for collections in cash at fixed rates, and it is scarcely likely that they should have encouraged payments in kind unless the risk of loss by sale was thrown on the cultivator.

[2] Purchasing direct from peasants was not entirely unknown, for in 1614 Nicholas Withington was buying indigo for the East India Company in the villages near Agra, but, as we shall see later on, indigo was almost the only agricultural product in demand for export to Europe, and the practice concerned only a very small number of peasants. The direct purchase for export of grain, oilseeds, and fibres is a much more recent innovation.

peasant had to sell, he was dependent on a system even less favourable to him than that which now exists, and which is justly regarded as one of the greatest drawbacks to the progress of agriculture. Under that system the peasant is the last person to benefit by a rise in price, while he is the first to suffer from a fall, and the greater and more frequent the fluctuations the worse is his position. I have found no materials for estimating directly the course of local markets in Akbar's time, but I think it is reasonable to infer that fluctuations were at least as great in the sixteenth century as in the first half of the nineteenth before the development of communications had unified the markets of the country. The conditions which prevailed at that time have been clearly described by Sir Theodore Morison in chapter xii. of *The Industrial Organisation of an Indian Province*, and a study of the figures given by him is the best way of realising the position of those peasants who had to sell their produce, and who had no alternative but to accept the price offered by the local dealers.

In ordinary times then the peasant did not derive much assistance from his environment. The same statement must be made regarding the exceptional periods of stress when agriculture was disorganised by the failure of the rains. We know that most parts of India were afflicted by famine at some time or other during the sixteenth and seventeenth centuries,[1] and the knowledge may be taken as an assurance that the climate has not changed materially in the intervening period. It is, however, impossible to compare the frequency of famines in the two periods because the significance of the word has altered in the interval: a famine is now a period when distress is such as to require the intervention of the State, but if we were to rely upon the chroniclers of the sixteenth century, we should define it as a period when men and women were driven by hunger to eat human flesh. Badaoni wrote as follows of the famine of 1555: "the author with his own eyes witnessed the fact that men ate their own kind, and the appearance of

[1] A list of recorded famines is given in Appendix A of Mr. Loveday's *History and Economics of Indian Famines* (1914).

the famished sufferers was so hideous that one could scarcely look upon them. What with the scarcity of rain, the famine and the desolation, and what with uninterrupted warfare for two years, the whole country was a desert and no husbandmen remained to till the ground." Of the same period Abul Fazl wrote that "men were driven to the extremity of eating each other," and of the later famine of 1596, we are told again that men ate their own kind, and that the streets and roads were blocked up with dead bodies. Akbar endeavoured to relieve distress in this latter case, but the organisation in existence at the time was probably unable to do more than provide food for the starving in the towns and cities, and the effect of these recurring visitations must have been a disorganisation of agriculture such as can scarcely now be conceived. It must be remembered then that the annalists tell us only of the extremity of distress; it was not worth their while to mention the recurrence of ordinarily unfavourable seasons which in modern times would be met by measures of relief, and we must not treat their silence as evidence that nothing was wrong. In forming our ideas of the condition of the industry, we must make allowances not merely for occasional periods of entire collapse, but for more frequent seasons of local or partial failure, and we must recognise that, alike in greater calamities and in lesser, the peasant was ordinarily left to bear the burden unassisted, except in so far as he might be able to secure a reduction in the revenue demand.

So far then as active measures are concerned, the rest of the community did little or nothing to promote the prosperity of agriculture: on the contrary, the peasant had cause to fear rather than to welcome association with the townsmen and the officers of Government,[1] and in particular he did not enjoy that security of tenure which is the first condition of

[1] As an instance of the normal risks of the industry may be quoted *Tavernier's* observation (p. 197), that at Delhi most of the State elephants were taken out daily to graze on branches, sugar-cane, or millet, to the great loss of the peasants. The tradition of free food for transport animals employed by the State unfortunately persists in this and other parts of the country up to the present day.

successful peasant-farming. The question whether a peasant had a legal right to remain in occupation of his holding was argued at great length during the early part of the nineteenth century: here we are concerned not with the juridical position but rather with the practical aspect of the matter. Could the peasant count on remaining undisturbed, or did disturbance in fact occur with sufficient frequency to cause a general feeling of insecurity? The evidence on this point is small in volume, but one fact alone appears to me to be conclusive. At the outset of his reign Jahangir tells us that he gave an order "that the officials of the Crown lands and the *jāgīrdārs* [grantees] should not forcibly take the ryots' lands and cultivate them on their own account." This order is one of a series designed to remedy popular grievances; from our knowledge of Jahangir's administration, we should not be justified in assuming that it had more than a slight and transient effect, but we may be sure that the grievance was sufficiently real and widespread to have attracted the attention of a new Emperor engaged in formulating a policy which should rally the people to his throne. The order applies, it will be noticed, to all land whether administered directly or granted as *jāgīr*, and we may safely infer that the ordinary peasant ran a real risk of having his holding taken from him. This inference finds strong confirmation in the account given by de Laet, who, after noticing the dispossession of important grantees, goes on to say that the common people were much harassed, and often compelled to change their land every season, sometimes because the Administration wanted it, and sometimes because it was to be given to some one else, so that the cultivation of the whole country was rendered inefficient. The risk of disturbance would not be great in a village distant from the administrative headquarters, or in the case of a holding without some special attraction of its own; but any one who might be inclined to work up his land to more than the average level of productiveness must have known that his tenure was at the mercy of any grasping officer or grantee whom accident might bring into his vicinity, and this knowledge would of itself be fatal to any profitable development of agriculture. That agriculture was in fact unprogressive at this period may be inferred from the observations of travellers of a later date like Mundy and Bernier. The former tells us that the peasants near Agra were treated "as Turks treat Christians," "taking from them all they can get by their labour, leaving them nothing but their bad, mud-walled, ill-thatched-covered houses and a few cattle to till the ground, besides other miseries." Bernier states that owing to the oppression of officials and grantees the ground was seldom tilled except under compulsion, that no person was willing and able to repair the water-channels, and that the whole country was badly cultivated; or, in other words, that the natural effects of insecurity of tenure were obvious. This evidence is applicable only to the Mogul Empire, and it is possible that conditions were more favourable in the Deccan kingdoms or in Vijayanagar, but I have found no observations regarding the position in these countries, and I do not know of any grounds for thinking that in the matter of security the southern peasant was in practice materially better off.

The influence of the environment was thus, on the whole, distinctly unfavourable to the progress of agriculture. The peasant obtained very little active help from the other classes of the community; he was placed at a disadvantage in his relations with the market, and any tendency which may have existed towards enterprise was sterilised by the nature of the Administration. Our next object is to consider the share of the peasant's income which the community claimed. We have seen in the first section of this chapter that Akbar demanded the equivalent of one-third of the gross produce, and that in the south the proportion was almost certainly higher, though it cannot be determined with precision. The share claimed by Akbar was in itself high,[1] whether it is

[1] It is perhaps desirable for the benefit of readers unfamiliar with Northern India to point out the difference between *rent* rates and *revenue* rates. At present the tenant cultivator pays rent, out of which his landholder pays the revenue: under Akbar there was usually no landholder, and the cultivator paid the revenue direct to the State. In studying the comparative incidence of the revenue it would be an obvious error to compare rent

judged by Hindu texts or by the standard of his Moslem predecessors. The texts indicate that from one-sixth to one-twelfth was considered reasonable, though as much as one-fourth might be taken in emergencies. The claims of Moslem rulers had varied widely, but had usually been pitched lower, and in the exceptional case of Alauddin Khalji, who demanded one-half, the motive was administrative rather than fiscal, the measure being avowedly part of a system "for grinding down the Hindus and for depriving them of that wealth and property which fosters disaffection and rebellion." Akbar's assessment was based on no such motives, but its severity will be at once apparent to any one who is familiar with the level of rents in Northern India at the present day; for readers who do not possess that knowledge, it may be worth while to go into the matter in some little detail, bearing in mind that the question at issue is the livelihood of a large proportion of the population of the Empire, and that while Akbar's assessment was high, the rest of India probably paid substantially more.

The burden of the revenue can be stated most clearly in terms of money. According to the calculations regarding the purchasing-power of the rupee which have been used in an earlier chapter, a peasant who wanted a rupee would have to offer in the vicinity of the Mogul capital more than seven times as much grain as in the years 1910–12, about eleven times as much oil-seeds, probably seven times as much raw sugar, or a quantity of cotton which is probably somewhat less, but cannot be determined accurately on the available data. It is therefore well within the mark to say that a rupee cost such a peasant at least as much produce as 7 rupees cost in the years before the war, and it is reasonably certain that at a distance from the capital the divergence in prices was even greater; consequently we shall be understating the

---

with revenue, but in the present section we are concerned with what the peasant paid, not with what the State received, and we have therefore to compare Akbar's revenue with the rent charged by modern landholders. As we shall see, Akbar's revenue was something like double the modern rent, and consequently it was four times or more the modern revenue, which is rather less than half the rent.

average burden on the peasant if for comparative purposes we take seven as the factor of purchasing-power. Making use of this factor, and taking the average of Akbar's assessment rates for the three provinces of Allahabad, Agra, and Delhi, we shall find that the amount claimed on an acre[1] was equivalent to the demand shown below in the money of 1910–12.

AKBAR'S REVENUE DEMAND PER ACRE CALCULATED IN MODERN CURRENCY

Crop.	Rupees.	Crop.	Rupees.
Wheat . . .	17·0 to 20·0	Linseed . .	8·5 to 10·25
Barley . . .	11·5 „ 13·5	Rape . . .	9·0 „ 10·75
Gram . . .	10·25 „ 12·0	Poppy . . .	36·25 „ 42·0
Jowār . .	9·0 „ 10·5	Sugar-cane (ordinary)	36·5 „ 42·25
Bajra . . .	7·25 „ 8·5	Cotton . . .	26·0 „ 30·0
Mandua . .	7·5 „ 8·75	Indigo . .	43·75 „ 50·75
Sāwān . . .	3·75 „ 4·5		

These rates, it must be noted, are for the crop, not for the year; a peasant would pay, for instance, about 4 rupees on an acre of the inferior millet *sāwān*, but if he followed it with a crop of gram he would have 10 or 12 rupees more to pay in the second half of the year. It is scarcely necessary to say that a rental demand based on these figures would be unthinkable at the present day; it is just conceivable that equivalent rents might be exacted for a short time from a village of exceptional fertility and resources by a landholder who set the provisions of the law aside, but these rates are not limited to exceptional cases, but are the average for a large part of Northern India, and no modern Settlement Officer would think for a moment of framing his assessment on any such basis.

The difference in the level of the demand may be further illustrated by calculating the revenue which would be due at Akbar's rates on the crops now grown in the country where

[1] The exact size of Akbar's bigha is uncertain, but it lay between 0·538 and 0·625 of an acre. The higher and lower figures in the text are based on these maximum and minimum values. It is probable that the actual demand lay between the limits given in the text, because the size of the bigha was affected by local variations in the standards of measurement employed, but that it was nearer the larger than the smaller figures. This question is discussed in the paper on "The Agricultural Statistics of Akbar's Empire," referred to under the Authorities to Chapter I.

they were in force. Such calculations are too long to give in detail, but as an example I may take the result for the crops grown in the year 1915–16 in the four large districts of the Meerut division. Assessing these districts on the lines adopted in Akbar's time, but giving all doubtful points in favour of the peasant,[1] and thus understating the theoretical revenue by a substantial amount, I find that the average sum which the Mogul would have claimed on an acre of occupied land exceeds the present average rent-rate by the following percentages:

District.	Excess percentage of Akbar's Revenue.
Saharanpur	112
Muzaffarnagar	99
Meerut	88
Bulandshahr	86
All four districts	96

That these high percentages are not due to some local cause may be inferred from the fact that the excess for the Oudh district of Unao is 97, while going farther east, the excess for Ghazipur is 128, and for Jaunpur as much as 193; and on the basis of these calculations I think it may be said that where the regulation system of assessment was in force Akbar claimed as revenue at any rate about twice as much as present-day landholders claim for rent. There are indications in his regulations of a possibility that the amount of the claim could be reduced by collusion with subordinate officials, but in that case it may be doubted whether the saving to the peasant would have been very great; unless the subordinates differed from their modern representatives, they would have claimed very nearly the whole of the fraudulent reduction, and left the peasant only sufficient to make the transaction worth his while.

[1] The calculations are only approximate, because there are, of course, no sanctioned rates for the crops introduced since Akbar's time. In such cases I have taken the rate for a crop of rather less value: maize, for instance, has been valued at about the rate of jowār. I have discarded Akbar's rates for cotton owing to the possibility that the quality of this crop has deteriorated, and have valued it at something less than wheat; and in cases where the rates varied with quality (*e.g.* rice and sugar-cane) I have used only the lower rate so as to be on the safe side.

These calculations leave out of account the legal and extra-legal cesses which the peasant now pays. The amount of these cannot be ascertained with precision, but they may fairly be set off against the similar payments made at the earlier period. We know of at least one general cess imposed by Akbar—the *dahseri*, a charge of about 25 lb. of grain on each acre cultivated—and we hear of other local cesses, such as that imposed on the neighbourhood to meet the cost of building the fort at Agra. I read the rules regarding the record of crops as imposing cesses to be paid for the maintenance of the officials engaged in the measurements made every season,[1] and in any case there can be no reasonable doubt that they "lived on the country," as similar officials hope to live at the present day. Where the land had been granted as *jāgīr*, the extra-legal charges were probably higher, especially after the lapse of Akbar's efforts to curtail this system. Hawkins, who acquired his knowledge as a grantee (though an unsuccessful one), depicts his fellows as "racking" the poor in order to get whatever they could before losing the grant, and Jahangir's accession edicts, already quoted, speak of various burdens "which the *jāgīrdars* of every province and district have imposed for their own profit." We cannot state in precise figures the total sums paid by the peasants, but we can be fairly certain that they were substantially in excess of the revenue calculated on the prescribed rates, and it is not impossible that they may have occasionally approximated to the proportion of "nearly three-quarters" of the produce, which, as we have seen, is given by de Laet.

We have no direct information regarding the demands made on peasants holding land administered by zamindars, but it may be conjectured that they were somewhat better off than

[1] In Book iii. of the *Ain-i Akbari* we read of *zābitāna* and *jarībāna*, the fees payable to officials engaged in assessment (*zabt*) and measurement (*jarīb*). It is possible that these fees were paid from the treasury, but I think it is much more probable that they were realised from the people. The word *jarībāna* has survived in parts of the United Provinces, but has acquired a new meaning: the peasants now apply it to any fine (*jūrmāna*) imposed by authority, and the pun, whether it be conscious or unconscious, suggests to me that *jarībāna* still means to the peasant some arbitrary exaction by State officials—which is also his view of a fine legally imposed.

those of their fellows who were subject to grantees. The grantee was ordinarily a stranger, concerned only to fill his pockets; the zamindar was a more permanent feature of the locality, and in some cases bound to the peasants by hereditary position and tribal relationship, while he was dependent upon their support in the contingency—never very remote—of his going, or being forced, into rebellion. It is probable therefore that the ordinary zamindar treated his peasants comparatively well, and this inference is supported by the fact recorded by Bernier half a century later, that "many of the peasantry, driven to despair by so execrable a tyranny, abandon the country" and sometimes "fly to the territories of a Raja, because there they find less oppression and are allowed a greater degree of comfort." Bernier also states that the fear of losing peasants in this way operated to mitigate the tyranny of the Mogul governors, and though it is probable that the tyranny was worse under Shahjahan than under Akbar, we may still believe that the jurisdiction of some at least of the zamindars offered a refuge from oppression at the earlier period.

In the Mogul Empire, then, the peasant who was assessed under the regulation system had to surrender in the form of revenue a very much larger share of his gross income than his successor now pays as rent. Of the provinces assessed on other systems, we know that in Sind the peasants paid one-third of the produce in kind, but less than half of this rate was taken in Ajmer, where the administration was not effective. The position in Bengal, Berar, and Khandesh is uncertain; they were recent acquisitions, and the maintenance of the old assessment systems may mean either that a change would have brought no more revenue, or that an immediate enhancement was considered dangerous on political grounds. I conjecture that the burden of revenue in these cases was lighter, but not much lighter, than in the regulation provinces, but I know of no evidence on the point. As regards the position in other parts of India, we have seen reason to believe that the revenue demand, stated as a share of the gross produce, was substantially higher in the south than in the north, and it follows that the peasants in the Deccan and in Vijàyanagar were probably worse off than those in Mogul territory. Thus the final result of our inquiry is that while the average of agricultural production per head of the rural population, taking India as a whole, was probably not very different from what it is now, the share left to the peasant for disposal was on the average very much less; the "average" peasant may have handled about the same gross income as now, but, if he did, he kept a much smaller share for his own use.

VI. The Conditions of Life in the Villages

The conclusions which have been reached regarding the condition of agriculture will be referred to again in subsequent chapters, but before leaving the subject for the moment we may bring together what we have learned regarding the lives of the men and women engaged in the industry. The ordinary village labourer was probably about as well or as badly off in ordinary years as he is now: there is, so far as I know, absolutely no direct contemporary information regarding his means of livelihood, but it is safe to assume that as a serf he had a little, but only a little, more than the bare minimum necessary for his subsistence. In unfavourable seasons his position was very much worse: he is now certain of finding employment on relief works when there is nothing to do at home, but in the sixteenth, and indeed far into the nineteenth, century he had the choice between the certainty of starvation at home and the probability of starvation on the roadside or in the jungle. Whether he had a reasonable chance of bettering his condition and rising in the world is a question on which there is no direct evidence. As a serf, he was not free to leave his village in search of work, and we may presume that his masters would allow him to go only when the number of labourers exceeded the requirements of the village. The demand for general labour was certainly much less than at present: there were no great factories or railways, and, except in the cities and the seaports, there are no signs of anything approaching to a labour market. I am inclined to think that the difficulty of leaving a village, coupled with the uncertainty of getting work elsewhere, must have discouraged any tendency to migration, and that the immobility of the agricultural labourer of the present day has its roots in the centuries during which there was little to tempt a man to venture away from his village, so long as the village could supply his food.

It is, however, quite possible that individual labourers could hope to rise to the position of cultivators, and that the aspirations, like the fears, of the modern labourers are founded on the experience of centuries. There is evidence in the *Report on Slavery*, already quoted, that servile labourers were in some cases allowed to hold plots of land, which they could cultivate when their labour was not required elsewhere, and, unless the attitude of the people has changed in the last three centuries, I do not think that an ordinary village—at least in Northern or Central India—would have prevented an individual from gradually extending his holding, provided that there was land to spare and that the supply of labour was sufficient. Promotion of this kind would have been facilitated in many parts of India, though not everywhere, by the existence of vacant culturable land, and it may perhaps be assumed that the difficulty of finding capital could be gradually overcome by a thrifty man with a recurrence of favourable seasons. It is possible then that a career was open to the exceptional labourer, though I know of no evidence bearing directly on the point; the ordinary labourer was probably resigned, as he still often is, to the position into which he had been born.

Regarding the actual cultivator of the soil, we have seen that he was much worse off in ordinary seasons than is the case at present; in any case he had less money to spend on clothes, comforts, and luxuries, and in some parts of the country he must sometimes have been short of food. In bad seasons his position was no better than that of the labourer; there is no trace of any systematic attempt to keep villages going through a period of calamity, or to restore them when the calamity had passed away, and when the stock of food was exhausted there was nothing for it but to take to the roads or the jungles, and, as we have seen, to sell off the children as the last realisable asset. Famine was not the only calamity to be feared; wars and rebellions might at any time paralyse the life of the villages while the oppression of the State officials might drive the peasants themselves into revolt. It would, however, be a mistake to look only on the dark side of the cultivator's life. In the intervals between famines and other calamities, a thrifty man, who understood the art of dealing with the revenue authorities, might gradually improve his position and extend his holding so as to secure a comfortable income, while in times of stress the more adventurous souls might migrate to less unfavourable surroundings, or, as Bernier says,[1] "seek a more tolerable mode of existence either in the towns or in camps." But when all possible allowances are made, the most probable conclusion seems to me to be that the ordinary cultivator was much worse off than he is to-day, paying a larger share of his present income to the sleeping-partners in his industry, and discouraged from almost every form of enterprise by the uncertainty which clouded the future.

Of the position of the zamindars it is not possible to say much. Those of them who appeared at Court and secured a definite rank (*mansab*) probably lived like the rest of the courtiers and officials; we get scarcely a glimpse of the life of the others who remained within their own jurisdictions, and can only conjecture that they lived like those of their successors—more common in the last century than in this—who distrust new ideas and maintain the old traditions of their country-side. Probably some of them performed valuable economic functions in helping and supporting their peasants, while others were parasites pure and simple; but it is impossible to say which class predominated, and of their general attitude we know only that it was such as to arouse strong disapproval in official circles.[2]

[1] *Bernier*, p. 205.

[2] Abul Fazl says that "the general custom of Indian *zamindars* is to leave the path of single-mindedness, and to have an eye to every side, and to join any one who is victorious or who is making increasing stir" (*Akbarnama*, translation, ii. 96), but we do not know how far economic motives influenced their conduct in matters of politics.

AUTHORITIES FOR CHAPTER IV

SECTION 1.—The third book of the *Ain* (vol. ii. of the translation) gives a large quantity of information regarding the revenue system of Northern India; this information has been discussed in a paper by Mr. Yusuf Ali and the present writer in *Journal R.A.S.*, January 1918, and the account in the text, which is based on that paper, differs in some important details from what will be found in some of the current manuals of Indian history. There is much less first-hand evidence regarding conditions in the south, where reliance must be placed on casual notices such as those in *Sewell*, 373, 379, and *Barbosa*, 289, 296. The quotation from *de Laet* is p. 125; the penalty for failure to cultivate is quoted from *English Factories* 1630–33, p. 233.

SECTION 2.—The observations regarding the course of agriculture are, as a rule, scattered and fragmentary. For the north of India most of the information comes from the *Ain* (Book iii. and "Account of the XII. Subas"); *Babur's* observations begin on p. 484; Finch's remarks are scattered through his journal in *Purchas*; for Terry, see *Purchas*, II. ix. 1468 ff. For tillage in the Deccan, see *Garcia da Orta*, 308, and compare *Imperial Gazetteer*, xi. 308. The crops of Northern India and the revenue rates are in *Ain*, translation, ii. 70-114; those of the south are collected chiefly from *Garcia da Orta* and from *Sewell*. For the acclimatisation of maize, etc., see *de Candolle* under the various crops. The use of dung as fuel is mentioned in *de Laet*, 116, and *Mundy*, ii. 71.

The observations quoted on irrigation in Northern India will be found in *Purchas*, I. iv. 431, 519, and *Babur*, 486. For the history of the canals, see *Imperial Gazetteer*, iii. 316 ff.; also a paper by Major Colvin in the *Journal A.S.B.*, March 1833. Wells and reservoirs are mentioned *passim* in *Sewell*, *Thévenot*, and other authorities besides those quoted.

SECTION 3.—The facts referred to in the earlier paragraphs of this section are drawn from the *Ain*, or such authorities as *Sewell* or *Hay* for the south, but the argument depends more on the general attitude of these and other writers than on their statements of particular facts. The instances given of scanty resources will be found in *Ain*, translation, ii. 44; Elliot, *History*, v. 138; *Letters Received*, ii. 103, 148; Maffeius, *Transactions*, 36. The facts regarding serfdom are from the *Slavery Report*, the whole of which should be read by any one who wants to realise the position; the quotations in the text are from pp. 38, 39, 93, 97, 113, 149, 157. The dictum as to the legal position of serfs is in Macnaghten's *Principles*, 130.

SECTION 4.—In this section I have used the results of the examination of Abul Fazl's statistics, to which reference has been made under Chapter I. Most of the statements of facts come from the "Account of the XII. Subas," in *Ain*, translation, vol. ii. For Bengal, see pp. 121-123 (also *Imperial Gazetteer*, iii. 204); for Bihar, p. 151 (also Fitch, in *Purchas*, II. x. 1736; *Roe*, i. 218; *Letters Received*, iv. 320); for Allahabad, p. 158; Oudh, p. 171; Agra, p. 179; Delhi, p. 278; Lahore, p. 312; Ajmer, p. 267; Malwa, p. 195; Berar, p. 229; Gujarat, p. 239. For Southern India, see (*e.g.*) *Thévenot*, 219, 240, and *Sewell*, 237.

SECTION 5.—Abul Fazl's references to irrigation works will be found in *Ain*, translation, i. 222, and ii. 38. For irrigation in the south, see *Sewell*,

162, and *della Valle*, ii. 338. *Mundy*, among other writers, mentions (ii. 84) that reservoirs and similar works were seldom repaired. The quotations regarding famines are from Elliot, *History*, v. 490, and vi. 21, 193; other references to the subject will be found under chap. vii. 4. Akbar's orders as to remission of revenue are in *Ain*, translation, ii. 45.

Jahangir's prohibition of forcible ejectment is in *Tuzuk*, i. 9; *de Laet's* remarks on the subject are on p. 125; oppression by grantees is noticed in *Thévenot*, 145, and *Bernier*, 226. The quotation from *Mundy* is ii. 73. Alauddin's revenue policy is expounded in Elliot, *History*, iii. 182.

For the purchasing-power of the rupee, see the present writer's paper in *Journal R.A.S.*, October 1918, 375 ff. The revenue rates used in the calculations are taken from *Ain*, translation, ii. 91 ff.; the modern data are from the *Season and Crop Report*, and the *Revenue Administration Report* of the United Provinces for 1915–16. For cesses, see *Ain*, translation, i. 275; *Badaoni*, ii. 74; Hawkins in *Purchas*, I. iii. 221; and *Tuzuk*, i. 7. For migration of peasants, see *Bernier*, 205, 231. The revenue rates charged in Sind and Ajmer are in *Ain*, translation, ii. 338, 267.

CHAPTER V

NON-AGRICULTURAL PRODUCTION

I. THE GENERAL POSITION

EVEN at the present day it is, as a rule, easier to study external trade than internal production, and no surprise will be felt that the statement is equally applicable to India in the sixteenth century, seeing that the bulk of our information is furnished by writers whose primary interests lay in commerce and who refer to production only so far as its conditions affected the supply of merchandise for export. Accordingly we have no contemporary description of the industrial position which can be regarded as complete or satisfactory. The "Account of the XII. Subas," included in the *Ain-i Akbari*, deals with mineral and industrial production, but the information it gives is far from being exhaustive, and Abul Fazl anticipates some modern writers in paying more attention to rare and curious products than to the articles consumed by the masses of the people. European travellers likewise were apt to ignore the staple products of the country because their interest was attracted mainly by the limited classes of goods which could bear the heavy cost of transport to Europe, and consequently it is not altogether easy to obtain a just view of the relative importance of different branches of production. In the sections which follow I have endeavoured to direct attention mainly to those goods which were quantitatively important, either because they were consumed by the masses of the people, or because they formed the basis of the export trade, and with this object I have drawn freely on the information available in regard to internal consumption and to foreign commerce.

Speaking generally, it may be said that at this period India was very nearly self-supporting, and that her imports were limited to certain metals and raw materials, together with a large number of articles of luxury required for consumption by a very small proportion of the population. The advantages enjoyed by a self-supporting community are in some quarters regarded as so important that it is perhaps desirable to say at the outset that I use the word to express an economic fact, and without any implication that the fact is either good or bad. The common people ate food and wore clothes produced in the country; it does not follow that they got enough to eat, or that the clothes they wore gave adequate protection against the weather. At the present day they are more dependent for their clothes on other parts of the world; the change may be either a good thing or a bad, and sometimes it is not very easy to say which is true, but such discussions are altogether irrelevant to my present purpose, which is to indicate the extent to which the term self-supporting is applicable. For this purpose we may class the principal goods for consumption very roughly as food, clothes, metal-ware, and articles of luxury or display, while goods required for production may be divided into raw materials, and tools or machinery. The country produced all the food and food-adjuncts which ordinary people required, though not always in sufficient quantities to satisfy all needs; imports under this head were practically limited to fruit, spices, and stimulants.[1] In the same way, all ordinary clothes were made in India, but silks, velvets, and broadcloths were imported

[1] The taste of the Moguls for fruit appears in almost every contemporary authority. Babur (*Memoirs*, 503-513) writes as a connoisseur; the sources from which Akbar's Court was supplied are detailed in the *Ain* (translation, i. 64-72); Jahangir's views are expressed in the *Tuzuk* (i. 5, and *passim*). The Portuguese brought wine and spirits from Europe (*Pyrard*, translation, ii. 211), while there was also a considerable import from Burma (*Linschoten*, c. 17), and coffee came from Arabia (*Jourdain*, 86). Imported spices were used very largely in the kitchens of the Moguls, and also, probably, of other classes; cloves and cinnamon appear in almost all the recipes given in the *Ain* (translation, i. 59, 60).

from various parts of the world. Metals, on the other hand, were undoubtedly scarce, and while nearly all the metal-ware used was made up in the country, much of the raw material was imported. As for articles of luxury or display, while their production employed many Indian artisans, the prevailing taste for novelty secured a market for the first supplies of almost any article coming from abroad, though, from the nature of the case, it was not usually a large or durable market.[1] Of goods required for production, there was no question of machinery at this time, and the tools used in India appear to have been locally produced. Imported materials included raw silk, ivory, coral, tortoise-shell, amber, and the like, in addition to the metals—gold and silver, lead, tin, zinc, and quicksilver, and, in some parts of the country, copper; some minerals, such as borax and sulphur, were also imported for use in manufactures; but with these exceptions, the industries pursued in India were based on the supplies of raw material afforded by the land. In the following sections I endeavour to bring together the information available regarding, firstly, the exploitation of materials other than those yielded by agriculture; and, secondly, the manufacture of all kinds of consumers' goods.

II. Forests and Fisheries

We have seen that in most parts of India, though not in all, the proportion of culturable land lying unoccupied was greater than now, and we may safely assume that it

[1] Some of the early disappointments of the English merchants arose from failure to grasp this fact: a small trial consignment would sell profitably, but when a larger stock was brought out on a subsequent voyage, the demand was found to be satisfied and the goods were almost unsaleable. Rareties, however, could always be sold or used for presents, and the volumes of *Letters Received* contain curious allusions to the demand for such commodities as English dogs, rare liqueurs, musical instruments, ladies' hats and hosiery, and other "side-lines" of the commerce of the time. This taste for novelty was not confined to the Mogul Court, and a missionary narrative (printed in *Hay*, 762-764) shows us the Emperor of Vijayanagar and his chief lords delighted by curiosities such as a glass box, a shell cup, or a heart worked in gold and silver, just as we read of Akbar's eagerness to possess an image of Ignatius "because it was new" (*idem*, p. 869).

was usually covered by some form of forest growth. The literature of the period contains no hint of the existence of anything comparable to the methods of conservation and scientific exploitation which have been introduced during the course of the last century, and if there were any restrictions at all, they were in all probability limited to the exaction of dues by the central or local authorities. We can therefore form a general idea of the condition of the forests in the time of Akbar, if we draw on our knowledge of the state of unregulated forests in India at the present day, and allow for the difference in the means of transport: inaccessible forests can have yielded no income, and inaccessibility was more common than now, while forests within reach of towns or villages furnished the inhabitants with timber, fuel, and minor produce on a scale which, roughly speaking, varied inversely with the pressure of the population. Such instances as we get of particular forms of produce having acquired a reputation in the markets fall in with this view: the bamboos of Bengal, which were in demand for fitting out ships, could be transported cheaply by the waterways of the country, while the teak of the Western Ghats was within reach of the sea-coast where large vessels were built, or it would be more accurate to say that ship-building was carried on at those places on the coast where suitable timber was available in sufficient quantities.

When we try to form an idea of the income derived by the country from forest produce, we find that it must be the resultant of various tendencies acting in different directions. Since there was more forest and less cultivation, we may be sure that a larger proportion of the rural population enjoyed an unrestricted supply of such produce than is now the case, and probably the difference was sufficient to justify the conclusion that the rural population as a whole was in this respect better off. On the other hand, the cities and towns probably had no greater facilities than now, for though forests may have been nearer, the means of transport were very much worse, nor had they the benefit of produce obtained from distant areas by organised exploitation. Against the advantage enjoyed by the rural population must be set the damage caused to their crops by the wild animals dwelling in the forests: every peasant who had unrestricted access to a supply of produce had his fields open to injury from this cause, and readers who have practical experience of the matter will probably agree that on balance there was no great advantage either way. In this case therefore, as with the yield of agriculture, while we cannot say definitely that the average income per head was greater, or was less, in Akbar's time than now, we can be fairly confident that, taking the country as a whole, it was of somewhere about the same order of magnitude.

A somewhat similar conclusion may be formed regarding the income from fisheries. The *Ain-i Akbari* tells us that fish formed an important part of the people's food in Bengal and Orissa, and also in Sind, and various travellers record that its use was common in the south of India, and that it was sometimes dried and salted for provisioning ships. Fish-oil was prepared in Sind, the use of fish-manure was established in Gujarat when Thévenot visited Surat in 1666, and, speaking generally, it may be reasonably assumed that the fisheries were conducted very much on the lines familiar at the present day. There may be some basis of truth for the popular complaint that the yield of the rivers has declined relatively to the demand, the extent of which depends on the numbers of the population within reach of the supply, and it is also possible that there has been some reduction in the quantity obtained from the fisheries on the coast, although their potential yield is practically inexhaustible; but if we bear in mind that the fish-eating population—the people to whom fish is a staple article of diet and not merely a luxury—form only a fraction of the total population of the country, it becomes highly improbable that the average income of the whole number can have been affected materially by any decrease in the yield of fisheries which may have occurred.

A few words may be added regarding the pearl-fishery of Southern India, which was one of the correct topics to be noticed by every visitor to that part of the country. The exact locality of the fishery varied from time to time, being situated in some years in Indian waters and in others off the coast of Ceylon, but wherever it was held it attracted a large crowd, stated by a missionary visitor to amount to as many as 60,000 persons. It may be gathered from the extant descriptions that the enterprise was highly speculative, as is still the case, but I have found no record which throws any light on its economic importance. Pearls were of course greatly in demand among the upper classes, but Indian waters had nothing approaching to a monopoly of their production, as they were imported from various places, particularly from the Persian Gulf, and the income derived from the enterprise, while it was important to the men engaged, cannot have been sufficient to make a material difference to the population of the whole country.

III. Mines and Minerals

As will have been gathered from the last section, we possess few records throwing direct light on the spontaneous animal and vegetable products of India at this period, but somewhat more detailed information is available regarding the exploitation of minerals, a subject which was considered to be of interest by the compiler of the *Ain-i Akbari*. Looking first at the precious metals, the production of gold appears to have been negligible: the silence of visitors to the south may be taken as conclusive evidence that the Mysore goldfields were not worked at this time, and Abul Fazl tells only of the metal being washed from river-sand in some parts of Northern India, a practice which still survives. Silver, too, was obtained in only trifling quantities: Abul Fazl states that a mine existed in the province of Agra, but that it did not pay for working; and apart from this theoretical source there are only vague statements that the metal was obtained by washing in river-beds, and that it was mined in "the mountains of Kumaun," a region of which the Mogul administration possessed very little definite knowledge.

The other metals chiefly consumed in India were quicksilver, tin, lead, zinc, copper, and iron. The first four of these were mainly imported,[1] though small quantities of lead and zinc were produced in Rajputana; the south of India obtained copper from overseas, but the north depended on supplies locally mined, while practically the whole country had to rely on its own resources in regard to iron. In order to form a just idea of the production of these two metals, it is necessary to remember that they do not occur in India in the metallic state, and that the reduction of the ores requires in both cases a large quantity of fuel, the supply of which is, in fact, one of the governing factors of the industry. Coal was not mined in India at this period, and the production of iron and copper was limited by the quantity of wood available within reach of the places where the existence of ores was known. The practical effect of this limit was demonstrated in various parts of India during the last century, when attempts were made to produce iron on a comparatively large scale: the industry usually made some headway at first, but the local supplies of fuel were soon exhausted, and the increasing cost of carriage gradually rendered the enterprise unprofitable. In these cases the point at which profits vanished was determined by the price at which imported metals could be sold in competing markets, and the limit was thus reached more quickly than would have been the case in the earlier period when importation was more costly; but the limit is nevertheless a hard fact which producers must have always been compelled to take into account; if they worked on a large scale, the fuel supply would soon become inadequate, and operations would have to be suspended until the trees had time to grow, while if production was kept down to the amount justified by the annual growth of fuel in the vicinity it can never have been conducted on any but the smallest scale. The descriptions available of the old workings and of the industry as it survived during the last century appear to me to prove that these

[1] There is a reference in *Letters Received*, iii. 63, to the discovery of a "quicksilver mine" near Agra, but the statement was made at a time when English merchants were offering imported supplies of the metal, and I take it to be an invention put about by the buyers in order to influence the market. I have not been able to find any evidence that quicksilver was produced at this period in India.

limitations had been actually felt: the industry was not organised on a large scale, but individuals set up small furnaces in places where ore and fuel were available and abandoned them when the supply of either necessary failed.[1] In cases where the supply of ore ran short, the abandonment would of course be permanent, but where ore was abundant, particular localities would be deserted for a time and left until the jungle should grow.[2] The industry was thus diffused rather than concentrated, inefficient when judged by modern standards, and altogether unsuited to attract capitalist enterprise, but nevertheless it formed in the aggregate an important item in the production of the country.

In the case of copper, we have to distinguish, as has already been indicated, between the north of India and the south. I have found no record of the metal having been produced at this period in the territories of Bombay, Madras, or Hyderabad, nor do I know of extensive old workings in those parts of the country, while the numerous references to its importation on both coasts show that the trade was firmly established, even the supply of copper coins depending on material brought from China. On the other hand, I have found no reference to imports by sea into Northern India, either through Bengal or by way of the Gulf of Cambay; Tavernier's account of the variations in the ratio of exchange between copper and silver coins indicates that in his time the principal sources of the former metal were nearer to Agra and Delhi than to the coast, and, apart from the evidence of old workings, we have the definite statements of Abul Fazl as to the existence of mines in various parts of the country. The sources which he indicates are, first, the Himalayas, and, second, certain localities which are now included in Rajputana: traces of

[1] The ordinary furnace seems to have yielded a quantity of iron varying from about 5 to 10 tons in a year; a modern blast-furnace of the type now in operation in India will yield in a single day about as much metal as an indigenous furnace would produce in the working lifetime of its owner.

[2] The question of availability appears, if we may judge by old workings, to have depended largely on depth. When mines are carried down into the ground they soon become flooded, and in the modern industry arrangements are provided for pumping out the water; but pumping was not understood in India at this period, and the workings were abandoned when they reached the level at which water accumulated.

old workings are numerous in these portions of the country, while they are found also on an extensive scale in parts of Chota Nagpur and Bundelkhand, and it is not improbable that these latter areas contributed to the supply in Akbar's time, since Abul Fazl's account of them is obviously based on very imperfect knowledge, and his silence in the matter is not conclusive. Rajputana seems, however, to have been the principal source at this period.

As regards the production of copper, there is no quantitative information, but we know that the metal was exceedingly costly. Akbar's mint paid 1044 dams for one maund, and at this rate a pound of copper would have cost the peasant about 84 lb. of wheat, whereas in the years 1910–12 the price in terms of wheat was about 16 lb., so that any one whose income was earned in agricultural produce had to pay at least five times the present price for articles made of the metal. We may be sure that this price was in practice prohibitive, and that the lower classes of Northern India exerted no effective demand for the metal, and consequently that the production was very small, compared to what it would have been if brass and copper vessels had been as generally used as at the present day. We may also be sure that the price was not materially lower in the south than in the north, for if it had been, importers would have diverted their supplies from the west coast ports to those of Cambay, an operation perfectly feasible in the commercial conditions of the period, and we thus arrive at the conclusion that in India as a whole goods made of copper and brass must in the sixteenth century have taken rank definitely as expensive luxuries instead of being conventional necessaries for the great majority of the population.

The production of iron was much more widely diffused than that of copper, and I think the output must have been much larger. There is no evidence that any large part of India depended on imports: [1] the ores are widely distributed, and

[1] The East India Company sold a trial consignment of iron at a profit in Surat, but this was due to the existence of a temporary local scarcity, and we are told that within a fortnight large supplies reached the city from up-country (*Letters Received*, i. 23). No further attempts to develop a trade appear to have been made at this period.

traces of old workings are found in almost every part of the country except in the alluvial plains; there was a regular, though not a large, export from the south of India, while in the north we have Abul Fazl's authority for the statement that production was carried on in the Mogul provinces of Bengal, Allahabad, Agra, Berar, Gujarat, Delhi, and Kashmir. The quality of the output was frequently high, and, in the south at least, the artisans had a method of making steel, which was, I think, the main form of export from the western coast. As to the quantity produced, we can form only a vague idea. Many of the modern uses of the metal were of course unknown, and we should not expect to find iron bridges, corrugated roofs, wire fencing, travelling trunks, or similar commodities in the India of Akbar's time: Indian constructional methods [1] are distinguished by the absence or economy of iron, and I take it that the output was devoted mainly to the manufacture of tools, implements, and arms, or such accessories as nails, screws, and horse-shoes. Abul Fazl gives a few data as to the cost of some of these articles in Northern India, but in most cases it is impossible to make a satisfactory comparison; horse-shoes, for instance, cost 10 dams for a set, but the amount of metal they contained is not specified, while in regard to such articles as nails or screws the cost of workmanship is an important but undetermined factor in the price. The only articles for which a comparison can be safely made are picket-pegs, which were valued at three dams per ser; this means that at the Imperial Court 1 lb. of iron in this form was worth 10 lb. of wheat, while about the year 1914 the value was just over 3 lb., and on this basis Akbar's peasants had to pay more than three times as much grain as their modern successors for the iron they required for tools and implements. The remaining figures given by Abul Fazl bear out the general conclusion that iron was dear, though not relatively so dear as copper, and we must regard the metal,

[1] *Pyrard*, for instance, mentions (translation, ii. 180) that comparatively little iron was used in building the Indian ships, which were consequently weaker than the Portuguese carracks, though the timber of which they were constructed was superior.

not indeed as a luxury, but as a costly necessity in the use of which the utmost economy was requisite.

Of minerals other than the metals the most important at this period were salt and diamonds ; and we may consider the latter first, not as being the more valuable product, but because the information which we possess regarding the methods of production supplements what has just been said of the mining industry, and enables us to form some idea of the conditions of employment. Diamonds, like the ores worked in India, are found near the surface of the ground, but their recovery does not involve the consumption of fuel, and consequently the industry is not subject to the limitation which, as we have seen, operated in the case of copper and iron ; accordingly, we find that very large numbers of labourers were collected at the diamond-fields, and we may take it that the organisation adopted there represents the highest stage reached by the industry of the period. This organisation is described most fully by Tavernier, who, as an expert jeweller, was particularly interested in the subject, and though his account dates from the middle of the seventeenth century, we may accept its main features as having persisted at least from the period with which we are concerned. At this time there were two diamond-fields in the Deccan, in one of which the diamonds were found in sandy soil, which required merely to be sifted and searched, while in the other the soil contained clay, which had to be washed away before these processes could be carried out ; the latter obviously required a larger labour force, and is therefore the more useful illustration of the contemporary industrial system. According to Tavernier's description, there was nothing approaching to organisation on a large scale : a merchant marked out a plot or " claim " of about half an acre in size, and employed a number of labourers, which may occasionally have been as high as 300.[1]

[1] Tavernier does not mention the number employed by individual merchants on this field, but he says that the system was the same in both places. At Raolconda, where washing was not required, he puts the number at 50, rising to a maximum of 100 ; allowing two carriers to a digger to provide for the extra work of washing, this would give a maximum of about 300.

The surface soil was dug out by men, and carried by women and children to a walled enclosure, where it was drenched with water brought in earthen pots; the slime was then allowed to run out through apertures in the walls; the residual sand was winnowed when dry with baskets such as were used at harvest; the coarser matter was thrown on the ground and beaten with wooden stamps, and finally the diamonds were picked out by hand. The whole process can be visualised at once by any one who has experience of Indian methods of work: there was a large crowd of workers, which Tavernier (perhaps with some exaggeration) puts at more than 60,000, but it consisted of a great number of working units, which individually were small, and each entirely independent of the others. The wages paid struck Tavernier as very low; even a skilled man earned, he says, only three pagodas in a year, and the temptation to steal was so great that there would be twelve or fifteen watchers to fifty labourers. Taking the pagoda at the value indicated in a previous chapter, the rate of earnings is less than a rupee a month, which cannot have been more than a bare subsistence-allowance; but a bonus was paid for the discovery of valuable stones, and probably the hope of a fortunate chance, or a fortunate theft, was prominent among the motives which attracted labourers to the field. Low as the wages were, it is obvious that in the aggregate large sums were disbursed, and since this field had in Tavernier's time been worked for about a century, we must conclude that on the whole it paid expenses, though (as commonly happens in speculative industries) the average rate of profit was probably very small; taking the wages bill as a basis, and making a generous allowance for other expenses, royalties, and profits, it is just barely possible that, when employment was at the maximum, the yield of all the sources taken together might have been worth as much as 20 lakhs of rupees yearly in the currency of the time. This figure is a maximum, and may well be an over-statement; but in any case the industry was of more than local importance, and the conditions in which it was carried on indicate an economic position by no means dissimilar from that which now exists—

a dense population with a low standard of life, attracted in large numbers to an industry where the work was of a familiar type, and content with low regular wages, which might be supplemented as the result of some fortunate accident.

The third source of diamonds described by Tavernier was of much less importance. In this case the gems might be found in the sandy bed of a river in Chota Nagpur, and the local population turned out and searched the sand annually from January or February onwards, that is to say, when the river was low and the autumn crops had been harvested; the work would thus come under the head of spare-time employment, and operations would be suspended after a few months, as they would obviously be impracticable from the beginning of the rains. The yield appears to have been very much smaller than that of the regular diamond-fields farther south, but doubtless the chance of a lucky find was sufficient to attract seekers to the number of 8000 which Tavernier mentions.

The production of salt was important at this period, and so far as I know it was not supplemented by importation on any considerable scale. The sources were those which are still familiar, the Sambhar lake, the Punjab mines, and the water of the sea, and the volume of internal trade appears to have been substantial. As in the case of the metals, we have no direct information as to the quantity produced, but can obtain some idea of its magnitude from a comparison of prices. Measured in terms of food-grains, a pound of salt was $2\frac{1}{4}$ times as dear in the vicinity of Akbar's Court as in Northern India about the year 1914, and since the Court was usually located near the main sources of supply, we may infer that the average price throughout the country was somewhat higher. The experience of the present century has shown that reductions in price lead to a substantial increase in consumption, and it is therefore probable that the relatively high price prevailing in Akbar's time meant a much smaller consumption per head than that to which the country is now accustomed. Opinions may differ on the question whether the larger consumption in modern times is fully accounted for by the quantity imported, but in any case it is obvious that production per head cannot have been much greater under Akbar, and possibly it was even less.

Of other mineral products in the same grade as salt, we know that saltpetre was produced, but it was at this time of very little importance compared with its position later on when the export trade to Europe had come into existence. Various other minerals, such as borax, alum, and ochres, were produced on a scale which was small, but sufficed, when supplemented by imports, to meet the industrial demand of the country. Among minerals of lower grade, building-stone was quarried for local use in most places where it existed, but the conditions of transport must have prohibited the development of larger markets, and the only case I have noticed of stone being carried to a distance is the use of Bassein stone at Goa, whither it was taken by sea. The use of broken stone for road metal and railway ballast is of course quite modern.

We may now attempt a rough comparison of Indian mineral production in Akbar's time and at the present day. The decreases are to be found under diamonds, iron, copper, and a variety of less important items, lead and zinc, borax, ochres, etc. I have put the loss under diamonds at the extreme figure of twenty lakhs of contemporary rupees. The purchasing power of the rupee at this time and place is doubtful, but it was almost certainly less than at Akbar's Court, so that the maximum loss under this head is substantially less than a crore of rupees (modern currency). For the other items, it does not appear possible to make a quantitative estimate, but we have seen that copper was a rarity, and, while its value was high, the quantity produced must have been very small indeed when compared with the consumption at the present day. Comparison in the case of iron is complicated by the very great expansion in production during the last few years; it is probable that the present output already approaches, if it has not yet reached, the yield in Akbar's times, but looking at the years about 1912, we must recognise that there had been a substantial decrease. Against these losses have to be set the entirely new production of coal, gold, manganese, and minor minerals, amounting before the War to an annual aggregate of about $7\frac{1}{2}$ million pounds sterling,[1] apart from the increase under saltpetre, and the large development of the stone quarries. Deducting from this figure the loss estimated under diamonds, and setting off minor losses against minor gains, we have still an aggregate compared with which the old production of copper and the excess of the old production of iron become insignificant, and after making allowance for the increase of population which has occurred during the last three centuries, the conclusion appears to be indisputable that the average income per head derived from mineral production, while it is still unduly low, is substantially greater than it was in Akbar's time.

IV. Agricultural Manufactures

A superficial study of the contemporary authorities is apt to produce the impression that at the close of the sixteenth century India was characterised by widespread and diversified manufacturing activity. In some respects this impression is misleading; the routes followed by travellers were comparatively few, and there are large tracts of territory of which we possess no account, so that we are entitled to infer only that industries had developed along certain main lines of transport, such as the Ganges and the Indus, or the roads from Agra to Lahore and to the west coast. Further analysis shows that along these routes industries were to a large extent localised in a comparatively small number of towns and cities, and the frequently repeated descriptions of the activities of centres like Ahmadabad or Lahore are apt to be applied to a much larger area than is warranted by the facts. Making every allowance for these sources of error, it is still to my mind

[1] In the official statistics, petroleum takes the third place in the list of Indian minerals, ranking next to coal and gold, but practically the whole quantity is produced in Burma, and in this book we are dealing with India excluding Burma, and consequently leave Burmese production out of account.

indisputable that in the matter of industry India was more advanced relatively to Western Europe than she is to-day; the recurring superlatives of travellers may fairly be allowed to possess so much of positive value, when supported by the concrete facts which their statements disclose. The relative rank of India among the nations is, however, a matter of very little importance for my present purpose, and my only object in alluding to it is to emphasise a distinction which is frequently overlooked. To recognise that India has lost ground relatively to Western countries is an entirely different thing from saying that the income she derives from industries has decreased, for it is quite possible that the country may be receiving a much larger supply of useful commodities even though the progress of other nations has been greater than hers. Whether the industrial income measured in commodities has increased or decreased relatively to the population in the course of the last three centuries is a question to which a direct answer cannot be given offhand, but we can approach it by a consideration of the evidence which is available regarding the nature and extent of the industries which were carried on at the earlier period. For this purpose some scheme of classification is required, and I shall deal in order with agricultural manufactures, handicrafts generally, shipbuilding and other forms of transport production, and lastly, and most important of all, the various textile industries.

The first of these classes comprises the different industries by which agricultural produce is worked up for consumption: in the aggregate they are of great industrial importance, seeing that they transform a large part of the raw material yielded by the land, whether grain, oil-seeds or sugar, fibres, drugs or dye-stuffs, and it is unfortunate for our present purpose that in Akbar's time, as at the present day, they commonly received less than their due share of attention compared with the more noticeable productions of artisans employed on other kinds of raw material.

Taking first the utilisation of food-grains, I think it is safe to conclude that there was practically no organised flour-milling industry in the sixteenth century: I have found no suggestion of anything of the kind, and I take it that the preparation of flour and meal was in general a purely domestic undertaking, as it still commonly is at the present day. It is possible that a certain amount of grain was milled at Surat and other ports in connection with the provisioning of ships, and at inland towns to meet the needs of travellers and visitors, but if there was any such concentration of the industry, the organisation can only have been rudimentary, consisting probably of a certain number of women using ordinary domestic hand-mills under the control of a grain-merchant. Similarly in the case of sugar, the bulk of the raw material must have been worked up by the cultivator for consumption in the form of *gur* or jaggery.[1] The production of sugar in the modern sense of the word was, however, practised in some parts of India. Bengal was the principal seat of the industry, and, as we have already seen, the product was carried round the coast to Malabar, and up the Ganges to the Mogul capital; I have found no description of the method of manufacture, but it is spoken of as "powder sugar," which probably means that it was of the fine-grained type still familiar in Northern India. This type of sugar was also procurable in quantity at Ahmadabad, while the more costly form spoken of as candy appears to have come mainly from the vicinity of Lahore, but was also produced in some other towns. The difference in value between the two types was considerable: Abul Fazl gives the prices at Court as 128 dams for a maund of powder and 220 dams for a maund of candy, so we may take it that the former was the standard type, and the latter a special product. Even the cheaper kind was, however, costly when judged by modern prices, since, allowing for the change in purchasing power, the rate quoted is equivalent to from 25 to 30 rupees for a modern maund, a price which would put the commodity beyond the reach of the poorer classes; we may therefore conclude that white sugar was a luxury in Akbar's time, and that the production was relatively much

[1] The product is mentioned by various writers, but the only reference I have found to the process is contained in *Thévenot's* remark (p. 219) regarding the Deccan that every peasant who grew sugar-cane had his own cane-press and furnace.

less than at present, the poorer classes and the confectioners who catered for them making use only of *gur*.[1]

The industry of oil-pressing was probably carried on by the exceedingly primitive methods still to be seen, but I have found nothing which can be called a description of the processes employed. I conjecture that this is one of the industries which have declined since Akbar's time, when mineral oil was unknown, but there appear to be no data to indicate the extent of the change which has taken place. Nor is it possible to speak with certainty regarding cotton-ginning on a commercial scale. Presumably both ginning and spinning were usually carried on by the grower and his family, but an observation recorded by Thévenot half a century later indicates that in some localities specialisation had already begun; near Ahmadabad he met a gang of workmen who had no fixed home but travelled from village to village, ginning and cleaning cotton, or doing any other work that was available, and we may infer that the seventeenth century was beginning to experience the need which has now been effectively met by the introduction of ginning mills throughout the principal cotton-tracts. The extent of this industry does not require discussion in this place, as it is covered by what is said further on regarding the production of cloth.

Tobacco manufacture can scarcely have started in India during Akbar's reign. The plant was unknown to his revenue officers, and consequently cannot have been grown to any extent during the sixteenth century. It is believed to have reached India through the agency of the Portuguese, and was established first in the province of Gujarat, where the leaf was obtainable in the year 1613, but the processes of manufacture were not understood. The preparation of opium was an old-established art both in Behar and in Malwa. The methods of making indigo practised at Biana,

[1] I have found no reference to sugar-refining in Rohilkhand at this period. It is not easy to believe that this industry, the most important of its kind in India, is of recent origin, but on the other hand it is improbable that its existence should have been overlooked by Abul Fazl, who mentions refining at places like Kalpi and Biana, south of the Jumna, but says nothing of it in any town of Rohilkhand.

the main centre of production in Northern India, are described by William Finch, and are substantially the same as those which were followed when the modern industry was at its height, though there have been various changes in organisation and in detail.[1]

A few words may be said in this place regarding the production of intoxicating liquors. The industry was officially discouraged by the Mogul Emperors: Akbar ordered the Kotwals, or city-governors, to restrict it so far as this could be done without interfering with the privacy of domestic life, and Jahangir—himself a heavy drinker—prohibited it altogether, but probably this latter regulation was not seriously meant, and in any case it was not carried out.[2] Spirits and fermented liquors were easily procurable throughout the country, as is apparent from the frequent references in the accounts of European travellers. In the south they were prepared mainly from the sap of the palm-tree, while the *mahua*-flower and molasses were used farther north; the materials employed in these areas were thus those which are still in use, and we may infer that the processes were of the types which are now being transformed under the guidance of the excise administration.

Taking this group of industries as a whole, I do not think there are adequate grounds for concluding that the income relatively to the population differed very materially from that which is now obtained. No tobacco was made, and less white sugar, but probably the amount of oil expressed was greater, and it is possible that the consumption of drugs and intoxicating liquor may have been larger than in these days of severe restrictions and heavy excise-duties. There can be no doubt that during the nineteenth century much more indigo was made

[1] The most important change is agricultural rather than industrial. The crop used to remain in the ground for three years, yielding annual cuttings, of which the second gave the best dye. With the extension of irrigation, a gradual change took place in agricultural practice until the crop became seasonal (*Letters Received*, iv. 237, 356).

[2] Prohibition was enforced much more strictly under Shahjahan, as appears from the complaints made by *Mundy*, *e.g.* ii. 97, 134; but even then it was not universal, for the same writer records that at Surat the *tari* trees were farmed by the Governor (ii. 32).

than in Akbar's time, but production had fallen to a very low figure in the years immediately before the War, which I have taken as the period for comparison, and it is possible that the industry was no greater then than at the end of the sixteenth century. If we set off the gains against the losses, we may reach the opinion that India as a whole was slightly better off, or slightly worse off, under Akbar than now, but I cannot detect in the information available any reasons for holding that a material economic change has occurred in the interval.

V. Handicrafts in General

Turning now to the second group of manufactures, the miscellaneous handicrafts (excluding textiles), the general impression left by the accounts of travellers is one of variety and skill, especially in imitation, rather than economic importance. Many of the craftsmen whose work receives most notice—jewellers, silversmiths, workers in ivory, coral, amber, or tortoise-shell, druggists, perfumers, and others—catered for an exceedingly narrow market, the extravagant ruling classes and a small and fluctuating demand on the part of foreigners: the commodities they produced were noteworthy, and, in some cases, of artistic merit,[1] but the volume of their industry was not great, and a large part of the value of their products was due to the cost of material rather than to the processes applied.

The products intended for larger markets deserve somewhat more detailed notice. Taking first the metal industries, we have seen in a previous section that articles made of copper and its alloys must have been luxuries, the price of the metal being almost prohibitive, and the evidence to be examined in a subsequent chapter regarding the standard of life suggests that such articles were in fact rarely owned by the poorer classes of the population; a working household might possess a small drinking-vessel, but large jars and dishes must have

[1] The complaint of artistic decay, so commonly heard in recent years, is not entirely novel. In the middle of the seventeenth century *Thévenot* (p. 140) remarked that some of the craftsmen at Delhi were not unskilful, but earnings were low, and they thought only of speed so as to get a livelihood.

been beyond their reach. It is not surprising, therefore, that we should be told practically nothing about the industry, which relatively to the population must have been very much smaller than at the present day. The position in regard to iron goods was also governed by the high cost of the metal: small articles were in common use, but heavy goods were practically unknown, and the amount of material handled must, relatively to the population, have been comparatively small. A substantial part of the demand came from the makers of swords and other arms, which were carried by large numbers of people, and there can be no doubt that the private manufacture of weapons has declined, but against this must be set off the modern output of the State factories and arsenals, which is very much greater than that of Akbar's workshops. Taking into account also the large quantities of heavy goods now produced by the foundries and iron-works established throughout the country, it appears to be probable that the industry as a whole yields a substantially higher income than was obtained in the sixteenth century.

The development of wood-working was not, so far as I can judge, retarded by the high cost of the raw material in the same way as the metal industries which have just been considered: the supply of particular qualities of timber may have been restricted by difficulties of transport, but it is probable that, with large areas of uncultivated land, materials for ordinary purposes such as house-building or the manufacture of agricultural implements were somewhat more easily obtainable than now. Of the more highly developed branches of the industry, I have reserved the building of ships and conveyances for separate consideration, leaving furniture and cabinet-making to be dealt with here. There can be no doubt that the output of these branches was, relatively to population, much smaller than at the present day, when the middle classes have come into prominence, and, like the upper classes, have adopted Western fashions to such a large extent: even in the palaces of the rulers there was very little furniture to be seen, and I have not come across any mention of the existence of either chair or table except among the Portuguese, or possibly among the Moslem merchants on the coast. Bedsteads, chests, and stools practically make up the list of bulky goods, while smaller articles such as ornamental boxes were also in demand. The Portuguese obtained most of their requirements from the ports on the Gulf of Cambay, and Pyrard mentions the import into Goa of lacquered bedsteads, inlaid cabinets, and similar goods. The houses of the Moslem merchants on the west coast were not in all cases so bare as those of other Indians, for Barbosa mentions that at Rander near Surat they were well kept and well furnished, but with these exceptions the absence of furniture appears to have been characteristic of the whole country, and, speaking generally, it may be said that the wood-working industry was limited by the absence of demand for its products rather than by any scarcity of material.

Leather goods receive little notice from the authorities available for this period, and the subject has to be approached indirectly. It is clear that the extensive export of hides and the import of various finished articles are quite modern phenomena, and that, in the time of Akbar, India as a whole was self-contained in this branch of industry. Now in the conditions which have prevailed since this period it is probable that the potential supply of hides and skins has varied roughly with the size of the agricultural population, and on this basis it may be contended that the leather industry must have been relatively more productive than at present, because in the absence of exports the quantity of raw material was greater, while no needs were met by imported goods. The validity of this argument depends on the truth of the underlying assumption that the available supply of hides was made into leather; if owing to the absence of effective demand a substantial portion was left unused, the production might be much smaller relatively to population than it is to-day, and I am inclined to think that this was actually the case. At the present day the bulk of the leather used in the country is devoted to the manufacture of boots and shoes, well-buckets, and harness and saddlery; compared with these main groups the rest of the production is insignificant, while I have been unable to discover any case of importance in which the use of leather has been discontinued since Akbar's time. If, therefore, all the raw material in the country was used, there must have been a relatively much greater consumption of some or all of the articles I have named, and of this I can find no trace. Foreign observers rarely say anything about the common people wearing shoes; discussion of the evidence they offer on this point will find a more appropriate place in a subsequent chapter, but I may anticipate the conclusion to which it leads, which is that in all probability shoes were less commonly worn than at the present time.[1] There is no reason to suppose that irrigation by means of buckets was relatively more common than now, and in some parts of the country it was certainly much rarer, so that, on the whole, less leather was required for this purpose. As regards harness and saddlery, the *Ain-i Akbari* gives very full details of the articles used in the Imperial stables, and it is remarkable how rarely leather finds a place in the enumeration: saddles were made mainly of cloth, and halters of rope; horses were seldom used for driving, and the harness of oxen—at that period the principal draught animals—has even now very little leather in it. Even, therefore, if more animals were employed than now, a point which is by no means certain, it does not follow that more leather was used in their equipment; its use is very largely a recent development, dating in fact from the nineteenth century. Thus the main markets for leather goods were relatively to the population smaller than they are to-day, while exports were quite unimportant, and the conclusion appears to me to be justified that the industry as a whole was less extensive than at present, and that the modern export of the raw material represents, not the destruction of an ancient industry, but the utilisation of matter which had been wasted in the earlier period.

Paper was at this period coming gradually into use throughout Southern India. Early travellers in this part of the country notice that all writing was done on palm-leaves, and

[1] The modern import of boots and shoes, about three million pairs annually, is in itself considerable, but relatively to the population it is too small to affect the argument.

as late as 1625, when della Valle obtained a specimen manuscript, it was written for him on this material. Pyrard tells us that the Portuguese at Goa imported their supplies of paper partly from Europe, partly from China, and partly from the Cambay ports; I have not found any definite information about the source of the Cambay paper, but I think it may be safely assumed that it was made at various places throughout Northern India by the hand-processes which have not yet entirely disappeared. The quantity used was, however, very small. There was little education, and most of what there was stopped at the primary stage, and was probably conducted by methods such as still survive, in which very little paper is used; the art of printing had been introduced at a few places by missionaries during the sixteenth century, but it was not practised for secular purposes till a later period; paper was used in the public offices, by merchants for their accounts, and by scholars and caligraphists in manuscripts, but there were no printed books, no newspapers, circulars or posters, very few letters; and the facts justify the conclusion that the production of articles of stationery was very small indeed.

The potter's industry appears to have been on the same footing as at present, producing chiefly coarse earthenware for the common people, though a few localities may have possessed a certain reputation for somewhat superior goods; porcelain was freely used by Moslems, but it was imported from China, and was an item of some importance in the Eastern trade. If, as has been suggested above, metal vessels were comparatively little used by the bulk of the population, the market for earthenware must have been relatively larger, and the potters busier than now, and this inference is confirmed, so far at least as Northern India is concerned, by the extent to which the men of this caste are now found to be engaged in agriculture; the Indian industry is typically unprogressive and has suffered because consumers have been able to find preferable means of satisfying their wants.

As to the building industry, the use of brick and stone was probably less extensive than now. The masses built their houses of mud or reeds, and roofed them with thatch, or occasionally tiles; the middle classes were almost insignificant in numbers; merchants were, as we have seen, averse from external display, and the upper classes, at least in Northern India, depended more largely on tents than on palaces. The consumption of bricks, stone, and timber in domestic architecture was therefore small when judged by the standard of the present day; construction for industrial purposes did not exist; and I can find no reason to think that the deficiency was made good by a more extensive programme of public works. Activity in this direction was spasmodic: a great work might occasionally be undertaken, and large quantities of material might be employed in its construction, but there was nothing like the modern organisation by which the State, the local authorities, and the railway administrations keep operations going steadily in every part of the country, and there can be no question that this system results over a series of years in the provision of a much larger amount of building than would be produced by the less systematic methods of an earlier age. Allowance must also be made for the time occupied in construction; to take one instance, the fort and palace at Allahabad constitute a very large undertaking even when judged by modern standards, but the work went on for half a century or more, and the annual increment of commodities is thus reduced to a comparatively small amount. If, then, we set modern textile factories against ornamental tombs, we must conclude that relatively to population the building industry has increased; we may regret that many of the modern buildings afford little scope for the display of taste and artistic skill, but we must at the same time recognise that from the economic standpoint they are much more useful than those of Akbar's days.

So far, then, as this group of industries is concerned, it appears to be reasonably certain that the income of commodities relatively to the population has substantially increased. There has probably been a decline in the production of pottery, the arms industry may have fallen off on balance, and (though no precise information is available) it is possible that the artistic crafts show a general reduction in output. On the other hand, we have seen reason to believe that relatively to numbers there has been a marked increase in the production of brass and copper goods, of iron goods other than arms, of articles made of wood, of paper and stationery, and of buildings of all descriptions except possibly the huts occupied by the poorer classes, while an increase in leather goods is more probable than a decrease. There can be no doubt how the balance stands between these two lists, and it is noteworthy that the changes tend uniformly in the direction of economic efficiency, seeing that nearly all the goods produced in increased quantities are either comparatively durable commodities or are destined to be employed in production.

VI. Production of Means of Transport

We now pass to a consideration of the production of means of transport, both of goods and of passengers, and since the last three centuries have seen a transfer of business from water to land, it is convenient to treat in one section the means of conveyance employed on both elements. It may be taken as certain that, relatively to population, the manufacture of vehicles for use on land was less important in Akbar's time than at the present day. We have seen in a previous section that there was no wheeled traffic in India south of Golconda, while the descriptions of the roads farther north indicate that, while such traffic was possible, there were many difficulties in the way; carts might be used in level country, but rivers and steep gradients were formidable obstacles, and the bulk of the heavy traffic was moved by means of pack animals, while carting was practised mainly in the case of valuable goods, such as treasure or indigo, where there were obvious objections to frequent loading and unloading. For passenger traffic, lighter carts drawn by trotting oxen were available in some parts of the country, but the palanquin was the more ordinary mode of conveyance. Horses or ponies were very rarely used for draught,[1] and the familiar middle-class conveyances of the present day—the *ekka* and the *gāri*—appear to have been developed since Akbar's time, the former from Indian, and the latter from European models. It is probable, therefore, that relatively to population there are now more road vehicles than there were, while if we take into account the work done in the various railway establishments, which in the years before the War employed over one hundred thousand hands in the construction and maintenance of rolling-stock, we shall arrive at a very substantial increment. To complete the account, we must reckon also the construction of railways and metalled roads, which had no counterpart in the sixteenth century, and there is thus a very large volume of new industry, against which the only set-off is the decline in the production of ships and boats.

This decline seems to me to be beyond question so far as the means of inland navigation are concerned. I have found no data regarding the Bengal waterways, where the development of the traffic in jute may have resulted in the maintenance, or even the extension, of the number of boats, but the river systems of the Ganges and the Indus certainly carried a much heavier traffic than they carry now. Fitch travelled from Agra to Bengal with a fleet of 180 boats; the vessels available on the Jumna sufficed on occasion to transport Akbar's enormous camp; and the accounts which we possess of Lahore and Multan indicate that the Indus system was at least equally well provided. The boats in use were fairly large: at Lahore they were 60 tuns[2] and upwards; vessels fit for the coasting trade were built at that city and also at Allahabad; some of the barges on the Jumna were of 100 tuns, while those on the Ganges ranged up to 400 or 500 tuns; and

[1] Among the presents sent by the East India Company to Jahangir was an English coach, which created some sensation at Court, and was used as a model by local craftsmen (*Roe*, ii. 320). Akbar's regulations made no provision for draught horses, his extensive stables being maintained solely for riding (*Ain*, translation, i. 136).

[2] For reasons to be explained in the next chapter, I adhere to the contemporary spelling of this word (or rather to one of them, for the spelling varies), to show that I am writing in terms of the unit of ship-measuremen employed in Akbar's time, and not of the modern shipping ton as defined under the Merchant Shipping Acts.

it is clear that a considerable volume of traffic could be carried by these means. It does not, however, appear to be possible to form even a rough guess as to the number of boats in existence or as to the annual output. The size of a particular fleet may be misleading unless we know also the frequency with which similar fleets moved: the dangers of robbery on the waterways were very real; probably merchants were willing to wait for a large party to travel by water, as was certainly the case on land; and I think it would be a mistake to suppose that a fleet such as Fitch mentions was often to be seen. All that can be said is that many more boats were built in Northern India, and that against them must be set off the much larger provision of means of land transport which is now made throughout the country. Taking into account the fact that there were only three important systems of waterways, and that the greater part of India lay far beyond their influence, it appears to me to be probable that the localised boat-building industry of Akbar's time was of smaller relative importance than the road-carriage and railway rolling-stock industries now distributed over almost every portion of the country; but even if the balance were equal, the modern production of railways and metalled roads indicates a large increase in favour of the present day.

The chief interest of the subject of this section concerns, however, the production of ships and boats on the sea-coast. Shipbuilding is at least as dependent as any other industry on convenience in assembling the necessary materials: it can be carried on only within reach of the sea, and on the coast it will be localised at those places where materials are most readily procurable. In modern times it is found in proximity to supplies of steel and fuel, but in the sixteenth century timber was the determining factor, and ships could be built only where suitable timber was available. It might therefore happen, as it happens now, that the commerce of a particular country might be carried in ships built elsewhere, and for our present purpose it is necessary to treat as a whole the shipping employed in the Indian seas between the Straits of Malacca and the Cape of Good Hope; some ships, mainly those belonging to the Portuguese, but also occasional visitors from beyond the Straits of Malacca,[1] entered these seas from outside, but the bulk of the local commerce was carried in vessels constructed within these limits. Regarded from this standpoint, the shores of the Indian Ocean presented sharp contrasts: there were extensive stretches of coast, notably on the Red Sea, where shipbuilding was rendered impossible by the absence of the essential material; there were other stretches, such as East Africa and the east coast of India, where it could be carried on; and there were others again, such as the west coast and the vicinity of the Gulf of Martaban, where the proximity of teak forests constituted a very marked differential advantage.

The lack of timber on the shores of the Red Sea has a particular interest for India, because it was a factor of primary importance in determining the success of the Portuguese attempt to dominate the commerce of the Indian Ocean. The Portuguese met with no organised opposition so far as the coasts of India were concerned, but early in the sixteenth century their position was threatened seriously by a fleet which was built at Suez with materials carried overland from the Mediterranean, and later on, as the Turks advanced southwards in Arabia, they made other efforts to serve a similar purpose; about the year 1586 they endeavoured to secure a footing on the coast of East Africa with the express object of obtaining timber for shipbuilding, and somewhat later they made serious attempts to import material from Pegu and Sumatra. In both cases, however, the Portuguese were able to frustrate the designs of their enemies, and their sea-power remained unchallenged until the arrival of the Dutch: the history of India might have been materially different had the Turks been able to build a fleet sufficiently powerful to ensure the success of their ambitions.

[1] It is sometimes stated that at this period Chinese ships had ceased to visit the Indian seas, but while it is true that they rarely came beyond Malacca or Sumatra, there are instances of their visiting India. A ship from China and another from Japan reached Negapatam about the year 1598 (*Hay*, p. 835); while Couto mentions a China junk at the same port in 1583 (*Decada*, X. i. 425), and another in 1585 (X. ii. 116).

I have found nothing to show that the resources of East Africa were extensively utilised at this period: coasting-craft were constructed there, and probably wherever else material could be had, but sea-going ships were not built—at least in sufficient numbers to attract the attention of travellers.[1] As regards Pegu, the evidence of shipbuilding is not clear. A visitor in the year 1583 wrote that there were ample materials for building a fighting fleet, but that ships were not built for want of " men to govern them, or to make them," a statement which suggests a lack of skilled workmen; on the other hand, the numerous channels of the delta were at that time full of boats of various types, which must have been built locally, and we may perhaps conclude that such talent as was available was devoted to building boats rather than sea-going ships. There is also some room for doubt about the position at Martaban, but I believe that very few ships, if any, were built there about this period. A certain amount of building was carried on in Tenasserim and Sumatra, but the general attitude of the authorities suggests to me that (apart from the Portuguese trade to Europe) the great bulk of the commerce in the Indian seas was carried in ships built in India, and that most of these, and certainly all the large ones, were constructed on the west coast, not at any one centre, but at various ports or inlets within easy reach of the forests. It is practically certain that India also built all the small boats required for the coasting trade from Bengal as far as Sind, and the aggregate volume of shipping was therefore very great when measured by contemporary standards.

The vessels in ordinary use were of small capacity. As we shall see in the next chapter, the sea-going ships were probably of less than 200 tuns burden on the average, and the coasting craft perhaps 40 or 50 tuns, while the number of the former class was much less than is sometimes supposed, but a discussion of the " tunnage " in use, and of the annual output, must be postponed until the information available regarding

[1] Friar Joanno Dos Sanctos speaks of " ships " being built on this coast, but I gather from his description that even the largest of them were only adapted for coasting (*Purchas*, II. ix. 1555).

sea-borne commerce has been considered. Mention may, however, be made of the great passenger ships, in the construction of which India appears to have taken the lead. Writing in the fifteenth century, Conti had recorded the existence of ships of 1000 tuns,[1] much larger than any with which he was familiar in the Mediterranean, and the early English visitors to Western India described vessels of even greater size, second only to the huge carracks built by the Portuguese. These Indian ships were used solely for the pilgrim-voyage to the Red Sea, and all told there were not, I think, more than half-a-dozen of them in existence at one time; they were not good sea-boats, and their draught was too great for most of the Indian harbours, but they represent a considerable achievement both in design and execution, and it is matter for regret that no account of their construction appears to have survived. To complete the tale of ships built in India, it must be added that the Portuguese constructed a few carracks at Bassein, on the coast north of Bombay, though the vessels of this class were usually built in Europe. Such enterprises must, however, be regarded as exceptional: the importance of the industry depended on the maintenance of an adequate supply of small ships for the sea-going trade, and small boats for moving goods along the coast.

VII. Textile Manufactures—Silk, Wool, and Hair

We now come to the last and most important group of Indian manufactures, those which produced cloth from various fibres—from silk, wool, and hair, from hemp, jute, and cotton—and we will take these materials in the order stated. So much has been written regarding the decay of the Indian silk industry that many people believe it to have been an important feature of the economic life of the country during an indefinite number of centuries. This view is, I think, exaggerated. Silk-weaving was a minor industry in the time of Akbar, and the subsequent decay on which so much stress has been laid did not affect the weaving industry so much as the production of the

[1] He says 2000 butts; one tun is equal to two butts.

raw material, which had greatly expanded as the result of the European demand arising after Akbar's death. Of the period about 1600 it may be affirmed that the export of manufactured goods was very small, that the home market was limited in size, and that it was supplied largely by the importation of foreign goods; silk fabrics were woven in a certain number of centres, but the total output was small, and it is possible that a substantial proportion of the raw silk consumed in India was used for the production of the mixed goods which are still a feature of the hand-weaving industry.

That Indian exports were very small is indicated by the silence of the men who wrote about trade at this period, and who were careful to notice every article which seemed to be of interest to Europe, as silk certainly was. Barbosa, who gives more details regarding exports than any other writer, says that at the beginning of the century some silk goods went from Gujarat to the coast of East Africa and to Pegu, but he indicates no other market, and the remaining writers, with one exception, pass the subject over in silence. The exception is Varthema, whose book asserts that Gujarat supplied "all Persia, Tartary, Turkey, Syria, Barbary, Arabia, Ethiopia," and some other places, "with silk and cotton stuffs." The book bears many signs of loose writing, and I cannot believe that Varthema had discovered a vast trade in silk goods which was concealed from his contemporaries; some of the countries named were, in fact, supplying silk stuffs to India at this time, and the most probable explanation of Varthema's statement is that he did not discriminate accurately between silk and cotton goods. It is fairly certain that substantial quantities of cotton goods went from India to many of the countries named by him, and it is probable that some portion of these contained silk as well as cotton yarn, but in view of the evidence of Barbosa, supported by the silence of a long series of writers, I do not think that a large export of silk goods can have been a feature of the commerce of the period.

The home market was more important than the export trade, for silk stuffs were widely worn by the upper classes, and the fashion of the times prescribed an extensive wardrobe for any one who desired to move in good society. Abul Fazl records that the taste for fine materials had become general at Akbar's Court, Barbosa had noted the prevalent use of silk by the nobles of Vijayanagar, and the luxury-demand was probably large relatively to the number of persons concerned. That number, however, was a very small fraction of the population of India, while there are clear indications that goods of foreign origin were preferred by many of the principal consumers. Silk goods of various kinds were brought to India from the Far East, from Central Asia, from Persia, and from the countries along the Eastern Mediterranean; Barbosa tells us that some of the silks he saw in Vijayanagar came from China, and a large proportion of the stuffs enumerated by Abul Fazl are assigned by him to one or other of the countries named above. Thus the Indian industry had at most a share in a market of limited size.

It so happens that information has been preserved which enables us to form an idea of the amount of raw material consumed in the industry. Apart from the small quantity of fibre produced and worked up in Kashmir, the only production of which we read in India at this period was that of Bengal. Tavernier obtained figures of the output in this region in the middle of the seventeenth century, when the Dutch had established themselves at Kasimbazar and had worked up a considerable export trade. At that period the total output was about 2½ million pounds,[1] out of which one million pounds were worked up locally, ¾ million were exported raw by the Dutch, and ¾ million distributed over India, most of it going to Gujarat, but some being taken by merchants from Central Asia. The Dutch export was, of course, a new feature of the trade: their demand was unsatisfied, and it is probable that production had responded to it, and was greater than in Akbar's lifetime. Making allowances, therefore, for minor sources which may have existed though they are not recorded, we cannot put the total yield about the year 1600 at more than 2½ million pounds, a small portion of which may

[1] Tavernier gives the figures in bales of 100 *livres*; I have added roughly 10 per cent to convert his figures of *livres* into pounds.

have beeu exported as raw material. The Indian supply was supplemented by imports, of which China was much the most important source, and the trade was closely controlled by the Portuguese. In the middle of the sixteenth century Garcia da Orta put the imports at a figure which may represent either 250,000 or 400,000 pounds;[1] Linschoten, writing about 1590, gives 400,000 pounds (3000 quintals), and this figure is probably official. The only other probable source of imports was Persia. Pyrard says that some raw silk was exported from Ormuz; he does not say that it went to India, but if it did, the quantity cannot have been great; the manufacturing centres of Gujarat, where Persian silk would naturally have gone, got their supplies chiefly from Bengal or China; the quantity available in Persia was not abundant,[2] and in the ordinary course of trade it went westward rather than eastward, for a few years after our period we find efforts being made to divert it from this course. We may therefore put the total imports to India at not more than half a million pounds, and the total consumption, imports and home production together, at about 3 million pounds of raw material as a maximum. The latest estimates I have seen of the present Indian production give a total of about 3 million pounds, while in the years before the War the imports (mainly from China) were about 2½ million pounds, so that, after allowing for the export of nearly 1½ millions, the industry consumed about 4 million pounds. On these figures the Indian industry taken as a whole has not kept pace with the probable increase in the population; the relative decline is important for the industry itself, but it does not represent a large decrease in the average income of the entire population of India.

[1] The translator in one place says the unit employed by Garcia da Orta was equivalent to 352 lb., but elsewhere it is equated to 600 lb., and I have not been able to ascertain which figure is correct.

[2] Richard Steele, who was an advocate of trade with Persia, and therefore not likely to understate its possibilities, wrote (*Purchas*, I. iv. 523) that, according to the King's books, Persia yielded yearly 7700 *batmans* of raw silk. The *batman* of silk was apparently equivalent to about 10 or 12 lb. (*Letters Received*, iii. 177, and notes), so that the total available was less than 100,000 lb. Ordinarily it was exported to Europe *via* Turkey (*Letters Received*, iv. 192, 246), so no large quantity can have come to India while the western outlet remained open.

The silk-weaving industry was localised, as might be inferred from the nature of its products. Contemporary writers speak chiefly of the fabrics of Gujarat, notably of Cambay, Ahmadabad, and Pattan, while weaving was carried on also at Chaul, a few miles south of Bombay.[1] It might be inferred from their descriptions that the industry depended wholly on material brought from China, but I think it is probable that supplies were also drawn from Bengal, as was certainly the case when Tavernier wrote. The same writer records a large local consumption in Bengal, and this too is probable, though travellers like Caesar Frederic or Fitch say very little on the subject. The production of Kashmir was worked up locally, but does not appear to have been extensive, and the industry was also carried on at Agra, Lahore, and probably some other cities, but such reputation as Indian silk goods possessed depended on the fabrics of Gujarat. It is noteworthy that Akbar devoted his attention to improving the production of the country. Abul Fazl states that the Emperor had studied the whole production of foreign stuffs, and that under his care foreign workmen had settled in India, silk-spinning had been brought to perfection, and the Imperial workshops furnished all the stuffs made in other countries; he names Lahore, Agra, Fatehpur, Ahmadabad, and Gujarat as having been affected by these measures. His account is coloured by conventional expressions of flattery, but is on the whole probable, and we may believe that patronage had led to an advance in the industry in its principal centre, Gujarat, as well as among the artisans directly dependent on the Court at the three northern capitals.

Apart from what was recognised as silk by travellers familiar with the material, Bengal produced at this period fabrics made of some fibre or fibres which they compared to silk. Pyrard speaks of the silk-herb; Linschoten of a kind

[1] The industry at Chaul seems to have been a recent development. When Barbosa wrote of the port at the beginning of the sixteenth century, it was a considerable centre of trade, but he does not mention silk and says nothing of any industry. Towards the end of the century Linschoten and other writers record an important silk-weaving industry, which must have grown up after Barbosa's time.

of cloth spun from an herb; Caesar Frederic of cloth of herbs, "a kind of silk which groweth among the woods"; and Fitch of "cloth which is made of grass, which they call Yerua, it is like a silk." What these fabrics were appears to be uncertain. I incline to the belief that the statements refer, in part at least, to the "wild" silks of Chota Nagpur, which are in fact gathered in the woods, and the origin of which might easily be attributed by oral tradition to a plant instead of an insect. It is also possible that some fibre such as rhea was at this period produced locally, but I know of no definite authority for this view. The evidence is not given at first-hand. Pyrard spent only a short time in Chittagong, and tells what he was able to hear; Linschoten did not visit Bengal; and the other authorities seem to have obtained their information in the towns. Whatever the fibre was, the manufacture of cloth appears to have been of at most local importance, and it need not be taken into account in estimating the produce of India as a whole.

Unlike silk, which is essentially a luxury-product, wool may be used for the clothing of both rich and poor, but, so far as contemporary authorities go, the poorer classes in India seem to have used very little of it at the period under consideration. I cannot recall a single instance in which a visitor to Northern India at this time mentions a woollen garment, or even a woollen blanket, being worn or used by an ordinary person, though several writers enter into particulars regarding cotton clothing, and would probably have recorded the fact if they had seen Indians wrapped in blankets during cold or wet weather as one sees them so frequently to-day. Common blankets, however, existed, for Abul Fazl includes them in his list of prices. The cheapest cost 10 dams, or say 46 pounds of wheat, in the markets near Akbar's Court, while about the year 1914 a blanket could be got for about 23 pounds of wheat; they were therefore substantially dearer at the earlier period. It is noteworthy that blankets were not supplied for even the best horses in Akbar's stables, the covering sanctioned for them being made of wadded cotton-cloth, and no doubt the same practice, which is still familiar, was followed in other large establishments of the period.

We have fuller information regarding the use of woollen goods by the upper classes. Bright-coloured cloth, especially scarlet, was in demand everywhere for purposes of display; woollen clothing was naturally little used at the various Courts in Southern India, but it was worn in the north, and Akbar's preference for dress of this material had doubtless an important influence on fashions at Agra and Lahore. In the case of wool, however, as of silk, much of the consumption of the upper classes consisted of imported goods: buyers sought for novelty in pattern and texture, and cloth from Italy, Turkey, and Persia was commonly sold in the principal cities. Importers found the market unsatisfactory owing to the vagaries of fashion, and the disappointments of the pioneer merchants of the East India Company are one of the most prominent topics in their reports: a few sample pieces of a new cloth would command a ready sale, but further shipments of similar patterns would be neglected, and there was no prospect of a steady off-take such as had at first been hoped for, while foreign patterns were quickly imitated by the local artisans. The number of these artisans does not appear to have been large enough to attract the notice of travellers: sheep were not an important element in the agriculture of the country, and apparently the Tibetan trade in raw wool had not been established,[1] so that the supply of material was limited. The only reference I have found to its quality is Terry's remark that the wool was generally very coarse.

Two special lines of manufacture deserve mention. The weaving of shawls, mainly from hair, belonged primarily to Kashmir, but under Akbar's patronage the art had been at this time established in Lahore[2] and perhaps elsewhere in

[1] In the "Account of the Twelve Subas" (*Ain*, translation, ii. 172, 280), Abul Fazl gives lists of goods imported into Oudh and Kumaun; raw wool is not mentioned in them, though woollen goods reached Oudh from the north.

[2] Abul Fazl says there were more than a thousand workshops in Lahore: I think he uses round numbers somewhat liberally, and stress should not be laid on the precise figure, but it may fairly be inferred that a substantial industry had been brought into existence. The outturn consisted largely of mixed goods.

the plains. Carpet-weaving also was fostered by Akbar, particularly at Agra and Lahore, but while some good specimens were produced, the output does not appear to have been large; Persian carpets retained their hold on the market, and some years later English merchants found that the industry was unprogressive, and that the craftsmen were in bad circumstances. The weaving of superior goods, whether of wool or of hair, must indeed be regarded as a "fancy-goods" business, not bulking largely in the economic life of the country. No data exist for a precise estimate of the total production of goods made of wool and hair, but taking plain and fancy goods together, the industry was probably less important relatively to population than now; the output of the large modern factories more than suffices to cover any decrease which may have occurred in the production of artisans.

VIII. Textile Manufactures—Hemp, Jute, and Cotton

We now come to the coarser fibres grown in India as field-crops. Regarding hemp we have very little information. Sann-hemp (*Crotolaria juncea*) was assessed in all the Mogul provinces for which revenue rates are on record, and we may infer that it was grown over a wide area though not in great quantity, but there is nothing to suggest that it was extensively used in industry, and probably it was cultivated mainly for domestic purposes, as is still the case in most parts of the northern plains; it is possible, however, that sacking made of this fibre was in local use, since the jute industry was at any rate not highly organised, and some coarse fabric must have been used for packing. Regarding jute, I have found only the single item of information that "a kind of sackcloth" was produced in the Bengal district of Ghoraghat (Rangpur), and it might be inferred that at this period jute was in Bengal what sann-hemp was farther west, a fibre grown for domestic use and of no industrial interest. There is some reason, however, for believing that in Akbar's time jute occupied to some extent the place of cotton as well as hemp. We are told on good authority that rather more than a century ago "the poor in Eastern and Northern Bengal were mainly, if not entirely, clad in a sack-cloth of jute"; and while it is conceivable that these classes wore cotton in 1600, jute in 1800, and cotton again in 1900, it appears to be more probable that the wearing of sackcloth as the cheaper material was an old practice, and that it persisted until the change in relative values which took place in the nineteenth century, when jute became an important industrial crop and the price of cotton goods was lowered as the result of the introduction of machinery. I have been unable to trace anything in the literature of the period which throws any light on this question, and the possibility has to be reckoned with in any estimate of the production of cotton goods: the masses of Bengal at this period wore either jute or cotton, and the province was so densely populated that its clothing must represent a substantial proportion of the entire textile consumption of the country.

Even if we conclude that Bengal wore sackcloth, the fact remains that cotton-weaving was by far the most extensive industry in India, and I think it is fair to say that the aggregate production was one of the great facts of the industrial world of the year 1600. Its magnitude certainly impressed the Portuguese, as may be seen from the statement quoted by Pyrard, that "every one from the Cape of Good Hope to China, man and woman, is clothed from head to foot" in the products of Indian looms. This picturesque phrase contains some serious exaggerations, and perhaps the best way of realising the actual extent of the industry is to strip off these exaggerations one by one until we reach the underlying truth. First as regards the market in India itself, it is nearly correct to say that "every one" wore cloth produced in the country, though, as we have just seen, it is possible that some of the cloth was made of jute; woollens, silks, and velvets were indeed imported from Europe and elsewhere, but their use was confined to the upper classes, who were numerically of very little importance, and the bulk of the people certainly wore home-made clothes. It is, however, very far from the truth to say that they were clothed "from head to foot," for the literature of the period shows that the clothing worn was exceedingly scanty, not merely in the warmer parts of India, where clothes are conventional necessaries, but in regions where they are absolutely required for efficiency. The evidence on this point will be considered in a subsequent chapter, and for the moment we must be content to correct Pyrard's statement by saying that most people in India wore clothes made in the country, but that their clothing was very scanty, being usually limited to a loin-cloth.

The case is even stronger as regards most of the countries outside India. The nakedness of the people living between the Cape of Good Hope and China is proved by a mass of concurrent testimony which would take many pages to reproduce; it was in fact the first and most obvious thing to attract the notice of European visitors, and it has to be borne in mind when we endeavour to estimate the importance of the various markets. Taking first the east coast of Africa, it is, I think, true that India supplied most or all of the clothes worn between Cape Gardafui and the Cape of Good Hope,[1] but the number of people who wore clothes was very small: Pyrard himself says tersely that all these nations go naked, Friar Joanno and other travellers say the same thing in greater detail, and the imports, which are nowhere to my knowledge described as great, were required only for the Portuguese garrison, the Moslem merchants, the Chiefs, and such of the native inhabitants as had begun to feel the influences of civilisation. Farther north there was a market of real importance: Arabia took substantial quantities of piece-goods, which were carried also to Egypt and distributed thence through the Mediterranean, though it would, of course, be incorrect to say that "every one" in these parts wore Indian clothes. On the other side of India, the kingdoms which now form Burma supplied a second market of import-

[1] *Barbosa* mentions (p. 234) that the Moslems had introduced weaving on the East African coast near Sofala. I have found nothing to show whether or not this enterprise survived until the end of the century.

ance during part, at any rate, of the sixteenth century; probably it was at its worst when the century closed, owing to the devastation which resulted from the Siamese war. The third important market was furnished by Malacca and the group of islands of which it formed the commercial centre: ships going from India for spices or for the produce of China carried large quantities of piece-goods, which were either sold at Malacca or bartered locally for cloves or similar produce. Here, however, as in India, individuals wore very little, as a rule "nothing but a cloth about their middles," and the extent of the market should not be overestimated. Beyond the Straits the markets were of much less importance. I have found no record of any large export of cotton goods to China, and it is noteworthy that the Portuguese, who knew this trade thoroughly, did not rely on piece-goods but carried silver from India to finance their purchases. There was some sale to Japan, but it does not appear to have been large, and an English factor, writing from that country in 1615, said that the people bought the sorts of Indian cloth carried there only "for the new and strange fashions and paintings thereof, being a people desiring change." Lastly, it may be noted that Spanish ships occasionally carried Indian cloth from the far-Eastern markets to the Philippines, and perhaps to Mexico, but it is not probable that the quantity so handled was large.

We may then restate Pyrard's picturesque and exaggerated account by saying that Indian looms had a practical monopoly of the home market for clothes, and in addition had three principal export markets, Arabia and beyond, Burma, and the Eastern Islands, besides minor outlets in various other parts of Asia and on the east coast of Africa. The production carried on to meet this demand was diffused throughout the country, but the distribution was not uniform: certain localities had acquired a reputation for special classes of goods, while facilities for carriage had led to considerable concentrations of the industry in particular areas either on the coast or along the inland waterways. Of the general diffusion there can be no doubt: wherever a European penetrated inland, he found cloth being produced along his route, and it is reasonable to conclude that the organisation, of which the remains are still visible, was at this period in full operation, and that all towns and most large villages produced the bulk of the cloth worn in the locality. Such everyday manufactures were not usually recorded in the *Ain-i Akbari*, and all the notices of weaving in this work appear to refer to goods which had obtained a wider reputation. Thus Abul Fazl noted the very fine muslin [1] produced in Sonargaon, the predecessor of Dacca; he spoke with approbation of the goods obtainable in places like Benares, Mau, or Agra in the Gangetic plain, and he recorded in general terms the excellence of the produce of Malwa, the Deccan, and Gujarat. Travellers and merchants notice in the same way the high quality of the goods obtainable in this town or in that, Lahore, Multan, Burhanpur, Golconda, and so on, and it is scarcely exaggerating the position to say that there was something approaching to a general market for superior qualities of cloth, though it must have been dominated by the high cost of transport.

Production for export was in the main drawn from four tracts, the Indus plain with its outlet at the port of Lahari Bandar, the country along the Gulf of Cambay and as far south as Dabul, the Coromandel coast, and Bengal. There were large communities of weavers at Lahore, Multan, Sukkur, Tatta, and other towns on the rivers of the Indus system, and much of their produce was exported by sea, some going towards Arabia, and the rest being taken at this period by the Portuguese. The Gulf of Cambay was the centre of the largest trade of all, drawing goods from Ahmadabad, Pattan, Baroda, Broach, Surat, and many smaller places, and exporting largely east as well as west: we meet Cambay cloth all down the coast of Africa, at Aden, and in the Persian Gulf; but we hear of it also in Ceylon, in Pegu, in Malacca, all through the Islands, and as far as the coast of China. The eastern side of India had a narrower range, and I have not

[1] The muslins of this part of the country had not, however, attained to the reputation subsequently enjoyed, which appears to have been due largely to the patronage of the Court of Shahjahan.

traced goods from the Coromandel coast in the Arabian Sea; it exported, however, largely to Pegu, Malacca, and the Islands, markets which it shared with Cambay and also with the fourth region, Bengal. It is not easy to ascertain the distance from which the centres of export drew their supplies. The English merchants found that some kinds of piece-goods could be profitably bought at Agra for shipment from Surat, although this involved land transport of about 700 miles as the road lay; but the instance is perhaps not altogether typical of ordinary conditions, for the merchants went to Agra primarily to sell their goods and to buy indigo, and the purchase of cloth was, so to speak, a "side-line" of their business in this part of the country. It is obvious that where waterways were available the radius of profitable export would be considerably greater than where land transit was required; Lahore is about 700 miles from the sea in a direct line, and more by river, and on this showing the Bengal ports may have drawn their supplies from as far up-country as Allahabad. No small part of India, therefore, was within the export radius, but at the same time the impression left by the narratives of travellers and merchants is that both in Gujarat and on the Coromandel coast the bulk of the cloth exported was woven in the immediate vicinity of the ports.

In addition to cloth, certain miscellaneous goods were manufactured from cotton. We read of cotton carpets, coverlets, ropes, bed tapes, and some other commodities, and the aggregate outturn was doubtless substantial, but there are no means of estimating the amount. Reference may also be made here to the subsidiary industry of dyeing, which depended mainly on cotton goods, though it handled also other textiles. Coloured goods were in large demand, especially for the countries which now form the province of Burma; the indigenous vegetable dyes were used,[1] and we may take it that the processes followed were in substance those which

[1] The dyes were not always fast: an English factor writing from Ahmadabad in 1613 complained of the local goods in this respect, adding, "they themselves confess that their colours are nought, and will not continue" (*Letters Received*, i. 302).

are still familiar, or which have recently been displaced by the products of European factories.

The details which have been given suffice to show that the cotton industry was at this period much the most important handicraft in India, but they do not enable us to form even a rough idea of the output of commodities. In order to approach this question, we require to take into account the data available regarding the Indian consumption and the volume of the export trade: the facts as to consumption can best be studied in connection with the standard of life, while the export trade will be considered in the next chapter, and we shall then be in a position to approach the question of the output of cotton goods, which has a material bearing on the income of the country as a whole.

IX. Industrial Organisation

Our authorities tell us very little concerning the manner in which Indian industry was organised at the close of the sixteenth century, and it is reasonable to infer that they are silent because they had nothing interesting to say. To the writers of the country the existing system—whatever it might be—would be too familiar to call for mention, and a knowledge of it would be tacitly assumed. Visitors from Europe would almost certainly have indicated any salient features which struck them as novel, and if we find no such features recorded, the inference is that the Indian system resembled in essentials that which prevailed in Europe at the period, or, in other words, that the management of business had not been separated from the work of manufacture, and that production was carried on by artisans without superior capitalist direction. This inference is rendered practically certain by the persistence of the same system in those branches of industry which have not yet been organised on modern European lines, and it is entirely in accordance with the few incidental observations which contemporaries have left on record. These observations are naturally to be found in the early correspondence of foreign merchants, who had to adapt themselves to the markets in which they were endeavouring to find a footing, and to learn by experience the best ways of buying the goods they required. Their first lesson was the need for provision in advance: it was little good trying to get cargo when the ships had come into port, but merchants had to be left in the country, and kept in funds so that they could order what was wanted and pay the price in cash as the goods were delivered. They learned too that some artisans at least were unsatisfactory, for when they gave a trial order to carpet-weavers at Agra, they found "the tardiness, slowness, and poverty of the workmen" to be so great as to prevent the establishment of a regular business. Elsewhere, however, they learned that buying through middlemen was less satisfactory than dealing direct with the artisans, and Sir Thomas Roe urged that attention should be paid to the piece-goods of Gujarat rather than of Sind and Bengal, on the specific ground that at Cambay or Broach "you may bespeak what sorts you will, what length, breadth, and fineness, and buy it from the loom at best hand." Working on these lines, purchases might have to be made of unfinished goods: cloth was thus bought from the weavers, and then dyers or bleachers were employed to get it ready for the market. One factor gives a vivid glimpse of the working of this system in unfavourable circumstances, reporting that when a consignment of Indian piece-goods was offered for sale somewhere near the Straits of Malacca, the cloth was found to be worn into holes owing to "the knavery of the washer that whites them, who to get opium hires them out a month to wear, whereby being foul he beats them to pieces to make them clean." Apart from such incidents, the impression left by this early commercial correspondence is that production was carried on by independent artisans with scanty resources and compelled to market their goods immediately upon completion.

The prevalence of the artisan system of production does not imply that India was unable to undertake great enterprises at this period. Such a suggestion can be immediately negatived by instances like the construction of the fort at Allahabad or the new capital at Fatehpur Sikri, as well as by the building of the great Portuguese carracks, each one of which must be regarded as a large undertaking when judged by the standard of the sixteenth century. The true implication I take to be that the organisation had to be brought specially into existence for each enterprise of the kind. A merchant who required a great ship could not apply to a firm which specialised in shipbuilding and would undertake all technical details: it is more probable that he had to arrange the whole business himself, from the felling of the timber onwards, or at least to organise the services of contractors for all the separate branches into which the undertaking was divided. The system of working a large number of small units was, as we have seen in a previous section, in operation at the diamond-fields in the seventeenth century; contracting and sub-contracting are still familiar in modern India, and I know of no facts which indicate the existence of any more elaborate organisation in ordinary industry at this period. The germ of another system is, however, to be found in the Imperial workshops maintained at the Mogul capital. Bernier, writing about sixty years after our period, described what he saw in the palace at Delhi in the following terms: "Large halls are seen in many places called karkhanas or workshops for the artisans. In one hall embroiderers are busily employed, superintended by a master. In another you see the gold-smiths: in a third, painters: in a fourth, varnishers in lacquer-work: in a fifth, joiners, turners, tailors, and shoemakers: in a sixth, manufacturers of silk, brocade, and fine muslins." These workshops probably represent the later development of those *karkhanas* which Abul Fazl mentions occasionally, though he does not describe their organisation in detail: they marked a different stage of production, in that the artisans worked under direction, and that the supply of materials was presumably arranged for by the officials in charge; and they offered the possibility of improvements in design and workmanship when, as was the case in Akbar's time, the Emperor took a personal interest in the products. It is possible that private workshops of a similar type may have been in existence in the case of some handicrafts, though our authorities say nothing about them, but the quotations already given appear to show that in the ordinary weaving industry at least the artisans worked independently.

The economic position of artisans was not a topic likely to interest the writers who have described portions of the India of the sixteenth century, and there is practically no contemporary information on the subject. A few later visitors took the question into consideration. Bernier, writing to Colbert, said: "No artist can be expected to give his mind to his calling in the midst of a people who are either wretchedly poor, or who, if rich, assume an appearance of poverty, and who regard not the beauty and excellence but the cheapness of an article: a people whose grandees pay for a work of art considerably under its value and according to their own caprice." He goes on to point out that the degradation of artistic handicrafts was retarded by the influence of the Imperial workshops, and by the protection of a few powerful patrons, which resulted in the payment of rather higher wages, and adds: "I say rather higher wages, for it should not be inferred that the workman is held in esteem, or arrives at a state of independence. Nothing but sheer necessity or blows from a cudgel keeps him employed: he never can become rich, and he feels it no trifling matter if he have the means of satisfying the cravings of hunger and of covering his body with the coarsest garment. If money be gained, it does not in any measure go into his pocket, but only serves to increase the wealth of the merchant." Bernier's description is corroborated by what Thévenot was told about the same period of the state of the arts in Delhi, and it may fairly be read as showing that the artisan in the middle of the seventeenth century was substantially in the same position as the artisan of to-day, working mainly for the benefit of merchants or middlemen, and with no prospect of advancement except through the influence of a wealthy or powerful patron. Some light is thrown on the position of the most important class of artisans by the experience furnished by the Gujarat famine of 1630–31. At this period Gujarat had benefited by the expansion of trade resulting from the appearance of foreign buyers in the markets, and it is reasonable to suppose that the weavers and workers in allied industries were at least as prosperous as their fellows in other parts of India. Their economic position was, however, unsatisfactory when judged by the familiar test of resistance to the stress of famine, for contemporary accounts show the complete collapse of the industrial organisation. By November 1630 the weavers and other artisans had abandoned their homes in such numbers that cargo for the English ships could not be procured, and when rain fell in the following June the merchants found it necessary to dole out grain to the weavers at Broach and Baroda, a "ser of corn" being given for each piece of cloth delivered.

On the whole, then, it may be said that not long after Akbar's death the economic position of the bulk of the artisans was at least as bad as at the present day: the workers were dependent on purchasers or middlemen for their current expenses and were destitute of means to face a period of stress. There is no direct evidence to show that this statement is applicable to the conditions which prevailed in the later years of Akbar's reign, but in the absence of any suggestion of an economic revolution in the intervening period it is reasonable to conclude that the position was substantially the same, and that, while individuals might benefit from powerful and enlightened patronage, the great majority of the workers had nothing to hope for beyond the continuance of the conditions which afforded them a bare subsistence.

Two factors in particular—the cost of materials and the burden of taxation—may be noticed as having probably exercised a material influence conducing to this result. We have already seen that the cost of metals was high, and consequently the metal-worker without sufficient capital would be entirely in the hands of whoever might provide him with material. In Northern India at least the price of raw cotton was also high, for in the revenue assessment the crop was charged with rates which indicate that it was much more valuable than wheat, and where this relation held, the strength of the middleman or financier was obviously greater than now.

There is no reason to think that the middlemen of Akbar's time had softer hearts than their modern successors, and since the conditions were favourable to exploitation, we need not question Bernier's assertion that exploitation was the rule. As regards taxation on handicrafts, we have little direct information. Abul Fazl tells us that Akbar remitted a large number of imposts, including a tax on the various classes of artificers and also taxes on particular products or occupations, on blankets, tanning, manufacture of lime and so on; but, as we have seen in a previous chapter, it is not permissible to regard these remissions as permanent, and what was renounced by the State was often collected by subordinate authorities. The existence of such taxes would not ordinarily be noticed by foreign visitors. Terry states definitely that the Mogul had "officers that spread over his Empire to exact money out of all the labours of that people who make the curious manufactures," and Tavernier mentions that at Benares the weavers had to take each piece of cloth to be stamped by the "farmer" (that is, the man who had contracted for the tax) before they could offer it for sale, but these are the only specific statements which I have found, though there are general assertions that all classes of the people paid taxes according to their means. While therefore there is not positive evidence to prove that artisans were heavily taxed in the latter years of Akbar's reign, the circumstances of the period render it probable that they had to contribute to the revenue, and the possibility should be borne in mind in any attempt to estimate their economic position at the period.

X. Urban Wages

It will be convenient to bring together at this point a few items of information regarding the rates of wages which prevailed in India at this period. The subject is relevant to town life rather than to country life, for, if I have correctly interpreted the economic condition of the villages, the labour market in Akbar's time was almost exclusively an urban phenomenon. The agricultural labourer was ordinarily a serf, receiving in return for his work an amount of commodities determined by custom, and about sufficient to keep him and his family alive: the village artisan was also, I take it, supported by the customary payments which are now gradually dying out; and it was only in the towns and cities that men were hired to work and that rates of wages can be said to have existed. This view does not imply a complete separation between the urban and rural population: there was, in fact, a drift from the villages towards the army and the cities, composed partly of the natural overflow of population, and partly of men who had abandoned cultivation under stress of bad seasons or of an environment unfavourable in other ways. Bernier indicates that this drift to the cities had become important at the period when he travelled in India: "It happens," he wrote to Colbert, "that many of the peasantry, driven to despair by so execrable a tyranny, abandon the country, and seek a more tolerable mode of existence either in the towns or in camps." Probably this particular cause operated with greater force under Aurangzeb than under Akbar, but it is reasonable to conclude that the labouring population of the cities was reinforced by men from the country, and that a certain amount of competition existed, which would influence wages indirectly even if their amount was not the subject of direct and open bargaining. The statement made by Terry that men stood to be hired in the market-place, as they may be seen standing in some cities at the present day, indicates that a labour market did in fact exist; but very little information as to its working appears to be on record, and, apart from the particulars given by Abul Fazl, I have found only a few incidental notes of the rates at which travellers and merchants engaged domestic servants.

The facts given by Abul Fazl are important, but their significance is limited.[1] He did not attempt to make a record

[1] The facts on which this paragraph is based are scattered through the first two books of the *Ain-i Akbari.* I have discussed some of them in the *Journal* of the Royal Asiatic Society for October 1917 (p. 815). For fines, see in particular the "Pagosht Regulation" (*Ain*, translation, i. 217). If a horse lost condition, the fines came down to the water-carriers and sweepers employed in the stable. When an elephant died through neglect,

of current rates of wages, but in describing the various departments of the Imperial household he noted the rates of pay which had been approved by Akbar, or what would now be called the sanctioned scales of the establishment. It would be a mistake to regard these scales as showing the exact earnings of the Imperial servants: in some cases they had to pay for petty supplies, the actual value of which cannot be ascertained; they were liable to frequent, and occasionally ferocious, fines; and, unless Akbar's Court was entirely unlike other Oriental establishments, they had to pay a portion of their wages to their superior officer. We may say, then, that Akbar had sanctioned the following rates of wages, and that his servants could not earn more, but probably in practice got something less.

Class.	Sanctioned Rate.	Modern Equivalent.
Ordinary labourers	2 dams daily	5½ annas
Superior labourers	3 to 4 „	8½ to 11 „
Carpenters	3 „ 7 „	8½ annas to Re. 1.4
Builders	5 „ 7 „	14 „ Re. 1.4

These rates, it will be understood, applied primarily to expenditure in the Imperial Camp, which by itself formed the largest city in the Empire; their purchasing power may therefore be calculated on the basis of the prices recorded by Abul Fazl, and I have shown the modern equivalents on this basis. So calculated, the rates are, broadly speaking, intermediate between those which prevailed in Agra and in Lahore when the Wage Census was taken in the year 1911,[1] and indicate that, if Akbar's workmen received the full sanctioned rates, they were rather better off than the modern workmen of the United Provinces, but not so well off as those of the Punjab: it is more probable that they got something less than the sanctioned rates and that their actual position was a little worse; but the general conclusion to which these

the attendants (some of whom drew less than three rupees a month) had to pay the price of the animal (*idem*, p. 132), a regulation which may be held to justify the epithet ferocious used in the text.

[1] The rates for builders form a partial exception to this statement: the higher limit of Re. 1.4 prevailed in the Punjab in 1911, but farther East the rates ranged about 8 as., as against the lower rate of 14 as. in Akbar's time.

figures point is that urban real wages in the north of India stood at somewhere about the same level in Akbar's time as in 1911, and that there has been no pronounced change in the standard of remuneration of these classes of the population. This conclusion is borne out by the monthly rates sanctioned for the infantry and for various departments of the Household: in several instances the lowest grades of servants were entitled to less than two rupees monthly (65 dams for a sweeper, 60 for a camel-driver, 70 for a wrestler, and so on), while the bulk of the menials and of the ordinary foot-soldiers began at less than three rupees. The minimum for subsistence at the Court is probably marked by the lowest grade of slaves, who were allowed one dam daily, equivalent to three-quarters of a rupee monthly in the currency of the time.

I have found no corresponding figures for the remuneration of men employed in more highly specialised work, and since we must assume that the separation between different grades of labour was at least as marked under Akbar as at the present day, it is not permissible to extend to their case the conclusion drawn from the rates for general labour. We have seen that artisans were, as a rule, badly off, and they can scarcely have been able to pay high wages to their journeymen, but what they actually paid is purely a matter of conjecture until fresh sources of information come to light.

The facts available regarding the wages paid by travellers and merchants come almost entirely from the south and west of India. Terry insists on the excellence of the servants obtained for five shillings, or say two rupees a month, and he adds that they would send half this sum home; probably this statement relates to servants hired in Surat, but in any case it refers to this part of the country, as Terry went no farther north than Mandu. Della Valle, writing of Surat about ten years later, put the rate at not more than three rupees, while de Laet's informants gave from three to four rupees, which could be supplemented in some cases by commission charged on purchases. A messenger between Surat and Masulipatam was in 1614 allowed seven or eight mahmudis (say something between three and four rupees) for the journey:

he took nearly two months over it, but he wasted time on the way, and probably one month would have been sufficient. These instances appear to justify the conclusion that early in the seventeenth century foreigners could secure capable servants for somewhere about three rupees a month. What this represents in real wages is uncertain: as has been indicated in a previous chapter, prices seem to have been higher on the west coast than in Northern India, but their precise level cannot be determined, while it would not perhaps be fair to compare this rate directly with the wages (approximately 30 rupees monthly with a reasonable prospect of commission on purchases) which Terry or della Valle would have paid if they had arrived in Bombay in the year 1914. The rates struck Europeans as extraordinarily low, and taken with those which prevailed in the northern capital they enable us to understand the great development of domestic employment which, as has been shown in a previous chapter, characterised the life of India at this period.

AUTHORITIES FOR CHAPTER V

SECTION 1.—*Nil.*

SECTION 2.—Travellers tell us little of the forests through which they passed; they were unpleasant features of a journey, to be hurried through as quickly as possible. Several of them, however, refer to the bamboos of Bengal and the teak of the Western Ghats; see, *e.g.*, *Pyrard*, translation, i. 338, ii. 180. The authorities in regard to fisheries are *Ain*, translation, ii. 124, 126, 338; *Linschoten*, c. 48; *Thévenot*, 77. For the pearl-fishery, see, *e.g.*, *Hay*, 735.

SECTION 3.—As regards gold, the silence of *Tavernier* seems to me conclusive. He was specially interested in the topic and devotes some space (p. 393) to a review of Asiatic production: he had travelled widely in Southern India, and if there had been any goldfield there, we may be sure that he would have visited the mines. The metal is referred to in *Ain*, translation, ii. 171, 280, 312; some of these passages refer also to silver, the mine in Agra being mentioned on p. 181.

For lead and zinc, see *Ain*, translation, ii. 268; for copper, 173, 182, 194, 268, 280; for iron, 124, 159, 181, 230, 280, etc. An idea of the location of old workings can be obtained by referring to the entries under Copper and Iron in the index of the *Imperial Gazetteer*. For imports of copper, see *Barbosa*, 285; Xth *Decada*, i. 364; XIIth *Decada*, 20; *Thévenot*, 318. For prices of copper and other minerals, see *Journal R.A.S.*, October 1918, 375 ff. Information regarding Indian steel is collected in *Hobson-Jobson* (art. Wootz.).

The account of the diamond-fields is in *Tavernier*, 326 ff. As to salt, the Punjab mines are described in *Ain*, translation, ii. 315; *Badaoni* refers to the Sambhar Lake (ii. 45); sea-salt is indicated in *Ain*, translation, ii. 139, etc. (Bengal); 256, etc. (Gujarat); 338 (Sind); while *Pyrard* (translation, i. 359) mentions salt-pans in Malabar. *Pyrard* (ii. 257) also mentions the use of Bassein stone at Goa. For saltpetre, see *Ain*, translation, ii. 231, 253.

SECTION 4.—*Gur* or jaggery is mentioned by various writers, *e.g. Barbosa*, 346, and *Linschoten*, c. 11. For the sugar of Bengal, see *Barbosa*, 362; *Linschoten*, c. 16; or Fitch in *Purchas*, II. x. 1736. For Ahmadabad and Cambay, see *Letters Received*, i. 302. For candy, see *Ain*, translation, ii. 181; *Letters Received*, iv. 291; *Linschoten*, c. 7. Prices are given in *Ain*, translation, i. 63.

For cotton-ginning, see *Thévenot*, 21; for indigo manufacture, *Purchas*, I. iv. 430. The availability of tobacco-leaf in Gujarat is recorded in *Letters Received*, i. 298; *Terry*, 96, notes the ignorance of the art of manufacture. Practically all authorities refer to intoxicating liquor of some sort. Akbar's regulations are in *Ain*, translation, ii. 42; Jahangir's orders are in *Tuzuk*, i. 8, and an account of his own habits will be found in *Purchas*, I. iii. 222. For examples of statements regarding the supply, see *Barbosa*, 346; *Purchas*, I. iv. 424; or *Jourdain*, 124, 132.

SECTION 5.—Mention of the artistic handicrafts is made by most visitors to the country; see for examples *Barbosa*, 278; *Linschoten*, c. 9; or *Thévenot*, 36, 140. As to the scarcity of furniture, see especially *Terry*, 185, but the evidence is largely negative, and the position can best be realised by noting what is missing from the various contemporary descriptions. For Portuguese furniture, see *Pyrard*, translation, ii. 245; for that of the merchants at Rander, see *Barbosa*, 287. The nature of Indian harness and saddlery is given in detail in *Ain*, translation, i. 126-153.

The statements in the text regarding paper are based mainly on *della Valle*, 291, and *Pyrard*, translation, ii. 175, 211, 245. References to the nature of houses will be found under the chapter dealing with the standard of life. For the time taken in building the Allahabad fort, see *Purchas*, I. iv. 437.

SECTION 6.—The best account of road travel is that given by *Tavernier*, 24 ff., also 121; it is rather later than our period, but I doubt if any marked change had occurred in the interval. For the extent of the river traffic, see *Purchas*, I. iv. 432, II. x. 1733; Elliot, *History*, v. 374; *Ain*, translation, i. 280. The size of the Ganges barges is given by *Jourdain*, 162; and of those on the Jumna by Finch, in *Purchas*, I. iv. 439. For attempts to build ships in Arabia and Egypt, see *Barbosa*, 246; Xth *Decada*, ii. 178; and *Hobson-Jobson* under "Teak." The authority for Pegu is Balbi, in *Purchas*, II. x. 1728. Conti's mention of the pilgrim ships is in *Major*, 27; they are frequently referred to in *Purchas* (see, *e.g.*, I. iii. 308, 396); even such a landsman as Terry mentions their size in tuns (*idem*, II. ix. 1470). *Pyrard*, among other writers, mentions the building of carracks at Bassein (ii. 114).

SECTION 7.—For export of silk goods, see *Barbosa*, 233, 366; *Varthema*, 111. Other authorities are silent, and it is noteworthy that neither Caesar Frederic, Fitch, nor Balbi (whose narratives are placed together in *Purchas*, II. x.) gives any hint of silk goods being exported from Bengal to Pegu. For the use of silk goods in India, see *Ain*, translation, i. 88, and *Barbosa*, 297. *Tavernier's* account of production is p. 290; imports of raw material are referred to in *Garcia da Orta*, 95; *Linschoten*, c. 23; and *Pyrard*, translation, ii. 239. I take the modern production from Professor Maxwell-Lefroy in *Journal Royal Society of Arts*, 1917, pp. 290 ff. The Gujarat industry is mentioned by most visitors; see, *e.g.*, *Linschoten*, c. 10. For Kashmir, see *Ain*, translation, ii. 349; for Akbar's improvements, *idem*, i. 88; for "herb-silk," see *Hobson-Jobson* under "Grass-Cloth" and "Moonga," and the references there given.

The references to woollen goods are *Ain*, translation, i. 55, 90-96, 136. The disappointments of English merchants are mentioned frequently in *Letters Received* (*e.g.* ii. 96, 103). Terry's remark on the quality of the wool is in *Purchas*, II. ix. 1469. Carpets are referred to in various places in the early volumes of *English Factories*.

Section 8.—The assessment rates on hemp will be found in *Ain*, translation, ii. 91 ff.: the single reference to jute is ii. 123. The statement as to the use of jute clothing is quoted from the *Imperial Gazetteer*, iii. 204.

For the attitude of Europeans to the cotton-trade, see *Pyrard*, translation, ii. 245; Pyrard's observation as to the nakedness of Africa is ii. 149; for Friar Joanno, see *Purchas*, II. ix. 1450 and *passim*. Remarks as to the scantiness of clothing in the Islands will be found in *Hakluyt*, v. 26, 372, and *Purchas*, I. iii. 165. *Pyrard*, translation, ii. 173, describes the course of trade with China at this period; the quotation as to Japan is from *Letters Received*, iii. 238; *Linschoten* (c. 22) mentions the trade beyond the Philippines.

Notices of cotton goods in India are scattered through the "Account of the XII. Subas," in *Ain*, translation, ii., and will be found in the narrative of practically every European visitor. The Indus Valley industry is referred to by *Manrique*, lxii-lxx. The distribution of Cambay, Coromandel, and Bengal goods can best be traced in *Barbosa*, *passim*.

Section 9.—To appreciate the position of the artisans in towns it is desirable to study the early volumes of *Letters Received* as a whole. Particular passages bearing on the subject will be found in i. 30, 302; ii. 112; iii. 84; iv. 249; also *English Letters*, 1618–21, 161. For State workshops, see *Ain*, translation, i. 88, and *Bernier*, 259; for the poverty of artisans, see *Bernier*, 228, and *Thévenot*, 140; for the effect of famine, see *English Factories*, 1630–33, 97, 146, 158, etc. The passages referred to in connection with taxation are *Ain*, translation, ii. 66, *Terry*, 397, and *Tavernier*, 81.

Section 10.—*Bernier*, 205, speaks of the movement to the towns; for the labour market, see *Terry*, 173; his praise of Indian servants is on the same page. For the other rates quoted for the south and west, see *della Valle*, 42; *de Laet*, 117; and *Letters Received*, ii. 101, iv. 28.

The wage census referred to in the text is that of the year 1911, the figures for which were given in *Prices and Wages in India*, 32nd issue, 233 ff.

CHAPTER VI

COMMERCE

I. General Features

In a previous chapter I have insisted on the essential stability of the main lines of Indian agriculture during the last three centuries: the position in regard to Indian commerce is entirely different, and in order to realise its nature and volume in the time of Akbar, we must put out of our heads almost everything we have learned regarding its features at the present day. The revolution is all the more remarkable for the reason that the general course of trade had remained substantially unchanged for at any rate more than a thousand years: Gibbon's mordant aphorism that "the objects of oriental traffic were splendid and trifling" is in substance as applicable to the sixteenth as to the second century of our era, but such epithets are ludicrously inappropriate to the piece-goods and machinery which India now purchases, or to the food-grains, oilseeds, and fibres with which she pays her debts. The change in question occurred after Akbar's death, and it is no part of my present purpose to trace its causes and development, but its occurrence must be borne continuously in mind if we are to arrive at a correct appreciation of the facts by which our period is characterised.

In the sixteenth century India, taken as a whole, exercised an effective demand for certain limited classes of foreign goods, and she was able to pay for them by exporting a variety of her own products. The list of foreign goods in demand has been given incidentally in the last chapter; of the principal articles, three may be classed as necessaries, three groups consist of raw material, and the remainder must be described as luxury goods pure and simple, their object being to minister to the tastes of the upper classes of the population. Two of the necessaries are gold and silver, which may claim this description on account of their use in coinage, though a large proportion of the supply was used only for display: taken together they formed much the most important item in the list of imports, and the maintenance of the supply was a definite aim in the regulations enforced on the coasts and frontiers of India. The other head in this class consists of animals, principally horses, which were required in large numbers under the prevailing military system. Here too the element of luxury was not entirely absent, for serviceable horses were bred in the north of India, and the imports thither from Persia and Arabia to some extent served the purposes of display; but in the kingdoms of the south there were practically no local sources of supply, and the maintenance of the trade was essential to the security of the States concerned. The groups of materials are—first, the raw silk required for the Indian industry; second, the metals—copper, tin, zinc, lead, quicksilver—the deficiency of which has been noticed in the last chapter; and third, the ivory, coral, amber, and other products required for the artistic handicrafts. The list of imported luxury goods is longer: all kinds of precious stones, costly textiles such as silks, velvets, and brocades, spices, perfumes, and drugs of all descriptions, the miscellaneous articles usually described as China goods, European wines, African slaves, and practically anything that could be called a rarity or novelty whatever the country of its origin. In payment for these imports India sent out her various textile fabrics, pepper, and a few minor spices, certain dyes of which indigo was the most important, opium and other drugs, and a variety of other articles of less account. She was eager to sell every kind of produce, and her insatiable appetite for the precious metals rendered trade a simple matter for customers who came with money in their hands.

The means of transport show a change not less marked than that which has occurred in the commodities transported. On land there were of course no railways, and there were no metalled roads; there were the river routes in the north, and, apart from them, goods were transported, mainly on pack animals, to the nearest point at which water-carriage became available. On the sea there were numerous small ships and a few of larger size, but none comparable in capacity with even an ordinary cargo boat of the present day. Whether small or great, the sea-going vessels depended solely on the winds, and not merely their speed, but their direction, was governed by forces entirely beyond human control. Harbours had not yet been created or transformed by engineering skill, but were located wherever the conditions permitted, and most of them were closed for a considerable portion of each year. Man had not begun to interfere seriously with nature, but was still in the stage when he must accommodate himself to the opportunities she provides.

In regard to the organisation of sea-borne trade, the sixteenth century was a period of unstable equilibrium, and in order to understand the conditions prevailing at its close it is necessary to go back to the year 1498, when Vasco da Gama sailed round the Cape of Good Hope. He found the Indian Seas from Madagascar to the Straits of Malacca practically in possession of the Moslem merchants, who owned and managed most of the ships and also took an important share in the trade on land. Traders of other classes could hire space on these ships for cargo, and could travel with their goods, but they had practically no influence on the shippers other than what was derived from their demand for cargo-space, except in the cases where they owned ships for themselves. Such cases were comparatively rare: from the accounts given by Barbosa and Varthema I gather that the Moslems controlled practically all the ships on the Malabar coast, the great majority of those plying from the Gulf of

Cambay, and a large share of those on the Coromandel coast and in the waters of Bengal. Whatever numbers might be owned by Bengali, Coromandel, or Gujarati merchants, the predominance of the Moslem interest is beyond dispute, and the result is seen in the remarkable uniformity which prevailed in nautical matters right round the shores of the Indian Ocean.

The Moslems had spread along these shores as merchants, not as conquerors, and they accommodated themselves readily to the conditions of the localities where profitable trade was to be had. On the eastern coast of Africa, where there was no civilised government, they established settlements of their own; but where, as in India, they found an existing civilisation, they settled under the protection of the authorities, and acquired a privileged position owing to the fact that they could make or mar the trade of a particular port; merely by staying away they could ruin the local merchants, and, what was probably more important, they could cause serious loss to the administration, which depended on the port dues for a large part of its revenue, or to the Governor, if he had farmed the customs for his private benefit. At the end of the fifteenth century their position in the Indian seas was firmly established, and there were no signs of the advent of any dangerous competitors. It is unnecessary for my present purpose to enter into details regarding the organisation of sea-borne commerce by the Moslem merchants. Its essential feature was the concentration of business on the west coast of India, particularly at the Malabar ports, of which Calicut was then the most important. The produce of the Far East was not as a rule carried direct to the Persian Gulf or the Red Sea, a process which involved a long and sometimes dangerous voyage; the ships from Pegu and Malacca came to Calicut or some neighbouring port, where cargoes for the further voyage were made up, consisting partly of Indian goods which had been brought down the coast, and in the same way goods brought from the Red Sea were landed there for distribution in various directions. Malabar was thus the entrepôt for almost the whole trade of the Indian seas, and was a commercial centre of the first importance.[1]

This situation was transformed by the appearance of the Portuguese in Indian waters. The Arabs did not take their ships round the Cape of Good Hope, and were thus limited to two sea-routes for the trade with Europe, one through the Red Sea, the other through the Persian Gulf, both of which were subject to interference from the policy of other countries. Goods sent by the Persian Gulf had to be carried overland through Syria, and at the end of the fifteenth century this route was practically closed by the Turks. On the other route goods had to be taken across Egypt; this line remained open, but the transit dues charged by the Egyptian Government were exceedingly heavy and involved high European prices for Asiatic goods. Portugal was at this time the most enterprising nation on the sea, and the decision was taken to attempt to secure the Eastern trade by opening up a route entirely independent of other nations, and bringing produce to Europe in Portuguese ships. Commerce was not, however, the only motive underlying this decision: the capture of the Indian trade would be a serious blow to the Moslem States, at that time regarded as the enemies of Christendom, while the enterprise would afford opportunities for missionary effort in the countries with which trade was to be carried on. This combination of religious and commercial motives is the key to the activities of the Portuguese during the sixteenth century, and much of their conduct which is inexplicable from the trader's point of view finds an excuse, though not always a justification, in the missionary zeal by which the rulers of the country were distinguished.

As has been said in a previous chapter, Portugal did not aim at establishing an Empire on land. Her policy was to dominate the Indian seas, and this required only a sufficient number of fortified harbours to afford shelter for the fleets

[1] A trace of this period may be found in the English word "calico," which is almost certainly derived from Calicut. Cotton goods were not made at Calicut in any quantity, but Calicut was the port from which they were shipped for Europe, and it gave them the name by which they became known in the West.

and to maintain the supply of fighting-men. These necessary harbours were rapidly acquired, in some cases by force, in others by negotiation, and within a very few years the new power was firmly established from Mozambique to Malacca. The next step was to regulate the course of commerce, which had hitherto been practically independent of political control: trade on certain routes, and in certain goods, was declared a State monopoly, and carried on for the benefit of the King of Portugal or his nominees; outside these limits private shipping was allowed to ply, provided that a licence had been taken out and paid for, but unlicensed ships were treated as prizes of war, and sunk, burnt, or captured as circumstances might determine. The administration was, however, exceedingly corrupt when judged by modern standards: the high officers were as a rule concerned only to make money as quickly as possible, and consequently the practical working of the regulations was more elastic than is suggested by their terms; perhaps it is not too much to say that under Portuguese domination Indian merchants could carry on almost any trade they wanted to, provided they understood how to set to work, and were prepared to pay the sums demanded for the privilege.

The Moslem ship-owners were by no means disposed to submit to these regulations, but they were not able to fight the new-comers on equal terms, and they accommodated themselves to the position in various ways. For one thing, they altered their routes, and Barbosa tells us that ships from Malacca were occasionally diverted to the Coromandel coast because their owners dared not face the Portuguese on the other side of India, while those which went west avoided the coast and took the outer passage through the Maldiv Islands, in spite of the danger of shipwreck in those waters.[1] In many cases, again, the Portuguese rules were accepted, and we find Indian ships sailing under licences granted by them to various

[1] The ships of the period could not be provisioned for the long voyage from Malacca to the Red Sea. When the coast of India was closed to them the Maldiv Islands offered the only chance of getting food and water, and consequently the dangers of navigation in their neighbourhood had to be faced.

places, in particular to the pilgrim ports on the Red Sea. Where, however, the conditions were favourable, the Moslems of the coast maintained a species of irregular warfare, and treated the Portuguese ships precisely as the Portuguese treated theirs. Contemporary writers describe this conduct as piracy, and they show that it constituted a very great danger to shipping, particularly on the Malabar coast, on parts of which the "pirates" were most firmly established; one of them, indeed, went so far as to imitate the system established by the Portuguese, and issued his own licences for trade, licences which are said to have been accepted even by Portuguese subjects. The Moslems therefore had by no means been driven off the seas, and they continued to conduct much of the maritime commerce, sometimes by licence, and sometimes in defiance of their competitors. By the end of the sixteenth century the power of the Portuguese had been very greatly weakened through a variety of causes into which it is unnecessary to enter; it was shortly to collapse before the Dutch and the English, who were now preparing to secure a share in the direct Oriental trade, but this event lies just outside my period, during which the commercial domination of the coasts was shared between the Moslems and the Portuguese.[1]

It will be noticed that none of the great Indian States played any part in this struggle for the seas. They were essentially continental powers, and while they appreciated the benefits of foreign commerce, and the revenue which it brought to their seaports, they did nothing to protect it on the way. Akbar sent ships from Gujarat to the Red Sea, but they sailed under licence from the Portuguese. The sea-borne trade of Vijayanagar was placed practically in Portuguese hands by the Treaty of 1547, while the Deccan kingdom of Bijapur appears to have been content to quarrel with the

[1] The first Dutch ships rounded the Cape of Good Hope in 1596, but their earliest voyages were directed to the islands beyond Malacca. By 1609 they were established at Pulicat on the Coromandel coast. The first voyage undertaken by the English East India Company reached Sumatra in 1602; it was not until the third voyage that one of the Company's ships visited an Indian port in August 1608.

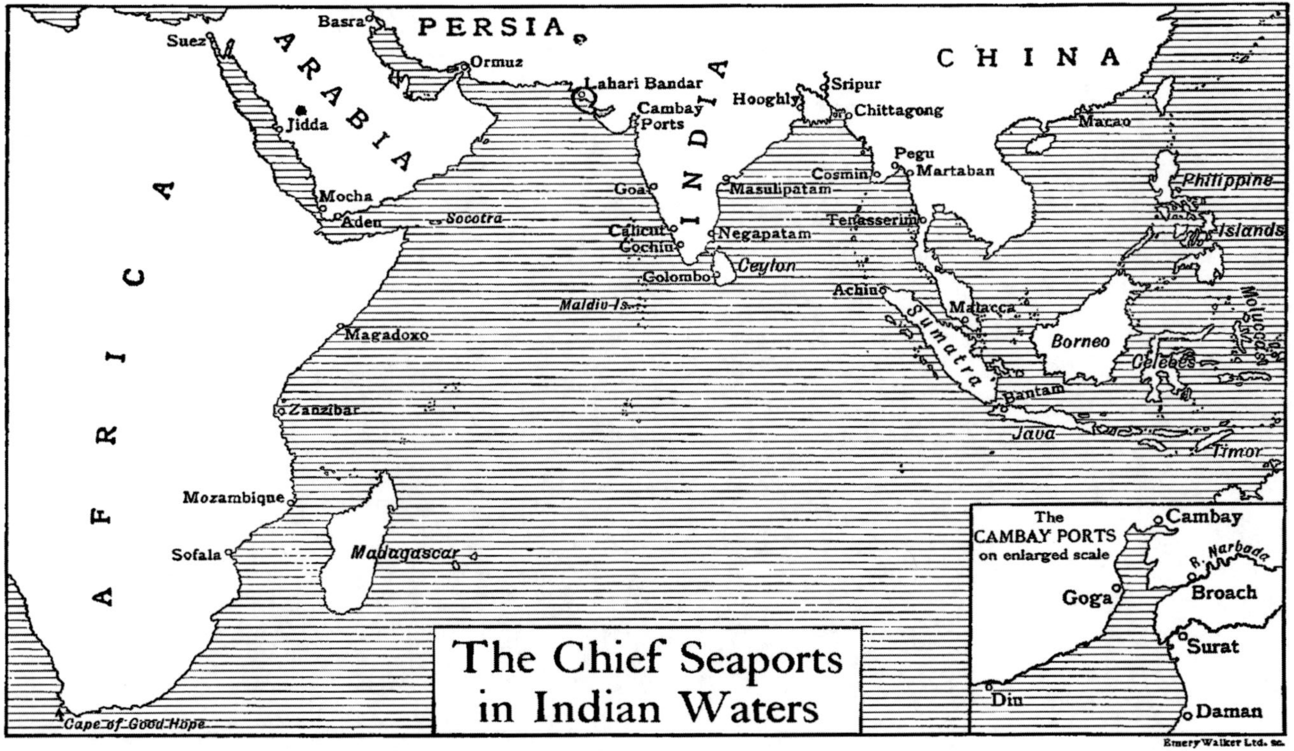

The Chief Seaports in Indian Waters
AFRICA
ARABIA
PERSIA
INDIA
CHINA
Suez
Basra
Jidda
Mocha
Aden
Socotra
Ormuz
Lahari Bandar
Cambay Ports
Goa
Calicut
Cochin
Colombo
Ceylon
Negapatam
Masulipatam
Hooghly
Sripur
Chittagong
Cosmin
Pegu
Martaban
Tenasserim
Achin
Sumatra
Malacca
Bantam
Java
Borneo
Celebes
Moluccas
Timor
Philippine Islands
Macao
Maldiv Is.
Magadoxo
Zanzibar
Mozambique
Sofala
Madagascar
Cape of Good Hope
The CAMBAY PORTS on enlarged scale
Cambay
R. Narbada
Broach
Goga
Surat
Diu
Daman
Emery Walker Ltd. sc.

Portuguese on land, and in any case could scarcely have hoped to drive them from the ocean. The Zamorin of Calicut did what he could to protect the "pirates," some of whom paid him tribute, but he too was unable to stand against the Portuguese in open warfare, and apart from his clandestine activities the merchants of the country could look to no protector, but were dependent on their own resources.

II. The Principal Indian Seaports

The actual position of Indian sea-borne commerce at this period can be described most clearly by taking each port, or group of ports, in turn, and indicating the relations which it maintained with other portions of the sea-board. Much of this ground will be unfamiliar to students knowing only the commerce of the present day. We shall not meet the names of Calcutta, Bombay, Madras, or Karachi, which now handle so large a proportion of the trade of India, or of Rangoon, Singapore, Hong-kong, Sydney, or Cape Town, in the wider Eastern seas; in their place, we have to deal with a longer list of ports, many of which are now of very slight importance, while of some even the names have disappeared from modern maps. The position of the Indian seaports is indicated on the map illustrating Chapter I., while the sketch on the opposite page shows how they lay with regard to the ports of other countries. The nature and size of the vessels which sailed from these ports will be discussed in a subsequent section: for the present, it must suffice to say that they fall into four classes—Portuguese carracks, pilgrim ships sailing to the Red Sea, ordinary sea-going merchant vessels, and small coasting craft. In terms of the system of ship measurement prevailing at the time, carracks were from 1500 to 2000 tuns,[1] pilgrim-ships varied from 500 to 1500 tuns, ordinary merchant vessels rarely exceeded 400 and averaged probably less than 200 tuns, while coasting craft were of all sizes from about 60 tuns downwards.

Starting from the north-west of India, it is evident from the

[1] For this word see the note on p. 167.

lie of the country that there must always have been a seaport somewhere near the mouth of the Indus, but the location has varied with changes in the river's course, and perhaps with other causes of whose nature we are ignorant. The port of Daibal or Dewal, which was familiar to the early Arab geographers, had by this time disappeared, but its name survived in the form Diūl, or Diūl-Sind, which was commonly applied to the whole region, and occasionally to the particular harbour in existence at the end of the sixteenth century. The usual name of this harbour was Lahari Bandar, and it was situated on one of the mouths of the river, in direct communication by water with Tatta, Multan, and Lahore.[1] Lower Sind (Tatta) had recently come under Akbar's rule, and Portuguese trading representatives were established in friendly relations with the Mogul officials at the port. The exports consisted of cotton goods, indigo, and a variety of country produce, carried either westwards to Persia and Arabia, or southwards along the coast of India; imports were of the usual type—metals (particularly silver larins from Persia), spices, and a variety of luxury goods for distribution in the cities served by the Indus and its tributaries. I have found scarcely any indications that sea-going vessels were at this period owned by local traders. The port was awkwardly situated with regard to the monsoons, and while it was visited occasionally by ships on the Ormuz route, most of its traffic appears to have been conducted by coasting boats to Persia and to the Gulf of Cambay.

Passing southwards from Sind, we come to the group of Cambay ports which, taken collectively, were at this period the most important in India. Surat, Broach, and Cambay itself were the largest, but several others were open; all were under the more or less effective rule of the Mogul Empire, and

[1] For the ports on the Indus, see *Hobson-Jobson* under "Diūl-Sind" and "Larrybunder," and the notes in Mr. Longworth Dames' translation of *Barbosa*, i. 105, 106. Daibal is mentioned frequently in the extracts from Arab geographers translated in the first volume of Elliot's *History*. *Barbosa* (p. 266) writes of "the kingdom of Diūl." Salbank, in *Purchas* (I. iii. 238), speaks merely of Sinde; Payton (*idem*, I. iv. 495) of Diūl; Withington (*idem*, I. iv. 485) of Lowribander; and this last name appears elsewhere with a wide variety of spelling.

while the Portuguese traded with them extensively, they were not established in force within the Gulf, but dominated its shipping from their fortified posts at Daman and Diu. This arrangement was effective from their point of view. The navigation of the Gulf was dangerous for large ships, and it was usual to load and discharge at Diu, Gogai, or some other convenient roadstead, whence flotillas of small boats could go as far as Cambay, through the shallow water at the extreme north of the Gulf. Diu is situated at the southern point of Kathiawar, Daman faces it on the mainland, and holding these two posts in strength the Portuguese could maintain an effective watch over the shipping which entered the Gulf, and could enforce their system of licences without reference to the Mogul authorities on land. Provided with licences, or occasionally defying the Portuguese, ships from this coast sailed west and south, carrying on trade with Arabia, Africa, and the Straits of Malacca: they exported to these markets large quantities of textiles and miscellaneous merchandise, and brought back metals, spices, and luxury goods of all descriptions. There was in addition an important passenger traffic, the only one which has to be taken into account at this period. The Gulf ports, and particularly Surat, were the starting-point of the pilgrim-route to the holy places of Arabia, and large numbers of travellers from India made this journey every year; it is probable that many of them carried goods for sale in order to meet the expenses of the later stages of the pilgrimage, and in any case the traffic in passengers and merchandise was closely interconnected.

The Gulf had at this time no direct trade with Europe. The Portuguese loaded their homeward fleet at Goa or further south, and Cambay goods for Portugal, together with provisions and other merchandise for the whole west coast, were carried down to Goa in fleets of "frigates," small coasting boats which could be propelled by oars.[1] A fleet of these

[1] This use of the word frigate is apt to mislead readers familiar with the literature of a later period, when a frigate was a large fighting-ship, the equivalent of the modern cruiser, and in point of size second only to the "ships of the line." At the beginning of the seventeenth century the word is used consistently in the sense indicated in the text. An erroneous idea of the

frigates, which was known as the *kafila* (caravan), might consist of as many as 300 boats, and usually two or three fleets sailed in each year: they were escorted by fighting vessels, but this precaution did not always ensure safety, for the "pirates" watched eagerly for this opportunity, and were occasionally able to destroy or capture a substantial number. The *kafila* was a prize worth fighting for. The cargoes included large quantities of piece-goods, indigo, and various other articles for foreign markets, besides wheat and other provisions, and most of the necessaries and comforts required by the Portuguese population.[1]

Going south from the Gulf of Cambay, we should expect to hear next of Bombay, but at this period the name was almost unknown to European writers, and the harbour was of no commercial importance.[2] Three ports, however, must be noticed on this part of the coast—Bassein, lying just north of the island of Bombay; Chaul, a short distance to the south; and Dabul, now known as Dabhol, a small port in the Ratnagiri district. Bassein was in the possession of the Portuguese; its trade was not large, but as has been mentioned in the last chapter it was a shipbuilding centre

---

kafila is given on page 423 of Hunter's *The Indian Empire* (edition of 1893), where it is stated that "a single fleet of Portuguese merchantmen sailing from Goa to Cambay or Surat would number as many as 150 or 250 carracks." At this period there were certainly never more than 10 carracks in Indian waters at one time: I have found no record of a carrack entering the Gulf of Cambay; and it is practically certain that if a carrack had ever got into those treacherous waters it would have been unable to get out. Sir William Hunter was misled by an error in the reference which he quoted without verification, by which "carracks" were substituted for "frigates," and the capacity of the fleet was consequently multiplied about forty-fold.

[1] The Portuguese stations on the west coast depended for their supplies far more on the coasting trade than on the resources of their immediate neighbourhood. *Pyrard* (translation, ii. 245) gives a long list of the articles obtained from Surat and Cambay, including, besides provisions, such commodities as paper, bedsteads, cabinets, opium, and wax. The coasting trade from Bengal was also of considerable importance to this region.

[2] *Barbosa* (p. 281), writing of a place which he calls Tana-Majambu, says there was "a right good haven, with a fair trade"; but in his scale of epithets the word fair means very little. In *Hobson-Jobson* the name is interpreted as Thana-Bombay, but Mr. Longworth Dames, in his translation of *Barbosa* (i. 152, note), suggests that the second portion most probably indicates Mahim, which is situated at the north of the island of Bombay.

of some importance. Chaul, also held by the Portuguese, had the silk industry to which reference has already been made; it had thus a connection with China, and it carried on a direct trade with the Red Sea and the Persian Gulf, but most of its silk goods were probably consumed in India. Dabul was not actually in Portuguese hands, but traded with Ormuz and Mocha, and Jourdain noted that it owned nine sea-going vessels.

Next, we come to Goa and Bhatkal.[1] Before its conquest by the Portuguese, Goa had belonged to the Deccan, while Bhatkal had served Vijayanagar, and had consequently enjoyed a very considerable trade; the Portuguese, however, obtained by treaties and other means a practical monopoly of the Vijayanagar trade, and Bhatkal appears to have declined, as we hear little about it at the end of the century. Goa, on the other hand, was a port of the first importance, and as an entrepôt occupied, along with Cochin, to a great extent the place formerly held by Calicut. Local exports were not great, but produce from a large part of India and from some adjoining countries was brought here to be made up into cargoes for distant destinations, or to be distributed along the west coast, and foreign imports were in like manner distributed from this centre over almost the whole coast-line of Western India. Local trade had been important while the Empire of Vijayanagar remained intact. Goa had then enjoyed the bulk of the luxury trade, and, what was still more profitable, commercially as well as politically, the import of horses for the southern kingdoms; the fall of Vijayanagar had however reduced the luxury trade to small dimensions, horses were not at the moment in very great demand, and at the end of the century Goa depended mainly on its business as an entrepôt.[2]

[1] There is occasional confusion between two places, Bhatkal and Baitkul. The former is marked on modern maps, while the latter lay between Bhatkal and Goa, close to Karwar. It is not always easy to make out which of these is indicated by the diversified spelling of the sixteenth century. See *Hobson-Jobson* under the two names.

[2] Mr. Sewell (*A Forgotten Empire*, pp. 156, 210), rightly lays stress on the decline of the Vijayanagar trade as a cause of the decay of the Portuguese power. Taken by itself, the blow would not have been fatal to an honest

The foreign trade of Goa and Cochin (for, as we shall see, the two ports were worked on a single system) followed four main lines—to the Far East, Persia and Arabia, Africa and Europe. The first destination of the East-bound ships was Malacca, the Moslem town in the Straits which had been one of the earliest acquisitions of the Portuguese. The ships carried textiles and other Indian merchandise to this market, and loaded for the return voyage spices, gold, and miscellaneous articles usually described as China goods—porcelain, lacquered ware, camphor, and various drugs and perfumes. Spices were the primary object of this branch of commerce: Sumatra and Java furnished pepper, cloves came from the Moluccas, mace and nutmegs from the island of Banda, and the quantities of these goods required to supply the whole of Europe and a large part of Asia made up in the aggregate a trade of substantial volume and very great value, when judged by the standards prevailing at the time. Gold could be obtained from Java, Sumatra, Borneo, and Celebes, while China and Japan supplied a large variety of goods not obtainable elsewhere. In addition to the commerce with Malacca and the Spice Islands, the Portuguese sent a few ships farther afield. Pyrard describes this adventurous voyage in some detail. The ships from Goa sold their cargo at Macao, the port for Canton, and reloaded with China goods for Japan. In Japan they sold these goods mainly for silver; then returning to Macao, they invested the silver in China goods for Malacca, where they concluded the circle of operations by buying spices for India. The whole voyage took about three years, and was "reserved" as a monopoly by the Portuguese authorities —that is to say, the privilege of taking a ship to China and Japan was granted, or more usually sold, to a grandee anxious to undertake the highly speculative enterprise.

Trade to Persia and Arabia centred in Ormuz, which was held in strength by the Portuguese, and where all goods were trans-

---

and efficient administration, which in the circumstances of the time would have found fresh outlets for its commercial energy, but the Portuguese power was decadent, and the fall of Vijayanagar did much to hasten a collapse which was already impending.

ferred to smaller vessels for the voyage up the Persian Gulf. The chief articles brought to India from this part of Asia were coined silver in the form of larins, pearls, horses, and silk goods, while cotton cloth was the staple of the export trade. With the Red Sea the Portuguese had at this time comparatively little concern: the principal ports—Aden, Mocha, and Jidda—had come under the power of the Turks; the first named was decayed, and ships from India discharged their cargoes at either Mocha or Jidda, but the Portuguese did not ordinarily pass the Straits. For the African trade they had an important fort at Mozambique and other stations at Sofala (farther south), Mombasa, Magadoxo (on the Somali coast), and elsewhere. These ports received Indian textile goods, spices, and provisions for the Portuguese inhabitants, while they exported ivory, amber, ebony, slaves, and especially gold. Gold was the real foundation of the trade with Sofala and Mozambique. This part of the coast was at the time commonly identified with Ophir, whence King Solomon had drawn his supplies, and in any case the quantity available was very great when judged by the standards then current. Mozambique was one of the most profitable centres of the Portuguese administration, and trade with it was "reserved" by the authorities at Goa on the same lines as the voyage to China and Japan.

Lastly, we come to the trade with Europe. A fleet sailed for India each year from Lisbon; it consisted of four or five carracks and perhaps some smaller vessels; it was not allowed to call anywhere except in case of need, and it arrived at either Goa or Cochin according to the weather experienced on the voyage. These fleets were conducted mainly for the profit of the Government, and carried on the King's account only coined silver, but private merchants were allowed to send out other goods, chiefly metals and articles of luxury. The annual return fleets were smaller, because losses by shipwreck were heavy, and there were usually no vessels fit for the voyage in reserve; thirty-three carracks sailed from India in the ten years 1590–1599, of which only sixteen reached Portugal in safety. Carracks which had reached Goa took on board part of their cargo at that port, but ordinarily completed their loading at Cochin; those which had arrived at the southern port loaded there, goods from Goa being forwarded in coasting boats. Part of each ship was reserved for pepper, which was shipped on account of the State, but the remainder of the space could be secured for private merchandise, and overloading was one of the causes which contributed to the frequent losses of ships on the homeward voyage.

South of Goa lay the various Malabar ports between Mangalore and Cape Comorin, of which Calicut and Cochin were the most important. Cochin was definitely Portuguese, and was second only to Goa in importance as an entrepôt, while it was the headquarters of the export trade in pepper. Calicut may be regarded as the centre of opposition to the Portuguese, and it was in this neighbourhood that the Arab "pirates" had their principal strongholds. The Malabar ports differed from those of Cambay in furnishing for export practically no goods of local manufacture: pepper was the chief product, and by far the most important export, and with this exception their local trade may almost be described as retail. About this period we hear of the Moslem shippers of these ports chiefly as endeavouring to send ships to the Red Sea without obtaining licences from the Portuguese; the endeavours bulk largely in the chronicles, but they do not represent a large volume of commerce, and much of the local activity related to the coasting trade, which brought grain and other provisions from the east coast, and distributed the various products of the coco-palm.

At the extreme south of India the Portuguese dominated the coast of Ceylon with a fortress at Colombo, but they were not on friendly terms with the people of the interior, and had much difficulty in maintaining their position. The island exported cinnamon and some precious stones, while India supplied it with provisions and clothing. The Indian ports facing Ceylon were apparently of little importance, and the first noticeable place on the east coast is Negapatam, where the Portuguese had a representative, but did not claim to exercise political authority. This port and others as far to the north as Pulicat carried on in the aggregate a substantial volume of trade: they exported piece-goods to the Straits, and received thence spices and various "China goods"; Pegu took piece-goods, yarn, and opium, and returned chiefly gold, silver, and precious stones, and there was also a considerable coasting trade with Bengal in one direction, and with Ceylon and Malabar in the other. Farther north again is Masulipatam, at this time the chief port of the kingdom of Golconda; it was an important place in 1590, trading with Pegu and Malacca as well as with other parts of India, and its commerce was shortly to be extended largely by the establishment of a Dutch agency, which developed a valuable business, importing spices, metals, and luxury goods, and loading textiles for the Far East.

North of Masulipatam there is a long stretch of coast on which we read of no important trade, and then we come to the harbours of Bengal. The names of these as given by contemporary writers are confusing, and the precise position is not altogether free from doubt: I have examined it in Appendix C, and here it must suffice to say that at this period there seem to have been three principal ports, Satgaon-Hooghly, Sripur, and Chittagong. The first of these was situated some way up the Hooghly river: Satgaon was the old port, but had silted up, and Abul Fazl tells us that Hooghly, about a mile distant, was the more important, and that it was the resort of Christian and other merchants. As a matter of fact it was largely a Portuguese settlement, though not under Portuguese administration: the inhabitants included numerous outlaws who had fled from Portuguese jurisdiction and formed a community of their own, living at peace with the officers of the Mogul, but accustomed to prey upon his subjects. Sripur was situated on the Meghna, close to Sonargaon, which was at this time the eastern capital of Bengal;[1] its site has been washed away, but the language used regarding it by Fitch and by the Jesuit missionaries

[1] Sonargaon lay about fifteen miles east of Dacca, which became the capital of Bengal in the year 1608. Dacca is not, I think, mentioned by any of the European visitors of this period.

shows that it was a place of great importance. As I have indicated in Chapter I., Chittagong was at this period probably outside the limits of the Mogul Empire and subject to Arakan, but here the Portuguese outlaws appear to have done very much what they pleased, and to have shared in the piratical enterprises for which the inhabitants were famed. The commerce of these ports was important: through the waterways of the Gangetic delta they were in easy communication with a large part of Bengal, and with Northern India as far as Agra: they exported textiles and large quantities of provisions (rice, sugar, etc.) and other country produce, and imported silver and other metals, spices, and miscellaneous goods from Pegu and Malacca as well as from other parts of India.

The general result of this survey of the coast may be stated in a very few words. The chief outlets for the produce of the country were (1) the Cambay ports, (2) Bengal, (3) the Coromandel coast, and (4) the Indus, the order in which I have given them indicating my view of their relative importance. To these must be added the Malabar coast with its valuable speciality, pepper, while lastly we have Goa as the great centre of collection and distribution in connection with the trade with distant countries. The next step is to review the position in the foreign seaports with which this trade was carried on.

III. The Principal Foreign Ports in the Indian Seas

In the last section we followed the coast of India as far eastwards as Chittagong. Beyond this port there is a stretch of coast-line which during our period belonged to the kingdom of Arakan and was of very slight commercial importance. The next kingdom, Pegu, had a much larger trade, which centred in three ports, Cosmin which was somewhere near the present Bassein, the Pegu river as far as the city of the same name, and, farther to the east, Martaban at the mouth of the Salween. The inhabitants of the country appear to have taken very little share in the foreign sea-borne trade, which was carried on by the Portuguese and by Indian Moslems; the former had agencies at the ports, but I gather that up to the end of the century they had not made good a claim to territorial authority. The main lines of trade ran to Malacca and Achin, to Bengal, and to the Coromandel coast, but there was also a direct connection with the Red Sea. Malacca and Achin supplied spices and China goods; India furnished textiles, dyed yarns, and some drugs, particularly opium; while the Red Sea sent European cloth and other luxury-goods. Merchants came to Pegu mainly to obtain gold, silver, and precious stones, the form of incense known as benzoin or benjamin, metals, and a variety of minor commodities, while there was a potential, if not an actual, export of shipbuilding materials from Martaban; apart from Indian textiles and opium, the country did not need imports very urgently, and Caesar Frederic insists naively that merchants lost on the goods they brought and looked for profit entirely to those which they carried away. At the end of the sixteenth century the trade of Pegu was disorganised as the result of the series of wars to which reference has already been made, and the description which has just been given applies to the normal position rather than to our precise period.

The next portion of the coast is Tenasserim, concerning which there is little contemporary information. It is true that Varthema purports to give an account of it, but he places it somewhere north of the Coromandel coast in India, and it is possible that he confused the names of Tenasserim and Orissa. Barbosa tells us that in his time there were Arab and "gentile" merchants, owning ships and trading to Bengal and Malacca, and that the volume of commerce was considerable. Caesar Frederic, writing after the middle of the century, makes little of the trade with the exception of the export of an intoxicating liquor known as *nipa*. Fitch mentions only the export of tin from Tavoy; and it may perhaps be inferred that the trade of this coast was of small volume, but that it furnished an important contribution to the limited supplies of metals which reached India.

We now come to Malacca, situated in the Straits between

Sumatra and the Malay Peninsula. As a commercial centre Malacca was a creation of the Moslem merchants, and before the arrival of the Portuguese was the entrepôt of the entire trade between the Indian and the China seas. Barbosa wrote that it "is the richest trading port, and contains the greatest merchants, and the most extensive shipping and traffic that exists in the whole world." The population was cosmopolitan, and besides the wealthy Moslem merchants, we hear of Chettis from the Coromandel coast, and of natives of Java and various other islands, being settled in the town. There were practically no local products, and even food was for the most part imported: the importance of the place consisted in its being the centre of exchange for goods from China, Siam, and the Islands, with those from India, Arabia, and Europe. At an earlier period the Chinese had been accustomed to take their ships as far as the entrance to the Red Sea and the head of the Persian Gulf, but they gradually curtailed their voyages, and in the fifteenth century they ceased to come even as far as the Malabar coast; the reason for the change is unknown, but we may assume that Chinese and Moslems alike found that commerce could be carried on most conveniently at the central market of Malacca, and that the trade settled down on these lines. As we have seen in the last chapter, ships from China occasionally reached the Coromandel coast even in the later years of the sixteenth century, but these visits were clearly exceptional; the bulk of the Chinese ships reached Malacca in the autumn, discharged their cargo there, and returned with merchandise which had been brought from the Red Sea, India, and the islands of the Archipelago. The ships from Western India arrived somewhat earlier, as they had to pass Ceylon before the opening of the monsoon, and they left Malacca on their return voyage about the end of December. Meanwhile smaller vessels brought the produce of Pegu, Siam, Cochin China, Java, Banda, Borneo, and the Moluccas, so that a great variety of goods changed hands in this central market.

It was inevitable that the Portuguese should aim at securing a place of such commercial value, and they occupied it forcibly in the year 1511, and organised much of the trade in their own interests. The importance of Malacca was maintained throughout the century, but owing to the fiscal measures of the Portuguese and to the severity with which they were enforced, its monopoly gradually passed away, and other centres of exchange came into competition with it as time went on; the early English merchants found that Bantam, on the western coast of Java, was a great centre for the purchase of Chinese products, while Achin, at the north-west point of Sumatra, was also of considerable importance, and was definitely hostile to the Portuguese pretensions. The distribution of trade had thus been widened, but its essential nature remained unchanged, and a share in it was the chief lure which brought the Dutch and the English into the Indian seas. The effect of their advent lies, however, outside the period now under consideration, during which Indian commerce with the Far East was conducted either through Malacca or through the neighbouring ports which had entered into competition with it. Malacca and its neighbours offered collectively one of the principal markets for Indian textiles, and also received substantial quantities of provisions and other goods, while their contribution to India's needs included spices, raw silk, gold, and a long list of commodities, nearly all of which come under the head of luxuries.

As regards the countries lying east of the Straits of Malacca, it must suffice to say that the Portuguese were established at Macao on the coast of China, at agencies in Japan, and in the principal islands of the Archipelago. Some way eastwards of Macao we meet the Spaniards settled in the Philippine Islands as an outpost of their American dominions, and thus pass beyond the limits of the authority of the Portuguese.[1]

[1] It will be remembered that "the Indies," in the widest sense of the term, had been partitioned between Spain and Portugal. At the period of which I am writing, Portugal had become temporarily subject to the King of Spain, but the separation of commercial interests between the two nations was strictly maintained, and everything that was done in the Indian seas was done in the name of "the King of Portugal," though that position was in fact occupied by the King of Spain. Couto gives instances of the commercial rivalry between the two nations, as for instance in the China market (XII. *Decada*, 243).

The Spanish trade in the Pacific Ocean had at this time little direct concern with India, though as has already been mentioned Indian textiles found their way to the coast of America; indirectly, its interest lies, I think, in the fact that it brought silver from Mexico to Asia, and so contributed to maintain the supplies on which India drew. Australia was still unknown to Europeans, and the limits of trade in this direction appear to be marked by the Portuguese settlement in the island of Timor.

Passing from Malacca across the Indian Ocean, we come to the coast of Africa. There were practically no signs of civilisation in the country now known as South Africa: ships from Europe occasionally put in at some point on the coast and obtained provisions from the inhabitants, but the first place which was a regular centre of trade was Sofala. From this place northwards to Cape Gardafui the commerce of the country had been developed by the Moslem merchants, who had established trading stations in suitable localities, independent of the native inhabitants, but usually in friendly relations with them: the most desirable of these stations had, however, been seized by the Portuguese, and the bulk of the East African trade was at our period firmly in their hands. As has already been indicated, gold was the most valuable product of the country, but there were also supplies of such luxury-goods as slaves, and of materials like amber, ebony, and ivory for the Indian luxury-crafts. Imports from India consisted mainly of the needs of the Portuguese stations, which could obtain comparatively little in the way of local supplies, and were dependent on the ships for much of their food and all their clothing; so far as I have been able to ascertain, the country itself took scarcely anything except beads, which were manufactured in Gujarat, and the small quantity of textile goods required by such of the inhabitants as had begun to wear clothing.

The Portuguese power was much less in evidence in the Red Sea. The occupation of Aden had indeed been one of the objects of the policy intended to secure complete control of the European trade, and the port was for a time in

Portuguese hands, but they had failed to hold it, and at the end of the century the Arabian coast was definitely under the domination of the Turks; Portuguese ships did not at this time usually enter the Red Sea, but they enforced the licence-system from their bases in India, or occasionally by means of fighting fleets sent to the Straits of Bab-el-Mandeb. The Indian ships did not pursue their voyage as far as the Gulf of Suez, but landed their cargoes at some port on the coast, where they were met by caravans as well as by vessels coming from the North. The location of this port of exchange, called the "staple" by contemporary writers, varied from time to time; about the year 1600, Aden was almost deserted, and trade centred either at Mocha which lies inside the Straits of Bab-el-Mandeb, or farther north at Jidda, the port of Mecca.[1] The trade from the North was valuable rather than extensive; merchants from Cairo, Constantinople, and various places in the Levant brought fine stuffs of wool or silk, and some metals, particularly coined gold and silver, but the volume of shipping was not great, and the season of trading was narrowly determined by the prevailing winds. Indian ships were more numerous; they brought a variety of piece-goods, as well as indigo and miscellaneous produce from India, and spices and other merchandise from farther east, while in addition they carried what was for the period a very large number of passengers, on their way to the sacred places in Arabia.[2] The opposite coast of the Red Sea contributed gold, ivory, and slaves, the Abyssinians in particular being in much demand, while Arabia itself furnished the market with horses, coffee, madder, and certain drugs and perfumes.

The coast of Arabia from Aden to Muscat was then, as now, of little commercial importance. Muscat was held by the Portuguese, but at this period their principal strength in these seas was located at Ormuz at the mouth of the Persian

[1] *Jourdain*, who was at Mocha in 1609, says (p. 103) that the "staple" had recently been removed to that port from Jidda.

[2] *Terry* (p. 130) speaks enthusiastically of "the ship" which usually went from Surat to Mocha, and says that in the year he left India it brought back 1700 pilgrim-passengers.

Gulf. This was the usual terminus of sea-going ships, the trade to Basra being carried on in smaller boats, and Ormuz was thus the "staple" of the Gulf as Mocha or Jidda was of the Red Sea. There was very little local trade, for the settlement was on a barren island and obtained even its ordinary provisions from the mainland, but much valuable merchandise changed hands. India and the countries farther east sent textile goods, spices, and other commodities in demand in Persia and as far as the Mediterranean, and the ships carried back coined silver in the form of larins, horses, dried fruits, and such luxury-goods as Persian silks and carpets, while the pearl fisheries at Bahrain on the opposite side of the Gulf also found their market among the merchants visiting the place. From Ormuz eastwards to Sind the coast was inhospitable and infested by pirates, and thus we have accomplished the peregrination of the Indian seas, which began at the mouth of the Indus. To complete our survey of the sea-borne commerce of India it remains only to take into account the trade with Ceylon and the smaller islands lying in the Indian Ocean; its volume was not great, and it was conducted mainly by coasting craft. We have still to follow the land frontier, which is, however, of much less interest than might be inferred from its geographical extent.

IV. Trade Routes on the Land Frontier

So far as can be judged from contemporary accounts, the merchandise passing the land frontiers of India was of small importance at this period; the routes open to trade were few, and long intervals elapsed between the passage of successive caravans. On the north-east there was a caravan route to China, but apparently it was not in regular use. Sir Thomas Roe was told in 1615 that a caravan went to China yearly from Agra,[1] but a few years earlier its departure was regarded as doubtful, and when in 1598 Father Hieronymus Xavier was planning a missionary journey, he decided not to

[1] Terry adds that the journey occupied more than two years "from Agra to the walls of China" (*Purchas*, II. ix. 1468).

take this route, though "some people" said it was open at the time, but to make for Kabul, whence the road to China was "worn" by the feet of merchants. We may perhaps conclude that there was some intercourse by way of the Brahmaputra valley, but that the stream of commerce was irregular and its volume very small. From the Brahmaputra to the Khyber Pass I have not come across any traces of a through trade-route: Abul Fazl tells of various commodities reaching India from the North, but most of them appear to be Himalayan products, and probably the trade with Tibet was of even less importance than is the case at present; while Finch notes that there was no passage for caravans from Kashgar to Kashmir, though a certain amount of merchandise was carried by porters. Practically, therefore, there were only two regular routes on the entire frontier—from Lahore to Kabul, and from Multan to Kandahar. Kabul was a large commercial centre, and a meeting-place for merchants from India, Persia, and the countries to the North, while it lay on the route from India to the main caravan-road between Western China and Europe: Kandahar was the doorway from India to the greater part of Persia, and both routes carried a considerable volume of traffic when judged by standards appropriate to the conditions prevailing at the time.

These conditions were inconsistent with the passage of any really heavy traffic as the term is now understood. Conveyance was effected by means of pack-animals, as the roads were not fit for vehicles, while the danger of theft and violence was usually too great to permit of the passage of small or unprotected convoys. Merchants were therefore accustomed to wait at the recognised starting-points until a sufficient number had gathered to form an effective caravan, one which would be able to resist attack, and they might have to wait for a considerable time. Thus the roads did not carry a steady stream of traffic: they were usually, I take it, empty, but at long intervals a large body of animals might pass. Manrique for instance tells us that, having missed a caravan at Multan, he found he would have to wait six months for the next. Fortunately for him, a nobleman with a large following was setting out for Persia, and he was able to join this party, but it is clear that ordinary mercantile caravans were few and far between, as indeed was commonly the case in large parts of Western Asia at this period.

Some idea of the journey to Kabul can be obtained from the account of the missionary Benedict Goez, who travelled by this route from Lahore to China. He started with a caravan of about 500 men. There were alarms of thieves between Attock and Peshawar: after passing the latter place they found it necessary to obtain a guard of 400 soldiers; and while going through a pass they had to clear the high ground of marauders, who were accustomed to roll stones down on caravans. The party was on one occasion attacked, and many were wounded, but eventually they reached Kabul, where they halted because "some of the merchants would go no farther, and others durst not, being so few." Goez, however, made up a party large enough to travel, and pursued his journey: we need not follow him farther, but he was by no means at the end of his adventures. The other route leading from Multan to Kandahar was followed a few years later by two English merchants on the affairs of the East India Company. They joined a caravan two stages beyond Multan, where it was waiting for an armed guard, and the party proceeded in safety as far as a fort maintained for the protection of travellers. No supplies were available on the route, and the inhabitants were throughout on the watch for an opportunity to steal, while the captain of the fort extorted blackmail from the travellers he was appointed to protect. From this fort the road was apparently safe for seven marches, but at the next post they were delayed for three days settling the amount of the commander's blackmail. After this they came to a pass where many caravans had been cut off, and again they paid blackmail, this time to the inhabitants. One more fort was passed, where again money had to be paid, and then they reached Kandahar. At this point the caravan broke up: the most dangerous part of the way had been passed, while the country ahead was so desert that only small parties could hope to find fodder and water sufficient for their needs. In the year 1615, when this journey was made, the sea route to Persia was closed by war, and the Kandahar road was consequently crowded; the number of camels passing in a year from Lahore was reported to be from 12,000 to 14,000, which would carry a total load of perhaps 3000 tons, including baggage and provisions for the journey as well as merchandise. In ordinary times, however, the number of camels was barely 3000, so that the total load would be about 600 or 700 tons; much of the road was desert, and supplies would account for a considerable portion of the total.

Other accounts of similar journeys present the same picture of delays, anxiety, blackmail, and occasional attacks; and these are accounts of caravans which reached their destination, not of those which were destroyed on the way. The scope for this method of transit was thus strictly limited to goods of high value in proportion to their bulk, and promising a very large proportionate profit at their destination; the traffic was not negligible, but it may be questioned whether it bore a larger proportion to the sea traffic of the time than the land trade of India bears to the sea trade at the present day.

V. The Direct Trade with Europe

The description of India's foreign commerce contained in the preceding sections aims at conveying only a general idea of the direction in which the principal commodities were carried, and it requires to be supplemented by an examination of the data which are available to indicate the volume of the flow. Before, however, we enter on this inquiry it may be worth while to turn aside for a moment in order to set out the causes which led to the development of the direct trade by sea with Western Europe, a subject in regard to which various misconceptions are prevalent, among them the idea that the foreign merchants were attracted by the lure of India's wealth. It is, I think, true that in the fifteenth century the Indies, in the widest sense of the term, were popularly supposed to be full of gold, silver, and precious stones, and it is probable that this idea influenced some of the individuals who took part in the early adventures to the East. Individual adventures, however, counted for very little: the new commerce was developed, not by individuals, but by States or powerful corporations, actuated by motives regarding which there is no room for uncertainty. The King of Portugal first, and later the Dutch and English Companies, sent ships to the Indian seas with the definite object of making money by trade: it was known that certain goods which commanded high prices in Western Europe were obtainable at low prices in the East; it was hoped that the Indies would be ready to buy many of the special products of Europe; and each seafaring nation in turn set to work to secure the largest possible share of this potentially important commerce.

The goods which Western Europe required from the Indies in the fifteenth century may be described shortly as spices and drugs: most of them were wanted in quite small quantities, but an exception must be made in regard to pepper, the use of which was widespread notwithstanding the high cost of transit, and there is really very little exaggeration in the statement that pepper is the historical foundation of the direct trade between India and Western Europe. To understand the intensity of the European demand for spices requires some knowledge of the social life of the time. Much meat was eaten in the more northerly countries, but under the prevailing system of agriculture animals could be killed for meat only in the summer and autumn, and provision for the rest of the year was made by preserving meat killed when it was in season. This was effected in two ways, by salting, or by "powdering": the latter process involved the use of a large quantity of mixed spices, and its importance may be gauged by the frequency of allusions to "powdered" meat in the English literature of the time. To this extent spices may almost be described as necessaries at this period, but the necessary demand was largely increased by the taste of consumers: practically every kind of food—meat, poultry, game, fish, fruit, and even bread —was flavoured in a way which would now be condemned as barbarous, and which can be realised only by a study of books on domestic management published before the culinary revolution that began in England in the reign of Charles II. The market for these spices was thus considerable when judged by the standards of the time, and in England at least it was organised at a very early period. The beginning of the London Company of Grocers was the Gild of Pepperers, which was in existence in the reign of Henry II., and in 1345 the membership was limited to "pepperers and spicerers," names which tell their own story.[1] The range of their interests in the fifteenth century may be gathered from the fact that in the year 1447 the Company was entrusted with the supervision of trade in "all sorts of spices and merchandise," including aniseed, cummin, pepper, ginger, cloves, mace, cinnamon, and cardamoms, in addition to "all sorts of merchandise, spices and drugs in any wise belonging to medicines."

Towards the end of the fifteenth century the goods required for this trade from the Indian seas were, as has been said in a previous section, obtained chiefly by way of Egypt. The transit was long and costly. A cargo might be made up on the Malabar coast, partly of local pepper, partly of other spices and of drugs, brought from Malacca or farther east; it would be transhipped at Aden or Mocha, then unloaded in the Gulf of Suez, and carried by land and water to the Mediterranean coast, paying very heavy duties for the passage across Egypt. Here it would pass to the Italian traders and be transported to Venice or Genoa, whence it might be sent farther west by sea, or might be taken by land over the Alps, and then down the Rhine to Antwerp, at that period the chief distributing centre for Western Europe. The trade therefore offered obvious attractions to Portuguese enterprise: there was the hope of large profit, which would be obtained at the cost of their own enemies the Venetians,

[1] The corresponding French word *épicier* is still in ordinary use to designate a grocer.

and of the enemies of Christendom farther east; and there was also the prospect of sailing into unknown seas and opening a road for the propagation of the Christian Faith. Commerce, however, came first, and from the outset we find the Portuguese commanders negotiating for trade; it is significant that their first open quarrel with the Moslem merchants at Calicut arose in connection with pepper, and that their determination to establish themselves at Cochin was based in large part on its facilities for supplying this commodity. When a few years later the Portuguese introduced their system of granting licences to Indian traders, spices were specifically excluded, and pepper in particular remained a royal monopoly; as late as the year 1585 the contract made for the fleet sailing from Lisbon provided for the annual import of 30,000 quintals, or say 1750 tons of pepper, an enormous quantity when judged by contemporary standards of commerce.

While Portugal was developing this trade round the Cape of Good Hope, Spain was obtaining spices from the Eastern Archipelago by way of America, and as early as 1527 we find an Englishman named Robert Thorne writing of this "new trade of spicery," and pointing out that it would be most profitable if the Emperor would follow the example of the King of Portugal and "become a merchant." Portugal, however, retained the principal position in the European market, especially in regard to pepper, which came mostly from India and was not within easy reach of the Spanish trade, and until political difficulties arose the prices charged in England were not such as to excite complaint. Pepper came to Lisbon in bulk, and Dutch and English merchants purchased it there for distribution to the chief consuming markets of England, Flanders, and Germany. The subjection of Portugal to Spain threatened the continuance of this trade. The Dutch were at war with Spain, the port of Lisbon was closed to their merchants, the price of pepper rose to a very high level, and the decision was taken to send ships to the sources of supply. At first, however, the Dutch did not come to India for pepper, but obtained it along with other spices from Java and Sumatra; their fleets were able to maintain themselves against the Portuguese, and by the end of the century their trade with the Archipelago was established. Their relations with India developed somewhat later: they found that they could bring from Europe no merchandise readily saleable in the Spice Islands, and that Indian piece-goods were the recognised medium of the trade, and consequently they established factories[1] in India as subsidiaries to their principal business, the supply of pepper and other spices to Europe.

The motives which brought English traders to the East were essentially similar to those which actuated the Dutch. England was at this time bitterly hostile to Spain. The English had seen the Dutch excluded formally from the Lisbon trade, and they apprehended that a similar prohibition would be applied to them: the price of pepper in England rose seriously; and the first step taken was to organise a series of companies to secure direct trade in Eastern products by way of the Mediterranean. This measure was not completely successful, and when at the end of the century the Dutch, having now obtained command of the market, raised the price of pepper to an exorbitant figure, the English merchants replied by founding the first East India Company. The Letters Patent granted to the Company were drawn in general terms. The objects of the enterprise were stated to be the honour of the realm, the increase of navigation, and the advancement of trade in merchandise; with these objects permission was granted to trade between the Cape of Good Hope and the Straits of Magellan, wherever " trade or traffic of merchandise " might be had, and the experimental nature of the first voyages was expressly recognised. A more clearly defined statement of the initial objects of the Company is contained in the preamble to the Laws and Ordinances framed in 1601, where it is affirmed that the first voyage was set out towards the islands of Sumatra, Java and the neighbourhood with the intention of trading for pepper, spices, gold and

[1] It is perhaps worth while to explain that the meaning of this word has changed. At our period it did not denote a place of manufacture, but merely a trading-post where factors or agents were stationed.

other commodities; while the current view of the enterprise is explained concisely in the sentence with which Purchas introduces the narrative of the first voyage: "The merchants of London, in the year of our Lord 1600, joined together and made a stock of seventy-two thousand pounds, to be employed in ships and merchandises, for the discovery of a trade in the East India, to bring into the realm spices and other commodities." That statement contains the whole truth. The English, like the Dutch, went to the East to buy spices; they first tried Java and Sumatra, and it was owing very largely to the difficulties experienced in opening trade at ports already occupied by competitors that the Company decided on a trial of the Indian mainland, and directed one of the vessels of their third voyage to make for Surat.

Thus the ships of three nations in succession came to the Indian seas in quest mainly of spices. They brought, however, merchants keen to establish trade, and the basis of commerce was quickly extended as the possibilities of the markets became known. So far as India itself was concerned, the export side of the business presented few difficulties, for Indian merchants were in general very ready to sell; on the other hand, there was no large or stable market in India or neighbouring countries for the goods which could be brought from Europe, and after constant disappointments with trial consignments the lesson was learned that trade with India could be effected only by exporting silver. William Hawkins, after two years' stay at the Mogul Court, wrote that "India is rich in silver, for all nations bring coin and carry away commodities for the same; and this coin is buried in India, and goeth not forth"; while a few years later Terry said that "many silver streams run thither, as all rivers to the sea, and there stay." This need for exporting silver was a serious obstacle to trade, for the European governments of the period were dominated by the theory that the value of foreign commerce was measured by the amount of the precious metals brought into the country, and were exceedingly unwilling to let coin be sent abroad. It is unnecessary for my present purpose to discuss either the fallacy of this theory or the important truths on which it rested; the theory was there, and merchants dealing with India had to take it into account. The English Company was authorised by its charter to carry a certain maximum amount of silver on each outward voyage, but was required to conduct its business in such a way that at least the same quantity should ultimately be returned; and while the latter condition could be complied with by sales of Indian goods in other European countries, the limitation of the amount to be carried out was a serious handicap; much of the interest in the early correspondence of the Company's merchants turns in fact on their systematic investigation of the markets to see what commodities could possibly be sold in order to supplement their limited stock of silver. The methods by which the difficulty was eventually met lie outside our period, but its existence requires to be clearly realised: at the end of the sixteenth century India was exceedingly ready to sell her produce, but would take very little except silver in exchange; there was no market for European goods among the masses of the people, while the upper classes cared for little but trifles and novelties, and tired of an article by the time it was offered for sale in quantity.

VI. The Volume of Foreign Commerce

We must now turn to the quantitative aspect of the commerce which has been described in the preceding sections. It is not possible to arrive at definite numerical conclusions regarding either the weight or the value of the goods entering or leaving Indian seaports, but sufficient data are on record to enable us to form a general idea of the volume of sea-borne trade, and to realise the extent of the change which has resulted from the development of the business of transportation. In order to understand these data it is necessary to take into account the influence of the seasonal winds; regular sailings are now so familiar that we are apt to forget their novelty, and assume that a ship can travel whenever and wherever the owners choose, but in the days when vessels were propelled by the wind their course was determined by the season rather than by choice, and in Asiatic waters one round voyage a year was the general rule. The conditions governing navigation at this period may be illustrated by the course of commerce on the west coast of India. The south-west monsoon set in, as it still sets in, about the beginning of June, and until its strength abated no sailing vessel would attempt to leave or enter port; the contrary winds rendered departures physically impossible, and while ships from the west would be carried towards India, they were much more likely to be wrecked on the coast than to succeed in entering one of the few harbours which offered protection at this season, so that from May to the beginning of September the ports were entirely closed.[1] The season for commerce came when the force of the monsoon weakened, and ships from the west could venture to approach the coast, but the time for arriving was by no means unlimited; during the autumn the winds work round gradually from south-west to north, and it becomes increasingly difficult for a sailing-ship to reach the more northerly ports, so that if time were lost the chosen market might prove to be unattainable. The northerly winds were, of course, favourable for departures, but here again time was important: sailing-ships could not travel against the south-west monsoon, and consequently they had to clear from India sufficiently early to get round Ceylon if going east, or the Cape of Good Hope if going west, before the next monsoon should set in. On the west coast, then, the busy season lasted from September to January so far as westerly trade was concerned, while that with Malacca continued until April. Other coasts had in the same way seasons of their own, and since the ship-owner had to consider both the time of departure and the time of arrival, the period available for any particular voyage was determined within narrow limits; if he started too late, he could not hope to arrive, or at least to arrive in time to make the return voyage.

[1] In some cases the close season lasted longer because the monsoon caused sandbanks to form at the entrance to the harbour, and some weeks might elapse before these obstacles disappeared. *Pyrard* states (translation, i. 437) that this was the case at Cochin, but his editor offers another explanation of the difficulty experienced at that port.

A few other examples may be given of the way in which the course of commerce was regulated in accordance with the seasons. The carracks for India had to leave Lisbon before Easter; if they were late in starting they might be unable to round the Cape of Good Hope, and in that case they would have to return to Europe to wait for the next year. If they rounded the Cape in good time, they sailed northwards between Africa and Madagascar, waiting until the monsoon should diminish, and then took advantage of the last of it to carry them across the Arabian Sea to Goa. There was, however, a risk of northerly winds setting in and making this course impossible, and consequently, if, as sometimes happened, they were delayed in rounding the Cape, they struck straight across for Cochin, giving up the call at Goa. They thus reached India in September or October, and they had to start back almost as soon as they could be loaded in order to pass the Cape before the next monsoon should set in; if they were late, they had to take shelter at Mozambique, and lose the best part of a year, with very great risk of losing the ships as well. In the case of the Red Sea traffic, April was the best time for passing through the Straits of Bab-el-Mandeb, so ships from India sailed about March; May and June were the busy months at Mocha or Jidda, wherever the staple was located, and the return ships commonly sheltered off the island of Socotra until the monsoon was sufficiently weakened to make it safe to start for India, where they hoped to arrive in September. As regards the Bay of Bengal, Caesar Frederic tells how the annual export of piece-goods from S. Thomé (Madras) to Pegu was carried in a single ship, which used to start on the 6th September: sometimes, however, the ship was delayed in order to get a full load, "and if she stay till the twelfth, it is a great hap if she return not without making of her voyage"; the wind might change to the east before the ship reached Pegu, and as no further change could be expected for three or four months, the ship would have to go back to S. Thomé, carrying her cargo still on board. In the same way we may read of ships "missing the monsoon" and being detained for long periods at Malacca or Macao or other Asiatic seaports; throughout these waters the season was the dominating factor, and a vessel which could not sail in the proper season had to lie rotting in harbour till the next season came.

In these conditions it is comparatively a simple matter to ascertain the volume of shipping on any particular route, since, if our authorities tell us, as they frequently do, the number of ships sailing in the season appropriate to that route, we know the total of its trade for the year, provided that we can estimate the carrying capacity of the ships employed. In the sixteenth century as now the unit of capacity was the shipping ton, but this unit has varied in magnitude in the interval, and the only statement which is generally applicable to both periods is that the shipping ton is a unit of capacity and not of weight; it must be thought of in terms of cubic feet and not of pounds avoirdupois. The comparison of shipping tons recorded at different times is a matter of much uncertainty: I have dealt with it in Appendix D, but for the present purpose it is best to confine our attention to the unit in common use at the close of the sixteenth century, and in order to avoid confusion I speak of this unit as the tun, reserving the modern spelling, ton, for the unit in use at the present day. European writers of our period meant by a tun a space available for cargo of about 60 cubic feet; when they wrote, for instance, of an Indian ship as of 200 tuns burthen, they meant that in their judgment it would hold about 12,000 cubic feet of cargo. Their statements are of course estimates; they did not measure the ships [1] whose size they noted, but most of them knew their business well, and the round figures which they give can be regarded as trustworthy within reasonable limits.

The merchant vessels employed in Indian seas may be described under four heads—carracks, pilgrim ships, ordinary Indian ships, and junks, but some account has also to be taken of fighting vessels of the galley type, and of the coasting craft,

[1] The only case I have noticed of Indian ships being actually measured is that of the two pilgrim ships the *Rahimi* and the *Muhammadi*, which were measured by Captain Saris in 1612 (*Purchas*, I. iv. 349); it was, of course, their great size that attracted his attention.

which occasionally travelled outside Indian limits. The carracks were the largest. Linschoten records that the ships composing the fleet in which he sailed from Lisbon ranged from 1400 to 1600 tuns; Pyrard a little later says that in his time they ranged from 1500 to 2000 tuns, and while carracks of smaller size are recorded, we may take the average capacity at about 1800 tuns for the European route, and somewhat less for the voyage to China and Japan. Pilgrim ships of about 1000 tuns were known to ply between India and the Red Sea as early as the fifteenth century, and Pyrard, writing of our period, recorded that some ships—but very few—approached 1000 to 1200 tuns. In the year 1612, when Sir Henry Middleton exacted reprisals from the Indian ships in the Red Sea, he laid an embargo on the *Rahimi* (1500 tuns), the *Hasani* (600 tuns), and the *Muhammadi*, all belonging to Surat: he gives the size of the last named as 150 tuns, but from the measurements made by Captain Saris she must have been nearer 1500 tuns, and I think the figure 150 is a mistake. Other ships noted at the same time were the *Salamati* of Diu (450 tuns), and the *Kadiri* of Dabul (400 tuns), so that we may take the pilgrim ships as ranging between 400 and a maximum of 1500 tuns.

The carracks and the larger pilgrim ships far exceeded in size the ordinary trading vessels employed in Europe at this period; the fleet controlled by the Levant Company in the year 1600 consisted of 30 ships averaging 175 tuns, while the average of the 57 "large" ships built in England in 1596–97 was less than 200 tuns,[1] and the greatest of them was below 400 tuns in capacity. These small boats, as they would be called to-day, were fit to make long and arduous voyages: the first fleet sent out by the East India Company included ships of 300 and 260 tuns; the French expedition on which Pyrard sailed consisted of one ship of 400 and one of 200 tuns,

[1] This use of the word "large" should be noted. We frequently read of "great" or "large" or "tall" ships, and are tempted to interpret the adjectives in terms of the present day. It will be seen from the text that "large" ships might average less than 200 tuns; ships of about the same size are spoken of as "great," and I think the adjectives indicate rather differences of build than any attempt to discriminate in regard to capacity.

while David Middleton in 1607 started from England in the *Consent* of 115 tuns, and returned with a cargo loaded in the Molucca Islands. It is no matter therefore for surprise that the ordinary Indian merchant vessels were very much smaller than the two special classes which have been described, and which were designed for traffic of an exceptional nature; the arithmetical average of size of all the Indian sea-going ships (other than pilgrim ships) recorded at this period in the works of Purchas, Linschoten, Pyrard, and Jourdain lies between 180 and 190 tuns, and even this is probably an exaggeration.[1] The figures given by these authorities are, as has been said, estimates, but estimates made by experienced men, and it appears to be reasonable to take the average size of ordinary merchant vessels at about 200 tuns in cases where there are no indications that larger or smaller ships were employed on a particular route.

The word junk means properly a ship of the distinctive Chinese build, with bow and stern shaped alike.[2] At the period under consideration junks reached India very rarely, but they were regular visitors at Malacca and Bantam. Jourdain says the junks from China were of 300 tuns or upwards, while various writers in Purchas mention junks of

[1] The size of every ship seen is not given in these records, but particulars of size are given in a substantial number of cases. I think that the writers were more likely to note the size of large ships than of small, so that the average of their observations would be greater than the true average of all the ships in use at that time. The tendency to record the capacity of large vessels is obvious in the case of the pilgrim ships; even a landsman like Terry speaks of them as "of an exceeding great burthen. Some of them I believe at the least fourteen or sixteen hundred tuns."

[2] The authors of *Hobson-Jobson* (*s.v.*) define junk as "a large Eastern ship, especially a Chinese ship." From a comparison of about twenty passages relating to the period of which I am writing, I infer that the definition given in the text is more appropriate. It is based on the description furnished by Garcia da Orta (and quoted in *Hobson-Jobson*); he was very careful in such matters, and most probably gives the meaning accepted by Portuguese seamen in his time. In all the passages referred to above, the ships called junks came from the east of Malacca, some from China, others from Java and neighbouring islands. The word is, however, used also with the wider meaning indicated in *Hobson-Jobson*; Captain Saris (*Purchas*, I. iv. 348 ff.) repeatedly speaks of Indian ships as junks, while *Mundy* (ii. 30) applies the term to the vessels belonging to Surat, including the pilgrim ships.

different sizes from 400 down to as little as 30 tuns; on the average, therefore, their capacity did not differ very greatly from that of the Indian ships.

The use for commercial purposes of galleys and similar fighting vessels [1] was at this time exceptional. Their distinctive feature was that they could be propelled by oars, and in addition to the armed forces they carried crews of slaves or prisoners for this purpose. So far as I know, the Turks and the Portuguese were the sole owners of galleys in the Indian seas. The former had two or three of them stationed in the Red Sea ports, but outside those waters employed them only for fighting; the Portuguese had perhaps a dozen in regular use, and they were ordinarily employed with the fleets of smaller vessels against the "pirates" of the west coast, but occasionally one or two of them were used to carry provisions to Malacca or Colombo, or even sent to Europe with pepper when the number of carracks available did not suffice. They ranged in capacity up to about 800 tuns, and Falcao takes 550 tuns as the average size.

Lastly, we have to consider the coasting craft, which occasionally took part in foreign commerce to Ormuz, the Red Sea, Pegu, and a few other places. Their capacity is rarely mentioned, but the largest I have read of was 60 tuns, and probably 30 or 40 tuns would be a fair average; since, however, the larger ones would probably be employed for the longer voyages, we may for our present purpose take them as averaging 50 tuns each. Their names are numerous and confusing, because they varied from coast to coast, and we read of *jelbas* off Arabia, *terradas* in the Persian Gulf, *proas* on the Malabar coast, and so on; but they served similar purposes, and so far as I can gather none of them was larger than the limit of 60 tuns which I have given.

With these particulars as to the capacity of the ships employed, we can attempt an estimate of the volume of trade on the various routes from India. Beginning on the west, the

[1] I include in this phrase the vessels called galleys and also the improved types known as galleons and galleasses. The miniature galleys called galliots are more properly classed with the coasting vessels.

size of the direct traffic to Europe can be readily ascertained. From 1590 to 1599, 33 carracks and no other vessels left India for Europe,[1] and taking the average size at 1800 tuns, we have an annual capacity of about 6000 tuns.

Taking next the east coast of Africa, we know that the commerce with Mozambique was reserved for the State or its nominees, and that Sofala and other ports carried on their trade with India through that centre. About two ordinary ships seem to have sufficed for Mozambique. I have not found details of the traffic with the more northerly ports and Socotra, but it was, if anything, on a smaller scale, and 1000 tuns will be a liberal estimate for the entire coast.

As regards the Red Sea trade, we know that it was concentrated at a single port, and Jourdain records that in the year of his visit about thirty-five sail of ships, great and small, came to Mocha from all places, while only two or three small ships came to Aden. All of these ships did not come from India; the number given includes vessels from Suez, Muscat, and the neighbouring coasts as well as those coming from Pegu, Malacca, and Sumatra. In the two seasons when Sir Henry Middleton operated in these waters, one-third of the vessels named by him came from places other than India; he was not concerned with the ships from Suez or the neighbouring coasts, so that his experience indicates that India's share of the total may have amounted to about twenty vessels in all. Downton gives particulars of the ships intercepted in the year 1612; these included all the Indian pilgrim ships and a variety of others, the former aggregating more than 4000 tuns, and the latter ranging about 200 tuns each. On these data the total Indian "tunnage" to the Red Sea may be put at less than 10,000, say 5000 at most for pilgrim ships, and probably not more than 4000 for the larger number of ordinary merchant vessels.

I have found no data for the volume of Indian trade with the Arabian coast and Ormuz at this period. Most of the

[1] Only sixteen out of the thirty-three reached Lisbon: most of the rest were shipwrecked, or captured at sea, but one was burnt in port and two were driven into Mozambique and rotted before they could be got away.

commodities brought from Persia were valuable rather than bulky, and very few tuns would be needed to convey the total imports of coined silver and silk fabrics; the horse trade, of course, required space, but it was less extensive at this period than formerly; and having regard to the lists of commodities, I should be disposed to infer that the total "tunnage" was substantially less than that going to the Red Sea. If, then, we allow 10,000 tuns we shall run no risk of understatement, and we may conclude that after reckoning minor items, such as the traffic with Ceylon and other islands, the total trade of India with the countries on the west was less than 30,000 and probably not more than 25,000 tuns.

On the other side of India we have to consider the trade to Pegu, Malacca, Java, and Sumatra. Trade with Pegu was temporarily disorganised, but we can infer its normal extent from the statements of Caesar Frederic and Fitch. Pegu expected one "great" ship yearly from S. Thomé, and another from "Bengala" (which I take to be Sripur), and these seem to have been the principal events of the commercial year, but a number of smaller vessels also came from the Bengal ports and the Coromandel coast, the voyage being open to coasting craft provided the seasons were observed, and the figure of 5000 tuns will be an ample allowance for all vessels, "great and small," going to the Pegu seaports and to Tenasserim.

The Indian trade to Malacca must be considered under two heads, the through voyages and those which terminated in the Straits. The principal through voyage was that from Goa or Cochin to China and Japan; it was reserved by the State, and Pyrard says that "two or three" ships started yearly, while I gather from Portuguese accounts that occasionally a single carrack was employed, and that in any case the vessels were of exceptional size. We may estimate this traffic at about 3000 tuns at the outside. The only other through voyage appears to have been that to the Moluccas; occasionally, at least, a galleon was employed for this purpose, and the voyage may be reckoned at 1000 tuns. As regards the ships plying only to Malacca, we have to take account of those coming from both the west and east coasts as well as

Bengal. An idea of the volume of the traffic to Goa and Cochin can be formed from the fact that in the year 1598, when the presence of a Dutch fleet rendered it necessary for the homeward merchant ships to sail in company, the convoy consisted of two ships from China, two ships loaded at Malacca, and two junks; excluding the ships from China, which we have already counted, this would represent barely 1000 tuns. There was at this period little traffic to the west coast other than that in Portuguese hands, and even if the Portuguese convoy was on this occasion below its ordinary strength, the total traffic to the coast cannot have exceeded 3000 tuns. On the east coast there was one ship to S. Thomé, and I gather it was of exceptional size; probably there were also ships to Negapatam and Masulipatam, though I have found no definite record, while an indefinite number plied from the ports of Bengal, carrying among other commodities such bulky goods as rice. In the absence of precise data, we may put the total of this traffic at 10,000 tuns in all; I do not think it can have been so large, but I am anxious to avoid under-statement. On these figures, the total volume of traffic between India and Malacca and beyond would not be more than 17,000 tuns. Regarding the competing port of Achin, we are told that during the busy season the harbour contained sixteen or eighteen sail, some from Pegu and Siam, the rest from Gujarat, Malabar, Calicut, and Bengal; the number belonging to each locality is not stated, but probably the bulk came from India, and we may put the total Indian trade of this port at about 3000 tuns. I have not found a similar record for Bantam, but Jourdain, who stayed there some time, wrote that every year "3, 4, 5, or 6" junks came from China and were 300 tuns or more in size, and on this basis we may perhaps take 2000 tuns as the maximum volume of trade between India and Java, including local produce but allowing for part of the China cargo going to other destinations.

We thus reach a total of 27,000 tuns for the trade of India with the countries lying to the east; I think this is an over-estimate, but in any case, taking east and west together, and reckoning the commerce with the islands on both sides of the peninsula, the total volume of Indian foreign trade was probably less than 60,000 tuns of the period, which are, speaking very roughly, equivalent to from 24,000 to 36,000 *net* tons of the present day. The annual *net* tonnage leaving India with cargo in the three years 1911–14 exceeded $6\frac{3}{4}$ millions,[1] and while there are many uncertainties regarding the detailed estimates I have offered, I believe that the contrast between these totals represents with substantial accuracy the change which has taken place since the time of Akbar, and that the volume of shipping has multiplied at least two hundredfold. The description which has been given of the general course of trade indicates that the contrast in regard to value must be much less marked; low-priced goods were shipped very rarely, and the average value of a tun must have been much higher when cargoes consisted of piece-goods, spices, and raw silk, than in these days when food-grains, oilseeds, and raw materials occupy so large a proportion of the space. It is not, however, possible to make even a rough estimate of this average value; practically the only information available consists of stories of the enormous losses resulting from the wreck of a particular vessel, and such statements are so obviously liable to exaggeration that it is not worth while to reproduce them. India's foreign commerce consisted of what we should now call an exceedingly small volume of comparatively expensive goods, but in order to form a just idea of its value it is necessary to discriminate between the prices of commodities before and after transport. The addition to export prices required to cover the cost and risk of transport was very great, and the essence of the business was to deal in those commodities in which the difference in prices afforded an adequate margin, a margin very much wider than any modern merchant can hope to secure. Some interesting information

[1] According to the *Tables of Trade and Shipping* issued by the Indian Department of Statistics, clearances with cargo from British Indian ports averaged 8,154,000 tons in the years 1911–14. The figures in the text are obtained by deducting the recorded clearances from the ports in Burma, and making a slight addition in rounding to allow for exports from French and Portuguese India, the tonnage figures for which are not within my reach.

on this topic is given in Mun's *Discourse of Trade.* He shows that the annual needs of Europe in spices, indigo, and raw silk could be obtained in the East Indies for about £511,000, while if the same quantities were purchased at Aleppo they would have cost £1,465,000, or, in other words, that the value would almost have trebled between the Indies and Aleppo; and further on he gives figures to prove that goods bought in India for £100,000 and brought to England by sea would be worth over £492,000 on arrival. Such figures as these help us to understand the way in which merchants estimated their profits; we read of goods being disposed of "at four for one," or even higher proportions; and it is not unreasonable to conclude that successful business in the Indian seas meant at least a doubling or trebling of the price paid at the point where goods were taken on board, while an even larger factor might be essential in the case of distant voyages. It must not, however, be assumed that these high profits on the turnover meant a high average rate of profit on the business. A merchant looked for a price of perhaps four for one if his venture was successful, but this return covered outlay, interest, and risk of loss. The items of outlay and interest were high because of the time occupied in transit; the risks from weather, enemies, and pirates were literally enormous, and in the case of the longer voyages a large proportion of the capital invested brought no return at all. We have seen that in the course of ten years sixteen carracks out of thirty-three were lost between India and Portugal, so that, taking hulls as well as cargo into account, more than half the original value of the exports disappeared. On the route from India to Japan, owners were satisfied if two ships out of three completed the outward voyage, and losses were equally frequent on the homeward journey, so that out of nine vessels starting on the three years' enterprise, four might be expected to return. On the shorter routes traversed by Indian ships the risks were less, but they were nevertheless substantial; Pyrard's narrative of his stay in the Maldiv Islands shows that those waters were death-traps; the Portuguese chroniclers record frequent captures of richly-laden ships by the "pirates" on the coast; and we must assume that Indian vessels were sometimes wrecked, though it was nobody's business to record the fact.

Apart from maritime dangers, there was the risk that goods might prove unprofitable at their destination. The markets were exceedingly narrow; the arrival of a single ship might convert scarcity into glut, and the commercial correspondence of the period contains frequent references to the uncertainty of business. Thus a merchant at Masulipatam complains that precious stones are too dear to invest in "because the ship of Arakan did not arrive this year." Local markets responded immediately to the appearance of customers, and another merchant writes that "upon the arrival of our ships all commodities do rise forty or fifty per cent." Another merchant complains that the local market had become overstocked with cloth, owing to unexpected arrivals; another writes that their stock was not in great demand, though "it had been gold" if it had arrived a little earlier; and speaking generally there were good grounds for the sententious remark made by John Gurney in Siam that "for these country commodities, quantity by others may breed gluts which may disappoint purposes."

In these conditions it is impossible to make even a rough estimate of the net profit obtained by India from foreign commerce. There is no doubt that successful merchants were wealthy men; we hear of the successes but not of the failures, and while we may be sure that a profit was made, we may suspect that, as happens in most highly speculative business, the average rate was not high. A large proportion of the profit was concentrated in the hands of the Portuguese; they received all that was earned by the direct trade with Europe, China and Japan, Malacca, Ormuz and Mozambique, and they levied heavy charges—either in licence-fees or in bribes—on as much of the remaining trade as came within their reach;[1] the profits of Indian merchants consisted of what was left.

[1] I gather that these charges were not in practice made on a fixed schedule but were a matter of bargaining. Finch notes (*Purchas*, I. iv. 422) that the original demand on a particular pilgrim ship was 100,000 mahmudis (about 40,000 rupees), but the charge finally settled was about 1000 reals (say 2000 rupees), with certain presents in addition.

VII. Coasting and Internal Trade

As has been explained in a previous chapter, the conditions of transport in India in the sixteenth century were such as to induce merchants to send their goods by water rather than by land, and these conditions operated with peculiar force on the western coast, where the country is difficult, and even now no direct railway exists from Karachi to Bombay or from Bombay to Mangalore. The coasting trade was therefore of much importance on both sides of India, but its organisation was not uniform; on the east coast small boats appear to have plied more or less independently throughout the trading season, but on the west the danger from the "pirates" was so great that practically the whole of the traffic was conducted under convoy. Each year when the monsoon weakened, the Portuguese sent out to the north and to the south of Goa fleets consisting of from ten to twenty armed "frigates" or rowing boats, usually with one or two galleys in support; these fleets patrolled the coasts, attacked the "pirates" in their harbours, and from time to time escorted convoys of merchants' boats between Cochin and Goa, or between Goa and the Cambay ports. Merchants waited for the opportunity of escort, and so we find that practically the entire season's trade between Cambay, Goa, and intermediate ports was conducted in large convoys which sailed two or three times in the season between September and May; the convoys, which were known as *kafila* or caravans, were not wholly dependent on the winds, because the boats composing them could be rowed, and their time of starting was regulated according to circumstances, the needs of Goa being probably the determining factor. The Cambay convoy consisted commonly of from 200 to 300 craft, which might aggregate from 8000 to 10,000 tuns, making the annual traffic each way something between 20,000 and 30,000 tuns; the volume was therefore great, but the figure given is not unreasonable if we consider that the convoys brought a large proportion of the goods which were exported from Goa or Cochin, and also of the needs of all the Portuguese settlements, including wheat and pulse, oil and sugar, furniture and miscellaneous goods. The protection of these convoys was by no means complete, and losses were occasionally heavy; in the year 1608 Finch heard of the capture by "pirates" of a ship and three boats from Ormuz, of sixteen boats out of twenty-five from Cochin, and of thirty boats bound for Diu, and the Portuguese chronicles contain frequent references to similar disasters.

The convoys between Cochin and Goa were conducted on the same lines as those from Cambay, but were not so large, and appear to have aggregated about 10,000 tuns in the course of a season. The third convoy on this coast was of a somewhat different nature; the ships coming from Malacca and the east were usually joined somewhere off Ceylon by coasting boats from Bengal and the Coromandel coast, and the whole fleet was convoyed by armed vessels to Cochin. I have not found data of the volume of shipping which arrived in this way from the eastern side of India, but it was certainly considerable, the trade in rice being particularly important. Nor have I come across any record which gives a precise idea of the volume of the trade passing up and down the east coast. One Portuguese writer says that early in the century he had seen 700 sail loading rice at Negapatam,[1] and perhaps this may be taken as an indication of exceptional activity; from such imperfect descriptions as exist, I should be inclined to infer that the ordinary volume of traffic was not so great as on the west coast, but its extent must for the present remain uncertain.

With regard to inland waterways, little need be added to what has been said in preceding chapters. Full use was made of the river systems of the Indus and Ganges, as well as of the network of channels in Bengal, and the rivers were undoubtedly the principal highways of Northern India. They were not, however, equally convenient at all seasons of the year; the strength of the flood and the direction of the wind were important factors, and it is probable that the traffic was

[1] Their cargo is stated to have been 20,000 *moios*, which may be equivalent to about 15,000 tuns; the boats would therefore be small, carrying a load of a little over 20 tuns on the average.

to a large extent seasonal. The seasons dominated the land routes also; traffic was practically at a standstill during the rains, and was reduced to small limits during the hot weather, when fodder and water were difficult to get, so that we find an English merchant at Surat complaining that there were four hot and four wet months, "in which time there is no travelling and therefore unfit for commerce." A striking illustration of the influence of the seasons is given by Tavernier in discussing the alternative routes from Surat to Agra. The western road through Rajputana was in his time the more dangerous of the two, owing to the attitude to travellers adopted by the chiefs and tribes, but it was nevertheless preferred by merchants whose time was limited; lying through sandy country with few rivers, it could be traversed directly the rains ceased, while the safer eastern road through Malwa was impassable for nearly two months owing to the heavy soil and the frequent obstacles presented by rivers still in flood. The ordinary traveller therefore would prefer to stay in Surat till the country had dried up, and then pursue his journey through Burhanpur and Gwalior, but a merchant who took this course could not return to Surat in time to sell the goods which he brought from Agra before the shipping season was over, and on the upward journey therefore he faced the greater risks of the western route. Later in the season the position was reversed; there was then little fodder or water to be had in Rajputana, and in the absence of special reasons travellers from the north naturally chose the road through Malwa, which presented fewer difficulties.

Allowing for the influence of the season, and for the varying degree of security in different parts of the country, inland trade was governed, as it is governed now, by differences in the level of prices, but since costs and risks were much higher the difference in prices had to be much greater to induce traffic to flow. The possibilities of trade at this period are indicated by the fact that when access to the Persian Gulf was closed by war, spices for Persia were carried right across India from Masulipatam to Kandahar, and various other illustrations might be quoted to show that valuable goods might be moved in small quantities for very great distances. The effect of the existing limitations was more obvious in the case of bulky goods such as grain, the trade in which was concentrated in the hands of the tribes known as Banjaras. I have found no contemporary accounts of their activities, but some details are given by later writers such as Mundy and Tavernier, and if we may assume that they are applicable in substance to the period with which we are dealing, we can form some idea of the bulk which could be moved. There might be about 10,000, or even 20,000, pack-oxen moving six or eight miles a day, and as each animal would carry something like 3 cwt.,[1] the total load would be from 1500 tons upwards. This is undoubtedly a large amount, being equivalent to the weight which could be carried by three or four ordinary goods trains at the present day, but such movements were not frequent; it is obvious that such large herds could be provided with fodder and water only during a few months of each year, and if we take their speed into account, we shall find that an entire season's traffic would be equivalent to an amount which a railway could carry over an equal distance in less than a week. India had thus developed a system of internal transit which, like her sea-going trade, was a remarkable achievement for the period, but which becomes insignificant when compared with modern results. Bearing this difference in mind, we may attempt to summarise the main currents of internal trade. As regards Northern India, the outstanding fact is that there was nothing corresponding to the great export of food-grains, oilseeds, and raw cotton of the present day. The country to the south was sparsely populated and was ordinarily self-sufficing, while the difficulties of the road would usually suffice to prevent the movement of such goods to distant Gujarat: the main traffic down the Ganges consisted of salt from Rajputana, while textiles and indigo were the most important commodities on the Indus. Bengal, on the other hand, had an important trade

[1] Tavernier says 300 to 350 livres, while Mundy says four great maunds, which would mean about 220 lbs. at that period. The ordinary load at present is about four modern maunds or 330 lbs.

in produce. Provisions of superior quality were moved in the direction of Agra, sugar was supplied by sea to "all India," that is to the western coast, and rice was carried in the same direction, as well as to Ceylon and even to Malacca. On the other side of India, Gujarat was not self-supporting: it had a large urban and seafaring population to provide for, and it imported food-grains largely from the north and east, rice from the Deccan, wheat and other grains from Malwa and Rajputana. It was doubtless this latter trade which attracted Sir Thomas Roe's attention on his journey up the Tapti valley to Burhanpur, and its existence indicates that the sparsely-populated regions of Central India had a substantial surplus for disposal. I have been unable to find indications of a similar outflow from the interior farther south: the Western Ghats presented very serious obstacles, and della Valle remarks that goods and baggage were more frequently transported upon men's shoulders than upon beasts' backs, while we know from various sources that provisions for the coast towns were brought from long distances by sea—wheat from the Gulf of Cambay, and rice from Bengal and the Coromandel coast. On the other side of the peninsula the export of rice was more important, but I have found no indication that it came from any great distance inland, and taking India as a whole, it does not appear that there was anything approaching to a general system of distribution of agricultural produce by land, although such a trade existed in particular localities.

One other point requires notice in connection with the internal commerce of the country. At the close of the sixteenth century forces were just coming into existence which subsequently led to a marked rise in the prices of various staples, and to a large development of trade. In discussing the decay of Portuguese commerce about the year 1610, Pyrard assigns a prominent place to the new competition of the Dutch; they appear to have been exceedingly expert in buying and selling, and their entrance into the market raised prices considerably, so that, according to this writer, "what formerly cost the Portuguese one sol now costs them four or five." Writing a few years later, Sir Thomas Roe attributes a similar result to the appearance of the English merchants; in his final letter to the East India Company (written in 1618) he insists that India had no grounds for complaint of the English trade, for "we have raised the price of all we deal in," and he goes on to point out the danger of continued competition with the Dutch, and to urge that it should be avoided by dividing the Eastern trade between the two nations. His apprehensions were well grounded, as appears in the history of the years which followed, and the rapid penetration of the country by foreigners competing for an increasing variety of its products resulted in a development of very real value to producers; but at the period which we are considering, this development had scarcely begun, and the inland commerce of the country was the result of forces which had been working for an indefinite period. I can offer no estimate of its volume; it was certainly very small when judged by modern standards, but looked at from the contemporary standpoint it represents a very substantial achievement.

VIII. The Organisation of Indian Commerce

The large volume of commerce which has been described in the foregoing sections was carried on by a comparatively small number of castes or races, the members of which had specialised in this direction, and I believe it is correct to say that there was less trading than now on the part of men not belonging to these particular fraternities. The three most prominent communities in the literature of the time are the Moslems of the seaboard, the banians of Gujarat, and the chettis of the Coromandel coast. I have already outlined the peculiar position held by the Moslems in the Eastern seas: we meet them at all important places on both sides of India, sometimes as shippers, sometimes as pirates, sometimes as merchants on land; and these occupations were by no means mutually exclusive, for Pyrard tells us that the pirates of the Malabar coast became good merchants, going hither and thither to sell their goods, at the season when their harbours were closed by the south-west monsoon. The

Moslems made no claim to sovereignty in the Indian ports, but at the same time they commonly held a privileged position, maintaining cordial relations with the local authorities, and enjoying, if I am not mistaken, more freedom than was granted to the ordinary inhabitants: their connections with foreign countries must have given them an unusually wide outlook on affairs, and in the seas between Africa and Malacca they may almost be described by the epithet cosmopolitan. The banians of the cities of Gujarat were more definitely localised, and were much more completely subject to the authorities, but they travelled freely by land and also by sea, and we read of them as established at Bantam, at the Red Sea ports, and in other distant places. The third community, the chettis, had not, I think, spread to the countries to the west of India, but they were well known in the Straits and the Archipelago, and their characteristics were so familiar on the Indian coast that "chetti" was the nickname commonly applied in Goa to those Portuguese who demeaned themselves in the eyes of their fellows by entering openly on a commercial career.

I have found no distinct notice of the trading races of Northern India at this period, but I think it is safe to assume that they were those whom we know at the present day. They were reinforced by Persians and Armenians, whose particular business was the overland trade westwards through Kandahar, and whom we meet in India as travellers, not settled for long in any one city, but going from one place to another until they had sold their goods and obtained what they needed for the return journey. Jews were established at Cochin and other places in the south, but they are also met with on the roads in the interior; Europeans were occasionally to be found engaged in private ventures,[1] and it may be fairly said that inland, as well as on the coast, commerce was distinctly of a cosmopolitan character. In some respects indeed

[1] Finch records, for instance, that when he arrived at Agra he found "Captain Thomas Boys with three French soldiers, a Dutch engineer, and a Venetian merchant with his son and a servant, newly come by land out of Christendom" (*Purchas*, I. iv. 427).

foreign merchants had advantages over natives of the country. A house, and still more a family, served as a hostage in the hands of the local authorities, who might have to be propitiated by occasional cheap loans or by sales under cost, and whose displeasure, if unhappily it were incurred, would be manifested in the traditional ways, ways of which the memory still survives. A stranger on the other hand did not risk more than the merchandise in his possession at the moment; in some cases he was protected by the prestige of his country; and at the period which we are considering, the demand for foreign curiosities was so great that the administration was disposed to favour the class of men most likely to maintain the supply. Sir Thomas Roe advised the East India Company, "you shall be sure of such privilege as any stranger, and rights when the subject dares not plead his," and I think the phrase may be taken as an accurate summary of the position in the greater part of India.

It is important to bear in mind that at this period there was in India no settled code of commercial law applicable to subjects and foreigners alike. The former were governed by the law of the land, which, as we have seen, depended largely on the individuality of the officer who applied it: foreign merchants on the other hand were treated with due regard to the international position of the State to which they belonged, and they commonly attempted to secure more or less formal treaties or agreements defining the conditions on which they might trade, and settling the particular rates at which customs duty should be charged. The negotiation of such treaties is a familiar incident of the early history of the Portuguese, the Dutch, and the English settlements, but I do not think the system was invented by European merchants; the privileged position held by the Moslems a century earlier at Calicut and other places seems to have been the result of similar, though possibly less formal, engagements between the authorities on one side and the merchants acting as a body on the other, and the conditions which prevailed in Asiatic waters render it probable that such agreements were the regular practice.

The distribution over a large area of the members of a few trading communities was obviously favourable to the development of business organisation, and this result is particularly noticeable in the matter of exchange. Very soon after the first English merchants arrived in Surat, we find them making use of the existing facilities for remitting money by bills, both locally as between Surat and Broach, and over greater distances as between Surat and Agra; but the system was not confined within the limits of India, and when a party of merchants was sent to Persia they were instructed to obtain bills in Agra either on Lahore or on Ispahan, and were provided with a letter of credit enabling them when in Persia to draw bills either on England or on Agra as might be convenient. I have found no contemporary description of the actual working of this system, but I think it may be assumed that the main features were identical with those described half a century later by Tavernier. According to him, a merchant requiring money to buy goods for Surat could obtain it on giving a two-months' bill on that town at any place as far up the country as Agra; east of Agra, as at Dacca, Patna, or Benares, he would give a bill on Agra, where it would be exchanged for a bill on Surat. The charges were, as Tavernier says, "high enough," ranging from 1 or 1½ per cent at Ahmadabad to 6 per cent at Benares and 10 per cent at Dacca,[1] but he points out that the risk was substantial, as the bill would not be met if the goods were stolen in transit: the charges were therefore inclusive of the risks of transport as well as of the current rate of interest. Tavernier adds that the rates might rise by 1 or 2 per cent when local chiefs were interfering with commerce and endeavouring to force it into particular routes for the sake of the transit dues, and that this nuisance was specially common on the road between Agra and Ahmadabad. He mentions further that at Surat advances could be obtained in the same way on goods des-

[1] These rates are clearly the actual charges for the time, not annual rates such as modern bankers would quote. Had they been the annual rates, Tavernier, as a man of wide experience in business, would not have thought it necessary to justify them. Some years earlier *Mundy* (ii. 290) found that the rate between Jhalawar and Ahmadabad was from eight to ten per cent.

patched to Ormuz, Mocha, Bantam, and even the Philippine Islands; in this case the rates charged were much higher (16 to 22 per cent for Ormuz, and still more in the case of the more distant ports), but again they included insurance against shipwreck and piracy, and these risks were, as we have seen, ordinarily very great.

The existence of this system of credit, extending over a wide area and quite independent of political limits, has been read as indicating a high level of commercial morality, and it would be possible to quote the evidence of some contemporary observers in corroboration of this view. It would be equally possible to give quotations on the other side, depicting Indian merchants as influenced by no considerations of conscience or honesty; but I think it would be useless to set out the evidence at length because its true interpretation is obvious. Indian merchants, like those of all other nations of equal experience, had developed a conventional morality of their own; they recognised certain limits within which their activities should be confined, and within these limits they could be trusted by foreigners as well as by their own community. The foreign merchants had also their own conventions, but their conventions differed from those which they met in India: sometimes they were agreeably surprised when an Indian merchant abstained from taking an advantage which they would have regarded as legitimate, but at other times they found that Indians would do what they would not have done themselves. Indian conventional morality in matters of commerce was not, and is not, perfect; its merit lay in the fact that it provided a system under which commerce could be effectively carried on, and like other such systems it was substantially fair to every one who knew "the rules of the game," though strangers who tried to take a hand had commonly to pay somewhat dearly for their experience, and some of them have recorded their resulting impressions for the benefit of later generations. The value of these impressions lies rather in the testimony they afford as to the quality and capacity of Indian men of business. In the sixteenth century, as at the present day, they must be ranked as merchants in the highest class. European visitors sometimes described them as superior to the Jews, and this evidence is conclusive to any one who appreciates the position held by Jews in the markets of the period; perhaps it is worth while to quote on this point the appreciation offered by Tavernier, whose wide experience made him an exceptionally competent judge. "The Jews engaged in money matters in the Turkish Empire are," he says, "usually considered to be exceptionally able, but they are scarcely fit to be apprenticed to the money-changers of India."

AUTHORITIES FOR CHAPTER VI

SECTION 1.—The position of the Moslem merchants at the beginning of the sixteenth century can best be realised by a study of *Barbosa*, *Varthema*, and the early books of the *Decadas*. *Whiteway* gives a useful summary of the growth of the Portuguese power. For changes in the routes of commerce due to the attitude of the Portuguese, see *Barbosa*, 353, 358, and *Pyrard*, translation, i. 279. The best account of the Malabar pirates is in *Pyrard*, translation, i. 438-447; they are mentioned by all writers of the time, but Pyrard had exceptional opportunities of observing them. The statement that Portuguese subjects took licences from a pirate is in *Hay*, 831; it comes from a Portuguese source, and is therefore probably true, since it is derogatory to the national pride. The grant of licences to Akbar's ships is mentioned in the *Decadas*, *e.g.* X. i. 441, and also by Moslem chroniclers, *e.g.* Elliot, *History*, v. 403; the terms of the Portuguese treaty with Vijayanagar are in *Sewell*, 186. The relations of the Zamorin with the Portuguese on the one hand and the pirates on the other bulk largely in the later *Decadas*.

SECTION 2.—An account of Lahari Bandar will be found in *Purchas*, I. iv. 49. The only statements I have noted of vessels belonging to that port are *Purchas*, I. iii. 273 ("a small bark of Sind"), and *idem*, 307 ("a small sail"). The Cambay ports are described by almost all writers of the period: for the *kafila*, see in particular *Pyrard*, translation, ii. 245, and for examples of losses by pirates, Finch in *Purchas*, I. iv. 21. For Chaul, see *Linschoten*, c. 10, and *Pyrard*, translation, ii. 259; for Dabul, see *Jourdain*, 198.

The clearest account of the commercial activity of Goa is perhaps that given by *Pyrard* in his second volume, but the later *Decadas* should be read by any one who wishes to know all about it, and also about Cochin. For the voyage to Japan, see *Pyrard*, translation, ii. 175 ff. The conditions prevailing in the Red Sea are best described in *Jourdain*, 74 ff.; those at Ormuz and on the east coast of Africa must be gathered from the later *Decadas*. An instance (not the only one) of the identification of Mozambique with Ophir will be found in *Purchas*, II. vii. 1022; Milton, in *Paradise Lost*, writes of "Sofala, thought Ophir."

For Ceylon, see *Pyrard*, translation, ii. 140; the Xth and XIIth *Decadas* give long accounts of the fighting on the island. For the Coromandel trade with Pegu, see *Purchas*, II. x. 1718, 1733, 1739. References to the Bengal ports are given in Appendix C; the position of the Portuguese residents can be learned from the missionary narratives in *Hay*, 728 ff.

SECTION 3.—Descriptions of the ports and trade of Pegu, given by Caesar Frederic, Balbi, and Fitch, will be found in *Purchas*, II. x. 1716 ff., 1625 ff., 1737 ff.; see also *Hobson-Jobson*, under "Cosmin," "Syriam," and "Martaban." For Tenasserim, see *Barbosa*, 369, *Purchas*, II. x. 1712, 1741, and *Hobson-Jobson* under "Tavoy," "Tenasserim," and "Nipa." The classical account of Malacca is that of *Barbosa*, 370 ff.; the curtailment of Chinese navigation is dealt with in Yule, *Cathay*, i. 83 ff. For Bantam as a competing centre of trade, see *Jourdain*, 308; and for Achin, *Purchas*, I. iii. 123, 157.

The conditions prevailing in South Africa are noticed by various travellers, *e.g. Purchas*, I. iii. 149; the nature of the trade farther north is indicated in *Barbosa*, 233 ff., and *Pyrard*, translation, ii. 224 ff., as well as in occasional references in the *Decadas*. For the Red Sea, see *Jourdain*, 77, 103, 353, and the narratives of Sir Henry Middleton and Downton in *Purchas*, I. iii. For Ormuz, see Fitch in *Purchas*, II. x. 1731, *Barbosa*, 260 ff., and *Linschoten*, c. 6.

SECTION 4.—The references to the north-eastern route are *Roe*, 97, *Hay*, 798, *Ain*, translation, ii. 172, 280, 312, and *Purchas*, I. iv. 434. Kabul is described by *Monserrate*, 617; *Manrique's* experience is in c. lxxi. The journey made by Goez is in *Purchas*, III. ii. 311; that of the English merchants in *Purchas*, I. iv. 519.

SECTION 5.—The European side of the matters dealt with in this section may be studied in *Cunningham*, *Thorold Rogers*, *Heath*, *Epstein*, and *Scott*. *Thorold Rogers* (V. c. xvii.) writes pungently regarding the style of English cookery which rendered spices necessary; readers who wish to know more of this subject will find a full description in a little book called *Health's Improvement*, by Thos. Muffett, corrected and enlarged by Christopher Bennet, published in London in 1655: incidental references will also be found scattered through the *Paston Letters*.

The motives and conduct of the Portuguese enterprise are clearly set out in *Whiteway*. The figures given for the export of pepper are taken from Xth *Decada*, ii. 121; *Garcia da Orta* (367) points out that little of it was consumed in Portugal, and gives the ultimate destination. Thorne's pamphlet will be found in the second volume of *Hakluyt*. For the Letters Patent of the English Company, see *Purchas*, I. iii. 140 ff.; for the Laws and Ordinances, *Stevens*, 198; and for *Purchas's* own account, I. iii. 147.

The quotations as to the flow of silver to India are taken from *Purchas*, I. iii. 221, and II. ix. 1470. The efforts to sell English goods in India can be read of in the early volumes of *Letters Received*.

SECTION 6.—The influence of the seasons on commerce is mentioned by most writers of the period: Lancaster's memorandum on the voyage from Europe may be consulted as an example (*First Letter Book*, 136). The course of the Portuguese carracks is given by *Pyrard* among other writers (translation, ii. 196 ff.). The season for the Red Sea is discussed in various places, *e.g.* Xth *Decada*, ii. 170; the case of the S. Thomé ship is taken from *Purchas*, II. x. 1716.

References to the history of the shipping ton are given in Appendix D. For the size of carracks, see *Linschoten*, c. 1., *Pyrard*, translation, ii. 180, *Purchas*, I. iii. 159; for pilgrim ships, *Major*, 27, and *Purchas*, I. iii. 308;

for contemporary European ships, *Oppenheim*, 168-9, *Purchas*, I. iii. 8, 147, 224, and *Pyrard*, translation, I. xv.; for junks, *Jourdain*, 316; and for Turkish galleys, Xth *Decada*, ii. 170. I have arrived at the number of Portuguese galleys by counting the despatches recorded in the Xth and XIIth *Decadas*; their size is referred to in *Pyrard*, translation, ii. 180, and *Falcao*, 205.

The number of carracks sailing for Europe is obtained from the annual records in XIth and XIIth *Decadas*. *Pyrard* (translation, ii. 148) refers to the reservation of the trade to Mozambique and some other ports. For the Red Sea, see *Jourdain*, 77, 103, and *Purchas*, I. iii. 260 ff.; for Pegu, *Purchas*, II. x. 1716; for Malacca, *Pyrard*, translation, ii. 173, Xth *Decada*, i. 212, 214, and XIIth *Decada*, 121; for Achin, *Purchas*, I. iii. 153, and for Bantam, *Jourdain*, 316.

Mun's "Discourse of Trade" is in *Purchas*, I. v. 734 ff. The rate of casualties on the Japan route is quoted from Maffeius, *Select Letters*, 7. The narrowness of markets is a very common topic; the illustrations given are from *Letters Received*, ii. 59, 84, 112; iii. 84.

SECTION 7.—*Pyrard*, translation, ii. 245 ff., gives a brief account of the *kafila* on the west coast; they are mentioned by various other writers, and their movements can be studied in greater detail in the *Decadas*. Finch's statement regarding losses is in *Purchas*, I. iv. 421; the reference to trade at Negapatam is taken from *Hobson-Jobson* (*s.v.* "Xerafine").

References to the seasons for land travel are *Letters Received*, i. 298, and *Tavernier*, 24. The overland trade in spices is mentioned in *Purchas*, I. iv. 520; the Banjaras are described in *Tavernier*, 26 ff., and *Mundy*, ii. 95. For the Ganges trade, see *Jourdain*, 162; for that on the Indus, *Purchas*, I. iv. 485. The export trade of Bengal has been referred to in previous sections; for the import into Gujarat, see *Ain*, translation, ii. 239, and *Roe*, 88; for traffic on the Ghats, see *della Valle*, 292.

For the rise in prices at the beginning of the seventeenth century, see *Roe*, 480, and *Pyrard*, translation, ii. 203.

SECTION 8.—The versatility of the Moslem traders is stated by *Pyrard*, translation, i. 447. For banians abroad, see *Purchas*, I. iii. 166, 263; for chettis, *Barbosa*, 373, and *Linschoten*, c. 30; for Armenians and Persians, *Roe*, 439, and for Jews, *Purchas*, I. iii. 232. *Roe's* statement regarding privileges is on p. 467.

For examples of commercial agreements, see *Letters Received*, iv. 28, and *Purchas*, I. iv. 458. The fullest account of the exchange system is in *Tavernier*, 23-25; it is mentioned frequently in *Letters Received*, *e.g.* i. 25, ii. 228, 266. *Tavernier's* appreciation of Indian men of business is on p. 18.

CHAPTER VII

THE STANDARD OF LIFE

I. Introductory

We have now examined the resources of each of the main classes into which we divided the population of India, and it remains to bring together such information as is available regarding the way in which those resources were used, or in other words, to attempt a description of the standards of life prevailing at the end of the sixteenth century. It is scarcely necessary to say that the literature of the period contains nothing like a complete or systematic treatment of this subject, for, as I have remarked more than once, Indian writers accepted the existing state of things, whatever it might be, as natural or necessary, while foreign observers were content as a rule to note such particular circumstances as happened to attract their attention; the information available is therefore incomplete and fragmentary, but it has the qualities corresponding to its defects, and appears to be entirely devoid of bias. The observers on whose statements we have to rely were governed by no economic theories, and had no case to prove: [1] allowances may have to be made for occasional errors, but there is no reason to suspect that the evidence is vitiated by prejudice or by the attempt to justify preconceived views,

[1] The nearest approach to an exception to this statement is Bernier, who had a definite economic creed, and whose generalisations may perhaps be subject to some discount in consequence: for our present purpose, however, he is of interest mainly because he states as observed facts results which might fairly be expected from the operation during half a century of tendencies which were already at work in the time of Akbar.

and as a general rule we can safely accept the facts as stated, even though it may be necessary occasionally to discard inferences drawn by their recorders.

The work of piecing together these fragmentary observations so as to present something like a connected description is greatly facilitated by the rarity of contradictory statements among our authorities. Allowances have of course to be made for differences of time and place, but the most definite impression produced by contemporary narratives is one of essential uniformity; whenever a traveller lifts the veil for a moment, the picture of which we get a glimpse is familiar in its main features, and each successive item of information becomes readily intelligible in the light of what has previously been learned. The nature of the evidence, therefore, justifies the attempt to speak of India as a whole, so long as we bear in mind that what is said of the whole does not apply necessarily to every individual member of the population; I have no doubt that frugal and parsimonious nobles could be found at the Courts, and that individual peasants or artisans may have been prosperous or even wealthy, but the broad facts remain that the mass of the nobles were steeped in luxury and that the mass of the people were miserably poor, poorer even than they are to-day. To realise the strength of the evidence in favour of this uniformity requires a first-hand study of the authorities: in the sections which follow, I attempt to bring together a sufficient number of passages to furnish an idea of its nature, but their effect is necessarily weakened by removal from their context, and it is only by following the succession of travellers in their journeys through the country that we can appreciate the full significance of their direct statements, and still more, of the chance expressions scattered through their narratives. The uniformity of which I have spoken will be apparent in the sections which follow, but one striking illustration may be noticed here. The Jesuit missionary Monserrate has left us a detailed account of his reception at Akbar's Court in the year 1580; other Jesuit missionaries have given descriptions of the Hindu Courts of the far south about fifteen years later, and in all essentials the two accounts might be transposed.[1] There are differences, of course, due largely to differences of climate and environment: in the south cotton fabrics take the place occupied in the north by wool, just as rice replaces wheat-flour, but these accessories are immaterial, and the main features of Court life appear with almost startling uniformity. Extracts, however, would not bring out the full weight of this evidence: to appreciate it properly, we must read the whole narratives, putting ourselves as far as possible in the position of the narrators, and seeing the country and people with their eyes; it is only by this process that we can obtain a complete and satisfactory view of the environment in which their experiences were obtained.

One result of the conditions which I have indicated is that we are told more of the life of the upper classes than of the rest of the community. As I have said above, our authorities noted such facts as interested them, and there can be no doubt that the life led by the nobles was intensely interesting to observe, while the food or clothes or homes of the common people afforded little scope for picturesque description; when you have said that people go nearly naked, you have practically exhausted the topic of clothing, and you can write little about furniture when the possessions of a family are limited to a couple of bedsteads and a scanty supply of cooking vessels. Some writers leave the common people entirely out of account, as when Conti tells us that the inhabitants of the country "sleep upon silken mattresses on beds mounted with gold," a statement which sufficiently indicates the limitations with which it must be understood; in the case of others the position is not always so plain, and some care is needed in order to make sure whether a particular statement applies to the people generally, or merely to some small class in whose affairs the writer was interested at the moment. This fact furnishes an additional reason for studying the original authorities, and it may be well to repeat that the sections which follow must not be read as a complete statement of the

[1] *Monserrate's* account will be found on pp. 559 ff. of his narrative. The experiences of missionaries in the south are printed in *Hay*, 750, 763, etc.

evidence available, but rather as an attempt to indicate its general nature.

II. The Upper Classes

The economic position of the upper classes may be stated in very few words. As we have seen in Chapter III., their incomes were as a rule received, or at least calculated, in money, and were very large indeed when the low prices of necessaries and reasonable comforts are taken into account, so that the members of the aristocracy had a substantial surplus available for investment, or for expenditure on luxuries, after providing for the ordinary needs of themselves and their establishments. Investment in the strict sense of the term was, however, comparatively rare. The methods with which we are familiar at the present day were not available: State loans were not openly placed on the market, stocks and shares did not exist, while land was held only at the will of the ruler, and could not be purchased except in small blocks for building houses or laying out gardens. It is possible that money could be placed on deposit with merchants, though I have found no mention of the practice, but in any case it can scarcely have been on the same footing as banking deposits in modern India. Probably some of the nobles undertook commercial ventures on their own account: we know that this course was taken by members of Akbar's family, and it is reasonable to assume that their example was followed.[1] In industry as distinct from commerce there was, as we have seen, practically no scope for the employment of capital, and commerce was a risky business in which ordinary men were likely to be less successful than those who gave it their undivided attention: probably it attracted some of the courtiers and officials, but as a rule money not immediately spent would be hoarded in the form of cash or jewellery for use at a later period, or possibly in the hope that on its owner's

[1] *Jourdain*, for instance, mentions (p. 164) that in the year 1611 the Queen-Mother had been buying indigo at Biana to venture on her ship to Mocha. This must have been the *Rahimi*, the great pilgrim ship, which is spoken of elsewhere as the Queen-Mother's ship.

death the accumulation could be concealed from the knowledge of the authorities.[1]

Spending, not hoarding, was, however, the dominant feature of the time. The example of magnificence set by Emperors and Kings was followed by their courtiers and officials, and while the resources of the country were freely drawn on, the taste of the period preferred novelties imported from abroad; indeed, the official encouragement given to foreign merchants must be attributed in great part to the fact that they were able to satisfy this insistent demand. This taste for imported goods had, from the nature of the case, least scope in the matter of food, the bulk of which was furnished by the grain and meat of the country: it appears partly in the lavish use of spices which has been mentioned in a previous chapter, and partly in the arrangements made to procure such auxiliaries as ice and fresh fruit. Abul Fazl gives details of the organisation of the ice-supply, then a comparatively recent innovation, and mentions that ordinary people used ice in summer while the great nobles used it all the year round; it might cost as much as 20 dams for a ser of the period, but the ordinary rate was nearer ten dams, or, allowing for the change in purchasing power, more than a rupee per pound, which fairly establishes its claim to be classed as a luxury. The Moguls appear to have been particularly fond of fruit: Babur writes of Indian fruits as a connoisseur, Akbar organised this department of his household on generous lines, while Jahangir's outbursts of delight at the quality of his supplies are a characteristic feature

[1] Half a century after our period, Tavernier, writing on the strength of his experience as a merchant, stated definitely that the demand for gold coins, which were difficult to procure, arose from the general desire to possess this metal "partly because it takes np little room and is easily hidden, partly because they delight to leave to their families large sums of which the King can have no knowledge" (*Tavernier*, ii. 15). *Bernier* (p. 167) quotes a letter from Aurangzeb to Shahjahan which speaks of the practice of sealing a dead man's coffers and torturing his servants until they disclosed the whole property, even "the most inconsiderable jewel." Probably the severity of the financial authorities had increased in the interval between Akbar and Shahjahan, but it is reasonable to suppose that even under the former ruler precautions were taken to ensure that the estate of a deceased noble should not be diverted from the Treasury.

of his *Memoirs*. So far as acclimatisation was effected, Akbar's efforts were doubtless beneficial to the country as a whole, but the organisation of imports primarily for his own use from such distant sources as Badakhshan and Samarqand can be classed only as a luxurious proceeding, as is indicated by the prices paid ; a melon from Badakhshan was priced at Rs. 2½, or the approximate equivalent of a pound sterling at modern values. Expenditure on food depended, however, less on the cost of these adjuncts, or even on the richness of the dishes, than on the profusion of the service : Akbar himself is said to have cared little about the quality of his food, but in his kitchen "cooks from all countries" prepared daily such dishes "as the nobles can scarcely command" ; the number of dishes served was very great, and the elaboration of the service even more remarkable. If Terry's often-quoted description of the dinner given by Asaf Khan to Sir Thomas Roe be compared with Abul Fazl's account of Akbar's table, a fairly accurate general impression can be obtained of the lavishness of provision and service maintained by the greatest men, and it is safe to infer that courtiers of smaller means followed the fashion set them so far as their resources permitted.

Dress afforded similar opportunities of expenditure both in the quantity of garments and in the costliness of the materials employed. If we may believe Abul Fazl, Akbar took much more interest in clothes than in food, and altered not merely the names of particular garments, but also the cut and the material ; his wardrobe was sufficiently large to require an elaborate system of classification, but when we read that 1000 complete suits were made up for him every year, allowance must be made for the practice of conferring dresses as a reward or distinction on persons appearing at Court. Abul Fazl distributed his entire wardrobe every year among his servants, and a variety of casual allusions indicate that a large stock of clothes was an ordinary feature of Court life. The range of materials was very great, as may be judged from the lists recorded in the *Ain-i Akbari*, in which a prominent place is taken by imported goods. Cotton fabrics could be obtained up to Rs. 150 per piece, woollen stuffs to Rs. 250, and silks to Rs. 300, while embroidered velvets and brocades might cost anything up to Rs. 700, or even (in one case) Rs. 1500; Abul Fazl speaks of a "piece" as containing sufficient cloth to make a complete dress, and on this basis we can form a general idea of the possibility of spending money on a wardrobe designed to render the wearer a conspicuous object at Court. As regards jewellery, it is hardly worth while to give details; it was worn in profusion; rare stones were eagerly sought, and outlay was limited only by the means available.

I am inclined to think that, with the possible exception of jewellery, more money was spent on the stables than in any other branch of a courtier's household. An adequate supply of elephants and horses was essential for the maintenance of a dignified position, and there were unlimited possibilities of expenditure on equipment and adornment. Elephants could be obtained at all prices, for Abul Fazl says that the cost varied from a lakh to Rs. 100. Horses suitable for gentlemen appear to have ranged from Rs. 200 to upwards of Rs. 1000,[1] and the maintenance of a large stable of high-priced animals must have been very costly even when the cheapness of grain and fodder is taken into account. As to the adornments, it is best to accept at once Abul Fazl's statement that they cannot be described, though it may be noted that an elephant's picket-chain might be made of iron, silver, *or gold*;[2] there was in fact no limit to the amount that might be spent under this head. Sport and gambling, which then as now went together, could also be costly amusements, which, under Akbar at least, were obligatory on the more prominent courtiers; the amount of bets was in some cases limited by regulation, but while we know that the practice was recog-

[1] The price of horses was rather higher in Southern India; Arabs and Persians sold for about 500 *pardaos*, or say Rs. 1000, at Goa, and would have fetched more at a distance from the coast (*Pyrard*, translation, ii. 67).

[2] This is apparently not mere rhetoric: *Badaoni* mentions (ii. 219) gold and silver chains, as well as housings of European velvet and Turkish cloth of gold, in a State ceremony of Akbar's time, while Thomas Coryat saw elephants wearing chains of beaten gold (*Purchas*, I. iv. 595).

nised, we are left to conjecture the extent to which the limitation was effective.

Expenditure on house accommodation was not, I think, an important item in the case of courtiers, for the Court was often on the move, and large camps seemed to have served as residences for most of those who accompanied it. In these camps the possibilities of spending money on display were practically unlimited, since the number, size, and decoration of tents were matters to be regulated by the aspirations of the individual, and a very high standard was set by the Imperial camp. Abul Fazl speaks of decorations of velvet and brocade, and of silken fastenings for the canvas screens, and we may be sure that the camp of a prominent noble presented a much more imposing spectacle than that which the word suggests in modern India. In the matter of furniture there was not the same variety as now, for tables, chairs, or couches were not in ordinary use. Carpets, bedsteads, mirrors, and utensils were, however, used in profusion, and their cost was limited only by the individual's means.

The style of living required a very large staff of servants, and, as I have said in a previous chapter, the extent of this domestic employment is an important economic feature of the time. A noble must have required servants almost by the hundred if we reckon his household on approximately the scale indicated by Abul Fazl, allowing four men for each elephant, two or three to each horse, a crowd in the kitchen, two crowds of tent-pitchers (one for the fore-camp and one for the rear), adequate transport, torch-bearers, and all the other elements of a respectable establishment; and while slaves were cheap, and wages were so low that a rupee would go as far as seven rupees in modern times, the cost must still have been very great. The crowd of attendants was by no means a feature peculiar to the Mogul Court, but was to be found in almost every part of India: when a traveller describes the life on the west coast or reaches one of the Courts in the Deccan, when an ambassador comes to Goa, when the Jesuit missionaries visit a noble in Vijayanagar, in each case we read the same thing; and it is significant that in this as in other matters the Portuguese at Goa followed the practice of the country, and a "man of quality" would not walk in the street without a train of attendants, pages, and African slaves.

Enough has perhaps been said to indicate that de Laet was justified in the conclusion which he drew from his materials, that the luxury of the nobles could scarcely be described, seeing that their one concern in life was to secure a surfeit of every kind of pleasure, a judgment which may be compared with Roe's dictum that "they are nothing but voluptuousness and wealth confusedly intermingled." One other object of expenditure has still to be mentioned—the presents to the Emperor and to persons of influence, the offering of which was prescribed by etiquette, while the value was determined mainly by the ambition of the donor. This practice should be distinguished from the secret bribery which also prevailed; presents were given openly, even ostentatiously, and they were part of the established system. No one could approach a superior empty-handed, and presents given to secure promotion may almost be regarded as akin to investments, just as Englishmen until the last century regarded the sums paid for posts in the public offices. In the atmosphere of Indian Courts, where novelty and riches were the things most desired, the practice assumed a form very different from the survivals of it which exist at the present day. Competition for appointment or promotion was keen; the prizes of a career at Court tended to go to the competitor whose gifts were most acceptable, and the results may be seen in the pages of Jahangir's *Memoirs*, where the offerings of each visitor or suitor in succession are described and appreciated from a strictly financial point of view. It is probable that the system became more and more burdensome as time went on, and that Jahangir's presents were more valuable than those of Akbar, but its existence in the earlier reign is beyond dispute, and the keenness with which gifts of the most varied kind were received by the Emperor, as well as by his contemporaries in the south, is clearly shown in the narratives of the Jesuit missionaries.

The natural result of the conditions which have been described was the impoverishment of the nobles, and we have Bernier's authority for saying that this result actually followed. "I was acquainted," he wrote, "with very few wealthy omrahs: on the contrary most of them are deeply in debt; they are ruined . . . by the costly presents made to the King and by their large establishment." The financial ruin of the aristocracy was by itself a matter of little moment, but it had an important bearing on the economic condition of the masses of the people: the provincial Governors and other officials had in practice very wide powers, and when their resources were running low it was on the peasants and artisans that the burden fell, so that there is no reason to question the substantial truth of the picture which Bernier draws of the misery of the masses at the end of Shahjahan's reign. The impoverishment of the nobles was a process requiring time, and it may be assumed that the deterioration in the condition of the people was also gradual, and that they were somewhat better off under Akbar, but in estimating the economic effects of his administration we must allow for the fact that it fostered the tendencies in question.

It must not, however, be supposed that every one at Indian Courts lived beyond his means; many, I think the great majority, did so, but there were thrifty men who built up large fortunes, and a few words must be said as to the disposal of these accumulations. So far as the wealth could be traced, it reverted, in Northern India at least, to the Treasury when its owner died, and since this result was distasteful, rich men endeavoured to dispose of it during their lifetime. One way of doing this was to bestow large dowries, like that which Raja Bhagwan Das provided for his daughter, which according to Badaoni included "several strings of horses and a hundred elephants, and boys and girls of Abyssinia, India, and Circassia, and all sorts of golden vessels set with jewels, and utensils of gold and vessels of silver, and all sorts of stuffs, the quantity of which is beyond all computation." Another resource was the construction of great buildings, and, as the surface of India still bears witness, the fashion of the time set less towards works of practical utility than to tombs and commemorative monuments.[1] Sometimes, though rarely, a noble might be permitted to leave the country and go to his home in Persia or elsewhere, or make a pilgrimage to the holy places of Arabia, carrying with him at least a portion of his accumulated wealth. Permission to take this course appears, however, to have been given only when it was desirable on political grounds, and the practice of carrying money out of the country was rigorously discouraged. A large fortune might thus prove to be nothing but an encumbrance, and while some men were apparently content to accumulate riches for the ultimate benefit of the State, the majority spent their income at least as quickly as it accrued, and spent it in the manner which I have illustrated in this section.

III. The Middle Classes

We know less of the life of the middle classes in the time of Akbar than of the classes which ranked either above or below them in the social scale; their numbers were certainly small, and we may fairly infer from the silence of our authorities that their life was at any rate free from ostentation. Professional men were, as we have seen, rarely to be found except at Court, where they might hope to attain to official rank, and probably lived more or less in accordance with the prevailing standards. Of the minor functionaries, who were certainly numerous at the various administrative centres, we get scarcely a glimpse, and in the absence of information regarding the current scale of salaries it is impossible even to conjecture how far they may have benefited by the cheapness of necessaries and reasonable comforts. In reading chronicles of the period, written presumably by men of this class, we occasionally notice that the economic outlook of the writers

[1] I have not been able to find anything which can be called a list of useful foundations or endowments established during the reign of Akbar. Mr. N. L. Law, who puts the educational achievements of the period considerably higher than I am disposed to, names only two foundations apart from those which Akbar himself created at Fatehpur Sikri and elsewhere (*Promotion of Learning in India during Muhammadan Rule*, Bk. II. chap. iv.).

is that of men who found life hard: they do not indeed indulge in any detailed analysis of the conditions, but when they sum up the features of a dynasty or an epoch they dwell on the price of food in a way which indicates that the subject was of vital interest. Such passages suggest to me that the literate classes, to which these chroniclers belonged, were probably in much the same economic position then as now, and that the question of prices may have possessed for the clerks of Akbar's time something of the same interest that it possesses for their successors at the present day, but until more positive evidence comes to light we should not be justified in forming any definite conclusion.

We know a little, but only a little, more of the position of the merchants of this period. We have seen that their economic condition must have varied greatly, and that while there were many rich men among them, their average income was probably not large.[1] If, however, they were wealthy, their possible ways of expenditure were confined within narrow limits, since ostentation was as dangerous in their case as it was desirable in the case of courtiers. Terry wrote that "there are very many private men in cities and towns, who are merchants or tradesmen, that are very rich: but it is not safe for them that are so, so to appear, lest that they should be used as fill'd sponges"; while Bernier observed that "rich men study to appear indigent," and that "let the profit be ever so great, the man by whom it has been made must still wear the garb of indigence." These observations are probably of general application so far as the interior of the country is concerned, and they help us to understand the thrifty, or even parsimonious, scale of living which characterises so many of the commercial classes at the present day. An exception must, however, be made regarding some of the merchants engaged in business on the west coast. Barbosa says of the

[1] Della Valle gives a striking instance of the instability of commercial fortunes. After describing a great reservoir at Surat, he records that it was constructed by a private citizen, "whose daughter they say, or rather one descended from him, is still living, and, I know not by what sinister hap of fortune, very poor so that she hath scarce bread to eat" (*della Valle*, 34).

Moslems settled in Calicut that they went well dressed, had large houses and many servants, and were very luxurious in eating, drinking, and sleeping, though he adds that their position had greatly deteriorated since the Portuguese came to India. The same writer says that the Moslems living at Rander were well dressed, and had good houses, well kept and furnished. A century later della Valle commented on the freedom of life at Surat, where he was told that there was no risk in splendour or the appearance of riches, and observed that "generally, all live much after a genteel way," a phrase which must be interpreted in the light of the writer's own position as a gentleman of culture and refinement. The exceptional position on the coast is probably to be explained by the privileged status of the Moslem merchants, and by their importance for the maintenance of the customs revenue, and the supply of rare commodities; being free to live well, they acted in accordance with their inclinations, while the merchants of the interior were very far from being free, and led the quiet and unostentatious life required by the circumstances of their position.

IV. The Economic Position of the Lower Classes

We must now turn to consider the life of the masses of the people, the peasants, artisans, and labourers. I know of nothing approaching to a complete contemporary account of their mode of living: all that we possess is a series of glimpses, furnished mostly by the records of foreign observers, who noted facts that appeared to them to be of interest, and, as has been said before, the value of these occasional observations depends largely on their congruence. The fact that a certain person observed a particular phenomenon in one part of India at a certain time has by itself little general significance; but when we find men of different tastes and pursuits describing substantially the same phenomena, now here and now there, over a period of upwards of a century, each observation in turn contributes something towards a proof of the accuracy of the whole, and we are justified in combining the different items into something approaching to the complete picture which the writers of the period omitted to provide. One set of facts indeed comes to us from Indian as well as foreign sources—the liability of practically the whole country, excluding Bengal, to recurring periods of famine, with heavy mortality, enslavement of children, and cannibalism as its normal accompaniments; these facts are quite certain, and the dread of such a calamity must always have been present to the minds of the people, but they form the background of the picture rather than the picture itself. Cannibalism was a normal feature of a famine, but famine itself was an exceptional rather than a normal characteristic of the country and the period, and for our present purpose its importance lies in the evidence which it furnishes that the mass of the people had no economic reserve. Early in the sixteenth century Barbosa wrote of the Coromandel coast, that although the country was very abundantly provided, yet if the rains failed, famine caused heavy mortality, and children were sold for less than a rupee; the writer goes on to tell how in such seasons the Malabar ships brought food to the hungry, and returned laden with slaves which had been obtained in exchange. A generation later, Correa tells of depopulation and cannibalism on the same coast; a decade after Correa, Badaoni records similar scenes near Agra and Delhi; Caesar Frederic describes the sale of children in Gujarat about 1560; Linschoten when living in Goa saw children brought to be sold, and adults seeking to be enslaved; towards the end of the century it was again the turn of Northern India, and the accumulation of evidence shows that the people were dependent on the season for their subsistence, and that a failure of the rains resulted in an immediate economic collapse. The background of the picture is thus easily grasped.

When we look for evidence of normal rather than exceptional conditions, we may begin with the earliest of the writers who can fairly be called modern, the Italian Conti and the Russian monk Nikitin. Conti has nothing to say about the common people, though he gives an enthusiastic account of the splendour of the upper classes. Nikitin, who travelled in parts of the Deccan and Vijayanagar early in the fifteenth century, says, if the translation of his narrative may be trusted:[1] "The land is overstocked with people; but those in the country are very miserable, while the nobles are extremely opulent and delight in luxury." The latter statement agrees with what we have found was the case in the time of Akbar, and the former need not excite surprise. Our next authority is Barbosa, who wrote at the beginning of the sixteenth century. He was struck with the poverty existing on the Malabar coast, since he insists on the inferiority of the rice shipped for the use of the common people, and he mentions that some of the lower classes in that region were very poor, some bringing wood and grass for sale in the city, others living on roots and wild fruits, covering themselves with leaves, and eating the flesh of wild animals; it is clear, therefore, that extreme poverty existed in Malabar, but we are not told the extent to which it prevailed. A similar impression is given by Varthema, whose experience was practically contemporary with that of Barbosa; he notes that at one place on the Malabar coast the people lived very miserably; he comments on the inferiority of house accommodation at Calicut and elsewhere, valuing houses at "half a ducat each, or one or two ducats at most"; while regarding Vijayanagar he remarks that the common people "go quite naked with the exception of a piece of cloth about their middle." These facts are relevant, and he says nothing to suggest that he was anywhere struck by the prosperity of the common people, while in most of the places described he passes over the subject in silence.[2]

[1] The narratives of Conti and Nikitin are translated in Major's *India in the Fifteenth Century*; the quotation is from page 14 of Nikitin's narrative. The translation of Nikitin is not altogether convincing in the case of a few passages, but I have not access to the original, and can say only that I suspect that a translator with personal knowledge of India might be able to throw light on some sentences which are at present obscure.

[2] The introduction to the translation of Varthema published by the Hakluyt Society states (p. lxxiii) that "another inference deducible from our narrative is the uniform prosperity of the inhabitants. Excepting the case of the outcast *paulias* of Malabar, the different classes of the population appear to have been in a thriving condition." I have not been able to find

About a quarter of a century after Varthema and Barbosa we come to Paes and Nuniz, the Portuguese chroniclers of Vijayanagar. Their evidence may be stated in the words of Mr. Sewell, who, after quoting Nuniz's description of the revenue system, says: "This statement, coming as it does from a totally external source, strongly supports the view often held that the ryots of Southern India were grievously oppressed by the nobles when subject to Hindu government. Other passages in both these chronicles, each of which was written quite independently of the other, confirm the assertion here made as to the mass of the people being ground down and living in the greatest poverty and distress." This evidence is important, because it relates to the period when Vijayanagar was at the height of its prosperity, and points to conditions prevailing over an area nearly as large as the modern Presidency of Madras.

The next witness is Linschoten, whose observations deal with conditions on the west coast between 1580 and 1590. He gives precise details of the poverty of the "common" Indians living in Goa, while of the country-people his account is even less favourable: they live very poorly, go naked, and "are so miserable that for a penny they would endure to be whipped, and they eat so little that it seemeth they live by the air; they are likewise most of them small and weak of limbs." After Linschoten we come to the incidental observations of the first English travellers. Hawkins, who spent some time at the Court at Agra about the year 1610, attributed the lawlessness prevailing over large parts of the Empire to the oppression practised on the country-people, who were "racked" by grantees hurrying to get money before their grants passed into other hands. Salbank, writing of the thickly populated country between Agra and Lahore, observes that some of the Mogul's subjects "are said to be very wealthy, such I mean as derive estates from him; but the plebeian sort

in the narrative itself a single positive statement in favour of this view, and in order to deduce the inference stated we should have to assume that when Varthema says nothing about any class, that class was in a prosperous condition, an assumption which seems to me to be absolutely unjustifiable.

is so poor that the greatest part of them go naked." Jourdain, who had seen the country between Surat and Agra, summed up his experience a little later in the aphorism that India lived "like the fishes in the sea—the greater eat the lesser." A few years later Sir Thomas Roe stated the same idea in more detail: the people of India "live as fishes do in the sea—the great ones eat up the little. For first the farmer robs the peasant, the gentleman robs the farmer, the greater robs the lesser, and the King robs all." Such remarks as these, the casual observations of men of affairs to whom the condition of the people was a matter of no immediate concern, throw definite though narrow rays of light on the subject with which we are concerned, and we may add the summary of what the English merchants were able to learn of the possibilities of Bengal as a seat of trade: they were told that the market was limited to the "gentry," of whom there were very few, and that most of the inhabitants were very poor. Meanwhile Pyrard had summed up his observations of life on the west coast, recording that the common people "throughout all these countries are much despised, vile and abject beings, just like slaves," while about the year 1624 della Valle gave incidentally a similar glimpse of Surat, which was then benefiting from the recent development of foreign trade. He explains the large establishments kept by almost "everybody" by pointing out that the people were numerous, wages were very low, and slaves cost practically nothing to keep. A few years later de Laet summarised the information he had collected from English, Dutch, and Portuguese sources regarding the Mogul Empire as a whole, in what is the nearest approach to a systematic description that has survived. "The condition of the common people in these regions is," he says, "exceedingly miserable"; wages are low; workmen get one regular meal a day; the houses are wretched and practically unfurnished, and people have not sufficient covering to keep warm in winter. It would be going beyond our period to quote the various later travellers who recorded similar observations, but it is important to note that before the end of the seventeenth century the poverty of the people had become so notorious in England that it could be employed as an argument in current political controversy.[1]

These glimpses of the condition of the common people are not sufficient to furnish the basis of a minute comparison with the position at the present day: we cannot deduce from them whether the masses were somewhat better off, or somewhat worse off, than now, but to my mind they afford adequate justification for the statement that there has been no great qualitative change, and that from the fifteenth to the seventeenth century the great majority of the population of India were exceedingly poor, when judged by contemporary European standards, which, it must be remembered, were lower than the standards which now prevail. We may conclude, then, that, speaking generally, the masses lived on the same economic plane as now, and can proceed to examine the evidence in more detail in order to see if it indicates changes in the degree of poverty.

V. Food, Clothing, and other Details

It is clear from contemporary accounts that the diet of the common people throughout India consisted essentially of the same articles as now—rice, millets, and pulses, with fish in Bengal and on the coasts, and meat in the south of the peninsula. Terry, writing chiefly of his experience in the Imperial camp in Malwa, makes it plain that "the meaner sort of people" did not eat wheat, but used the flour of "a coarse, well-tasted grain," which from the locality we may reasonably set down as jowār. The condition of agriculture in the Mogul provinces from Agra to Lahore makes it to my mind highly probable that wheat was less commonly eaten than now by the peasants in that part of the country; millets were largely

[1] In a pamphlet of 1697, styled *The Great necessity and advantage of preserving our own Manufactures*, by "N. C., a Weaver of London," the East India Company were bitterly attacked for injuring home industries by "having their goods cheap wrought by the wretched poverty of that numerous people." A copy of the pamphlet is in the British Museum; it is quoted in Cunningham's *English Industry and Commerce* ("The Mercantile System," p. 463).

grown, and they must have been intended for local consumption, while it is unlikely that importation of supplies of wheat for the Court would have been necessary if ordinary people were accustomed to consume that staple. I have, however, found no direct evidence on this point, as the food of the common people in the north is not described by any authority. On the question of greater interest, the quantity of food, there is also almost complete silence; indeed the only writer who touches on it seems to be de Laet, who noted that the principal article of food was "kitsery," composed of pulse and rice, which was eaten with a little butter in the evening, while in the daytime the people chewed pulse or other parched grain. According to de Laet, then, there was only one regular meal a day; his statement is made in general terms, but we should scarcely be justified in applying it to the whole country, nor may we extend the application of Linschoten's observation of definite under-feeding beyond the west coast where it was made; and apart from these two writers there is nothing to show that in ordinary times the people had either more or less to eat than they have now.

As regards fats, sugar, and salt, the principal adjuncts to the diet of ordinary people, there are not sufficient materials to furnish conclusions applicable to the whole of India, but it is permissible to take the prices of these articles recorded by Abul Fazl as indicating with substantial accuracy the position in the Imperial camp and the surrounding country, and as suggesting more vaguely the conditions prevailing in a larger area of Northern India. The figures in question show that fats, that is to say, butter (*ghi*) and the seeds furnishing edible oils, were, relatively to grain, distinctly cheaper than now, and in this respect the lower classes were better off as consumers, though not as producers. This inference is borne out, to some extent, by de Laet's mention of butter, which has just been quoted, and incidental remarks made by other writers are consistent with the same view. On the other hand, salt and at least the better qualities of sugar were dearer than at present. In terms of grain, salt was more than double the present price, and remembering that the Court was usually located comparatively near to the chief centres of supply, we may conclude that the extra cost was still greater in the country farther south and east. The case of sugar is more doubtful, but I think the probabilities are in favour of the view put forward in Chapter V., that refined sugar was a luxury beyond the means of the poor, and that sweetmeats must have been made almost entirely of the raw product (*gur*). The extent to which sweetmeats were eaten is uncertain; travellers say nothing to indicate that they were as now a staple food, and sugar was so expensive in Europe at this period that we should expect them to have noticed this form of consumption if it had been a conspicuous feature of the halting-places on the roads. I am myself inclined to think that the large consumption of sweetmeats is a comparatively modern feature of Indian life, but the evidence in favour of this view is wholly negative and does not justify a definite conclusion. Perhaps the changes in regard to this group of adjuncts may be taken as unimportant on balance; consumers have certainly benefited by cheaper salt and refined sugar, while they have suffered through the rise in the price of *ghi*, and it is not improbable that different parts of the country have been affected in different ways by alterations in the supply of the commonest forms of saccharine products.

The position in regard to housing accommodation is clear. No traveller has a good word to say for the houses occupied by the masses in any part of India, and it is scarcely worth while to reproduce their contemptuous descriptions in detail; even Terry, who usually looked on the bright side of things, wrote that the cottages in the villages were "miserably poor, little and base," and we have similar accounts from all sides of India. Unfortunately this general condemnation is still substantially deserved: in some parts of the country, notably Bengal and Central India, progress has of late years been rapid in the matter of making the buildings weather-proof, but apart from this change, the housing of the people can still be described in the terms used three centuries ago, and the descriptions afford no basis for a comparative estimate of the degree of wealth or poverty. There are some indications that the class of houses occupied by the masses in the cities has improved; it would not now be correct to say of Agra, for instance, what Jourdain said of it, that "most part of the city is straw houses, which once or twice a year is burnt to the ground," but the change in this case is probably to be explained by the fact that most of the population of the capital had to be prepared to follow the Imperial camp, and ordinary people were not likely to go to the expense of providing permanent homes.

The supply of furniture was scanty, as is still the case. De Laet records that furniture was exceedingly rare, consisting only of a few earthen vessels, bedsteads, and thin and scanty bedding, while Linschoten, writing of the west coast, says that "the household stuff of the people is mats of straw, both to sit and lie upon," and that their "tables, tablecloths and napkins" are made of plantain-leaves. Such descriptions still hold good in the main, but there is a definite change to be recorded in regard to articles of metal, and particularly household utensils. We should expect travellers on the look-out for unfamiliar things to take special note of the brass or copper vessels now so commonly seen, which are rendered conspicuous to foreign observers by their shape as well as by their lustre, and by the scrupulous etiquette with which they are handled, but as a matter of fact such possessions are very rarely mentioned. Linschoten wrote that the common people at Goa drank out of a "copper can," but used earthenware pots for cooking, while the country people in the same region "drink out of a copper can with a spout, which is all the metal they have in their houses"; but with the exception of this writer I have found no mention of such utensils. Nikitin in the fifteenth and de Laet in the seventeenth century spoke only of earthenware,[1] and even Terry said nothing of brass vessels, though he was careful to note the use of "thin iron plates" for baking bread, and might be expected to pay equal attention to the more conspicuous utensils had they

[1] Nikitin's translator writes (p. 17) of "a stone pot," which, I take it, signifies earthenware.

come under his observation. The view suggested by the silence of the authorities that ordinary people used much less metal than now, is rendered probable by the facts regarding prices given in a previous chapter. Copper coins circulated, it will be remembered, at the value of the metal they contained, and not as is now the case as tokens, so that a drinking-cup or dish would have cost approximately its weight in coins. In the neighbourhood of Akbar's Court copper cost five times as much grain as now, and we have seen that it cannot have been materially cheaper in the south; a supply of vessels comparable to that which the people now possess would thus have represented a large aggregate of wealth, and it is reasonable to conclude that to ordinary people metal goods in general were luxuries, desired perhaps as they are desired now, but too costly to be obtained in the quantities which are now available.

Contemporary evidence is more copious in regard to clothing than to furniture, but its general effect is rather to lay stress on the nakedness of the people than to enter into details regarding the various garments worn. The importance of clothing depends so much on the climate that it will be well to review the evidence under two heads, taking first the observations relating to the south, where the question is mainly conventional, and then passing to Northern and Central India, where, for some part of the year, adequate clothing is necessary for efficiency. The tradition of the nakedness of the south is of old standing, and can be traced through various writers onwards from the beginning of the fourteenth century, when John of Montecorvino wrote that tailors were not required as the people went naked, covering only the loins. In the fifteenth century, Nikitin said that the Hindus of the Deccan "are all naked and barefooted." Barbosa notes that the Hindus of the Deccan go naked from the waist upwards and wear small turbans on their heads. Varthema records of the Hindus of Gujarat that "some of them go naked, and others cover only their privities," while as regards Vijayanagar he states that "the common people go quite naked, with the exception of a piece of cloth about their middle." Fitch writes that at Golconda "the men and the women do go with a cloth bound about their middles without any other apparel." Linschoten says that the peasants in the neighbourhood of Goa "go naked, their privy members only covered with a cloth," and della Valle writes regarding the population of that city that "the people is numerous, but the greatest part are slaves, a black and lewd generation, going naked for the most part or else very ill clad." Of the people of Calicut the same writer remarks that "as for clothing they need little, both men and women going quite naked, saving that they have a piece either of cotton or silk hanging down from the girdle to the knee." De Laet does not describe the clothing of the common people, but he notes the scantiness of their bedding, "convenient during great heat, but of little use when the weather is really cold," and the remark may serve as a summary of the foregoing observations. It will be noticed that nothing is said of coats or upper garments, which are now common, though by no means universal.

For the north of India we have in the first place the observations of the Emperor Babur, according to whom "peasants and people of low standing go about naked. They tie on a thing which they call *lunguta*, a decency-clout which hangs two spans below the navel. From the tie of this pendant decency-clout, another clout is passed between the thighs and made fast behind. Women also tie on a cloth (*lung*), one half of which goes round the waist, the other is thrown over the head." This description is so detailed that it appears reasonable to accept it as exhaustive. Towards the end of the sixteenth century Fitch made some notes on the clothes worn in the Gangetic plain. At Benares he says that "the people go all naked save a little cloth bound about their middle. . . . In the winter, which is our May,[1] the men

[1] Fitch does not give his dates in detail, but he left Agra at the end of September, and reached Bengal in five months, so he may have been in Benares during the real "winter." The reference to May is an obvious error. The Portuguese on the west coast spoke of the rainy season as "winter," and travellers who entered India from that side occasionally say that winter begins in May; I suspect Fitch had this use of the word in mind when he inserted the parenthesis, which strikes the reader as ridiculous.

wear quilted gowns of cotton . . . and quilted caps." At Tanda, near the old capital city of Gaur, he writes that "the people go naked with a little cloth bound about their waist"; he uses the same expressions regarding the people of Bacola, which was situated near Chittagong; while as regards Sonargaon, the capital city, he tells us that the people "go with a little cloth before them, and all the rest of their body is naked." These statements are corroborated as regards Bengal by the remark in the *Ain-i Akbari* that men and women for the most part go naked, wearing only a cloth; unfortunately for our present purpose, Abul Fazl did not give similar information regarding the remaining provinces of the Empire, for which we are dependent on the statements already quoted, and on the incidental observation of Salbank regarding the country between Agra and Lahore, that "the plebeian sort is so poor that the greatest part of them go naked in their whole body save their privities, which they cover with a linen [1] coverture." The most striking feature of these accounts is the absence of any covering for the upper part of the body, and in this respect they are certainly not applicable to Northern India at the present time; we should expect also that a writer like Babur would have described the turbans now so commonly worn in the Panjab if they had come under his observation; and it appears reasonable to conclude that less clothing was generally worn. I have found no mention of woollen garments in any part of India, and no record of blankets being used or carried by the common people.

The tradition of nakedness in the south extends to the feet. John of Montecorvino reported that shoemakers were as little required as tailors. Nikitin said, as we have seen, that the people of the Deccan went barefoot. Paes says the same thing of "the majority of the people, or almost all," in Vijayanagar; and since Linschoten describes the shoes of the better classes in the vicinity of Goa, we may regard his silence

[1] The word "linen" was frequently applied at this period to cotton cloth by visitors from Europe, to whom linen was the more familiar fabric of the two. *Della Valle*, for instance, says (p. 43) that "the linen is altogether of bumbast or cotton, there being no flax in India."

regarding the lower classes as significant. So far as Northern India is concerned, the evidence on this point is almost entirely negative. Barbosa states that in his time the common people in the city of Bengala wore shoes, but with the exception of this statement I have not found a shoe mentioned anywhere north of the Narbada river, and while this fact is not conclusive, the silence of such a writer as Babur appears to me to be at least suggestive; it is possible that shoes were as widely worn as now, but the probability lies in the contrary direction. If, as I believe, shoes were less worn than now throughout India, the cause is not to be found in the high cost of leather, which, as we have seen in a previous chapter, was probably abundant, at least in the raw state, and we must assume that, though the cost was small, the means of the people were insufficient to provide articles which were not strictly necessary for subsistence. In regard to other garments, the cost of material may have been a factor of some importance; the statistics of prices given by Abul Fazl suggest that both cotton and woollen goods were dearer than now in terms of grain, but they are not by themselves sufficient to justify a definite conclusion, and the most that can be said is that they point in the same direction as the statements of travellers, and make it easier to understand their insistence on the nakedness of the masses of the population.

In other matters, people seem to have lived under Akbar much as they live now, and a quantitative comparison of their expenditure is impossible. Pilgrimages were popular, and in the absence of means of rapid travel they may have cost more than now, but we do not know the proportion of the people who were able to make them. Marriages were celebrated in the style which is still familiar, but we are not in a position to compare the expense incurred. Jewellery and metal ornaments were largely worn, but there is nothing to show the extent of the practice, and our knowledge may be summed up in della Valle's remark that "those that have them adorn themselves with many gold-works and jewels." There were almost certainly fewer possibilities than now of spending money on the trifles and small conveniences obtainable everywhere at the present day—pocket-knives, buttons, looking-glasses, and similar goods; they were not then on the market, and probably the want of them was not felt. Intoxicating liquors, opium, and drugs appear to have been readily obtainable in most parts of the country, and, as I have said in an earlier chapter, the restrictions contained in Akbar's regulations were probably not systematically enforced, but we have no information regarding the consumption of the masses, and it can be said only that over-indulgence did not occur on a scale to attract the attention of foreign visitors. Tobacco was not as yet generally available, and I have found no suggestion that the common people smoked any indigenous product, so that apparently we must conclude that the practice is comparatively novel. It is reasonable to infer that little money was spent on litigation: professional lawyers did not exist, and I doubt whether many high officers of the period would have given much time to the investigation of disputes among those of the common people who were not in a position to offer really substantial bribes. On the other hand, rather more was probably spent than now in satisfying the demands of petty officials of various classes, but it is impossible to form any definite idea of the expenditure necessary under this head.

To complete our review of the circumstances of the people, a few words should be said regarding the benefits which they were able to enjoy without payment. So far as the activities of the State were concerned, these benefits appear to have been very scanty indeed. There were some unmetalled roads, and a very small number of bridges; there was nothing in the way of organised medical assistance; I can trace no signs of a system of popular education;[1] and the day had not come for schemes of industrial or agricultural develop-

[1] I make this statement with all respect to the remarks of Mr. N. L. Law (*Promotion of Learning in India during the Muhammadan Period*, pp. 160-162) on the improved "system" of education introduced by Akbar. The chapter of Abul Fazl on which Mr. Law relies cannot be read as indicating that anything was actually done: it is true that Akbar suggested a new and exceedingly ambitious curriculum, but, as I have said in a note to Chapter III., the absence of administrative details shows that the matter stopped there.

ment, or for the provision of veterinary treatment or other modern forms of State activity. In all these matters the masses are economically better off at the present day. The question of the benefits arising from charitable endowments is not quite so clear, but, if one might judge from the surviving institutions, I should be inclined to conclude that for the people at large these benefits were of small account, though they may have been substantial in the case of particular localities or special classes of the population; speaking generally, the common people had to provide what they needed for themselves.

At the beginning of this chapter I suggested that the scattered and fragmentary observations, which alone are available, could be pieced together so as to make something like a picture of the economic life of India at the close of Akbar's reign. The picture which I see is this. The upper classes, small in numbers and consisting largely of foreigners, enjoyed incomes which were very great relatively to reasonable needs, and as a rule they spent these incomes lavishly on objects of luxury and display. They did practically nothing towards promoting the economic development of the country, and such part of their income as was not spent was hoarded in unproductive forms. The single benefit resulting from their activities was indirect: their patronage of foreign merchants, dictated solely by the desire for novelty, in fact facilitated the opening of new channels of trade, and thus paved the way for economic developments in the future. Enjoying this patronage, the merchants on the coast adopted a somewhat similar style of living, but elsewhere it was dangerous for traders or men of business to indulge in open expenditure, and, like the rest of the middle classes, they lived inconspicuous and probably frugal lives. The great bulk of the population lived on the same economic plane as now: we cannot be sure whether they had a little more or a little less to eat, but they probably had fewer clothes, and they were certainly worse off in regard to household utensils and to some of the minor conveniences and gratifications of life, while they enjoyed practically nothing in the way of communal services and advantages. That is the picture itself: in the background is the shadow of famine, a word which has changed its meaning within the last century. In Akbar's time, and long afterwards, it meant complete if temporary economic chaos, marked by features which, repulsive as they are, must not be left out—destruction of homes, sale of children into slavery, hopeless wandering in search of food, and finally starvation, with cannibalism as the only possible alternative. It is against this background that the splendours of Agra or Vijayanagar must be viewed.

AUTHORITIES FOR CHAPTER VII

SECTION 1.—*Nil.*

SECTION 2.—Details regarding the supply of ice are given in *Ain*, translation, i. 56. For fruit, see i. 65, also Babur's *Memoirs*, 503, and *Tuzuk*, *passim*. For the style of food, see *Ain*, translation, i. 57; *Terry*, 195, and *Manrique*, lxvi. Terry's account of Asaf Khan's banquet is quoted at length in V. Smith's *Akbar*, 504.

The particulars given regarding dress are taken from *Ain*, translation, i. xxviii and 87-94; those regarding the stable are from i. 118, 126, 129; for gambling and sport, see i. 219. Tents are described in i. 45-55.

Particulars as to the staff of servants at the Mogul Court have been given in Chapter III.; the references for other parts of India are *della Valle*, 42; *Thévenot*, 307; *Pyrard*, ii. 75, 80, 135; *Hay*, 750 and *passim*. *De Laet's* general conclusion is p. 119, and Roe's corresponding observations are in *Letters Received*, vi. 298.

For presents, see *Tuzuk*, i. 103, 132, 134, etc.; *Hay*, 723, 762, 869; *Roe*, 110; *Sewell*, 281; *Manrique*, lxiv; but this list of references is very far from being exhaustive. The references to *Bernier* in the text are to pp. 213, 226, 230. The dowry provided by Raja Bhagwan Das is described in *Badaoni*, II. 352. *Tavernier* in particular refers (p. 75), to the difficulty of carrying money out of the country, and *Manrique*, lxxi, illustrates the practical importance of this rule.

SECTION 3.—Instances of the economic outlook of the chroniclers will be found in Elliot's *History*, iv. 246, 476. The risks of display are referred to by *Terry*, 391, and *Bernier*, 223, 229. For the merchants of the west coast, see *Barbosa*, 280, 342, and *della Valle*, 42.

SECTION 4.—The references to famine conditions are *Barbosa*, 358; *Hobson-Jobson* (*s.v.* Xerafine); Elliot's *History*, v. 490, vi. 193; *Purchas*, II. x. 1703, and *Linschoten*, c. 41; the list is by no means exhaustive. The passages cited as to normal conditions are, *Major*, 14; *Barbosa*, 295, 338, 339; *Varthema*, 129, 132, 136; *Sewell*, 379; *Linschoten*, c. 33, 39; *Purchas*, I. iii. 221; *Letters Received*, iv. 307, vi. 182; *Jourdain*, 162; *Roe*, 397; *Pyrard*, translation, i. 386; *della Valle*, 42.

SECTION 5.—For the nature of the food ordinarily consumed, see especially *Ain*, translation, ii. 122, 151, 239, 338; also *Barbosa*, 291; *Sewell*, 366; *della Valle*, 42; *Linschoten*, c. 33, and *Terry*, 198; for the quantity, see *de Laet*, 116. For the prices of food adjuncts, and of clothing, see *Journal, R.A.S.*, October 1918, 375 ff.

For housing, see, amongst other authorities, *Monserrate*, 152; *Purchas*, II. x. 1732–35; *Terry*, 179; *Thévenot*, 48, 104, 129, 281, and (in Agra) *Jourdain*, 162. For furniture, see *de Laet*, 116; *Linschoten*, c. 33, 39; *Major*, 17, and *Terry*, 198.

The references to clothing in Southern India are Yule, *Cathay*, iii. 57; *Major*, 12; *Barbosa*, 290; *Varthema*, 129; *Linschoten*, c. 39; *della Valle*, 157, 360; *Purchas*, II. x. 1732, and *de Laet*, 116: in the north, *Babur*, 519; *Ain*, translation, ii. 122; *Purchas*, II. x. 1735–37; *Letters Received*, vi. 182. For shoes, see Yule, *Cathay*, iii. 57; *Major*, 12; *Sewell*, 252; *Linschoten*, c. 38, 39, and *Barbosa*, 365.

For pilgrimages, see, *e.g.*, *Hay*, 719; for marriages, *Purchas*, II. x. 1732; for jewellery, *della Valle*, 45.

CHAPTER VIII

THE WEALTH OF INDIA

I. Contemporary Ideas

The question whether India was a rich country in Akbar's time can be answered in different ways according to our choice of a criterion of the wealth of nations. Ordinary Europeans of the period would, I think, have pointed as evidence of wealth to the visible stock of what they knew as costly commodities, while statesmen and financiers would have laid stress rather on the persistent influx of the precious metals, and although both these criteria are obsolete, their historical significance calls for a brief notice before we pass to an examination of the question as it presents itself to economists at the present day.

In the sixteenth century the ordinary European had, as I have said in the first chapter, very vague ideas about that large portion of the world which he spoke of in general terms as the Indies. He knew them at best as distant countries possessed of apparently unlimited supplies of commodities like spices, with which he and his neighbours were inadequately furnished; these commodities commanded high prices in Europe, and the fact that they were held in little account in their place of origin did not enter into the calculations of consumers in the West. The Indies were undoubtedly well supplied with spices and similar goods, travellers told tales, not necessarily exaggerated, of the splendours of Courts and Monarchs, and the popular idea of India's wealth required no further confirmation. The strength of its hold on the

Western imagination is perhaps best seen in the fact that it persisted even when the fear of India's cheap labour had become established; India was still accounted fabulously rich when India's population was known to be miserably poor.

It is unnecessary at the present day to discuss the validity of the alternative criterion adopted by Elizabethan statesmen and financiers. If the theory be admitted, their judgment was undoubtedly correct, for the influx of gold and silver into India is one of the permanent outstanding features of the commerce of the world. In the early days of the Roman Empire, as in the sixteenth century, India was eager to sell her produce, but wanted little merchandise in return, and then, as now, the balance of trade was adjusted by imports of the precious metals to an amount sufficient to excite alarm. At the period with which we are concerned, the topic was a commonplace among those travellers who were also men of affairs; it was discussed at length by Bernier in his Letter to Colbert, and referred to by various other writers, but for our present purpose it is perhaps sufficient to quote Sir Thomas Roe's remark that "Europe bleedeth to enrich Asia" as a concise illustration of the contemporary point of view.

The influx of treasure came from various sources. As has already been noticed, the official exports of Portugal consisted almost entirely of silver, which was expended on Indian commodities for shipment both eastwards and westwards. The Red Sea trade brought large sums, for a great part of the Indian exports were sold for cash at Mocha. The Persian trade contributed a substantial flow of silver, while the gold obtainable in East Africa was the main object of the Portuguese settlements at Sofala and Mozambique. Treasure was brought from the East as well as from the West, from Pegu, Siam, the Archipelago, and Japan, that is to say, from practically all countries except China, where the export was prohibited. A similar rule appears to have existed in India: as Terry wrote, the people of any nation were "very welcome, that bring in their bullion and carry away the other's merchandise; but it is looked on as a crime that is not easily answered, to transport any quantity of silver thence." Thus there was a large and regular influx, with at most a small outflow, and consequently a continuous addition to the stocks possessed by the country. The destination of this influx of treasure is a matter of much economic importance. Part of it was gradually used up in coinage, which consumed chiefly silver in the north and both gold and silver in the south. Industries also absorbed a substantial amount: gold thread was employed in the more costly cotton fabrics, silver plate was common in wealthy households, jewellery was worn by all who could afford it, and there was a wide scope for the display of both metals on animals, conveyances, and other objects of luxury. Only a part of the influx was, however, devoted to these purposes, and the balance of the precious metals was stored up in circumstances which prevented their employment in production. The accumulation of large hoards was essentially a feature of Hindu civilisation: the hoards were concentrated in the temples and the Courts, and while religious institutions appear to have steadily added to their possessions, the story that a king never touched his predecessor's treasure but accumulated a new hoard for himself was so widespread during the sixteenth century that it probably had a real foundation in fact. Paes, for instance, records that in Vijayanagar the treasury was sealed on the death of each Emperor, and opened only in the case of great need; while Babur says that Bengalis regarded the amassing of treasure as a glorious distinction, but it was disgraceful for a new ruler to expend what his predecessors had collected. The best evidence of the magnitude of these hoards is our knowledge of the violent dissipation which occurred from time to time. Thus the early Moslem invaders during the eleventh and twelfth centuries swept the north of India practically clear, and the stock of treasure remained low till it was replenished by Alauddin's campaigns in the Hindu south, when the soldiers threw away the silver because it was too heavy to carry, and the loot of gold, pearls, and diamonds was recorded in maunds. The fifteenth century again saw a depletion in the stock of Northern India; we are told that under Ibrahim Lodi gold and silver were procurable only with the greatest difficulty, and the deficiency continued until the Moguls replenished the north from Gujarat, Central India, and the Deccan. It is scarcely worth while to reproduce the chroniclers' statements of the sums which changed hands on these and similar occasions, but as a single instance it may be mentioned that after the battle of Talikot the royal family of Vijayanagar are said to have carried away treasure in gold, diamonds, and precious stones valued at more than a hundred millions sterling.[1] Compared with this sum, Akbar's accumulations, estimated by Mr. Vincent Smith at forty millions sterling in cash alone, appear comparatively modest, but it must be remembered that Akbar started with very little in hand, while the Vijayanagar treasure was probably in part at least of old standing.

It is not easy to determine how far this habit of hoarding prevailed among the people generally, as distinct from the rulers and the custodians of religious institutions. Tavernier asserts that many of the nobles at the Mogul Court accumulated gold, and, though I know of no direct authority for the statement, it is highly probable that the chiefs of Vijayanagar were intent at this period on amassing treasure in view of the political situation. Successful merchants must have held in the aggregate a large stock of cash, representing what would nowadays be called reserves and funds awaiting employment, and it is hard to draw a line between reserves and hoards. The lower classes can have hoarded very little gold, because of its high value in terms of commodities; a single gold *muhr* would have cost a peasant the entire produce of from two to three acres of wheat, and to a town labourer would have represented the wages of 200 days.[2] We are bound, however, to recognise that the habit, which is still

[1] I think we get a glimpse of a part of this treasure in a letter of a Jesuit missionary (*Hay*, 780), who in the year 1599 saw the treasure kept by the Vijayanagar Commander-in-Chief, and was told that much of it had once belonged to the Emperor.

[2] This illustration relates primarily to Northern India. In the south, where gold was in active circulation, and coins of small denomination were current, the lower classes may have been able to absorb a substantial amount.

prevalent, of keeping a few coins or jewels laid away and adding to the store when possible bears the marks of its antiquity on its face, and I have no doubt that a certain proportion of the influx of silver was absorbed by the more prosperous members of the lower classes. In one way or another, then, the precious metals were disposed of as they flowed into India, or as Hawkins wrote at the time, "All nations bring Coin, and carry away commodities for the same; and this Coin is buried in India, and goeth not out."

II. Modern Ideas

So far we have reached the position that India was regarded as rich by Europeans of the sixteenth century, either because of her visible stock of what they knew as costly commodities, or on account of her continued absorption of the precious metals, and in both cases opinion was substantially in accordance with the facts; we have now to inquire whether India was rich in the sense which the term conveys to modern economists. The modern criterion of wealth is the income of commodities, or more precisely the relation of that income to the numbers of the population: when we pass from wealth to well-being, we have further to take into account the way in which the income is distributed, because a nearer approach to equality will usually yield a greater aggregate of satisfaction, but so long as we are dealing with the wealth of a country as a unit, the question of distribution does not arise. In the foregoing chapters I have tried to estimate the changes which have taken place in the "average income," that is to say, in the income of commodities yielded relatively to the numbers of the population by each source in turn, and we may begin this inquiry by summarising the results which have so far been reached.

In the case of agriculture we have seen that while different parts of the country have been affected in different ways, it is improbable that for India, taken as a whole, the gross income per head of the rural population has changed by any large proportion: it may possibly be somewhat smaller, more probably it is somewhat larger than it was, but in either case the difference would not be so great as to indicate a definite alteration in the economic position. We may reasonably assume that the proportion of rural to total population has not changed materially; in Akbar's time, as at the present day, the population was mainly agricultural, and if there were proportionately more soldiers and domestics then, there are more town-workers now, so that we may conclude that the average income from agriculture per head of the total population is somewhere about the same. The summary of the results which have so far been reached will then stand as follows:

As regards primary production, agriculture yielded about the same average income as now; forests yielded about the same; fisheries perhaps somewhat more; and minerals almost certainly less.

As regards manufactures, agricultural industries show on balance no material change; the average income from miscellaneous handicrafts, wool-weaving, and transport production other than shipbuilding, has substantially increased, but silk-weaving shows a decline.

No estimate has yet been made of the average income from shipbuilding, cotton and jute weaving, or foreign commerce, while for our present purpose it is unnecessary to take internal commerce into account, commodities being valued at the place of consumption rather than of origin.

In combining these results, allowance must be made for differences in the importance of the various items. The silk industry, for instance, was of small volume, and even a large decrease in its total income would be almost negligible when spread over the entire population of the country, while the other probable decrease, that from fisheries, loses much of its significance in the same way. These two losses are probably much more than counterbalanced by the gains under mineral and transport production and miscellaneous handicrafts, but these gains in turn, substantial though they are, become very small when we set them beside the preponderating item of agricultural income, representing the results of the efforts of a majority of the whole population. So far then as those estimates are concerned, we may conclude that India was almost certainly not richer in Akbar's days than now, and that probably she was a little poorer; if there has been any change so large as to be capable of recognition by the rough tests which alone are available, we must look for it under the three sources of income for which estimates have not yet been offered, sources which, as we shall find, are very closely inter-related. If India was richer than now, the additional income must have consisted of the ships which she built, the textile goods which formed the most important single item of their outward cargo, and the excess value of the foreign goods which they brought back.

We have no direct knowledge of the annual output of shipping, but it is possible to make a rough estimate of the amount in existence in India at this period, and to calculate within wide limits the output required to maintain the existing supply. We have seen that the vessels leaving annually for foreign ports aggregated probably less than 60,000 tuns, so that by taking this figure as a basis we shall at any rate not underestimate the annual production. A deduction must be made for the ships built in Europe (about one-tenth of the total), but on the other hand an addition is required for the Indian ships employed in the direct trade between the Red Sea and Pegu, Malacca, Java, and Sumatra, and we may set this item off against the former, though it was probably not so large. No allowance need be made for ships in reserve, because, under the conditions imposed by the seasons, owners were practically compelled to send their ships out; if a vessel did not start at the proper time, the whole year's income was lost, and the deterioration resulting from a prolonged stay in harbour was perhaps an even more serious matter.[1] We may therefore take the aggregate of Indian sea-going merchant ships at a maximum of 60,000 tuns; 40,000 tuns is probably a liberal allowance for coasting craft, and 20,000 tuns for fighting ships,

[1] The injury to ships in Indian ports is mentioned by several navigators of the period. Payton, for instance, insists on the need for double-sheathing ships bound for Surat, where the danger from worms was particularly great (*Purchas*, I. iv. 522).

making 120,000 tuns in all.[1] The annual output required to maintain this amount of shipping depends on the annual rate of loss, which was very high according to modern ideas. The average life of a carrack seems to have been about three years, for Pyrard says that they usually made only two, or at most three, voyages, but a large proportion of the losses of these ships occurred in waters where Indian vessels did not ply, off the Cape of Good Hope or still farther west, and it is safe to say that the latter on the average lasted longer. How much longer they lasted is a matter of conjecture; from a consideration of such details as have been recorded regarding shipwrecks and losses by fire and capture, I think the average life must have been more than five years, but I doubt whether it can have been as much as ten, and on these lines the annual output would lie somewhere between 12,000 and 24,000 tuns, while it would be less if the average life was longer than I have conjectured. The figures I have given are the equivalent in carrying capacity of from 6000 to 12,000 net registered tons, and are thus greater, but not very much greater, than the output in the years before 1914, when from 4500 to 7800 net tons were built annually.[2] Allowing then for the difference in population, the shipbuilding industry has fallen off, but the loss in income is obviously insignificant when spread over the inhabitants of the whole country.

Turning to the income derived from foreign commerce, it will be remembered that no estimate has been offered of the rate of profit obtainable in the time of Akbar. We can, however, form some idea of what foreign trade meant to the country as a whole by comparing the amount of shipping

[1] The estimate for fighting ships includes the Portuguese navy and the forces maintained by the "pirates." The size of the former can be deduced from the detailed accounts of the fleets given in the later *Decadas*; the boats owned by the "pirates" were certainly fewer and smaller than those of the Portuguese, and I have taken their total as a little more than half that of their enemies.

[2] These figures are taken from Table No. 183 of the *Statistical Abstract relating to British India*: I have ascertained from the India Office that the tonnage shown in this table is *net*. Possibly the figures given should be raised to allow for construction in ports belonging to Indian States, but information on this point is not readily available, and the error cannot in any case be of much importance.

space per head. We have found that the probable maximum of space was equivalent to 36,000 net registered tons, and using the minimum estimate of population suggested in Chapter I. we can see that, in order to obtain the average income, the profit (whatever it was) which was obtainable from one ton of space must be divided among about 2800 persons at least. For the modern period, the profit from one ton has to be spread over fewer than 45 persons, and without going further into hypothetical calculations, the conclusion may fairly be drawn that the average income derived from sea-borne commerce may well have been less than now, and in any case cannot have been so much greater as to make a material difference in the average total income of the entire population of India, while the information which we possess regarding trade on the land frontiers shows that whatever the rate of profit may have been, its volume was even less significant for the country as a whole.[1]

The remaining source of income, the manufacture of cloth from cotton and jute, requires somewhat more detailed examination. We have seen that a substantial portion of the population may have worn jute clothing in the time of Akbar, while it may be conjectured that coarse cotton cloth was at that period used for packing other goods outside the very limited area where jute was grown, and since the uses of the two fibres have been interchanged, any attempt at comparison involves the abandonment of the distinction based on the nature of the material; we must think simply of cloth, and state the facts in terms of yards. The error introduced by neglecting differences in material and quality is much less than it looks, because the value of the material has already been taken into account as part of the income derived from

[1] For the benefit of readers who have not studied the comparative statistics of shipping, it may be worth while to give a few figures for other countries by way of contrast. Just before the war, the ships which cleared with cargo from Japan represented about two-fifths ton per head of the population, or say fifteen times the figure for India (including Burma). At the same period the United States had more than half a ton per head, Australia had one ton, and the United Kingdom nearly one and a half ton; a nation living largely by sea-borne commerce must send out yearly about one ton or more per head of the population.

agriculture, and we are now concerned only with the increase in value resulting from the processes of manufacture; we must recognise that the average of quality was probably higher in the sixteenth century than now, because a larger proportion of the cloth was made of cotton, but on the other hand we must take into account the greater width of much of the modern mill-woven cloth. A yard of "average" cloth was thus smaller as well as better in Akbar's time than now, and on the whole it forms a not unsuitable unit for the rough comparison which alone is possible.

Starting then with the facts of modern times we may say that, on the average of the years 1911–14, and taking production, imports, and exports into consideration, India consumed annually about 18½ yards of jute and cotton cloth per head of the population, while on a similar basis the production was from 15 to 15½ yards per head, leaving a net import of 3 yards or rather more: the question which we have to consider is thus whether production at the end of the sixteenth century was greater or less than 15 yards per head. At that period there were no imports of cloth made of these materials, and consequently production represented the total of exports and internal consumption. We can arrive at a rough measure of the possible exports from the volume of shipping space available, which we have taken at a maximum of 60,000 tuns. Cloth was the principal article carried, but other exports were numerous, and some of them were bulky; it is rare for a single class of goods to furnish as much as half the exports of a large country, and we shall not run any risk of underestimation if we assign two-thirds of the total space to cloth. On this assumption it is just barely possible that exports may have reached 200 million yards, though I think myself that this figure is probably far in excess of the truth; and using the minimum estimate of population previously suggested, we may thus put exports at a maximum of about 2 yards per head. Deducting this from present production, there remain 13 yards, and we have to ask whether the former consumption exceeded or fell short of this figure. Consumption falls under two main heads, packing (at present 2½ yards), and clothing (at present about 16 yards). The use of packing varies roughly with the volume of commerce, and the figures already dealt with show that this was trifling compared with the present standard; we may therefore infer that the cloth required for packing at the earlier period amounted to only a small fraction of a yard per head. As to clothing, we have seen in the last chapter that all over India clothes were probably less worn by the masses than now, and the present figure (16 yards) is therefore in excess of the standard of the time of Akbar. The amount of this excess is, in the present state of our knowledge, a matter of conjecture: if we guess that the average for clothing was 12 yards, then the total consumption must have been less than 13 yards, and the total production less than the present figure of about 15 yards; if we guess that clothing took 10 yards, then the total production must have been much less than now, while in order to arrive at a larger production per head we must assume that people in general used nearly as much cloth as now, though they certainly did not wear it in public. Finally, allowance should be made for the large modern export of yarn, to which there was nothing comparable in the time of Akbar: even if the production of finished cloth was as large as now, the scale would be turned against the earlier period by including these partially manufactured goods.

The general result of this somewhat tedious analysis is that we must choose between the following possibilities: (*a*) a total population of much less than our estimated minimum of 100 millions: (*b*) a volume of export-shipping much greater than our estimated maximum of 60,000 tuns; (*c*) internal consumption much larger than is suggested by contemporary accounts; (*d*) a production of cloth per head almost certainly not greater, and probably somewhat less, than now. Readers who accept the inferences drawn in previous chapters regarding the economic conditions of the period will conclude that the fourth alternative is the most probable, while those who seek to prove that production was substantially greater in Akbar's time than now must show that some or all of those inferences are mistaken. The average quality of the cloth produced was doubtless higher than now, but the difference may easily be exaggerated: the export markets took a very small proportion of the total, the consumption of the upper classes in India was quantitatively insignificant, and we must regard the great bulk of the cloth woven as similar to the coarse but durable fabrics which are still produced. I do not think, therefore, that the difference in quality requires any large allowance beyond that which has already been made in neglecting the greater average width of the modern production.

Thus a detailed examination of these sources of income—shipbuilding, foreign commerce, and textile manufactures—appears to me to justify the conclusion that they cannot have yielded so much more than now as to raise the average income of the country materially above its present level. The result can perhaps be stated more concisely as follows: If it be admitted that the mass of the people wore fewer clothes than now, then the whole question turns on the proportion of shipping to population. In order to establish the proposition that India was richer under Akbar, it would be necessary to show that a large proportion of the population was employed in building ships and manufacturing cloth with which to load them: it may be conceded that such an impression might have been formed by a traveller whose observations were limited to the coast from Diu to Goa, but it is to my mind inconceivable that the impression could have survived a journey across the thickly populated Deccan from Surat to Golconda, from Golconda northwards to Lahore, and then from Lahore to the mouth of the Ganges. When we look at India as a whole with the eyes of travellers who made these journeys, we see a population predominantly agricultural, and realise that the numbers employed in connection with foreign commerce can have formed only an inconsiderable fraction of the total.

We have thus passed in review all the important branches of production existing at the end of the sixteenth century, and are in a position to answer in general terms the question which we asked at the beginning of this section, whether India was rich in the sense of having an adequate income per head of the population. The answer is that India was almost certainly not richer than she is now, and that probably she was a little poorer. It is true that the country produced commodities which were eagerly sought for by other nations, and that by the sale of these commodities a steady influx of the precious metals was secured, so that people who viewed India from outside, and under the influence of economic theories which are now discarded, might be excused for forming an erroneous judgment of her wealth; but when we escape from the fascination exercised by a spectacular foreign commerce, and concentrate our attention on the resources of the country as a whole, our final verdict must be that, then as now, India was desperately poor. The information which is available suggests to me that the average income of commodities was probably even smaller than now; it does not suffice to afford definite proof that the stream of wealth has increased, but it justifies the conclusion that the deficiency of production which is the outstanding fact at the present day was, at the least, equally prominent at the close of the sixteenth century.

III. Distribution

We have now to consider the actual distribution of the income which we have hitherto treated as an aggregate, divisible in equal shares among the whole population of the country. The main conclusions which we have reached on this subject may be summarised as follows:

(1) The upper classes were able to live much more luxuriously in the time of Akbar than now.

(2) The middle classes appear, so far as our scanty knowledge goes, to have occupied more or less the same economic position as at present, but their numbers were proportionately much smaller, and they formed an unimportant section of the population.

(3) The lower classes, including very nearly all the productive elements, lived even more hardly than they live now.

The economic system of the period was so simple that it is easy for us to see how these differences arose. Speaking of India as a whole, we may say that producers enjoyed practically no communal benefits, and kept for themselves so much of their produce as was not taken from them, while the consuming classes took from the producers as much as they could; and since the bulk of the consuming classes were dependent mediately or immediately upon the State, the chief agent of distribution was the revenue-system in force. The effect of this system upon the great mass of producers, the cultivators of the soil, has been studied in some detail; we have seen that in the regulation-provinces of the Mogul Empire, comprising practically the whole of the northern plains as far as the west of Bengal and a substantial portion of the country farther south, the standard of the revenue-demand was about double the modern standard of rent, and we have found reason to infer that the share of the State was at least equally great in the territories of Vijayanagar and in the kingdoms of the Deccan.[1] In order to realise the significance of this fact, it is necessary to bear in mind that, while the revenue was calculated on the gross yield, it had to be paid from the net income. If the productivity of a holding is to be maintained, a substantial proportion of the gross yield must be expended in ways which are, strictly speaking, necessary; the peasant must keep himself and his family alive and fit for work, he must maintain the efficiency of his cattle and provide for their replacement, he must renew his implements, and he must pay wages and various other expenses of cultivation. The burden of this necessary outlay varies, but on a representative holding in Northern India it probably approximates to one-half of the gross yield which the peasant

[1] It may be repeated that this conclusion does not apply to those parts of the Mogul Empire where the regulation-system of assessment was not in force, notably Bengal and Berar, or to portions of some other provinces, comprising for the most part the least productive areas. We do not know the burden of the revenue in these tracts, but we may conjecture that it was not very much lighter than in the remainder of the Empire.

hopes to secure in favourable seasons. The revenue or rent is the first charge on the net income left after these expenses have been provided for, and when it has been paid, the balance is at the disposal of the peasant for comforts or luxuries, improvements, and investment or repayment of personal debts; his financial position depends, not on his gross income, but on the amount of the free surplus which remains at his disposal. The surplus for which Akbar's peasants could hope was at the best very small; if half the produce was required to cover necessary expenditure and one-third was claimed as revenue, there remained only one-sixth of the gross income expected in favourable years, and a very slight loss due to accidents of season would absorb the whole of the anticipated balance. Reduction of the revenue-demand by one-half would obviously double the amount of the free surplus, and thus leave the peasant a comparatively much larger sum of money to spend in prosperous times, while enabling him to carry on his business unaided in less favourable years. Speaking broadly, that is the difference between Akbar's times and the present day; the modern tenant-cultivator has more money to spend when seasons are good, and he can stand greater losses when seasons are bad. The peasant holding directly under the State ought to occupy a still more favourable position, since in modern times the revenue is less than the rent, and if the distinction is not so marked in practice as in theory, the reason is that the direct holder has commonly attained to a somewhat higher standard of life, particularly in regard to conventional necessaries. In any case, the reduction in the burden of compulsory payments which has taken place since the time of Akbar is quite sufficient to account for the observed improvement in the position of the peasant; he may not handle a larger gross produce than formerly, but he is able to keep a larger share of it for himself.

We may reasonably infer that the standard of life of the rural labourers was set by that of the peasants who employed them, in the sense that they were ordinarily somewhat worse off than their masters, and we can thus understand the contemporary observations summarised in the last chapter so far as they apply to the rural population as a whole: the standard of life was generally lower than now, for the simple reason that a larger proportion of the income obtained in the villages was diverted to the expenditure of the State. It is not possible to speak with the same confidence regarding the craftsmen and artisans, because we possess very little information regarding the burdens which they bore, but so far as they paid anything in the way of taxes or dues they were correspondingly worse off; their numbers were, however, small relatively to the agricultural population, and it is the contribution of the villages rather than the towns which marks the system of distribution in existence at the end of the sixteenth century.

The absorption by the State of so large a proportion of the peasants' free surplus is not necessarily to be considered as an economic evil. So far indeed, the conditions prevailing in the days of Akbar are in accordance with the ideals of some modern socialists, and the advisability of this distribution must be judged by the uses to which the appropriated surplus was devoted. Had it been expended in meeting the peasants' needs and in enabling them to lead a more reasonable life—in furnishing the various factors of agricultural production, in providing opportunities for education, or in securing medical relief and proper sanitary conditions—then the task of the critic would have been to determine whether the well-being of the people was on the whole promoted or not, and whether the benefits provided by the State gave more or less satisfaction than would have been obtained if the income had been left in the hands of those who earned it. This question, however, does not arise. Apart from a varying and imperfect measure of security, the peasant obtained no return whatever, and the large share of his free surplus which was taken by the State was expended in the interests of other classes forming a very small minority of the population. We have seen in earlier chapters how the share of the State was eventually disbursed; the bulk of it went on the purchase of articles of luxury, the increase in the stock of treasure, and the maintenance of a large mass of unproductive employment, and while these features still characterise the economic life of India, there can be no doubt that their relative importance has diminished. To complete our comparison between the two periods, it is desirable to trace the destination of that portion of the income of the country which has been diverted from these objects.

So far as I can see, the account is balanced by three main items, increase in communal expenditure, growth of the middle classes, and the modest improvement which, as we have found, has been effected in the standard of life of the masses of the people. The extension of communal expenditure is obvious in the provision now made for education, medical relief and sanitation, means of communication, and assistance to production in various forms; it cannot indeed be asserted that the needs of the country have yet been adequately met, but the mere enumeration of the objects of a modern administration is sufficient to mark the change since Akbar's days. The growth of the middle classes in numbers and resources is at least equally obvious. We may regard the great territorial magnates as in part the successors and representatives of the official nobility of the sixteenth century, but the ordinary landholder of Northern India is a new and distinctive feature, as is practically the whole of the professional class, lawyers, doctors, teachers, journalists, engineers, and the rest. Here again it cannot be maintained that, except perhaps in the case of landholders and lawyers, the needs of the country have been adequately met, but the progress already made is substantial, and speaking generally, our conclusion must be that, though the average income of India may be no greater than it was three centuries ago, the changes which have taken place in its distribution have resulted in a material increase in the well-being of the people taken as a whole. I should not like it to be thought that I regard the existing distribution as entirely satisfactory: unsolved problems which directly concern it are important now, and will be more important in the near future, but the standard of well-being, while it has improved, is still so deplorably low that nothing but a large increase in the national dividend will suffice; vary the distribution as we may, there is not at present enough to go round, and if this comparison of two widely different periods has any lesson for modern statesmen and administrators, it is the paramount need for concentration of effort to secure an adequate increase of production.

IV. Conclusion

We have now reached the final stage of our study. We have seen that the economic life of India at the end of the sixteenth century was characterised essentially by inadequate production and faulty distribution, and it remains only to take account of the tendencies at work; did the situation existing at the death of Akbar hold out a promise or a threat for the future prosperity of the country? The answer to this question must be that the whole tendency of the economic environment was still further to discourage production, and to enhance the existing faults of distribution, so that a period of increasing impoverishment was to be expected, but that other and less conspicuous forces were just beginning to operate which offered a more hopeful prospect for the distant future. In regard to the immediate outlook, we need only recall that producers as a whole were at the mercy of an administration conducted by men who were accustomed to extremes of luxury and display, who were discouraged by the conditions of their tenure from taking measures to foster the development of their charge, and who were impelled by the strongest motives to grasp for themselves the largest possible share of each producer's income. Productive enterprise was penalised, while the demands on the existing stream of commodities were certain to increase; the incentive to effort was bound to diminish, and the superior attractions of an unproductive life to become more and more apparent to all the most active elements of the population. Such was the immediate prospect: the history of the seventeenth and eighteenth centuries will show to what extent it was realised, but we are justified in saying that the position was unstable, and that the seed had been sown of economic and political collapse.

An Indian statesman of the period might well have recognised the dangers that lay ahead, but he could scarcely have detected the first inconspicuous signs of a further change. We have seen in a previous chapter that the demand of the upper classes for luxuries and novelties led to the patronage and encouragement of foreign merchants, and it is to the extension of the area of trade that the change in the economic situation is ultimately due. The foreigners who were attracted to the country pursued indeed a strictly self-regarding policy. Incidentally their activities stimulated production through the increased demand for commodities and the introduction of new staples and improved processes, but they did not at first exercise any influence on the administrative exploitation, which in Akbar's time and from a much earlier period dominated and sterilised the energies of the population of India. Contact with this root-evil was established only through the political changes of the eighteenth century, and thenceforward the main interest of Indian economic history lies in the gradual transition from the régime of exploitation, through indifference, to conscious effort for improvement. According to the theories current in England during the nineteenth century, the transition to administrative indifference should have sufficed, but subsequent experience has shown that the lesson of the past had been learned too well, and the slow and halting progress which has been achieved in recent years proves at once the force of the old evil tradition, and the need for conscious and organised effort directed towards its complete and final eradication.

AUTHORITIES FOR CHAPTER VIII

SECTION 1.—The absorption of the precious metals is referred to in *Bernier*, 202; *Roe*, 496; *Purchas*, I. iii. 221; *Terry*, 112, and various other writers. The sources are indicated by *Bernier*, *l.c.*, also by *Tavernier*, 393, and by other authorities quoted in Chapter VI. For the position in the early days of the Roman Empire, see Chap. II. of Gibbon's *Decline and Fall* (with Professor Bury's note, i. 55, of the edition of 1900); the evidence on the subject is noticed in *Rawlinson*.

The violent movements of accumulated wealth are recounted in Thomas' *Chronicles*, and can be followed in detail through the pages of Ferishta's *History*. For gold coins in Northern India, see *Tavernier*, 14-16, and *Terry*, 112, 113; for the sanctity of hoards, see *Sewell*, 282, and *Babur*, 483; for the scarcity of gold and silver under Ibrahim Lodi, see Elliot's *History*, iv. 476; for the Vijayanagar treasure, *Sewell*, 199; and for that of Akbar, V. Smith, *Akbar*, 347.

The remaining sections recapitulate results which have been reached in previous chapters, and it is unnecessary to repeat the references which have already been given.

APPENDIX A

THE CROPS GROWN IN INDIA IN THE SIXTEENTH CENTURY

1. The crops specified in the revenue statistics of the *Ain* may be arranged in modern classification as follows:

Cereals. Wheat. Barley. Rice.

Summer-rice is entered distinct from the two grades (*not* varieties) enumerated among the autumn crops.

Millets. Jowar. Bajra. Chena. Sawan. Kodon. Kakun. Mandwa. Kudiri or Kuri. Barti.

Bajra is entered as lahdara, a name now almost obsolete. Kakun is shown as Kal or Gal, with Kangni as synonym. Kudiri (or kuri) and Barti are both described as resembling sawan, and probably denote the lowest-grade millets such as kutki or mijhri: it is possible that one of these inferior crops may have gone out of cultivation, but the descriptions given are not sufficiently detailed to make this certain.

Pulses. Gram. Lentils (masur). Peas. Mung. Urd. Moth. Lubiya. Kulthi. Arhar.

Two varieties of gram were assessed under the names nakhud-i Kabuli and nakhud-i Hindi.

Kisāri is not shown in the tables of rates, but in the description of Bihar (for which no rates are given) it is mentioned as eaten by the poor, but unwholesome.

Oil-seeds. Til. Linseed. Rape. Toria. Safflower.

Sugar-cane. Two grades are distinguished, common and thick (paunda).

Fibres. Cotton. Hemp.

Dyes. Indigo. Al.

Drugs, etc. Poppy. Betel.

Miscellaneous. Various minor crops are specified, including vegetables, spices or relishes, water-nuts (singhara), melons (both Persian and Indian), and a long series of gourds and pumpkins.

2. Outside the provinces where the regulation-system of assessment was in force, the only indications I have noticed of additional crops in the Mogul Empire are (1) the statement referred to in the text that a kind of sackcloth was made in Bengal, which I take to indicate that jute was grown; and (2) the cultivation of tobacco in Gujarat, where it had just been acclimatised.

3. As regards Southern India, the following crops are mentioned by Paes, Nuniz, Garcia da Orta, or other sixteenth-century writers.

FOOD GRAINS. Rice. Wheat. Jowar. Ragi (mandwa). Millets in general.

Jowar appears as *milho zaburro,* the meaning of which is discussed in the next appendix. Barley is mentioned in one translation, but I doubt whether this is accurate.

PULSES. Gram. Mung. Horse-gram. Various pulses (unspecified).

OTHER CROPS. Sugar-cane. Cotton. Indigo. Til. Linseed. Pepper. Coconut. Ginger. Turmeric. Betel. Cardamom. Areca. Various vegetables (unspecified).

APPENDIX B

" INDIAN CORN " IN VIJAYANAGAR

Two passages in Mr. Sewell's *A Forgotten Empire* (pp. 237, 333) suggest that Indian Corn, or Maize (*Zea Mays*), was one of the commonest grains in Vijayanagar in the first half of the sixteenth century. This suggestion is rendered highly improbable by facts known to botanical students, which indicate that maize first reached India through Portuguese agency (vide *de Candolle*, under *Maize*), since in that case it could scarcely have become a staple crop on the upland within a very few years of the Portuguese settlement at Goa ; the expression translated " Indian Corn " is *Milho Zaburro* (literally, zaburro-millet), and while this rendering is justified by all the Anglo-Portuguese dictionaries within my reach, further investigation shows that it is not applicable to our period, when the expression meant not maize but the great millet Sorghum, known in India as jowār. A few details of this investigation will be useful to students as indicating the kind of precautions necessary in handling the evidence of sixteenth-century writers.

The word *zaburro* occurs in the works of various Portuguese writers on botany, while the allied form *ceburro* is used in Spanish. Regarding the meaning of these expressions, Dr. Stapf of Kew writes that " all the botanical authorities whom I have been able to consult, from Grisley, 1661, to Coutinho, 1913, connect Zaburro with Sorghum," while Sir David Prain, to whose kindness I am indebted for this information, has also given me a reference to Dodoens' *Frumentorum . . . Historia,* on p. 71 of which it is stated, under the heading *Sorghum,* that the Portuguese call it zaburro-millet (" *Lusitanis milium saburrũ appellatur* "). The date of this book is 1566, while the narratives translated by Mr. Sewell date from 1525 to 1535, so that we are justified in concluding that, whatever the modern signification may be, *Milho Zaburro* meant jowār, and not maize, at the time they were compiled.

Before this information reached me, I had tried to ascertain the meaning by tracing the derivation of the word *zaburro* (which is not explained in any of the modern dictionaries), but had failed to find any probable or even plausible origin in any of the Latin languages or in those of Northern Africa, the sources from which millets might be expected to have reached the Iberian peninsula, while the first records of the discovery of maize in America showed that the word could not have come from there. When these inquiries had yielded no result, Mr. R. Burn, C.S.I., suggested to me that the word might be of Indian origin and represent a corruption of jowār, and this appears to be the truth. The Portuguese had no letter with the sound of the Indian *j*, and they represented this sound by *z*; they had no *w*, and used either *b* or *v* in its place, while they commonly added an *o* in borrowing a substantive; examples of these changes can be easily found in *Hobson-Jobson* (*e.g.* Zedoaria from Jadwar, Baçaim from Wasai, Mungo from Mung), and it is clear that jowār might easily become zubāro, or with a natural change of stress, zubarro. At this point the suggestion was referred to Sir George Grierson, who wrote that metathesis of the *u* and the *a* need cause no difficulty, and that the word zaburro might be treated as most probably a corruption of jowār.

We thus reach the conclusions that *zaburro* certainly meant jowār in the sixteenth century, and that it is most probably the same word, transformed in the mouths of the Portuguese. Why it should now be given the sense of maize is a different question. If, as the dictionaries say, maize has assumed a Portuguese name belonging to a millet, the assumption can be paralleled in various other languages: in English, maize is commonly called corn ("Indian Corn"); in French, it is wheat ("blé de Turquie"); in South Africa, it is "mealies," that is *milje*, or millet; and in Oudh, it is "great jowār." It is, however, more probable that the Anglo-Portuguese lexicographers have been misled regarding the word, which is described correctly as a variety of Indian millet in Figueiredo's dictionary published in 1913, but at this point the interest of the topic becomes purely philological.

APPENDIX C

THE SEAPORTS OF BENGAL

When Portuguese writers of the sixteenth century speak of a voyage to Bengal they usually refer either to the Great (*grande*), or to the Little (*pequeno*), *Porto*. These names were adopted by writers of other nations (e.g. *porto piqueno* in *Purchas*, II. x. 1736), and the missionaries latinised them as *Portus Magnus* and *Portus Parvus* (e.g. *Hay*, 728 ff.). The word *porto* in these names seem to have been usually taken as the equivalent of the English "port," and hence modern writers have looked for only two important seaports in sixteenth-century Bengal; when this view is taken, the literature of the period leads at once to the identification of Hooghly (or Satgaon, which was close to it) as the "Small Port," and of Chittagong as the "Great Port," as is done by the authors of *Hobson-Jobson*. I believe this view to be mistaken. It seems to me that the word *porto*, in the mouths of seafaring Portuguese at this period, referred primarily to a gap in the coast-line, and not, as landsmen are apt to assume, a town on the sea-shore; in other words, *porto* might signify a gulf or estuary, which might contain several seaports. Modern Portuguese dictionaries recognise this meaning of the word, but their authority is not of great importance in a matter of the kind; my view that it is the primary meaning is based mainly on the language of Father F. Fernandus, a Jesuit missionary who was sent to Bengal in 1598 to attempt the reformation of the Portuguese settlements. His letter describing his journey is printed in *Hay*, 727 ff.

Fernandus embarked at Cochin for the *portus parvus* (*sic enim vocant*); the words in parenthesis indicate that he was giving the current name (*Porto pequeno*) of his destination. After describing various anxieties on the sea voyage, he speaks of a greater danger within the *portus*, when the ship ran aground; they succeeded, however, in getting off the shoal, and then after sailing for eight days, still in the *portus*, reached the Portuguese "station"[1] of Hooghly. It is clear, therefore, that Fernandus meant by *portus* the river, and not the town, of Hooghly, and I think it is equally clear that he must have taken his nomenclature from ordinary Portuguese, whether sailors on the ship or the men among whom he worked on land; he cannot have invented these names, and there is no reason to suppose that he did not follow the ordinary usage. Thus *Porto pequeno* does not necessarily signify any single town, but may denote the river Hooghly, on which Calcutta now stands.

After some months' stay, Fernandus went on to the *Portus magnus*; this was not a sea voyage, because he mentions the danger from tigers on the way, and doubtless his boat travelled by some of the inland waterways. He first reached Sripur, which he describes as a "station" belonging to the *Portus magnus*, and he dated his letter from this place, but he added a postscript to announce his arrival at Chittagong, also a "station" in the *Portus magnus*. Thus Fernandus certainly did not mean only Chittagong when he wrote *portus magnus*; the expression covered both Chittagong and Sripur. The situation of Chittagong is well known; that of Sripur is fixed by Fitch's description of his visit to Sonargaon,[2] the eastern capital of Bengal (*Purchas*, II. x. 1737). Sripur was on the "river of Ganges" and was six leagues from Sonargaon; it was a sea-going port, for Fitch sailed thence on a small ship for Pegu. Thus in the language used by Fernandus the *Porto grande* extended at any rate from the Karnaphuli river to the immediate neighbourhood of Dacca, and since he was probably using terms in their current meaning, we are not bound to limit the expression to any single port. The use of the expression becomes clear if we look at a map of the Bay of Bengal, and remember that the Portuguese came to Bengal by sea. On the left they would have the estuary of the Hooghly (*Porto pequeno*): on the right lay that of the Meghna stretching from the Backergunje district to Chittagong, and the whole of this constitutes the *Porto grande*. It may well have included numerous other ports in the landsman's sense of the word, but in any case it included both Chittagong and Sripur. We are not therefore bound to say that Bengal had only two seaports; it had, and has, two estuaries, with room for an indefinite number of seaports within them, and at the end of the sixteenth century there were

[1] The Latin word is *statio*. Is this the ancestor of the Anglo-Indian "station," a term of which the origin is not traced in *Hobson-Jobson*?

[2] Fitch writes phonetically: Sonargaon appears in his narrative as Sinnergan, and Sripur as Serrepore, but I think there can be no doubt as to the identification. Fernandus writes the latter name as Syripur.

at least three of sufficient importance to be noticed by our authorities, Hooghly on the river of the same name, Sripur some distance up the Meghna, and Chittagong.

This primary use of the word *Porto* was not, however, universal at our period; Fitch, for instance, definitely identifies the town of Satgaon with *Porto Pequeno* (*Purchas*, II. x. 1736), and some other writers can be read in the same way. The change in meaning may, I think, be attributed to the fact that the Portuguese did not to any great extent trade directly with Sripur; their communications were with either Hooghly or Chittagong, that is, with only one "station" in each *porto*, and in these circumstances the transfer of the name from the *porto* to the "station" might easily take place, just as "the Mersey" has become almost a synonym for Liverpool. The passages cited from Fernandus show, however, that up to the end of the sixteenth century the derivative meaning had not been universally adopted, and justify the view that *porto* may be read as estuary in any case where this interpretation is consistent with the context.

The question will naturally be asked which of these seaports represents the "city of Bengala" described by Barbosa at the beginning of the century. My own opinion is that Barbosa was referring to Sonargaon with its adjacent port, but the question is too intricate to be discussed here, and readers may wisely suspend judgment until the completion of Mr. Longworth Dames' translation of Barbosa.

APPENDIX D

THE SHIPPING TON

The origin of the shipping ton is the tun of wine. In European ports the practice grew up of describing a ship's capacity for cargo in terms of the number of tuns of wine which could be carried. A tun of wine consisted of two butts, and was equivalent to 40·3 cubic feet; adding the size of the casks, and the loss of space due to their irregular shape, the space occupied by a tun comes to about 60 cubic feet.[1] Originally the number of tuns was not reached by any process of measurement: the capacity of a ship which had carried wine would be known by experience, and practical men would acquire sufficient knowledge to judge the capacity of other ships by their appearance and build. It is such estimates as these that are available in regard to the period we are considering: they are all given in round numbers, and obviously are not intended to be accurate to a tun; on the average, they are probably fairly close to the truth, though there are doubtless errors in particular observations.

Towards the end of the sixteenth century the number of tuns for particular ships became an important question in England, because it determined the amount of the subsidy paid for shipbuilding, and estimates such as had hitherto sufficed became subject to bias; a system of measurement was therefore worked out to supersede such estimates. At the first attempt the number of tuns which could be carried in a particular ship was determined by experiment; the length, breadth, and depth of the ship were then measured, and the volume in cubic feet calculated; the rest was a sum in simple proportion. It was found that each actual tun required about 97 cubic feet of volume measured on

[1] *Oppenheim* gives 60 cubic feet: *Holmes* says that the tun is 42 cubic feet *plus* at least one-third of 42; this gives 56 cubic feet as the minimum. I take 60 as a convenient round number with a possible error small in comparison with the other factors to be considered.

the lines adopted, and this relation was made the basis of a general rule; find the volume of a ship by a particular set of measurements and divide by 97.

The effect of this rule was to alter the definition, but not at first the size, of the tun. The unit was still the space required by a tun of wine, and this space was found to be 97 cubic feet *measured in a particular way*. This system has survived up to the present day, but both the method of measurement and the divisor adopted have been varied from time to time. A "registered ton" is now defined as 100 cubic feet of space measured according to the precise specifications made under the Merchant Shipping Acts; it is a conventional unit, which has lost its original relation to the tun of wine, and its present relation could be determined with precision only by filling a series of modern cargo boats with tuns, a measure which nobody is likely to undertake. For our purposes, the important point is that the changes in the method of measurement have been in the direction of a closer approximation to the actual cargo space. The original method of measuring the length, breadth, and depth of the ship as a whole could give the actual cargo space only if the ship was rectangular and there were no internal structures below the topmost deck; the fact that 97 cubic feet (measured in this way) were required to accommodate 60 cubic feet (actual) shows that the cargo space was greatly overstated. This overstatement has now disappeared, because each deck is measured separately, and allowance is made for the curve of the sides; hence substantially less than 100 cubic feet (a measured ton) would now be required to accommodate a tun of wine, and in fact the volume of ordinary goods carried in recently-built vessels is, generally speaking, in excess of the volume given by the measurement. It follows that we shall not understate the cargo-capacity of Indian ships of the sixteenth century if we say that a tun of wine would require from $\frac{4}{10}$ to $\frac{6}{10}$ of a modern registered ton, instead of requiring a whole measured ton as was the case when measurement was first introduced. At this rate 1000 tuns of wine would require from 400 to 600 modern tons of shipping; and we should reduce the "tunnage" calculated for Indian trade in the sixteenth century by from $\frac{2}{5}$ to $\frac{3}{5}$ in order to compare it with the returns of shipping published at the present day. In the text I have arrived at 60,000 tuns as the probable maximum volume of Indian commerce: this would require from 24,000 to 36,000 tons present measurement, and since this figure has to be compared with about $6\frac{3}{4}$ million tons (the volume of Indian trade before the War), it really matters very little which fraction we take.

A word must be added regarding the modern distinction between gross and net tons. The shipping statistics which have just been quoted are given in *net* registered tons, but landsmen's ideas of ships are usually based on *gross* tons,[1] and the difference between the two is important. The gross tonnage of a ship includes space occupied by machinery, etc., and not available for cargo ; the net tonnage excludes the space so occupied. The relation between gross and net tonnage varies greatly among different classes of ships, but for modern cargo boats we shall not be very far from the truth in taking the net tonnage as on the average 60 per cent of the gross. If, then, we conclude that the Indian sea-borne commerce at the end of the sixteenth century could be carried in from 24,000 to 36,000 tons *net*, we may say that it would require from 40,000 to 60,000 tons *gross*, or at most one modern cargo-boat of moderate size sailing in each month of the year.

[1] Gross tons are given in the ordinary shipping advertisements, which are probably the most important sources of the landsman's rather vague ideas on the subject.

APPENDIX E

LIST OF AUTHORITIES

THIS list is arranged in the alphabetical order of the abbreviations or 'key-words' which have been used in the notes and references to the text.

ABDUR RAZAK. See under Major.

AIN. The Āīn-i Akbari. By Abul-Fazl-i 'Allāmī. Persian text, edited by H. Blochmann. Printed for the Asiatic Society of Bengal.

Translation by Blochmann and Jarrett. Printed for the Asiatic Society of Bengal.

AKBAR-NAMA. The Akbar-nāma. By Abul-Fazl-i 'Allāmī. Persian text issued by the Asiatic Society of Bengal.

Translation by H. Beveridge. Issued by the same Society, but not yet complete.

BABUR. The Memoirs of Bābur, a new translation of the Bābur-nāma, incorporating Leyden and Erskine's of 1826 A.D. By Annette S. Beveridge. London. Luzac & Co.

BADAONI. Muntakhab-ut-Tawārīkh. By al-Badaoni. Translation issued by the Asiatic Society of Bengal.

BARBOSA. Livro de Duarte Barbosa. Issued by the Lisbon Royal Academy of Sciences, as vol. ii. No. VII. of Colleção de Noticias para a Historia e Geographia das Nações Ultramarinas.

The translation issued for the Hakluyt Society in 1865 is now being superseded, and the first volume of the new rendering by Mr. Longworth Dames has been issued for 1918. Had this rendering been complete, I should have given references to it, but as only one volume is available, I have quoted the original text.

BERNIER. Travels in the Mogul Empire, 1656–68. Revised edition by A. Constable. London, 1891.

CLIFFORD. Further India. By H. Clifford. London, 1904.

CONTI. See under Major.

COUTO. See under Decadas.

CUNNINGHAM. Growth of English Industry and Commerce. 3rd edition, 1903.

DANVERS. The Portuguese in India. By F. C. Danvers. London, 1894.

DECADAS. (Decadas) da Asia. By J. de Barros and D. de Couto, 24 vols. Lisbon, 1777–88.

DE CANDOLLE. Origin of Cultivated Plants. By A. de Candolle. English translation. London, 1884.
The references given are to this translation. I have used the French edition of 1883.

DE LAET. De Imperio Magni Mogolis. By J. de Laet. Leyden, 1631.

DELLA VALLE. Travels in India. Hakluyt Society, 1892.

DODOENS. Frumentorum . . . Leguminum . . . Historia. By R. Dodonaeus. Antwerp, 1566.

DU JARRIC. Thesaurus Rerum Indicarum. By P. du Jarric. Cologne, 1615–16. (I have not had access to the original French edition.)

ELLIOT—HISTORY. The History of India as told by its own Historians. Edited from the posthumous papers of Sir H. M. Elliot. By J. Dowson. London, 1867–77.

ELLIOT—RACES. Memoirs on the History, Folklore and Distribution of the Races of the North-Western Provinces of India. By Sir H. M. Elliot. Edited by J. Beames. London, 1869.

ENGLISH FACTORIES. The English Factories in India. By W. Foster. Oxford.

EPSTEIN. Early History of the Levant Company. By M. Epstein. London, 1908.

FALCAO. Livro . . . en que se contem toda a fazienda e real patrimonio. . . . By L. de Figueiro Falcão. Lisbon, 1859.

FARIA Y SOUSA. The Portuguese Asia. By M. de Faria y Sousa. Translated by J. Stevens. London, 1695.

FIRST LETTER BOOK. The First Letter Book of the East India Company. By Sir G. Birdwood and W. Foster. London, 1893.

GARCIA DA ORTA. Colloquies on the Simples and Drugs of India. Translated by Sir C. Markham. London, 1913.

HAKLUYT. Collection of the Early Voyages, Travels, and Discoveries of the English Nation. Edition of 1809–12.

HAWKINS. The Hawkins Voyages. Edited for the Hakluyt Society, 1877.

HAY. De Rebus Iaponicis, Indicis et Pervanis. By John Hay. Antwerp, 1605.

HEATH. Some Account of the Worshipful Company of Grocers. By J. B. Heath. London, 1854.

HOBSON-JOBSON. A Glossary of Colloquial Anglo-Indian Words and Phrases. By Yule and Burnell. Edited by W. Crooke. London, 1903.

HOLMES. Ancient and Modern Ships. By Sir G. C. V. Holmes. Part I. London, 1900.

IMPERIAL GAZETTEER. The Imperial Gazetteer of India. 26 vols. Oxford, 1908.

IRVINE. The Army of the Indian Moghuls. By W. Irvine. London, 1903.

JOURDAIN. John Jourdain's Journal of a Voyage to the East Indies, 1608–17. Edited for the Hakluyt Society, 1905.

JOURNAL R.A.S. The Journal of the Royal Asiatic Society of Great Britain and Ireland. London.

JOURNAL A.S.B. The Journal of the Asiatic Society of Bengal. Calcutta.

LAW. The Promotion of Learning in India during Muhammadan Rule. By N. L. Law. London, 1916.

LETTERS RECEIVED. Letters Received by the East India Company from its Servants in the East. Vols. I.-VI. London, 1896–1902.

LEVASSEUR. La Population Française. By E. Levasseur. Paris, 1889.

LINSCHOTEN. The Voyage of John Huyghen van Linschoten to the East Indies. Edited for the Hakluyt Society, 1884.

LOPES. See under Sewell.

MACNAGHTEN. Principles of Hindu and Mohammedan Law. By Sir W. H. MacNaghten. Edited by H. H. Wilson. London, 1885.

MAFFEIUS—SELECT LETTERS. Selectarum Epistolarum ex India Libri Quatuor. By J. P. Maffeius. Antwerp, 1605.

MAFFEIUS—TRANSACTIONS. Rerum a Societate Jesu in Oriente Gestarum Volumen. By J. P. Maffeius. Coloniae, 1574.

MAJOR. India in the Fifteenth Century. Edited by R. H. Major for the Hakluyt Society, 1858.

(Contains translations of the narratives of Conti, Nikitin, and Abdur Razak.)

MANRIQUE. (I have not had access to the original *Itinerario* of Fray Sebastian Manrique. Some information derived from it is given in Murray (below), but the references in the text are to the translation of some chapters published by Sir Edward Maclagan in the Journal of the Panjab Historical Society, 1911, Vol. I. 83, 151.)

MONSERRATE. Mongolicae Legationis Commentarius. By Father A. Monserrate. Memoirs of the Asiatic Society of Bengal, Vol. III. 9, pp. 513–704.

MOOKERJI. A History of Indian Shipping. By R. Mookerji. London, 1912.

MUNDY. The Travels of Peter Mundy in Europe and Asia, Vol. II. Edited for the Hakluyt Society, 1914.

MURRAY. Historical Account of Discoveries and Travels in Asia. London, 1820.

NIKITIN. See under Major.

NUNIZ. See under Sewell.

OATEN. European Travellers in India. By E. F. Oaten. London, 1909.

OPPENHEIM. History of the Administration of the Navy. By M. Oppenheim. London, 1896.

PAES. See under Sewell.

PURCHAS. Purchas: His Pilgrimes. By S. Purchas. (I have used the reprint issued for the Hakluyt Society in 1905, but the references I have given are to the paging of the original edition, which is shown in the margin of the reprint.)

PYRARD. The Voyage of François Pyrard, of Laval, to the East Indies. Translated for the Hakluyt Society, 1887–89. (The references are given to this translation, but I have used the French text of the Paris edition of 1679.)

RAWLINSON. Intercourse between India and the Western World. By H. G. Rawlinson. London, 1916.

ROE. The Embassy of Sir Thomas Roe to the Court of the Great Mogul, 1615–19. Edited for the Hakluyt Society, 1899.

SCOTT. Constitution and Finance of English, Scottish and Irish Joint-Stock Companies to 1720. By W. R. Scott. Cambridge, 1910.

SEWELL. A Forgotten Empire. By R. Sewell. London, 1900.
(This contains translations of the Portuguese narratives of Paes and Nuniz. The text of these narratives is given in Chronica dos Reis de Bisnaga. By D. Lopes, Lisbon, 1897.)

SLAVERY REPORT. Slavery (East Indies). Despatch from the Governor-General, dated February 8, 1841 (No. 3). Printed by Order of the House of Commons, No. 262.

V. SMITH'S AKBAR. Akbar, the Great Mogul. By Vincent A. Smith. Oxford, 1917.

STEVENS. The Dawn of British Trade to the East Indies. By H. Stevens. London, 1886.

TAVERNIER. Les Six Voyages de J. B. Tavernier en Turquie, en Perse, et aux Indes. Seconde partie. Paris, 1692.

TERRY. Voyage to East India. By Edward Terry. (Reprint.) London, 1777.

THÉVENOT. Les Voyages de M. de Thévenot aux Indes Orientales. Amsterdam, 1727.

THOMAS—CHRONICLES. The Chronicles of the Pathan Kings of Delhi. By Edward Thomas. 1871.

THOMAS—RESOURCES. The Revenue Resources of the Mughal Empire in India, 1593–1707. By Edward Thomas. 1871.

THOROLD ROGERS. History of Agriculture and Prices in England, 1259–1793. By J. E. Thorold Rogers. Oxford. 1866–1902.

TUZUK. Memoirs of Jahangir, translated by A. Rogers. Edited by H. Beveridge for the Royal Asiatic Society. London, 1909–14.

USEFUL TABLES. Useful Tables, forming an Appendix to the Journal of the Asiatic Society (of Bengal). Calcutta, 1834–36.

VARTHEMA. The Travels of Ludovico di Varthema, translated for the Hakluyt Society, 1863. (I have not had access to the original text of this book.)

WHITEWAY. The Rise of Portuguese Power in India. By R. S. Whiteway. London, 1899.

YULE—CATHAY. Cathay and the Way Thither. By Sir Henry Yule. Edited by H. Cordier for the Hakluyt Society, 1913–16.

YULE—MARCO POLO. The Book of Marco Polo. By Sir Henry Yule, 3rd edition. London, 1903.

INDEX

Abd-un Nabi, Shaikh, 86
Abdur Razak, 11, 91
Abul Fazl, 20, 46 ; on Akbar's Court and Household, 66, 67, 68, 69, 71, 74, 78, 82, 84, 87, 92 (*note*), 186, 189, 190-91, 257, 258-60; local agriculture, 118, 119, 121, 123, 125 ; famine, 128 ; industry and mineral wealth, 146, 148, 149, 150 ; prices, 271, 277 ; silk trade, 173, 175 ; sugar, 157, 158 (*note*) ; textile trade, 177 (*note*), 182, 219
Abyssinian slaves, 26, 217
Account of the XII. Subas, 107, 118, 126 (*note*), 141
Achin, 213, 215, 236
Aden, 209, 216-17
Administration of Mogul Empire : civil, 77-82 ; Imperial Services, 65-77 ; judicial, 34-7 ; revenue, 3-5, 31-4, 46-50, 99, 100, 102-4, 131-6, 297-300
Afghanistan, 3, 5
Africa, trade with, 180, 181, 182, 199, 209, 216, 234, 283
Agra, 7, 8, 13, 14, 273 ; Imperial capital, 7, 8 ; land revenue, 99-100, 134 ; population, 8, 13, 14 ; productivity of province, 121-122 ; security in, 36, 41 ; textile industries, 175, 177-8, 182, 183, 185
Agriculture : crops grown, 102-5, 118-24, 178, 270, 271, Appendices A. and B., 303-6 ; environment unfavourable to, 125-30 ; implements, 105, 106 ; income of commodities from, 115-18, 286, 287 ; land-tenure, 96-100, 129, 130 ; manufactures dependent on, 156-60, 178-84 ; methods of, 100-102 ; population and, 9, 20, 22, 189, 190 ; yield, average, 115-18, 124
Ahadis, 73-4, 77. 94
Ahmadabad, 8 ; silk, 175 , sugar, 157
Ahmadnagar, 2
Ain-i Akbari quoted, 20, 37, 53, 54, 56, 65, 83, 86, 91, 118, 119, 121, 145, 182
Ajmer, 8 ; crops, 122 ; revenue, 135
Akbar : accession, 3, 4 ; army, 20, 65, 66, 73-6, 88, 192 ; city government, 37-9 ; Court, 14, 24, 26, 27, 65-73 ; currency, 54-6, 59, 60 ; customs duties, 46-50 ; dominions, 5, 6, 33 ; dress, 177, 258, 259 ; education and, 263 (*note*), 278 ; famine relief, 125 ; foreigners and, 24, 26, 69, 70, 76, 83, 84 ; Household, 87-9, 190-92, 257, 258; Imperial Service, 65-73, 94; intoxicants restricted by, 159, 278 ; irrigation works, 125 ; judicial system, 34-7 ; patronage of art and science, 83-5 ; religious grants, 86 ; revenue administration, 3, 4, 32-4, 46-50, 79-81, 97-100, 103, 111, 116 (*note*), 117, 122, 130-36, 188-9, 297-300 ; silk production improved by, 175, 177 ; slave trade and, 92 ; textile industries and, 175, 177, 178 ; treasure, 285 ; weights and measures, 52-4
Āl, 102
Alauddin Khilji, 98, 131, 284
Aleppo, 238

Allahabad, 8, 15; crops, 120-21, 122; fort, 165, 185; shipbuilding, 167
Alum, 154
Amalguzār, 33
America, Indian textiles in, 216
Amīr, 65, 69, 77
Amir-i-Azam, 66
Antelope, 7
Arab merchants, 23, 24, 42, 200, 213
Arabia: pilgrimages to, 205, 217, 263; trade with, 180, 181, 197, 208-9, 217-18, 234-5
Arakan, 9, 29, 212
Armenians, 23, 39, 246
Armies of India, 16-20, 73-6, 77; Mogul, 20, 65-6, 73-6, 88, 192
Arms, manufacture of, 161, 165
Artisans: economic position of, 187-9, 297; production by, 185-7
Artists patronised by Akbar, 83-5
Asaf Khan, 258
Ascetics, 27
Assignments of land revenue, 67, 72, 80, 84, 86, 129, 134
Aurangzeb, 190, 257 (*note*)

Babur, Emperor, 100, 106, 108, 257, 275, 276, 277, 284
Bacola, 276
Badaoni, 67, 81, 82, 127, 128, 262, 266
Bahadur's rebellion, 43
Bahar, 53, 54
Bahrain, 218
Bājra, 103, 121
Bamboo, 144
Banda, spice trade with, 208
Banians of Gujarat, 245, 246
Banjaras, 243
Bantam, 215, 236
Barbosa, 11, 17 (*note*), 32, 91, 92, 114 (*note*), 162, 172, 173, 175 (*note*), 198, 201, 206 (*note*), 213, 214, 264-5, 267, 274, 276
Barros, 14
Bassein, 23, 171, 206-7
Behari Mal, Raja, 69
Benares, 182, 189, 275-6
Bengal: clothing in, 119, 276; crops, 104, 119-20, 144, 178-9, 243; jute, 119, 178-9; kidnapping in 92, 93 (*note*); population, 10, 13, 22; rebellion in, 40; seaports, 211-12, Appendix C., 307-9; silk, 173, 175; slaves, 113; sugar, 105, 157; thieves in, 45; treasure-hoarding in, 284; waterways, 167
Berar, crops of, 123
Bernier, 13, 27, 69, 120, 130, 135, 138, 186, 187, 189, 190, 253 (*note*), 257 (*note*), 262, 264, 283
Bhagwan Das, Raja, 262
Bhatkal, 207
Biana, 44; indigo, 105, 158, 159; sugar, 158 (*note*)
Bidar, 3, 91
Bigha, 99 (*note*), 132 (*note*)
Bihar: crops of, 119, 120, 121; opium, 158
Bijapur, 3, 6, 8; doctors in, 85; Portuguese and, 202-3
Birbal, Raja, 70, 71
Blackmail levied, 50
Blankets, wool, 176, 276
Blochmann, 69, 71
Boat-building, 167-8
Bokhara, 9
Bombay, 114, 206
Borax, 154
Brahmans, 23, 70, 86
Brass vessels, 149, 166, 273
Bribery, 35-6, 37, 61, 261
Broach, 182, 185, 188, 204
Building industry, 164-5, 166
Building-stone, 154-5, 164-5
Būmi, 34, 74
Bundelkhand mines, 149
Burhanpur, 43
Burma, trade with, 180-81, 183

Calicut, 48, 79-80, 199, 200 (*note*), 224, 275; Zamorin of, 4, 79, 89, 203
Cambay, 23; paper, 164; ports, 25, 163, 182, 204-6, 240, 241; silk, 175
Camels, 221
Canals, 107-8, 122
Candy, 53, 54
Candy sugar, 157
Cannibalism, 266, 280
Caravans, 218-20, 221, 243
Carpet-weaving, 178, 185
Carracks, Portuguese, 186, 203, 205 (*note*), 209-10, 230-31, 289

Caste system, 23
Cattle, 106-7
Cesses, 134
Ceylon trade, 210, 218
Chaul silk, 175, 206, 207
Chettis, 245, 246
"China goods," 197, 208, 213, 215
China trade, 9, 148, 164, 169 (*note*), 173, 174, 181, 208, 218, 236, 283
Chittagong, 26, 28, 176, 212, Appendix C., 308
Chota Nagpur: diamonds, 153; mines, 149; "wild" silk, 176
Cities of India, 8-9; peasants drift to, 190; security in, 37-41; size of, 13-15
City dues, 49-50
Classes of population, 23-8; Court officials, 63-73, 94; lower State employments, 73-82, 263-4; professional and religious, 83-7; servants and slaves, 87-94; standard of life of, 256-80
Clerical services of Mogul Empire, 78-81
Cloth production, 158, 177, 179-82, 255, 290, 291-3
Clothing, 119, 177, 179-82, 255, 258, 259, 274-7, 290-93
Coal, 147, 154
Coasting craft, 233, 289; trade, 240
Cochin, 207, 208, 224, 236, 240, 241
Coinage, 55-8, 284; a form of merchandise, 59-60
Colebrook, Sir Edward, 113
Colombo, 210
Commerce: coasting trade, 240-41; exports, 180-84, 197-8, 204, 209, 212, 213, 215, 216, 218, 291-2; imports, 142-3, 179, 180, 196-7, 204, 208, 209, 212, 213, 215, 216, 218, 283, 291-2; organisation, 245-50; textiles, 179-84; transport, 166-71, 197, 243-4
  foreign: cash basis of, 57; European, 221-7; income from, 289; regulated by seasons, 230-33; sea-borne, 198-212; shipping employed, 233-9; volume of, 233-9, 288-9, Appendix D., 310-12
  internal, 241-5; agriculture and, 126-7; charges on, 46-52; security of, 37-46
Commercial law and morality, 247, 249-50
Conti, 11, 91, 171, 255, 266, 267
Coorg, serfdom in, 114
Copper, 146-7, 148-9, 154, 160, 166, 273-4; coinage, 55, 56, 148, 274
Coromandel coast, 92, 266
Correa, 266
Coryat, 13
Cosmin, 212
Cotton, 102, 103, 104, 105, 119, 122, 132; industry, 158, 171, 172, 179-84, 290-91; revenue assessment, 188-9
Court of Akbar, 14, 24, 26, 27, 65-73, 143 (*note*), 190-92, 254-5, 257-63, 300
Court of Vijayanagar, 63-5, 260
Covad, 54
Cowries, 56
Crop-statistics: compilation, 81; as an index to population, 20-22, 109-11; revenue assessment by, 99-100, 102-4, 131-3
Crops cultivated, 102-5, 118-24, Appendix A., 303-4, Appendix B., 305-6
Crowther, 46, 107
Cultivation: density of, and population, 20-22, 109-11; enforced, 97; extension of, 116-17
Currency, 54-60
Customs duties, 46-50

Dabul, 206, 207
Dahseri, 134
Daibal, 204
Daman, 25, 205
Dames, Mr. Longworth, 17
Dams, 53, 55, 60
Debts, recovery of, 35-7
Decadas, 11
Deccan, Moslem kingdoms of: administration, 32-3, 295; agriculture, 123, 125, 130, 136; armies, 18-19, 76-7; arts neglected in, 85; population, 11, 19; servants and slavery in, 89, 91
Delhi, 8, 13, 14; craftsmen, 160 (*note*), 186-7

Diamonds, 151-3, 154, 186
Diu, 25, 205
Diūl, 204
Doctors, 84, 85
Downton, 234
Dress, extravagance in, 258-9
Ducat, 57, 60
Dutch in India, 173, 202 (*note*), 211, 215; Companies, 222, 224-5; competition by, 244-5

East African timber resources, 169, 170
East India Company: first visit, 202 (*note*), 231; chartered, 225-6, 227
Education under Akbar, 263 (*note*), 278
Egypt and Indian trade, 200
Elephants, 7, 128 (*note*), 259
English merchants in India, 40, 46, 47, 143 (*note*), 177, 183, 202 (*note*), 215, 222, 224, 225, 245, 248
Espionage, 39, 51
Europe: cities of, compared with Indian, 13-15; trade with, 209, 221-8, 234, 238, 246-7
Europeans: their ideas of India, 1-2, 282; Indian estimation of, 42; as traders, 246-7
Exchange system, 248-9
Exports: general, 197-8, 204, 209, 212, 213, 215, 216, 218; textiles, 180-84, 291-2

Famine, 266; 1540, 11; 1555, 127-8; 1596, 22 (*note*); 1630-31, Gujarat, 187-8, 266
Fanām, 57
Far East, trade with, 199, 208, 211, 215
Faria y Sousa, M. de, 10
Fatehpur Sikri, 8, 13, 44, 185
Faujdār, 33
Fauna of India, 7, 22
Fernandus, Father F., Appendix C., 307-9
Fertility, alleged decline in, 115-18
Finch, William, 12, 21, 27 (*note*), 36, 42-5, 47 (*note*), 107, 159, 219, 239 (*note*), 241, 246 (*note*)
Firoz Shah, 98, 108
Fisheries, 145-6, 287
Fitch, Ralph, 13, 45, 119, 167, 168, 175, 176, 211, 213, 235, 274-5
Flores, 47
Flour-milling, 156-7
Food-grains, 102-4, 132; milling of, 156-7
Foreigners at Akbar's Court, 24, 26, 69, 70, 76, 83, 84, 300; in India, 23-8, 30, 247, 279
Forests of India, 7, 21-2, 143-5
Frederic, Caesar, 175, 176, 213, 229, 235, 266
Frigates, 205-6
Furniture, 161-2, 273-4

Galleys, 233
Gama, Vasco da, 198
Ganges river traffic, 167, 241, 243
Gaur, 14
Gaz, 54
Goa: Bassein stone used at, 154; currency, 57, 58; famine, 266, 268; furniture in, 162; horses in, 76; maund, 53; paper imports, 164; poorer classes in, 275; Portuguese in, 4, 25, 207, 260-61; servants and slaves in, 89, 90, 91, 260-61; trade of, 205, 207-8, 236, 240-41
Goez, Benedict, 220
Golconda, 3, 6, 8, 33; army of, 76; doctors in, 85; Kotwal of, 38, 39; poor in, 275; servants in, 89
Gold, 146, 154; coinage, 55, 56, 57, 58, 60, 257 (*note*); imports of, 197, 208, 209, 283-6
Gregorovius, 13 (*note*)
Grocers, London Company of, 223
Gujarat: banians, 245, 246; crops, 123; currency, 55; famine, 187-8, 266; fish-manure, 145; population, 12, 13, 22, 274; revolt, 40; silk export, 172, 174, 175; textiles, 182-3, 185; tobacco, 58; trade, 202, 244
Gurney, John, 239

Hair shawls, 177
Hakim Ali, 71
Handicrafts, 160-66, 185-9, 287, 290-293
Harness-making, 162, 163
Hawkins, William, 46, 67 (*note*), 134, 226, 268, 286

Hemp, 102, 171, 178
Hindu territories of the south, 2
Hindus: Akbar and, 70, 86; Alauddin Khilji and, 131, 132; caste system among, 23; slavery and, 91, 92
Hoarding of treasure, 284-6
Horses: trade in, 76, 95, 163, 166, 197, 218, 235, 259
Housing of poorer classes, 272-4
Hūn, 57

Ibrahim Lodi, 285
Ilahi gaz, 54
Imperial Household, 87-9, 190-92, 260
Imperial Service, Akbar's, 63, 65-73, 94; appointment, 69-70, 72-73; duties, 65-6, 70-71; rewards, 66-9, 71-3
Implements, agricultural, 105-6
Imports: general, 196-7, 204, 208-9, 212, 213, 215, 216, 218, 283; textiles, 179-80, 291-2
Income of commodities, 115-18, 124, 145, 155-6, 165, 286-94, 294-300
Independent States, 4-6
India, 1-2, 12; administration, 31-60, 295-300; agriculture, 102-5, 118-24, Appendices A. and B., 303-6; armies, 16-20, 65-6, 73-6, 77, 78, 192; castes, classes, etc., 23-8, 63-73, 83-7, 87-94; divisions, 2-6; European idea of, 1-2, 282; industry, 141, 146-60, 160-66, 166-71, 171-84, 287; population, 9-22, 23-8, 286-295; relations with neighbouring countries, 9, 29; surface, 6-9, 29; wealth, 283-94
Indian corn, Appendix B., 305-6
Indian merchants' commercial morality, 249, 250; wealth, 264, 265
Indigo, 102, 103, 104, 105, 112, 119, 126 (*note*), 132, 158, 159, 160, 197, 256 (*note*)
Indus river traffic, 167, 243
Industry: organisation, 184-9
production, 141, 155-6, 287; agricultural manufactures, 156-60; handicrafts, 160-66, 185-9, 287, 290-93; mineral, 146-55; shipping and vehicles, 144, 166-71, 186, 288-9; textiles, 171-84, 185
Intoxicants, manufacture of, 159, 278
Iron, 106, 146, 147, 148, 149, 150, 154, 161
Irrigation, 101, 102, 107, 108, 118, 125, 126, 163
Irvine, Mr., 20, 68 (*note*)
Italian traders, 223

Jāgīrs, 67, 72, 80, 84, 94, 129, 134
Jahangir: commander of 10,000, 65; Court of, bribery at, 35, 261; *jāgīr* system, 67, 73, 94, 129, 134; *Memoirs* of, 7, 40, 257-8, 261; prohibition by, 159; rebellions against, 40, 43; road control and tolls, 46, 49, 50; servants, 88 (*note*)
Japan, trade with, 181, 208, 215
Japanese in India, 26, 30
Jaunpur, 8
Java trade, 224, 226, 235
Jesuit missionaries, 11, 29, 65, 83 (*note*), 211, 254, 260
Jewellery, 259, 277
Jews, 23, 246, 250
Jiddah, 209, 217, 218, 229
Jitals, 56
Joanno, Friar, 180
John of Montecorvino, 274, 276
Jones, Sir William, 92 (*note*)
Jourdain, 207, 217 (*note*), 236, 256 (*note*), 269, 273
Jowār, 103, 121, 123, Appendix B., 305-6
Jumna vessels, 167
Junks, 232, 233
Justice, administration of, 34-7
Jute, 119, 167, 171, 178-9, 290-91

Kabul, 219, 220; rebellion, 40
Kachka, 31, 32, 33
Kafila, 206, 240
Kamargha, 27 (*note*)
Kanauj, 8
Kandahar, 219
Kanungos, 80
Karkhanas, 186-7
Karoris, 73, 81-2
Kashmir silk, 173, 175
Kasimbazar, 173
Kāzi, 34

Khām, 31
Khandesh, 2
Kotwal, 34, 36, 37-41, 51, 159
Krishna Raya, Emperor, 125
Kūch, 5, 10
Kumaun: serfs in, 114; silver mines, 146

Labour, wages of, 189-93
Labourers, landless, 112-15, 136-7
Laet, de, 98, 129, 134, 192, 261, 269, 271, 273, 275
Lahari Bandar, 47, 182, 204
Lahore, 8, 13; shipbuilding, 167; silk, 175; sugar, 157; textiles, 177-8, 182
Land: assignments of, 67, 72, 80, 84, 86: measurement, 81, 134; revenue assessment and collection, 3, 31-4, 97-100, 102-4, 111, 117, 122, 130-36; tenures, 96-100, 129-30
Larin, 57, 60, 209
Law, commercial, 247, 249
Law, Mr. N. L., 263 (*note*), 278 (*note*)
Lead, 146, 147
Leather manufactures, 162-3, 166
Levant Company, 231
Linschoten, 91, 174, 175, 176, 231, 266, 268, 273, 275, 276
Lions, 7
Livre, 54
Lower classes: clothing, 119, 177, 179-81, 274-7; expenses, 277-279; food of, 270-72; hoarding by, 285, 286; housing, 272-4; standard of life, 265-70, 279, 280, 295
Lucknow, 13

Macao, 208, 215
Macnaghten, Sir William, 113
Madras, 8, 114
Magadoxo, 209
Mahmudi, 55, 60
Maize, Vijayanagar, Appendix B., 305-6
Malabar coast: ports, 198-9, 200, 202, 212, 223; poverty, 267; serfs, 114
Malacca, trade with, 181, 183, 185, 199, 208, 212, 213-15, 223, 228, 235-6
Maldiv Islands, 201, 238
Malwa, 122, 158, 242
Manar, 11
Manrique, Father Sebastian, 49, 219
Mansabdār, 65, 69, 74, 77, 78, 138
Manufactures, 148-50: agricultural, 156-60; handicrafts, 160-66, 185-9, 287, 290-93; shipping and vehicles, 166-71, 186, 288-89; textiles, 171-84, 185
Martaban, 169-70, 212, 213
Masulipatam, 47 (*note*), 48, 211
Maunds, 52, 53, 54
Medical profession, 83, 84, 85
Mendicants, 27
Merchants: charges on, 46-50; risks and profits, 50-52; security of trade, 37-46; wealth, 263-4, 279, 285
Metals, 143, 146-51, 188, 197
Middle classes under Akbar, 26-7; standard of life of, 263-5, 294
Middleton, David, 232
Middleton, Sir Henry, 231, 234
Millets, 102, 103, 121, 122, 132, Appendix A., 303
Milling, 156-7, 158
Mines and minerals, 146-55
Mir Adl, 34
Missionaries introduce printing, 164
Mocha, 209, 217, 218, 229, 234, 283
Mogul the heir of all his subjects, 51, 71, 94, 257, 262, 263
Mogul Empire: army, 20, 65-6, 73-6, 88, 192; classes in, 23-28, 63-73, 73-82, 83-7, 87-94, 256-80; extent, 2, 3-6, 28, 29; Imperial service, 63, 65-73, 94; judicial administration, 34-7; population, 10, 11-15, 21, 22; rebellions against, 40; revenue administration, 3, 4, 32, 33, 34, 46-50, 79-81, 99-100, 103, 111, 116 (*note*), 117, 122, 130-36, 189, 297-300; slavery in, 26, 27, 91-2; treasure of, 285
Mohur, 60
Moluccas, spice trade with, 208, 235
Mombasa, 209
Money, dealing in, 59, 60
Monserrate, Father, 8, 13, 23, 29, 49, 254
Moors, 25 (*note*)
Morison, Sir Theodore, 127
Moslem kingdoms of the Deccan:

administration, 32, 33; agriculture, 123, 125, 130, 136; armies, 18-19, 76-7; arts neglected in, 85; population, 11, 19; servants and slaves in, 89, 91
Moslem merchants, 24, 162, 180, 198-202, 210, 214, 224, 245-6, 247, 265
Moslems: Akbar and, 70, 86; and slavery, 91-2
Mozambique, 26, 209, 234, 283
Muhammadi, the, 230 (*note*), 231
Multan, 8, 219, 220
Mun, 238
Mundy, 23, 49, 130, 159 (*note*), 243
Munsiff, 80
Muscat, 217
Muslin, 182
Mylapore, 8, 32 (*note*)

"Narsinga," 2
Navsari, 23
Negapatam, 210, 241
Nikitin, 11, 91, 267, 273, 274, 276
Nobles: commercial ventures by, 256-7; extravagance of, 257-263; revenue collectors, 32-3, 64, 98: Vijayanagar, 63-5, 76, 85, 86, 173, 260
Nuniz, 16, 17, 35, 45, 98, 99, 268

Ochres, 154
Officials, Court: Mogul, 63, 65-73, 94; Vijayanagar, 63-5
Oil-seeds, 102, 103-4, 122, 132; pressing, 158-9
Olala, 125
Omrahs, 65 (*note*), 69
Ophir, 209
Opium, 213, 278
Ormuz, 208, 209, 217, 218
Orta, Garcia da, 23, 102, 174, 232 (*note*)
Oudh, 121

Paes, 11, 13, 268, 276
Pagoda, 57-8
Pakka, 31, 32
Paper-making, 163-4, 166
Pardao, 58, 60, 64 (*note*)
Paris, population of, 13
Parsis, 23
Patna, 8; exports, 119, 120 (*note*)
Patronage, 83-5
Payton, 288 (*note*)
Pearl fisheries, 11, 145-6, 218
Peasant cultivators: condition under Akbar and now, 106, 107, 111, 112, 124, 190, 295-9; implements and power supply, 106, 107; income of commodities, 115-18, 124, 145, 155, 156, 165, 295-8; not helped by community, 125-30; revenue payments, burden of, 97, 99, 100, 131-6
Pegu, trade with, 9, 29, 169, 170, 182, 183, 211, 212-13, 229, 235, 283
Pepper trade, 208, 210, 212, 222-5
Pepperers, Gild of, 223
Persia: horses from, 197, 218, 235, 259; slaves from, 26; textiles, 177-8: trade with, 9, 57, 105, 173, 174, 208-9, 218, 235, 246, 248, 283; trade-routes, 219, 221, 242
Persians in India, 23-4, 42
Peshrau Khan, 71
Petroleum, 155 (*note*)
Philippine Islands, 215
Pilgrim-ships, 171, 203, 217, 230, 231, 232 (*note*), 239 (*note*)
Pilgrimages, 277; to Arabia, 205, 217, 263
Pimenta, Father N., 11, 28, 32 (*note*)
Pirates, 4, 202, 203, 206, 212, 218, 233, 239, 240, 241, 245, 289 (*note*); Portuguese, 26, 202, 212
Police system, 37-41
Poppy, 102, 103, 104, 119, 132
Population of India: city, 9-15; country, 17, 20-22, 109-11; divisions of, 23-8, 63-94; income of commodities and, 286-294; strength of armies an index to, 16-20
Porcelain imported, 164
Portuguese: convoys, 240-41; cotton industry and, 179-81, 182; currency, 57-8; decay of commerce, 244-5; English competition, 47, 224; furniture, 161-162; horse trade, 76, 95; idea of India, 1-2, 12; licence system, 201-2, 205, 210, 215, 217, 224,

239; missionary zeal, 112, 200, 224; Moslem merchants and, 24-5, 200-203, 210, 214, 224, 245-6, 265; pride, 42 (*note*); servants and slaves, 89, 91, 261; settlements, 4, 24, 25, 30, 204-12, 213-18, 283; shipbuilding, 168-71, 186, 203, 205 (*note*), 209-10, 230-31, 289; spice trade, 222-3, 236; tobacco introduced by, 158; trade supremacy, 204-18, 283
Pottery, 164-5
Pound, 53, 54
Prinsep, 54
Printing, 164
Professional classes, 27, 83-5, 263-4
Prohibition under Mogul Emperors, 159, 278
Pukhta, 31, 47
Pulicat, 202 (*note*)
Punishment of crime, 40
Punjab salt mines, 153
Pyrard, 29, 48, 76, 79-80, 89, 90, 150 (*note*), 162, 164, 174, 175, 179-80, 181, 208, 231, 235, 238, 244, 245, 269, 289

Quicksilver, 146, 147 (*note*)
Quintal, 53
Quota system, military, 16, 34, 64, 65-6

Races inhabiting India, 23-6
Rahimi, the, 230 (*note*), 231, 256 (*note*)
Raichur, 17 (*note*)
Raiyats, 97 (*note*)
Rajputana: mines, 147-8, 243; travel in, 242
Rajputs in Akbar's service, 70
Ramayana, 83 (*note*)
Rander, 162
Raolconda, 151 (*note*)
Real, 57 (*note*), 58
Real-of-eight, 57, 60
Red Sea trade, 199, 200, 202, 207, 210, 213, 216, 217, 234, 283
Religious classes, 83, 85-7
Rent-rates, 130-31, 133, 135
Revenue assessment and collection, 3, 4, 32-4, 46-50, 79-81, 97-100, 103, 111, 116 (*note*), 117, 122, 130-36, 188-9; distribution, 295-8
Rhinoceros, 7
Rice, 104, 119, 121, 123
River highways, 7, 167-8, 241-2; tolls, 49
Roads, 6, 7, 278
Rohilkhand sugar-refining, 158
Rome, population of, 13 (*note*)
Routes of travel, 6-7, 9, 12-13
Rupee, 55-6, 60, 131, 154
Rural population: crop-statistics and, 20-22, 109-11; income of commodities of, 286-7; serfs among, 90, 112-15, 136-7; standard of life of, 296-7
Rural servitude, 90, 112-15, 136-7

Sa, Father Simon, 11, 28
Sadr, 84, 86
Salbank, 41, 46 (*note*), 268, 269, 276
Salt, 151, 153-4, 243, 271-2
Saltpetre, 154-5
Sambhar lake, 153
S. Thomé, 8, 25, 32 (*note*)
Sann-hemp cultivation, 178
Saris, Captain, 230 (*note*), 231, 232 (*note*)
Sarkārs, 33-4
Sarkhej, 105
Satgaon-Hooghly, 211
Seaports: foreign, 212-18; Indian, 204-12, Appendix C., 307-9
Security: of travel, 35; in cities, 37-41; in country, 41-6
Sequin, 57, 60
Serfdom, rural, 90, 112-15, 136-7, 190
Sers, 52, 53
Servants and slaves, 26, 27, 76, 87-93, 112-15, 136-7, 190-92, 193, 260-61
Sewell, Mr., 16, 17, 85, 125, 268
Shahjahan, 135, 159 (*note*)
Sher Shah, 80, 81, 99
Shipbuilding, 144, 167-71, 186, 288-9
Shipping: vessels used and their capacity, 203, 230-33, 288, 289, 290, Appendix D., 310-12
Shoes, 162-3, 276-7
Sikhs, 23
Silk industry, 171-6, 207, 287
Silver, 146; coinage, 55, 58, 60, 148,

218, 284; imported, 197, 209, 216, 218, 226-7, 283-6
Sind land revenue, 99, 135
Slave trade, 26, 92, 216-17
Slavery, predial, 90, 112-15, 136-7
Slavery, Report on, 90, 92 (*note*), 93 (*note*), 113, 137
Slaves, 26-7, 76, 89-93, 192
Smith, Mr. Vincent, 48, 68 (*note*), 79 (*note*), 285
Socotra, 234
Sofala, 209, 216, 234, 283
Sonargaon, 182, 211, 276, Appendix C., 309
Spanish trade, 215-16, 224, 225
Spice trade, 208, 222-6
Sripur, 211-12, Appendix C., 308
Standard of life, 254-6, 279-80, 294-5; upper-class, 256-63, 294; middle-class, 263-5, 294; lower-class, 265-70, 295; rural labourers, 296-7
"Staple," the, 217, 218, 229
State employment, lower: military, 73-7; civil, 77-82, 263-4
Steel, manufacture of, 150
Steel and Crowther, 46, 107
Steele, Richard, 174 (*note*)
Stone, 154-5, 164-5
Sūbas, 33
Suez fleet, 169
Sugar, 271, 272
Sumatra, 208
Surat: customs duties, 47 (*note*), 48; exchange system, 248; freedom in, 265, 269; Kotwal of, 39; Parsees in, 23; population, 12, 269; prices in, 58; serfs and servants in, 88, 89, 91, 114, 192-3; weights and measures in, 53, 54
Surat-Agra routes, 12, 242, 248
Surface of sixteenth-century India, 6-9
Sūwar rank, 66

Talikot, battle of, 2, 17, 19, 65
Tanda, 276
Tavernier, 11, 49, 85, 128 (*note*), 148, 151-3, 173, 189, 242, 243, 248, 250, 257 (*note*), 285
Tavoy, 213
Teak, 144, 169
Temples, endowment of, 86-7
Tenasserim, 213, 235
Terry, 23, 26, 46, 88 (*note*), 101 (*note*), 189, 190, 192, 217 (*note*), 218 (*note*), 226, 232 (*note*), 258, 264, 270, 272, 273
Textile manufactures, 171-84, 185, 189
Thana, 112
Thévenot, 11, 14, 23, 33, 38, 39, 47 (*note*), 49, 50, 76, 123, 145, 157 (*note*), 160 (*note*), 187
Thorne, Robert, 224
Tibet, 9, 219
Tiger, 7
Timber the determining factor in shipbuilding, 168-71
Tin, 146, 213
Tobacco manufacture, 158, 159, 278
Todar Mal, Raja, 70, 81, 82
Torture practised, 39, 40, 82
Trade routes: inland, 241-4; land, 218-21; sea, 199-200, 201, 223
Traffic: road, 166-7; water, 167-171, 227-39
Transit dues, 48-50, 248
Transport, means of, 166-71, 198, 219-20, 238
Treasure, imports and hoards of, 283-286. *See under* Gold *and* Silver
Tribes, uncivilized, 27
Tulsi Das, 83 (*note*)
Tun, shipping, 167, 230, Appendix D., 310-12
Turks, 9; in Red Sea, 169, 209, 217; timber-supply and, 169

Ujjain, 8
Umda, 66
United Provinces, crops of, 120-21
Urban servitude, 90-93; wages, 189-193

Valle, della, 12, 88, 91, 125, 126, 164, 192, 244, 264 (*note*), 265, 269, 275
Varāhu, 57, 60
Varthema, 45, 172, 213, 266, 274
Vasco da Gama, 198
Vehicles, 166-7
Vijayanagar, City of, 8, 13, 38, 49-50
Vijayanagar, Empire: agriculture, 123, 125, 130, 305-6; army, 16-19, 76-7; Court, 35, 63-5; de-

cline of, 207; judicial system, 34, 35; lower classes, 267-8, 274, 276; nobles, 32, 33, 63-5, 76, 85, 86, 98, 173; Portuguese and, 202, 207; revenue administration, 32, 33, 64, 98, 295; security in, 45; servants and slaves in, 89, 91; transit and city dues, 49, 50; treasury, 284-5
Villages, 8; life in, 136-8

Wages, urban, 189-93
Water-lifts, 101, 102, 106
Wealth of India: gold and silver, 283-6; commodities, 286-94
Weights and measures, 52-4
Wells, 101, 108, 125
Wheat, 102, 103, 119, 120, 132
Winds, prevailing, and commerce, 227-30
Wine imports, 142 (*note*)
Withington, Nicholas, 126 (*note*)
Wood, 106, 165-6; supply determines shipbuilding, 168-71
Wood-working, 161-2
Woollen goods, 176-8, 259, 276

Xavier, Father Hieronymus, 218

Zabt, 99
Zamindars, 3, 4, 27, 34, 74, 99, 114, 134-5, 138
Zamorin of Calicut, 4, 79, 89, 203
Zanana, Akbar's, 87, 88
Zinc, 146, 147

THE END

BY THE SAME AUTHOR

Crown 8vo. 6*s.* 6*d. net.*

AN INTRODUCTION TO ECONOMICS FOR INDIAN STUDENTS

ECONOMIC JOURNAL.—"A creditable attempt at a straightforward account of the broad elementary principles of economics, with useful illustrations from Indian experience. . . . Unquestionably it should prove a useful volume for teachers of economics in India, suggesting ways of bringing out differences between Indian conditions and the ordinary social assumptions underlying the text-books to which English students are accustomed."

LITERARY WORLD.—"We can with the greatest confidence recommend this book to the ordinary reader. He will have no difficulty whatever in reading it, as the style is most lucid, and he will not be troubled with statistics. . . . Mr. Moreland's extensive experience of agriculture and business in India is everywhere apparent in this book, and the exceptional opportunities he had for observation of the facts and study of the various problems render extraordinarily interesting the opinions he freely expresses on many matters of the greatest importance to India at the present time. Indian students will certainly not be the only persons who will derive pleasure as well as profit from this work."

INDIAN EDUCATION.—"This excellent book will fill a long-felt want in the Indian educational world, that of a fairly elementary treatise on Indian Economics, if the term be permissible. The Indian youth who reads this work will be in a far better position to understand the Economic classics than one who plunges into them straight away. . . . We strongly recommend it to all Indian teachers and students of Economics."

THE PIONEER (ALLAHABAD).—"The most important contribution to the study of economics which has been made for a considerable time by any Anglo-Indian writer. . . . Mr. Moreland has done for Indian students what Dr. Marshall (in his smaller book) has done for English students of economics. He has given us a book such that he who runs may read, and reading understand."

LONDON: MACMILLAN AND CO., LTD.

OTHER NEW WORKS ON ECONOMICS

8vo. 18*s. net.*

INDIAN FINANCE AND BANKING

BY

G. FINDLAY SHIRRAS

DIRECTOR OF STATISTICS WITH THE GOVERNMENT OF INDIA; FELLOW OF THE UNIVERSITY OF CALCUTTA; ON SPECIAL DUTY IN THE FINANCE DEPARTMENT OF THE GOVERNMENT OF INDIA, 1910–1913; READER IN INDIAN FINANCE AND CURRENCY IN THE UNIVERSITY OF CALCUTTA, 1914

CONTENTS.—I. Introductory. II. The Indian Currency System before the War. III. In War Time. IV. and V. In the Nineteenth Century. VI. and VII. Indian Currency, 1900–1919. VIII. The Paper Currency. IX. The Gold Standard Reserve. X. A Gold Currency and a Gold Mint. XI. Council Drafts. XII. Balances. XIII. and XIV. The Indian Banking System. XV. The Effect of the War on Indian Banking. XVI. Problems of Indian Banking Legislation.

8vo. 8*s.* 6*d. net.*

THE ECONOMIC CONSEQUENCES OF THE PEACE

BY

JOHN MAYNARD KEYNES, C.B.

FELLOW OF KING'S COLLEGE, CAMBRIDGE

8vo.

THE ECONOMICS OF WELFARE

BY

A. C. PIGOU, M.A.

PROFESSOR OF POLITICAL ECONOMY IN THE UNIVERSITY OF CAMBRIDGE

LONDON: MACMILLAN AND CO., LTD.

A SELECTION OF WORKS ON ECONOMICS

DICTIONARY OF POLITICAL ECONOMY. By Various Writers. Edited by Sir R. H. I. PALGRAVE. Three Vols. Medium 8vo. 25s. net each. Appendix to Vol. III. Separately. Sewed. 3s. net.

PRINCIPLES OF ECONOMICS. An Introductory Volume. By ALFRED MARSHALL. Seventh Edition. 8vo. 12s. 6d. net.

ELEMENTS OF ECONOMICS OF INDUSTRY. By ALFRED MARSHALL. Third Edition. Crown 8vo. 4s. 6d.

INDIAN CURRENCY AND FINANCE. By JOHN MAYNARD KEYNES. 8vo. 7s. 6d. net.

STATE CREDIT AND BANKING DURING THE WAR AND AFTER. By ROBERT BENSON. 4to. 6s. net.

PAPERS ON CURRENT FINANCE. By H. S. FOXWELL, M.A., Professor of Political Economy in the University of London. 8vo. 10s. net.

PRINCIPLES OF ECONOMICS. By Dr. N. G. PIERSON. Translated by A. A. WOTZEL. Two Vols. 8vo. 12s. 6d. net each.

PRINCIPLES OF ECONOMICS. By Prof. F. W. TAUSSIG. Second Edition. Two Vols. 8vo. 10s. 6d. net, each.

THE ECONOMIC ANNALS OF THE NINETEENTH CENTURY. By Prof. W. SMART, M.A., D.Phil. 8vo. Vol. I. 1801–1820. 21s. net. Vol. II. 1821–1830. 21s. net.

WEALTH AND WELFARE. By Prof. A. C. PIGOU, M.A. 8vo. 10s. net.

THE FINANCIAL SYSTEM OF THE UNITED KINGDOM. By HENRY HIGGS, C.B. 8vo. 6s. net.

NATIONAL ECONOMY: an Outline of Public Administration. By HENRY HIGGS, C.B. Crown 8vo. 3s. 6d. net.

THE THEORY OF INTERNATIONAL TRADE, WITH SOME OF ITS APPLICATIONS TO ECONOMIC POLICY. By Prof. C. F. BASTABLE, M.A., LL.D. Fourth Edition, Revised. Crown 8vo. 4s. 6d. net.

PUBLIC FINANCE. By Prof. C. F. BASTABLE, M.A., LL.D. Third Edition. 8vo. 16s. net.

ELEMENTS OF INDIAN TAXATION. By LEONARD ALSTON, Litt.D. Crown 8vo. 2s. 6d. net.

A STUDY OF INDIAN ECONOMICS. By P. BANERJEA, M.A. Second Edition. Crown 8vo. 4s. 6d. net.

LONDON: MACMILLAN AND CO., LTD.